In God's Shadow
The Collaboration of Victor White and C. G. Jung

C. G. Jung with Victor White at Bollingen

Ann Conrad Lammers

In God's Shadow

THE COLLABORATION OF VICTOR WHITE AND C. G. JUNG

Paulist Press
New York ◇ Mahwah, N.J.

ACKNOWLEDGMENTS

The Publisher gratefully acknowledges use of the following material: excerpts from *Soul and Psyche: An Enquiry into the Relationship of Psychotherapy and Religion*, by Victor White, copyright © 1960, Harper and Brothers, NY; excerpts from Victor White's essay, "Kinds of Opposites," from *Studien zur Analytischen Psychologie C.G. Jung: Festschrift zum 80. Geburtstag von C.G. Jung* (herausgegeben vom C.G. Jung-Institut Aurich, Rascher-Verlag, 1955); excerpts from *Memories, Dreams, Reflections* by C.G. Jung, Edit. A. Jaffe, trans., R&C Winston, copyright © 1961, 1962, 1963 and renewed 1989, 1990, 1991 by Random House, Inc. Reprinted by permission of Pantheon Books, a Div. of Random House, Inc.; excerpts from Victor White's lecture "Good and Evil," pp. 16–34, courtesy of *Harvest*, Volume 12 (1966), Analytical Psychology Club, London, England, in consultation with Editor; excerpt from Victor White's review, "Eranos 1947, 1948," pp. 395–400, from *Dominican Studies*, vol. II, October 1949; excerpts from St. Thomas Aquinas, *Summa Theologiae: Latin Text and English Translation*, London and New York: Blackfriars in conjunction with Eyre and Spottiswode and McGraw Hill, copyright © 1964; excerpts from *Scholasticism*, by Victor White, pamphlet #R126, copyright © 1934, The Catholic Truth Society, London; excerpts from "Religious Tolerance" by Victor White, from September 4, 1953 issue of *The Commonweal*, pp. 531–534; selected excerpts and one photo from Jung, C.G., *Letters, Volume I: 1906–1950*, copyright © 1973; Jung, C.G. *Letters, Volume II: 1951–1961*, copyright © 1973; Jung, C.G., *Collected Works, Volume 9ii, Aion: Researches into the Phenomenology of the Self*, copyright © 1959 (Bollingen, second edition); Jung, C.G., Collected Works, Volume II, *Psychology and Religion: West and East* (Bollingen) Copyright © 1958, 1969, all published by Princeton University Press, Princeton, New Jersey. Reprinted by permission; Additional material from C.G. Jung's letters to Victor White, courtesy of L. Niefus and P. Jung for the Erbengemeinshaft C.G. Jung; excerpts from Victor White's essay, "Thomism and Affective Knowledge," pp. 126–131; *Blackfriars*, XXIV, April 1943; excerpts from "The Frontiers of Theology and Psychology," Victor White's Guild Lecture Number 19 (1942), courtesy of the Guild of Pastoral Psychology; Victor White's handwriting on cover and correspondence courtesy of Adrian Cunningham, for the English Dominican Province; C.G. Jung's handwriting on cover, courtesy of L. Niefus and P. Jung for the Erbengemeinschaft C.G. Jung.

Library of Congress Cataloging-in-Publication Data

Lammers, Ann Conrad.
    In God's shadow : the collaboration of Victor White and C.G. Jung
    Ann Conrad Lammers.
        p.   cm.—(Jung and spirituality series)
    Includes bibliographical references and index.
    ISBN 0-8091-3489-6
    1. Jung, C. G. (Carl Gustav), 1875–1961—Religion.   2. White, Victor, 1902–1960.   3. Psychoanalysis and religion.   4. Catholic Church and psychoanalysis.   I. Title.   II. Series: Jung and spirituality.
BF109.J8L36   1994
150.19′5—dc20   94-15329
                                                              CIP

Published by Paulist Press
997 Macarthur Blvd.
Mahwah, N.J. 07430

Printed and bound in the United States of America

Contents

DEDICATION

To my daughters

SERIES FOREWORD

The *Jung and Spirituality* series provides a forum for the critical interaction between Jungian psychology and living spiritual traditions. The series serves two important goals.

The first goal is: *To enhance a creative exploration of the contributions and criticisms that Jung's psychology can offer to religion.* Jungian thought has far-reaching implications for the understanding and practice of spirituality. Interest in these implications continues to expand in both Christian and non-Christian religious communities. People are increasingly aware of the depth and insight which a Jungian perspective adds to the human experiences of the sacred. And yet, the use of Jungian psychoanalysis clearly does not eliminate the need for careful philosophical, theological and ethical reflection or for maintaining one's centeredness in a spiritual tradition.

The second goal is: *To bring the creative insights and critical tools of religious studies and practice to bear on Jungian thought.* Many volumes in the Jung and Spirituality series work to define the borders of the Jungian and spiritual traditions, to bring the spiritual dimensions of Jung's work into relief, and to deepen those dimensions. We believe that an important outcome of the Jung-Spirituality dialogue is greater cooperation of psychology and spirituality. Such cooperation will move us ahead in the formation of a post-modern spirituality, equal to the challenges of the twenty-first century.

Robert L. Moore
Series Editor

Preface

All my life I have had what might be called a binocular habit of mind. Looking back, I think I had already developed a desire to reconcile opposing perspectives when at sixteen I took up the study of German. I wanted that language for the sake of singing Mozart; but partly also, I recall, because I had begun to see my deepening knowledge of French language and culture as one-sided. I was aware of the bitter history between Germany and France, and I knew my heritage derived from both. These facets of the European world (known to me then mainly through their literature and music) seemed equally worth cherishing; yet between them was an abyss of distrust and misunderstanding. I had the adolescent idealism to hope, if only half-consciously, that by mastering both languages I might become, myself, the missing connection.

This book, a close study of a collaboration between two fields that have often come into conflict, is thus built on a dialectic that springs from a personal habit of thought. To that extent the methodology is natural. But two-sidedness exacts an effort. Approaching the insights of even one complex field—psychology or theology—one sees that no single authority represents the whole discipline. Rather, a chorus of voices, not always in harmony, speaks from several directions. Institutionally approved teachings and orthodoxies exist, to be sure. But in each field more than one school can claim to define orthodoxy—to say nothing of heretics camped outside the walls. And even the best-guarded orthodoxies are subject to change.

Beside the conflicts of internal authority, a serious challenge arises when one tries to coordinate the methodologies of separate fields of knowledge. Representatives of two fields, such as Christian theology and analytical psychology, well trained in

1

their own schools of thought, may either ignore or fundamentally misinterpret each other's language and logic. And, contrary to my adolescent hope, the potential for conflict is not lost when an individual studies both fields. The argument is then merely taken inside, to continue within the bilingual mind and heart.

Within these limitations, the effort to view human life and healing from two vantage points at once, theological and psychological, has been a compelling task for me since 1978. That year I first came to study depth psychology and Christian theology at the General Theological Seminary in New York. My interest in both fields carried me first through the Master of Divinity degree at seminary, and then on to doctoral work as an "independent" student in the Religious Studies Department at Yale, where I sought not so much to answer as to sharpen the theological-psychological questions in whose vortex I continued to find myself. The doctoral dissertation on which this book is based was accepted by the university in 1987.

Until recently I avoided asking myself the origins of my passion to study both theology and psychology, or what led to my concentration on the painfully convoluted relationship of Victor White and C.G. Jung. When the Managing Editor for the Jung and Spirituality series of Paulist Press, Dan Meckel, urged me to write about the source of my fascination with my subject, I was reluctant at first. But the quality of my resistance hinted that something more important might be at stake. When I finally faced the matter within my own soul, I discovered that, to use Kierkegaard's phrase, I had been about the work of love in remembering one who is dead. This book is directed to a person who has died, or rather to the image of that person which goes on living in myself.

Before I discuss that person, I must first write about another. Professor Hans Wilhelm Frei was, while he lived, the leading spirit of the Religious Studies Department at Yale. It was he, more than anyone else, who persuaded me that Yale would provide a good academic home for my interdisciplinary work. A deep and generous soul, Frei personally shared Karl Barth's doubts about religious subjectivity; yet as a scholar he was open to the questions raised by depth psychology. He encouraged me to study independently, promising that (subject to departmental supervision and testing) I could design my program in large part myself. In the years I was at Yale, Frei kept his promise, though mainly from the background. With unfailing tact he opened gates and suggested paths, so that I never became quite lost in Yale's byzantine ways or confounded by the complexity of my own project.

The death of Hans Frei in 1988 hit me at many levels. I felt it as a personal loss. He had been not only a faithful mentor and friend, but also in some symbolic sense a father in the spirit. Of course, he was aware of that role in a general way (we talked once about the curse of *paternalism* in contrast with the gift of *paternity*). But he could not have known, since while he lived I could not have told him, that in his person—his humor and humility, his way of being present to others—but most of all in his steady support of my work, he had allowed me to begin the healing of an old wound. Through this book, and the doctoral study behind it, a part of that healing process is nearing its completion.

I must go back to early years to explain. After my father, Howard M. Lammers, died of cancer just before my first birthday, my mother was married again to an Episcopal priest. This quiet, bookish man, Arthur Corson Kelsey, who became my stepfather when I was four, was later for nine years Chaplain at the General Theological Seminary in New York. It was he who unwittingly set me to work on the fundamental problem to which this book, and, I suspect, much of my study of theology and psychology since the late 1970s, are addressed. I apprenticed myself to two fields of learning in order to say to him, at last, on my own authority: No, you were wrong. No one need endure the division between God and the soul from which you suffered. No teacher of Christian doctrine should teach, as you did, the negation of human feeling in the name of Christ.

As parents never really leave, my internal image of my stepfather has continued to pose the challenge he put to me all the years we knew each other, but especially the summer before he died. I had been in Germany that summer for eight weeks, while my family—mother, stepfather, half-sister and twin half-brothers—were on vacation at our house in northern Vermont. Now back from my adventure, more self-confident than when I left home, I wanted to tell my stepfather one story of my trip that I thought he would especially enjoy: the story of how I had gone to church with Presbyterians.

I was, of course, a confirmed Episcopalian—or, more accurately, a very young dyed-in-the-wool Anglo-Catholic. That summer, while staying in Frankfurt, I had had a brief but important encounter with a Protestant worshipping community, an encounter that was, I knew vaguely then and can say now with certainty, a brush with the church universal, my first experience of ecumenicity. It happened as follows.

A regular churchgoer at home, I was lonely for church after two weeks in a foreign country. The Lutheran service to which I had been taken in Berlin had made me feel like a stranger; the language and setting had been too far from what I knew. I felt I would give anything to say some prayers and sing some hymns in English, just to feel that I was part of a worshipping family. It turned out that, to serve the rather large American population, there was something in Frankfurt called the American Church. I found the name and address listed in a newspaper.

The pastor of the American Church welcomed me outside the building when I arrived early on Sunday morning. This was a congregation of Presbyterians, he explained. I would be welcome to join them. Yes, I could certainly partake of Communion with them if I felt comfortable doing so. It was up to me; I had my choice in the matter. Going into the church I felt a sort of spaciousness enlarge within me: my personal sense of truth and aptness was being called into play, to pronounce a private judgment on the presence of God and the meaning of church for me. Soberly I found my way to a seat and waited to see how my newly evoked conscience would make its choice.

When the time came for the congregation to partake of the bread and wine, I hesitated. I could feel myself keenly balanced between "no" and "yes." Finally my desire to be part of a body of Christian worshippers prevailed over my reluctance. In the context of this service, basically familiar in form and content though not echoing the Book of Common Prayer, it seemed clear to me that the acts we were invited to perform were in essence the same as the acts performed by Episcopalians at home. With a little feeling of daring and a rush of happiness, I joined with the others to eat the bread and drink—to my mild surprise—a cup not of wine but of grape juice.

This was the happy story I had saved to tell my stepfather. I caught his attention one afternoon in the dimly lighted dining room. (All the downstairs rooms in that house were dark and cool, shaded by huge trees and by the overhanging roof of an encircling porch.) I began my narrative. As I reached the part about receiving Communion, his face grew somber; then anger deeply engraved it. "You did what?" he asked. There was no going back. I felt as though I had been caught asleep in a brothel. Nothing for it now but try to explain how I arrived there.

"I was lonely," I stammered. "I had been feeling out of communion." My stepfather stared at me. "You're in communion if you're on the moon." His tone was dry and hard. I believe those were the last words spoken between us that day. He was a priest, my stepfather, and I was only nineteen. The spiritual promiscuity I had disclosed, my presumption in thinking that an unaided conscience could discern Christ among the Presbyterians, were never spoken of again.

What my stepfather answered that day, standing in the dining room of the old house on the lake, was false. His definition of the church and the sacraments, splitting human feeling and experience from metaphysical reality, was wrong. I could not challenge him then. But I can say now that I acted faithfully, and so did the pastor who trusted me to discern the sacred reality that might become present to me in worship. Not supernatural certainty alone; experience and feeling also measure religious truth. God is *for* and *with* people in their personal lives, not an absolute metaphysical reality separate from human loving and knowing.

There is something else that I can now say with certainty. Before my stepfather was wrong, he was himself wronged. He delivered to me only what had been handed over to him. If I suffered by it, he suffered first and longer. I suspect that his first teachers of false doctrine were not his professors at seminary, but his parents: the mother who committed suicide when he was fifteen and the father who sent a grieving boy to France for a year, to live with strangers.

In that cold year abroad my stepfather must have learned

the teaching he later handed on to me: "You're in communion if you're on the moon." To survive his young agony, he invented a definition of love from which touch was missing. Feeling was unnecessary, he taught himself, both to human life and to God. Presence is discerned in absence. Abstract thought suffices. It is remarkable that, with this circle of teachings as his hidden fortress, my stepfather would later minister so well to so many, with the gentleness that was his trademark.

If the corruption of the best is worst, the corruption of the best news is the worst news of all. One of the most terrible uses of the Gospel, therefore, is its use to punish the faithful. The tortuous tale of Victor White's later career, viewed from a certain angle, is an illustration of that abuse. I intuit but cannot prove that Victor White was also the victim of early losses. Perhaps they were not as serious as those which marred my stepfather's theology at its root. Perhaps White had opportunities to affirm the place of closeness, feeling, and touch as parts of love even within the church. It is certain that he committed himself to promoting "affective knowledge" in place of theological intellectualism and validating "experience" in place of mere abstraction. It was that theological commitment, in part, which led him to the psychological friend and ally, C.G. Jung, whose developing thought would later contribute to White's professional downfall.

I began my doctoral work already well acquainted with the writings of C.G. Jung and the practice of Jungian analysis. Halfway through my program, however, I realized that I needed a conversation partner on the Jungian side, someone who could help me in a scholarly way to shape my interest in the religious and theological implications of analytical psychology. Through a mutual friend I was fortunate to find the person I was looking for, a Jungian analyst and teacher, Charles H. Taylor. Mr. Taylor, formerly on the faculty at Indiana University and later for some years Provost at Yale, now teaches at the C.G. Jung Institute in New York.

While I was facing my first qualifying exam, Charles Taylor suggested that I read Jung's letters to Victor White. These letters, he said, might help me to focus my discussion of the relation between Jung's psychology and Christian theology. In our ensuing conversation and friendship for almost a decade Mr.

Taylor has repeatedly helped me crystallize the issues central to my work, bringing to bear both his practiced analytic eye and his deep appreciation of religious values.

Another conversation partner and friend emerged over time in the person of Franz Jung, C.G. Jung's son. Our conversation—first by letter and then in person—now spans many years. Mr. Jung first opened a window on the content of Victor White's letters and later played a decisive role in their release for scholarly use. Thanks to his ongoing interest in my work, I have had the joy of coming to know Franz Jung not only as a conscientious keeper of his father's heritage, but also as a man who, after following a path separate from his father's, came late in life to a unique appropriation of C.G. Jung's vision.

To several others on the Jungian side, for information and suggestions, I owe special thanks. William McGuire, executive editor of Jung's *Collected Works* and editor at Princeton University Press, now retired, put me in touch more than once with key resources. Dr. Gerhard Adler, Jungian analyst and primary editor of the *C.G. Jung Letters*, wrote to me from London in the last year of his life to share his impressions of Victor White. Dr. Joseph Henderson, founder of the C.G. Jung Institute of San Francisco, shared his memories of White's visits to California and of Jung's attitude toward religious questions in the Western world.

On the Catholic side, too, help was generously given. Fr. Christopher Mooney, S.J., professor of theology at Fairfield University, Fairfield, CT, spent the better part of an afternoon instructing me in the recent history of Roman Catholic theology and suggesting sources for research. Dr. John P. Dourley, O.M.I., Jungian analyst and professor of Religious Studies at Carleton University in Ottawa, engaged me in lively conversation about my research and shared the results of his own during his 1987 sabbatical in Berkeley. Dr. Paul M. Parvis, O.P., Subprior at Blackfriars, Oxford, sent me information from the house archives pertaining to Victor White's career in the Dominican Order.

Extraordinary resources became available to me when I met Fr. Aelred Squire, O.S.B., Camaldolese—formerly Dominican. A published patristics scholar, historian and linguist, Aelred Squire was Victor White's student at Oxford and later his friend and colleague. (An account of Aelred Squire's life and career appears below as Appendix C.) Fr. Aelred has contributed tangibly and intangibly to my understanding of White's world and of crucial events in Fr. Victor's life. With a deft touch he complexified for me aspects of White's theological project that I was mistakenly seeing as simple, and simplified others that I had made needlessly complex.

The Rev. Paul J. Philibert, O.P., who recently completed a term as Prior Provincial of the Dominicans in the southern states and now directs the Institute for Church Life at the University of Notre Dame, supported my fledgling work at a crucial point. In 1987 when I finished my dissertation I was on the faculty of the Church Divinity School of the Pacific, which is a member of the Graduate Theological Union in Berkeley. That fall, happily for my project, Fr. Philibert became president of the Dominican School of Philosophy and Theology, another seminary in the ecumenical consortium. At his warm invitation, one evening in spring 1988 I presented a portion of my research to a gathering of scholars at the Dominican school. It was the first, and for some time the only, public forum for this work, and I am heartily grateful to Paul Philibert for his collegial support.

In 1990 the Dominicans of the English Province requested and received from the Jung family copies of Victor White's letters to C.G. Jung. (Circumstances of the 30-year custody of White's letters by the Jung family, and of their release, are discussed below in Appendix A.) At the urging of Franz Jung, and with permission from the then English Provincial, Fr. Timothy Radcliffe, O.P., and with permission also from White's literary executor, I too received copies of the Jung-White correspondence in 1991, so that I could revise this book in the light of that primary source.

Though not himself a Dominican, Dr. Adrian Cunningham, chair of the theology department at the University of Lancaster in England, has devoted himself for many years to studying the life and work of Victor White. Since 1990 he has represented the English Dominicans as White's literary executor. I owe him special thanks for his patient contributions to my late-stage revisions of this work, although its conclusions and final form, of course, are entirely my responsibility. I am deeply grateful to him for giving official permission to quote White's letters in my book.

In this connection I wish also to thank Fr. Bede Bailey, O.P., archivist for the English Dominican Province. Although the perspective of this work sometimes diverges from his own, especially regarding the political and theological context in which White worked, Fr. Bede kindly joined Dr. Cunningham in giving me permission to quote White's letters.

People at Paulist Press have earned my gratitude many times over for their patience in attending the delivery of this project. Dan Meckel, Managing Editor for the Jung and Spirituality series, saw the manuscript through a prolonged phase of revisions and permissions. It fell then to Fr. Lawrence Boadt, Senior Editor, and Karen Scialabba, his able assistant, to guide the book through all the stages of production. This they accomplished diplomatically, efficiently, and with unfailing good humor.

Before closing this preface I must acknowledge one more major scholarly debt. In the chapters that follow, Jung's psychology and White's theology are often described as language systems, using a hermeneutical lens that is derived mainly from the cultural-linguistic theory of doctrine, as proposed by George Lindbeck in his book *The Nature of Doctrine*. While it is hard to be completely even-handed when writing about a deeply-rooted conflict, I have tried to honor the principle of neutral description and evaluation implicit in Lindbeck's proposal. This is the best way I know to do justice to Jung and White and to the hardships that arose because of their collaboration. An attitude of equal respect for the two men and their respective "languages" was woven into the fabric and feeling of the original study. It is maintained here for reasons of practicality as well as principle. To abandon that approach, taking sides with one man against the other, would have required an entirely different work by a different writer.

Ann Conrad Lammers
Albany, CA
December 1993

Chapter One

Builders of Bridges

A. THE SHAPE OF THE QUESTION

1. *Bridges and Borderlands*

One dream of some, though by no means all, twentieth-century theologians and clinicians has been to create better understanding between two communities—the religious and the scientific. These communities of theory and practice, rivals since at least the age of Galileo, have distrusted each other all the more vehemently since the Age of Reason when Voltaire, representing a scientific view of the church, recommending rubbing out the monstrosity. Nevertheless, a vision of collaboration, translation, and even marriage between the two fields continues to arise.

The dream arises most often perhaps among those whose professional work is the healing of souls and who therefore contact the inner symbolic springs of human life as well as attending to its mechanics. A concern for religious or symbolic levels of healing invites one inevitably to take up a theological perspective; but at the same time, the practice of caring for human souls involves psychological theory and skill. Indeed, to talk believably about divinity, holiness and salvation one must also be able to talk about physical pain and desire, psychic growth and transformation. Theological terms have to be "brought home" in terms of the subjectivity of daily human experience, or they ring hollow.

But a sober observer might question whether a theoretical bridge can be expected to unite the theological and psychological disciplines in the way the healer wishes. The success record of interdisciplinary bridge-builders is uneven. Bridges from one language world to the other have usually fallen into either of two categories of failure. Some have been completed and displayed only to have observers point out that one theory has appropriated the other, so that both feet of the bridge are now standing on the same side of the water. The presuppositions and concepts of one discipline control the agenda for both. Other attempted bridges stand with their feet on two shores and a defiant gap in the middle. The internal logic of each field refuses to engage the basic premises of the other.

Carl Gustav Jung and Victor White used the metaphor of "bridges" more than once to express the hopes and frustrations of their theological-psychological collaboration. As an example of the effort to live out an intellectual marriage between these two fields, the collaboration of White and Jung deserves to be honored in the history of Western civilization. As an experiment in conceptual and practical bridge-building, however, it occupies the second category of failure: when these two builders stopped their work, a large gap remained.

It seems that when Jung and White began to correspond in 1945, neither fully grasped the meaning of the other's key assumptions. They perceived some differences of language and concept; but they thought the differences could be got over with time and diligence. At first their areas of tension were fruitful. The two men respected each other's contributions, and their collaboration led to important writings on both sides. Then, partly for reasons extrinsic to the relationship, their conversation devolved into painful conflicts and in 1955 was bitterly broken off. Unresolved differences between them continued to echo in the writing of each man until he died.

The failure of such a collaboration, so hopefully begun between knowledgeable representatives of two fields, should be of interest to any who hope to engage in similar work. It may be that the risks of such a venture may be reckoned in advance, like the dangers of ocean sailing or rock-climbing, so that collaborators can prepare to meet difficulties when they arise. In his last book, *Soul and Psyche*, written after the end of the collaboration, White remarks:

> As Jung has said, "It is certainly a difficult task to find the bridge connecting the standpoint of dogma with the direct experience of psychological archetypes. . . ."

To this he ruefully adds:

> But it is important that bridges should really bridge, and
> this means that the two sides of the structure should really
> join.
>
> (*Soul and Psyche*, p. 44)[1]

Over time, as Jung and White became more aware of each
other's philosophical standpoints, and especially of their respective theories of knowledge, they began to despair of joining the
two sides of their conceptual structure. Their work foundered,
in part, because neither would allow his philosophical commitments to be co-opted or compromised. Their final state of in-
completion was honorable, for they sacrificed the bridge, but
not their moral and professional integrity. It was this same integrity that had made the conversation intrinsically worth having.

My purpose in this book will be to examine several levels of
the theological and psychological conversation between White
and Jung, including relevant aspects of their personal histories
and the politics and processes of their relationship. To study the
circumstances of the Jung-White collaboration and its failure
cannot, of course, constitute an exhaustive exploration of the
debate between "theology" and "psychology" as such. The two
fields are far too complex; neither could be adequately represented by a single spokesman or the work of a single decade. All
the same, a particular example may shed light on a whole class
of problems. Anyone interested in bridge-building on the same
territory may use this paradigm to locate some of the dangers
that might threaten such a project.

2. *Jung and White*

Approaching the subject as experts in their respective
fields, Jung and White agreed initially about what constitutes
the inner experience and objective welfare of the human soul.
But they disagreed from the start about other concepts essential
to their common enterprise, such as the source and extent of
human knowledge about God, the warrants of religious faith,
and the ultimate destiny of creation. It could be argued, there-

fore, that even if the personal and historical variables that endangered their relationship are discounted, their basic commitments still produced conflicts too basic for negotiation. It seems
apparent that the bitter falling out that began when Jung published *Answer to Job*[2] exposed, but did not create, the basic ob-
structions to the collaboration. This observation is significant
because it points to indelible obstacles that may even now prevent the full cooperation of Jungian psychology with any school
of Christian theology that shares metaphysical commitments
like White's.

On the other hand, it also can be demonstrated that the
collapse of the Jung-White collaboration was contingent on personal and historical factors, such as Jung's stubborn rejection of
metaphysical arguments and White's equally stubborn loyalty to
the orthodoxy of his religious order. One must reckon with the
impact on White's work of the narrow doctrinal boundaries
within which official Roman Catholic theologians of the 1950s
were expected to think and speak. If such contingent historical
factors were major reasons for the collaboration's failure, other
bridge-builders, starting out from similar shores, might yet succeed where Jung and White failed. Much hinges on the argument that the failure of this collaboration resulted not from irresolvable incompatibilities between the essentials of Thomistic
theology and analytical psychology, but rather from the personal and historical circumstances of the collaborators.

In support of this second viewpoint, features implicit in the
thought of the two men suggest that there was room for more
agreement in principle than they achieved in practice. Jung's
bias against metaphysics, for instance, belies the underlying
philosophical foundation of his work. His psychology betrays a
basic teleological thrust, an area of metaphysical common
ground which White identified in the beginning. White's wish
to promote the theological warrants of experience, unusual in a
Thomist of his time and place, led him to appreciate Jung's
experiential methods. And precisely because White could embrace Jung's neo-Kantian epistemology to the extent he did,
Jung saw him as an invaluable partner.

At the level of practical application, too, the two men
shared basic presuppositions. Both were motivated by concern

for the spiritual health of individuals in the modern age and for the survival of civilization. Both wanted to articulate grounds for hope. White's concept of salvation, as an object for human hope, is paralleled by Jung's concept of the endurance of meaning. Each in his own language related hope to wholeness, understood as spiritual health, completeness, and the integrity of the human personality. With this much agreement, we might suspect that contingent historical factors, not irreconcilable principles, caused the collaboration to fail.

But along with their agreements, Jung and White found profound discrepancies between their ways of thinking. Some of these discrepancies were methodological: for example, Jung's avoidance of anything smacking of metaphysics. If aversion to philosophical abstractions is essential to Jung's psychology, must not competent Jungians be committed to it as he was? If so, the common ground with virtually any school of Thomistic theology disappears. Also, Jung's commitment to individual rather than collective moral authority, his suspicion of truth claims made by institutional religious powers, and some of his psychologically justified claims about the God-image (e.g., his insistence that God has a moral shadow) are not easy to reconcile with Catholic doctrine as White understood it. These features, all central to Jung's thought, may be as difficult for a Christian theologian to swallow today as they were for Victor White.

The questions posed by these conflicting hypotheses can only be answered if one pays attention to the personal stories of Jung and White, as well as to theoretical issues that arose in their collaboration. For this reason the following chapters will weave considerable biographical and historical commentary together with discursive analysis.

3. Process and Form

One difficulty that arises, when one tries to sort out the discussion and to see what was at stake for Jung and White, is due to Jung's dislike of abstract concepts and philosophical methods. The grounds for his objection to conceptual abstraction may be implicit in the very fabric of his thought. But if so, then a project like the one in hand runs the risk of violating the premises of Jungian psychology, because there is no way to compare and examine two systems of thought without using a philosophical meta-theory, i.e., a theory that can compare salient features of two other theories. As far as possible, in constructing such a meta-theory, I have relied on metaphors springing from the conversation between Jung and White. Bridge-building, as we have seen, is one metaphor. Language, or linguistic systems (syntax, vocabulary, grammar), will be another.

As to Jung's rejection of metaphysics, it is possible to show that, even though he has no patience with the abstractions of metaphysical argument as he understands it, essential features of his own psychology are metaphysical. Victor White was right in pointing to this fact.[3] In her incisive work, *Philosophical Issues in the Psychology of C. G. Jung*,[4] Marilyn Nagy traces Jung's commitment to a certain kind of neo-Kantian epistemology from his college years into his old age. She shows that although dislike of metaphysics is consistent with his neo-Kantian starting place, other parts of his thought are indelibly idealist and metaphysical. Central features of her work are discussed below, both here and in Chapter Four.

In certain contexts, Jung was ready to admit that his thinking had been shaped by the philosophical perspectives he had absorbed in his early education. For example, in one of his last essays, "Approaching the Unconscious," he called the study of Kant and Schopenhauer the "greatest spiritual adventure" of his youth (*Man and his Symbols*, p.56).[5] In 1929, evaluating the differences between himself and Freud, he wrote that it was "a great mistake on Freud's part to turn his back on philosophy" ("Contrasts," p.118).[6] And in 1959 he remarked on British television that as a young man, unlike Freud, he had been "steeped" in the philosophy of Kant ("Face to Face," p.431).[7]

Jung's unwillingness to engage in abstract conceptual arguments springs from a process-oriented pragmatism that he learned from William James, as well as from his neo-Kantian subjectivity. Although Nagy disputes the label "pragmatist," pointing out that Jung emphasized his prospective vision of psychic wholeness at the expense of immediate concreteness (Nagy, pp.19, 87 n.21, 91 n.1), his thought was certainly marked by a Jamesian practicality. Jung's focus, as he converses with White, is usually in terms of therapeutic process and development. White's tends to be more systematic; he thinks in terms of intellectual form, logic, and classification. At times, each borrows the other's approach; but for the most part they seem to operate out of these distinct perspectives.

The difference surely reflects temperamental as well as philosophic leanings. The two men are almost perfect representatives of the complementary tendencies that philosopher-anthropologist Gregory Bateson refers to as "process" and "form," Jung favoring the former and White the latter. These tendencies, which express themselves in distinct patterns of thought and styles of communication, actually require each other in principle, Bateson observes. Both are needed at alternating moments in any complex mental activity, such as learning. Bateson describes their relationship as "a *zigzag ladder of dialectic between form and process*" (*Mind and Nature*, p.215).[8] In a dialogue such as Jung's and White's, however, where the partners have strong opposing preferences, such a contrast in habitual perspectives can foster tension. Heraclitus is Bateson's prime example of the thinker who specializes in process at the expense of form (*Mind and Nature*, pp.222f). Readers of Jung will recall that he more than once expressed admiration for Heraclitus, the "very great sage" whose refrain was "mutability."[9]

Jung's resistance to formal rational argument—the kind he dismissed as metaphysical—was no doubt one-sided. On the other hand, White's preference for the logic of conceptual argument, reflecting his training in Thomistic philosophy, could be equally one-sided in its insensitivity to processive thought. Yet Victor White very much wished to cultivate a psychologically sensitive and therapeutic line of thought, to complement the formal bent of Catholic dogmatics. This wish was reflected not only in his involvement with Jung's psychology, but also in his focus on the theological impact of "experience" and in his important three-part essay on "affective knowledge."[10] In the end, according to most of his Dominican colleagues and superiors, White's conceptual work as a whole was tuned only too well to Jung's key.

4. Levels of Disagreement

Theoretically and methodologically, we may see the conversation tending to break down between White and Jung on at least three levels: doctrine, hermeneutics and epistemology. We can think of these three as if they were built upon each other, each providing the necessary foundation or context for the next. Epistemology is the base for the other two: it provides a context for hermeneutics, as hermeneutics does for doctrine.

White's arguments with Jung are sometimes stated at the doctrinal level, as assertions about which the theologian and psychologist disagree. The hermeneutical disagreement enters when we compare the ways the two men read the same text, using conflicting principles of interpretation. The most basic difficulty for Jung and White, however, is at the epistemological level. They both claim to know important aspects of reality, and even to know God; but they describe their "knowing" in drastically different ways. The epistemological level of disagreement could be called a deep syntax. It influenced the discussion on both sides, in ways of which the two speakers only gradually and painfully became aware.

When we study the record of the debate, we notice the three levels of disagreement. At the level of a doctrinal dispute, White says (for example), "God is absolutely good." Jung replies, "God (by which I mean the God who is actually known by human beings) is both good and evil." In an effort to untangle the roots of the doctrinal argument we come to the hermeneutical level. White's reading of the book of Job is correlated with established church teachings; Jung reads it as a creative product of the collective unconscious.

Just below the surface of the hermeneutical thicket we find a profound disagreement about epistemology. White's presupposition is that human beings know the nature of God, the world and themselves through reason and objective biblical revelation; and this knowledge is—*must* be, if God is trustworthy—consistent with what we know through the inner life of the soul. The eternal truths of Catholic Christian doctrine are, White affirms, borne out by human experience. Jung's epistemological starting-place, on the other hand, is his conviction that the only meaningful way to speak about the human knowledge of God, the world and ourselves is to predicate this knowledge entirely upon psychological experience. This, he hastens to add, is the nature of the church's knowledge as well. There is thus no such thing as an "absolute" truth for Jung; all truth is based on empirical observation, open to further refinement and change.

Faced with epistemological differences of this sort, there is no meta-context to which one can appeal except an existential faith commitment. But such commitments rise before the soul with unchallengeable authority. They are the nonnegotiable prior context, or what George Lindbeck calls the "irrefutable framework," grounding every other statement of belief or fact (*Nature of Doctrine*, p.10).[11] In disagreeing with each other, White and Jung can each only fall back upon an irrefutable and irreducible framework of faith.

A. DOCTRINE

The word "doctrine" is familiar from theological discourse, but it is unusual in psychological usage. I use it here to refer to an objective point of teaching in either field. Jung's later work often discusses major theological doctrines such as the Trinity and the nature of Christ, all of which he recasts in psychological terms. His psychological doctrines include, e.g., the concepts of shadow, animus and anima, the Self[12] as a complex of opposites; the individual's subjective "containment" within the psyche; the ethical requirement of sacrificing ego to Self; and the teaching that evil is a positive and equal contrary to good, rather than (as the Catholic Church classically teaches) a "privation" of it. In "The Integration of Evil," the ninth chapter of White's last book, *Soul and Psyche*, White discusses Jung's psychological proposals about the figure of Christ, the nature of God, and the problem of evil, as if they were flawed doctrines to be understood and criticized at the same level as the basic Christian teachings (*Soul and Psyche*, pp.146–51).

B. HERMENEUTICS

Jung and White differ also at the hermeneutical level, the level which asks, "How should we understand what is meant by the text?" Most strikingly, they read the Bible through different

interpretive lenses. Disagreement about hermeneutical principles entails disagreements about moral authority, the relevant
interpretive community, and even what shall be counted as a
"text." Jung, for instance, vests almost as much authority in
dreams, myths, and alchemical writings containing religious
symbolism (snake, child, mandala, etc.) as he does in canonical
biblical writings.

The effect of hermeneutical differences may be complex
and subtle. For example, in Appendix V to *Soul and Psyche*
(pp.233ff), White proposes an alternate reading of the book of
Job, applying a "Jungian" interpretive lens but arriving at conclusions very different from Jung's own. Thus we are concerned here not only with differences of hermeneutical theory
between Jungian psychology and Catholic theology, but also
with the fact that two readers, using ostensibly the same theoretical lens, may arrive at different readings of the same text.

This phenomenon is explained in part by differences in the
two readers' respective communities and contexts. Basic to hermeneutics is the issue of membership in the community in light
of which the text is read. The term "hermeneutical circle"
means that we experience and understand our central texts
within a community which also defines itself through those
texts. Thus one is likely to read biblical passages, in the context
of a consciously Christian community, differently from the way
one would read them outside it. (Not to mention the likelihood
that any two Christian communities may read texts in diverging
ways.) Freed from their place in Christian self-understanding,
the biblical texts can appear primarily as works of world literature, dream residues, or historical-political deposits.

Finally, we cannot interpret texts without ourselves becoming part of the interpretation, because we carry our personal
social and intellectual context with us as yet another lens
through which the text is read. The idea of the hermeneutical
circle does not negate the private and personal act of interpretation. We are dealing here with matters of variable degree and
priority. A complex mental world, consisting of more than one
community simultaneously, is almost inevitable for readers in a
pluralistic society. In such a society it is misleading to posit sharp
disjunctions between believers and nonbelievers, or to assume

that anyone is purely inside or outside a given community of interpretation.

It would be especially wrong to make such a disjunction when dealing with the interpretive world of C.G. Jung, who was simultaneously by his own account both inside and outside the mental world of Western Christendom, and loyal to both Protestant and Catholic self-understanding. Nevertheless, the concept of the hermeneutical circle helps us to ask a useful question: how well did Jung read "theologically," or White "psychologically"? Could either hope to interpret texts in ways acceptable to the other's primary community of interpretation?

C. EPISTEMOLOGY

The third level, creating a context for the other two, is the epistemology that governs all of Jung's and White's claims to know whatever it is they know about God and the world. We must review the difference between Jung's neo-Kantian epistemology, which attends only to psychological warrants, and White's more complex theory of knowledge. If there is a Gordian knot obstructing the conversation, it is pulled tight by their contrasting theories of knowledge.

One way to state the basic epistemological issue for Jung and White is to ask whether subjective experience is completely self-authenticating, especially regarding the claim to know or know about God. If religious concepts may be said to refer to a reality beyond the psyche, then there must be an objective measure by which such concepts may be judged true or false. If not, experience needs no justification beyond itself. It carries its own truth claim with it.

The epistemological question is thus also a question of authority, for it asks what is the court of last resort: whether the subjectivity of the individual, or the mythic consciousness of the collective, or some source of "objective" revelation against which the images of the psyche, individual and collective, may be seen and measured. Is there a "north" for the compass of human knowing, or is truth to be judged contextually? If the latter, is it to be tested by the *consensus gentium*—the standard of common consent—or by the inner convictions of individuals? To use theological language, the question of authority soon

leads to the question of canon: what is the standard of measure-
ment for the truth of human statements about God?

To raise the question of an objective "north," a reality outside of psychic perceptions against which to measure the truth
of an interpretation, is to ask whether we may go beyond the
intrapsychic to metaphysical language about God *in se* or Being
as such. But the very question is suspect, for Jung was determined "to know only the soul" (Nagy, Part I), i.e., to claim only
such knowledge as inner experience directly yields. Metaphysical inquiry ignores empirical evidence and abstracts attention
away from the soul, where real value is located. Jung saw the
arguments of metaphysics in any case as inappropriate to the
modern thought-world.

> It would be an anachronism, i.e., a regression, for the man
> of the twentieth century to solve his conflicts "rationalisti-
> cally" or metaphysically, therefore, *tant bien que mal*, he has
> built up for himself a psychology.
>
> (Foreword, *God and the Unconscious*, p.xxxvi)[13]

Beneath this observation about the modern temperament,
Jung's subjectivism is rooted in deep philosophical soil. Sympathy with Kant's critique of pure and practical reason, and especially with the second *Critique*, which "makes the fact of moral
values tantamount to knowledge of God" (Nagy, p.79), implicitly shapes all his psychological conclusions. In his insistence on
the primacy of the subject, Jung approaches psychomonism: a
conviction that no reality exists outside of subjective psychic
perceptions. Jung himself resisted the label, insisting that he
was merely agnostic about any extra-psychic truth. But Nagy
argues persuasively (pp. 63–79) that, on this question, Jung's
whole psychology can be summed up in the conclusions of
Kant's second *Critique*:

> (1) *Esse in anima* means to affirm inner values as over against
> either nominalist or purely rationalist views. (2) *Esse in anima*
> also means that reality itself equals the inner value of the
> subject. What is valuable is what is real.
>
> (Nagy, p.79)

Jung denies to the empiricist any observation post outside human subjectivity, making psychology powerless to test metaphysical claims objectively. He cannot invoke or recognize "absolute" truth, all truth being a function of the inward consciousness of the individual soul. Thus Jung stands in principle against any claim of extra-psychic or objective knowledge of God, and by extension against the magisterial authority of White's church which makes such claims.

White, on the other hand, operates in the intellectual world of Catholic Thomism, which appeals to the authority of a collective magisterial tradition and to the objectivity of the dogma supported by that tradition. Although he respects Jung's experiential starting-place, he also has a primary and unshakable commitment to the notion that absolute truth is grounded outside the subjective psyche, through reason and biblical revelation, as well as inside it through personal experience. Supported by his reading of Aquinas, whose epistemology he believes allows such an interpretation, White tries to join classic theological authorities—Scripture, reason, creed, tradition—with the subjective (Kantian) authority of experience.

White's ability to fit some aspects of Jung's psychology into his Thomistic thought-world is due to the fact that he interprets the writings of St. Thomas through a Platonizing, Augustinian lens. Why he does so, and the impact on his theology, are matters that will concern us in Chapter Two. Whereas his Platonizing lens permits him to follow Jung's subjectivism up to a point, he still insists on combining subjective experience with objective metaphysics. Thus he recognizes two kinds of human knowledge, both—he asserts—arising from and leading to the same eternal truth. It would be impossible, in White's opinion, for metaphysics and experience ultimately to conflict. According to Jung, however, their agreement would be impossible to demonstrate. And for his purposes, the attempt to do so is at best distracting.

Jung's systematic subjectivism gives him a formal advantage: his underlying epistemology is clearer and more single-minded than White's. Whether this formal advantage is judged a real advantage at the end of the day, however, depends on whether one believes that "the truth" is really known better through a single subjective lens, or through the more diverse and complicated lenses of White's theology. This choice seems to depend ultimately on the kind of personal commitments characteristic of faith.

B. THE LIMITS OF LANGUAGE

1. *Linguistic Metaphors and True Belief*

Both White and Jung use a metaphor of "language" to describe the difficulties in their conversation. For example, White's view of the collaboration in 1952 is suggested in this statement in the Author's Preface to his first book of essays on Jungian psychology:

> The worker on the borderlands of religion and psychology must be bilingual, and there is no dictionary which will supply the exact equivalents of the two languages he must employ.
>
> (Preface, *God and the Unconscious*, p.xxx)

Jung's view of the same set of difficulties is reflected in his Introduction to the same book:

> I do not presume to know what the theologian misunderstands or fails to understand in the empirical standpoint, for it is as much as I can do to learn to estimate his theological premises correctly. If I am not mistaken, however, one of the main difficulties lies in the fact that both appear to speak the same language, but that this language calls up in their minds two totally different fields of associations. Both can apparently use the same concept and are then bound to acknowledge, to their amazement, that they are speaking of different things.
>
> (Foreword, *God and the Unconscious*, pp.xviiif)

For the "worker on the borderlands," to be bilingual, then, means to unravel divergent meanings of terms that seem on first sight to be the same. To be bilingual one must also be bicultural, with a foot in both worlds. Even those who live and work on the "borderland" may share no consensus about language.

The cultural-linguistic model[14] has rich possibilities for a comparison of two systems of thought, and I use it frequently in the present essay; but it has limitations as well. "Language" cannot suggest all that is involved in the doctrinal, hermeneutical and epistemological stakes of the conversation between Jung and White. The model is both faithful and unfaithful to the reality it conveys. One serious difficulty with using a linguistic metaphor for religious systems of thought is that to call such a system a "language" (even when we view language as a "form of life" in Wittgenstein's sense) implies much about the objective coherence of *belonging*, but need imply nothing about the subjective condition of *believing*. To say that a statement is "true" in a cultural-linguistic sense may mean only that it makes sense in its context and fits coherently with other parts of the system to which it belongs. Such a "coherent" statement need not correspond, however, to any reality in heaven or on earth.[15]

A person might talk coherently about God and salvation, in that case, without necessarily believing that someone or something exists as "God," or that anyone will really be "saved." To claim that a statement is true then has no meaning, apart from saying it is coherent with the language system to which the statement belongs. But this is perhaps not what religious people mean by truth. Arguably it makes a profound difference, to people who speak in religious terms, whether their statements are to be conceived of as rooted in ontological reality or only in systemic coherence and behavioral correspondence.

The cultural-linguistic metaphor also has a relativizing implication which can make believers uncomfortable when applied to their own beliefs. One language is usually as adequate as any other, so long as each language is taken within its particular social context. Indeed, since growth of languages is mainly by historical evolution and not by conscious choice, the adequacy of a language must be judged "adaptationally." Past a certain point of complexity, it is of questionable value to compare one language with another as to truth, or even beauty— though it's a chauvinistic temptation to claim superiority for one's own dialect.

In defining key elements of Christian doctrine, contextual coherence is probably not an adequate definition of truth. Is it simply parochial chauvinism, when Christians claim that salvation comes to all humanity through Christ? Modern theologians who want to avoid turning *solus Christus* into a warrant for religious imperialism frequently wrestle with this claim, but find they cannot disconnect it from their whole web of Christological and soteriological meaning. The struggle to achieve universalism, yet not abandon the centrality of Christ, underlines the importance of that claim itself for the tradition.

According to the "cultural-linguistic" theory of theological doctrines, the truth of a belief is definable as behavioral coherence within a community's self-description or central "story."[16] The truth of what is spoken, then, includes behavior—both individual and collective—within a social context over a period of time. The patterns of communal life are thus an integral part of what is meant by religious "language"; and in acting true to the context of the communal faith, a member of the community testifies to the truth of belief. We not only "speak Christian" for example; we "do Christian" (or Muslim or Hindu); and the coherence of our doing, as judged by our linguistic culture, is what is meant, in this theory, by its truth.

The cultural-linguistic metaphor undergoes its hardest test when we consider "true belief" as a pledge of human hope, especially hope concerning life after death, meaning in the midst of suffering, and the reliability of a goodness which redeems the world. These existential questions seem to demand a referential standard of truth. Consciousness of mortality presses us to seek grounds for a hope that is more than merely culturally coherent, a hope as firm as the fact of death. Many Christians—White among them—claim that such a reality is known to us, rooted not merely in the coherence of human culture but in a transcendent reality beyond it. In the Jungian epistemology such a claim is unverifiable; his best warrant for hope is that human lives can undergo visible transformations over time.

Thus it may be that to talk about religious "systems," using the linguistic metaphor, engages us in paradox from the beginning. Part of the very coherence of religious language is its claim that it is *not* merely a "language," but refers to some ultimate reality. Many theists would take the statement, "there is God," to have ontological as well as cultural-linguistic significance. It is part of the very syntax of the religious language system of Victor White, for one, to claim that the accuracy of Christian language is warranted by reference to a relationship and reality ontologically prior to culture and language, a relationship and reality which make possible both culture and language.

2. Epistemological Syntax

In Lindbeck's typology, Victor White operates in the cognitivist or propositionalist doctrinal world of neo-scholasticism. He tries to convert that world, however, to a cultural-linguistic tolerance of religious differences.[17] Jung's doctrinal context is the experiential-expressive world of post-Schleiermacher Protestantism; he insists that religious statements are to be understood only as they operate within the psyche—individual or collective. Jung's approach to doctrine can work two ways: he either takes the meaning of religious statements from cultural-linguistic context, or he refers the question of meaning to the pure individual subjectivity of experiential-expressivism.

Jung's conviction as an empiricist is that the image of God in the human psyche is real in precisely the empirical sense that a linguistic metaphor says statements are true. That is, Jung understands the God-image to be contained in individual and communal mental process. He makes no claim about God's existence "outside" that psychological frame, even when he says he *knows* that God exists ("Face to Face," p.428). What Jung can claim to "know" is that the image of God exists in the psyches of his patients, in collective memory, and in his own experience. He consistently disclaims knowing whether the God-image refers to something outside the psyche—personal or collective— that experiences it. This sort of objective knowledge, he says, cannot be had.

It is possible to accept the metaphor of language in the sense that Jung and White both invoke it, but to carry it a step further than they do (and in a direction somewhat different from Lindbeck's), to talk about the "grammar" or "syntax" of the two languages. Syntax in this sense refers to what Gregory Bateson calls the meta-context, and what Lindbeck calls the irrefutable framework. When Jung presses White to learn a new language and White dwells on the problems of translation, they are facing not merely verbal discrepancies, but differences in syntactical pattern, in the deep structures of presuppositions that frame their ideas.

In his second letter to White, Jung enlisted his help and suggested the asymmetrical terms of their collaboration. He wrote:

> You cannot preach to a man who does not understand the language. To shout and to repeat makes no sense. But you feel as I do, that the theologian ought to learn a new language. . . . It is a gigantic task indeed to create a new approach to an old truth. . . . The old way of interpreting has itself to be interpreted. . . .
>
> (*Letters I*, p.387)[18]

"*The theologian ought to learn a new language.*" It is significant that, for Jung, the challenge ran only one way. The empirical language of analytical psychology, he thought, was already suited to the modern era. He could see no point in learning to speak an archaic language that forced one into metaphysical tautologies. Christian theology would have to catch up, or else remain largely irrelevant to people in the modern era.

It is common to refer to "misunderstandings" between Jung and White. Victor White wanted to call their dispute by this name and tried sometimes to blame the toughness of their dilemma on the contrast between psychological "types" (implying that Jung's argument is that of a feeling type and his own that of a thinking type). He writes this way, for example, in his 1955 paper, "Kinds of Opposites."[19] The dispute between himself and Jung about the problem of evil, he says, "is probably not insoluble; and may be largely due to misunderstanding, and typological differences" ("Opposites," p.146). The body of the article, however, gives no reason to think this is the case. In 1959 he again alludes to disagreements arising from nothing more than divergent life experiences and temperaments:

> I think you will agree that your work itself will be moribund
> if there is not some disagreement about it, and some
> *Auseinandersetzung* with those of different backgrounds and
> experiences—and perhaps different typologies!
>
> (VW to CGJ, 18 Oct. 59)[20]

Even White's next-to-last letter to Jung regrets "some strange misunderstanding—or non-understanding—which has arisen between us" (VW to CGJ, 6 May 60). But looking at all the evidence, one must conclude that their difficulties do not arise just from a failure to understand, which could in principle be corrected. The two men disagree about how to speak of reality. In their history together, the closer they come to understanding each other the more they disagree.

White tries to show, as he argues in his essay "Thomism and 'Affective Knowledge,' "[21] that a subjective epistemology of personal experience can be included and coordinated with discursive, intellective syntax (found, for example, in *Summa Theologiae*). The attempt to coordinate two kinds of knowledge supports White's apologetic project; as a theologian he wants to show that the church's teaching is confirmed "from below."

Jung denies White's priorities. If subjective experience is merely the second sail on a boat driven by the oversized sail of intellective reason, he argues, that boat will capsize. The only sail Jung ever raises is subjective experience. Conceptual, discursive reason and abstract concepts may possibly be allowed in the conversation if they support the authority of experience; otherwise, they threaten to undercut the all-important subjective evidence. Instead of dealing with religious reality, then, we would have to do merely with an intellectual game.

Before his rhetoric had had time to sharpen in the long debate, Jung compared dogma with experience as follows:

> A dogma is always the result and fruit of many minds and
> many centuries, purified of the oddities, shortcomings, and
> flaws of individual experience. But for all that, the individ-
> ual experience, by its very poverty, is immediate life, the
> warm red blood pulsating today. It is more convincing to a
> seeker after truth than the best tradition.
>
> (*Psychology and Religion, CW 11*, §88)

If Jung had said no more than this, White might almost have agreed with him. Jung's word "convincing" might be read in terms sympathetic to White's own work on the subjectivity of affective knowledge; for White agrees that knowledge of God can arise immediately, nonrationally and personally. He even insists that the doctrines of the church should be available to empirical examination and justification.

In his own work, before and after the break with Jung, White argues that there ought to be room for psychological verification of theological assertions. The truths of faith cannot be mere abstractions. So in 1958, in his review of Raymond Hostie's book on Jung,[22] White writes:

> [Hostie] seems to relegate the *privatio boni* to a purely philo-
> sophical sphere which escapes empirical examination. This
> will not do much to overcome the endless misunderstand-
> ings which must arise between those who regard good and
> evil as two components of a whole and those who regard
> goodness and wholeness as equivalent, and evil as a defect in
> goodness itself.
>
> ("Hostie," pp.63f)[23]

But Jung's diction in *Aion* and other late works goes further, until he sets the warrants of metaphysics and experience
irreconcilably against each other. It does not help matters that
he often does this while claiming that he is not doing it, as in the
following statement:

> Psychology is an empirical science and deals with realities. As
> a psychologist, therefore, I have neither the inclination nor
> the competence to mix myself up in metaphysics. Only, I have
> to get polemical when metaphysics encroaches on experience
> and interprets it in a way that is not justified empirically.
>
> (*Aion, CW 9ii,* §89)[24]

As White points out, Jung's experiential epistemology is not
itself justifiable by experience. It is an interpretive lens directed
toward experience; and the choice of the lens is *a priori*. White
maintains that Jung's denigration of metaphysics is therefore

itself a metaphysical move. For example, in his largely negative review of Hostie's book, White grants Hostie one point: Jung habitually mixes talk about the "God-imago" with talk about God. Although Hostie "can and does quote Jung himself to show that philosophical assumptions, taken from Kant and the positivists, are invoked to justify this usage," White continues,

> It should be clear that the assertion that empirical knowledge is the *only* valid human knowledge, and that any other (e.g., by deduction) is "downright impossible," is itself nonempirical and incapable of empirical verification. . . . On the other hand, it is an observable psychological fact that some people do make statements about God on rational grounds, whatever Kant may think of the validity of their procedure, and the fact is one of paramount psychological importance to themselves which should not be dismissed by the psychologist for *a priori* reasons.
>
> ("Hostie," p.62)

A possible conclusion from White's observations is that in order to be self-consistent, Jung ought to reject neither systematic theology nor metaphysics as such. He should simply join White in criticizing the penchant of some religious thinkers (Catholic and Protestant) to build "one-sided" abstract conclusions at the expense of subjectivity.

This view of Jung's position is only tenable if Jung has no principled objection to metaphysics, but was driven to reject philosophical abstractions by a reductive argument that, in a more clear-sighted moment, he himself would call "inferior thinking." It would suit White's argument, then, if we could show that in trying to keep the focus on experience, Jung accidentally threw the baby out with the bath.

We can test this hypothesis by asking whether Jung would tolerate having the philosophical baby brought back in. Would he accept metaphysical argument as a coordinate, albeit secondary, support to the conclusions of empirical evidence? Jung's objection to metaphysical argumentation goes deeper, I believe, than this proposal allows. Like Goethe and the German Romantics whom Jung so admired, he holds that systematic philosophi-

cal inquiry represents a death-threat to the warm life-blood of
subjective experience.

If this is really Jung's position, its closest philosophical relative is found in Ludwig Feuerbach's *The Essence of Christianity*.[25]
Jung ridicules the materialism of Feuerbach when he finds it in
Freud;[26] but he rejects systematic theology for reasons that, if not
identical with Feuerbach's reasons, do not conflict with them.
Feuerbach posits a stage in religious history, and in the psychological life of individuals, when it was possible to experience a
wholehearted primitive identification with religious myths. Rationalistic academic theology, he asserts, breaks and supersedes
this naive identification with the holy. In the aftermath, it is impossible for civilized humanity (or the educated individual) to re-
capture the original wholeness of the unconscious projection.
Feuerbach looks forward, however, to a third and final stage of
religious self-awareness: the synthesis which resolves the conflict
of the first two stages. The rebirth of our religious wholeness, he
affirms, is when we take the God-symbols "inside" and consciously recognize that "what a man declares concerning God, he
in truth declares concerning himself" (*Essence of Christianity*, p.29).

Jung need not adopt Feuerbach's Hegelian logic to agree
with other features of his argument. Like Feuerbach, he sets
intellectual concepts of God against the immediate personal
experience of the holy, and anticipates a stage in history—
already realized, he believes, in some individuals—when the
reality of "God within" will become a psychological principle of
wholeness, overcoming the warring opposites. Seen from this
viewpoint, Jung rejects theological metaphysics not by an accident of rhetoric, but because he is convinced that religious experience outweighs theological concept. Like Feuerbach, he sus-
pects that discursive analysis only destroys the integrity of the
soul's connection to God.

For his part, Victor White also had objections to academic
theology as practiced by some of his contemporaries. He wanted
nothing to do with a desiccated doctrine that treated experience
as unimportant. Indeed, his criticism of arid theological intellectualism made him something of a maverick in his Order even
before his collaboration with Jung. All this predisposed White to
favor Jung's empiricism, though he wanted to turn it to a pur-

pose foreign to Jung's thinking. White hoped to integrate Jungian psychology with the warrants of discursive reason, to yield a truer and more modern interpretation of St. Thomas.

So, although he was sympathetic to Jungian empiricism, as he understood it, a frontal attack on metaphysics as such could only seem foolish to White, who had, as required by his training with the Dominicans, studied Thomistic philosophy for four years before formally beginning his study of theology. Indeed, White had no intellectual tools but what his Dominican training provided, since he had entered the Order at nineteen and gone to no other school. He was, for all his discomfort with neo-scholasticism, a thoroughly orthodox theologian. His conception of orthodoxy depended on the faithful use of an objectively grounded philosophy.

As one might predict, neither White nor Jung could ultimately give way to the other's basic presuppositions. On Jung's side it was a point of intellectual integrity to question statements made from a metaphysical standpoint. On White's it was a point of integrity to rely on them. White's sacramental ecclesiology saw the church as a collective center of consciousness and experience, whose knowledge of God was equal to that of the individual. Jung saw the individual, not the collective, as the center of both knowledge and moral autonomy.

Perhaps if the two thinkers could have allowed for two equally useful kinds of religious grammar, applying metaphysical arguments in one kind of discourse and suspending them in the other, their disagreements might have been got over. But for this to be the case, Jung would have had to relax his Kantian epistemological dogmatism enough to give metaphysics a place in modern thought, and White would have had to allow for some kind of discontinuity between metaphysical and experiential reality. Barring such profound and unlikely compromises, the best bilingual dictionary could not create harmony.

C. THE SHAPE OF THE RELATIONSHIP

Although White was a full generation younger than Jung,[27] we should not consider him simply as the junior partner in their professional relationship. White spoke the language of Thomistic theology in his time as skillfully and coherently as Jung spoke that of analytical psychology. They undertook their intellectual collaboration to this extent as equals. Intellectual and personal asymmetries were discernible, however, from the start.

Jung's social community was the scientific-analytical world in Zurich, a circle he had created around himself and of which he was the unquestioned head.[28] White's was the Dominican college of Blackfriars, Oxford, where he taught theology, and other Roman Catholic communities in Oxford, Cambridge and London. White also enjoyed a circle of Jungian friends and associates outside of his church affiliations.[29] These friends, however important to him personally, had little to say about his standing as a Catholic theologian.

When Jung received his first letter from Victor White he had just celebrated his seventieth birthday (*Letters I*, pp.381f). He was thus in the final stage of a phenomenally fruitful career. He had fought professional battles, suffered losses, collected followers; he could negotiate on his own terms. Unlike Victor White, who had taken a vow to obey his ecclesial superiors, C.G. Jung labored in his own vineyard. This degree of professional independence, won at great personal cost, allowed Jung to pursue his convictions without risking his career. At a point when their collaboration had all but ended, Jung acknowledged these crucial differences of social context in a letter to White:

> Somehow I can afford my independence, but I am fully aware that there are many who cannot do the same. . . .
> Only the free-lance can risk saying something beyond the conventional and thus cause discomfort to himself without endangering his very existence.
>
> (*Letters II*, p.242)

Jung treated the question less charitably and somewhat less accurately[30] when he snapped, in a letter to Howard Philp:

> What Victor White writes about the assimilation of the shadow is not to be taken seriously. Being a Catholic priest

he is bound hand and foot to the doctrine of his Church and
has to defend every syllogism.

(Soul and Psyche, p.259)[31]

Jung's professional autonomy started with his traumatic
break from the orthodoxy of Freud. White's security as a professional theologian, on the other hand, was predicated on his
adherence to the orthodoxy of his church. While his conscience
may have been free in theory, that freedom was—at least from
Jung's point of view—heavily conditioned. Given all that both
men invested in their collaboration, its ultimate deterioration
was costly to them both. In Jung's view, the loss might have been
avoided if White's work had not been subject to such tight ecclesial constraints.

In view of their differences of age and reputation, it is all
the more remarkable that Jung at first relied so confidently on
his younger partner. The early stage of collaboration seemed to
represent a genuine meeting of minds. White wrote to Jung for
the first time as soon as the Second World War had ended in
Europe. With his letter, dated 3 August 1945,[32] White sent four
articles he had written since discovering Jung's work: "The
Frontiers of Theology and Psychology," 1942;[33] "St. Thomas
Aquinas and Jung's Psychology," 1944;[34] "Psychotherapy and
Ethics," 1945;[35] and a "Postscript" to the latter,[36] reviewing a
book by a Freudian psychotherapist on the ethical implications
of psychotherapy.

When White first contacted Jung he had already been
through a period of Jungian analysis and had spent considerable time studying the modern masters of psychology. Dissatis-
fied with Freud and Adler, he turned to Jung as the one major
psychologist whose work cohered with the theology of Aquinas
as White understood it. He saw Jung as the personification of
the best "new science," with whose help he would create a modern Thomistic synthesis, recasting divine truth in modern psychological categories. His purpose was apologetical: in this recasting the true meaning of Christian faith might be conveyed
better to the modern mind.

Jung, meanwhile, had for some time been looking for a
reputable Roman Catholic theologian with a deep, personal

grasp of psychology, who would work with him to refine his interpretation of Catholicism. His goal seemed on the surface highly compatible with White's, for both viewed Christianity as the only remedy for the soul-sickness and self-destructive tendencies of the modern world, and both cared deeply about revitalizing the central symbols of Christian life in Western culture.

Jung's first letter to White (26 Sept. 45) mentions some Catholic theologians with whom he has worked previously and expresses his great interest in the Roman Catholic point of view. His second letter (5 Oct. 45), written after studying White's monographs, expresses an outpouring of confidence and expectation. His delight at having a psychologically informed theologian to work with spills over in a joke:

> Excuse the irreverential pun: you are to me a white raven[37] inasmuch as you are the only theologian I know of who has really understood something of what the problem of psychology in our present world means.
>
> (*Letters I*, p.383)

He adds, significantly, "You have rendered justice to my empirical and practical standpoint throughout" (Ibid, p.384). This was a powerful endorsement, for it was exactly in relation to his empiricism and pragmatism that Jung had found himself perpetually misunderstood by representatives of the church. For contrast, he comments on a Catholic theologian whose point of view is very different from White's:

> I enjoy the most valuable help of Prof. Hugo Rahner, S.J. . . . . But I see him only rarely and it is most difficult to find out how far his psychological understanding reaches. I think he is too careful.
>
> (Ibid, p.386)

The phrase "too careful" may be Jung's judgment of Rahner's theology or psychology; but it was probably also a reflection on the other man's personality. Jung apparently could not get close enough to Rahner to find out how deeply the theologian understood either Jung's theory or his own inner life. These comments about Rahner were thus also hints as to what Jung expected of any theological collaborator: to communicate the depth of his psychological understanding and to take personal risks for the sake of a shared task whose "gigantic" importance White had already recognized.[38]

A sign of Jung's enthusiasm about his new partner was that he soon invited White to visit him at Bollingen. In a letter of 30 April 1946, he lyrically evoked the atmosphere of the place and promised White that here he need wear no "disguise,"[39] since the local residents were accustomed to clergy, and the monastery of Einsiedeln was nearby.[40]

A hint of the risks White was taking by collaborating with Jung can be seen in his dream, which he sent to Jung after his first visit to Bollingen. In the dream,[41] as summarized by Adler and Jaffé, White found that

> he was sailing, with Jung at the helm, from Norway to England. They were passing through perilous rocks at great speed, but there was no feeling of fear "because the wind was taking care of us."
>
> (*Letters I*, p.448n)

Jung's comments on White's sailing dream show an exhilaration which, from the point of view of normal Jungian dream interpretation, is either less than candid or signals that Jung was so swept up in the mutual adventure that he failed to notice the obvious danger to them both. On 6 November 1946 he wrote:

> I had all sorts of feelings or "hunches" about you and about the risks you are running. We are indeed on an adventurous and dangerous journey!
>
> (*Letters I*, p.448)

It seems odd that Jung failed to comment on the psychological dangers—which must have been obvious to him as a sailor—represented by rocks, speed, and the dream ego's lack of conscious attention. Jung, of all people, did not trust the wind entirely in either the literal or the archetypal sense. In various writings he comments that the Holy Spirit is an ambiguous power which always unsettles human structures, including the church.

If the adventure was dangerous for White, it posed risks for Jung as well. A heart embolism struck a week or so after he wrote his glowing response to White's dream. It put him close to death. The letter of November 1946 may have been one of the last letters he wrote before falling ill.

After Jung's heart attack, White wrote at first to Jung's secretary, Marie-Jeanne Schmid, and then to Mrs. Jung, to avoid tiring his friend. His next letter directly to Jung was a brief typed note on 11 December 1946, which referred again to the "wind" of his dream, this time identifying the wind as the Holy Spirit:

> I am very well and in good spirits and hope that the *pneuma* will continue to blow and keep us both off the rocks. Any way, He knows best. . . .
>
> (VW to CGJ, 11 Dec. 46)

White's note elicited an immediate and lengthy response. Jung's next (18 Dec. 46) letter to White was a long letter that he wrote by hand, while lying in bed, about a month after he suffered the embolism.

A footnote by Adler and Jaffé, attached to Jung's letter of 18 Dec. 46 but reflecting on the whole correspondence, gives an excellent overview of the relationship as viewed from the perspective of Jung's letter-writing:

> It is the first of a long series of handwritten letters, often of many pages, showing [Jung's] great personal interest in the correspondence with White, who seemed able to give Jung what he felt he needed most: a man with whom he could discuss on equal terms matters of vital importance to him. It is significant that with the growing estrangement over the problem of the *privatio boni* . . . the handwritten letters are replaced by dictated, typed ones, except for the very last two . . . written during White's final illness.
>
> (*Letters I*, p.450n)

The causes of the eventual break between the collaborators were related to intellectual as much as to personal differences. That is, their differences were intellectual first and became personal only later. The work, undertaken in good faith, ran into massive disagreements, misunderstandings and contrary assumptions. If Jung's feverish little book, *Answer to Job*, can bear the comparison, one would say it was the tip of an iceberg, the visible occasion but not the underlying cause of disaster. And there were other forces at work as well, winds that blew against White from his church and his Order, which made the outcome of the story more disastrous than it might otherwise have been.

The relationship began with an upward curve from the initial enthusiasm of discovery, rising up five years of productive but increasingly labored work (1945–50), and arriving at an uneasy plateau of three years (from White's first reading of *Answer to Job* in 1951 to the publication of its English translation). Then followed a downslope of distance, delays, misunderstanding and frustration, finally verging on mutual hostility (1954–55). After that came a break of four years (1956–59). The coda of the last few months (early 1960) was marked by affection and regret. The two men's concluding correspondence resonates with the mutual wish that, even if they could not agree, each might still hear and respond to the other's best argument.

Chapter Two

Thomism and the
Warrants of Experience

A. VICTOR WHITE, AN INTRODUCTION[1]

1. *The Thomistic Climate*

To understand Victor White's situation as a theologian it is essential to know something of the historical context in which he was working. Of particular significance is the political climate for theologians in the twentieth century Roman Catholic Church. White was a Thomist, and Thomistic scholarship is influenced by political (ecclesiastical) forces in an important way. Without undertaking a detailed study of the history of modern Thomism and the response to it by church authorities, we can nonetheless see something of White's situation.

Pendulum-swings recur in the history of church teaching. Periods of doctrinal expansion and contraction succeed each other with some regularity. Theologians synthesize ancient faith and modern knowledge, in response to which the hierarchical arm reinforces an accustomed order. Many theologians acquiesce to this reminder of official boundaries; but others, pursuing their vision of a developing doctrine, continue to run "out of bounds" until official church theology is forced upon them by some sort of disciplinary action. In the twentieth century one example of the interaction between Catholic theologians and the official forces of orthodoxy can be seen in Pope Pius X's efforts to discipline the Modernists. The effort to halt what was seen as the wrong kind of doctrinal development led in some circles to an atmosphere of theological reaction and stagnation. A Roman Catholic scholar, J. A. Weisheipl, summarizes the process:

Ecclesiastical legislation during and following the Modernist crisis failed to achieve the broad goals of Leo XIII. A narrow legalized Thomism, out of touch with modern movements after World War II, created resentment and a "new theology" that found inspiration in evolutionism, phenomenology, and the teachings of P. Teilhard de Chardin. Pius XII, an ardent advocate of modernity, found it necessary to condemn dangerously extreme views of the *théologie nouvelle* in *Humani generis* (Aug. 12, 1950).

(*NCE*, vol.12, p.1168)[2]

In Victor White's day the conservative Thomism of the Roman pontifical universities was endorsed as the theological platform upon which sound Catholic doctrine must be built. This doctrinal foundation applied in principle for all Roman Catholic theologians. Many scholars and administrators in White's order, conscious of the heritage of St. Thomas and the Dominican teaching tradition, felt especially delegated to maintain conservative neo-Thomistic standards. These standards, reinforced by Pius XII in the encyclical *Humani generis* (1950), had a chilling effect on some, like Victor White, whose theological genius was the more speculative and creative development of doctrine.

Victor White should be numbered among modern theologians who have worked to create a more open, less intellectualist Thomism, avoiding an excessive abstraction and rationalism by attending also to the more subjective aspects of faith and knowledge. One of his important essays, "Thomism and 'Affective Knowledge,'" argues for a Thomism grounded in St. Thomas' writings, which would be consistent with knowledge generated by subjective experience. White found in Aquinas' work a plain recognition of the direct, experiential knowledge of God. He justified his own theological attention to the warrants of experience (of which more below) by referring to Aquinas' Platonizing and Augustinian tendencies.

White was readier than many of his contemporaries at Blackfriars to recognize, and to claim that St. Thomas also recognizes, a knowledge of God which does not depend on (though it does not contradict) knowledge arising from the discursive use of intellect. His desire to found theological knowl-

edge on an experiential basis was one of the factors predispos-
ing White to Jung's psychology. But it placed his theology in a
somewhat unique position relative to many of his colleagues.
The conservative Thomism which prevailed in his day, exemplified by the work of Garrigou-Lagrange, among others, maintained an attitude of caution, verging on severe distrust, toward
theological arguments claiming "experience" as a warrant.[3]

The term *experience* requires clarification. White wanted his
use of this term to be understood in the broad English commonsense tradition. In an endnote to his last work, *Soul and Psyche*,
he turned to a current dictionary definition to explain what he
meant:

> We use the word "experience" in the broadest sense as it is
> defined by the *Oxford English Dictionary*: "The fact of being
> consciously the subject of a state or condition, or of being
> consciously affected by an event. Also an instance of this: a
> state or condition viewed subjectively; an event by which one
> is affected."
>
> (*Soul and Psyche*, p. 274, note 1)

White quickly adds that his use of the word can be distin-
guished from its use in Modernism, which he says "exalted the
'religious sense' . . . at the expense of voluntary intellectual assent. . . ." (Ibid)

Appropriately, White never claims that Aquinas uses *experientia* the way he, White, uses "experience."[4] Aquinas uses the
word rarely and narrowly, unlike the medieval Cistercians whose
usage is closer to that of a modern writer like White.[5] Aquinas
limits himself to the Aristotelian sense, defining experience as
remembered sense-perceptions (*ST* 1a.54,5).[6] The closest Aquinas
comes to using the word in a sense similar to White's is his admission that a human being may know something about the working
of grace

> inferentially by perceptible signs . . . for in fact he who re-
> ceives it knows by an experience of sweetness which is not
> experienced by him who does not receive it.
>
> (*ST* 1a2ae.112,5)

"Yet," Aquinas significantly adds, "this knowledge is imperfect" (Ibid), since inferences about God based on sense-perception are bound to be uncertain. In view of these passages, White cannot appeal to Aquinas' use of *experientia*. He argues instead that important tendencies in Aquinas' thought leave the way open for a theological orthodoxy which is psychologically informed and experiential—though in a sense closer to the medieval Cistercians than to Aquinas.

After White's death his colleague at Blackfriars, Thomas Gilby (whose philosophical work was close to the dominant school of Thomism at the time), took over the task, which had been White's, of translating and editing the first volume of the Blackfriars edition of the *Summa Theologiae*. In his Acknowledgement at the beginning of the first volume of that edition, Gilby succinctly describes the difference between White's approach and his own:

> [M]any will not have to read between the lines to perceive that [the editor] is not so warm to the *mythos* of depth psychology as Fr Victor was, nor so cool towards the *logos* of the scholasticism of Cajetan and the theologians of Salamanca, the Baroque, and the Leonine revival.
>
> (*ST* Vol.1, p.xvii)

In what follows I will use "revisioned Thomism" or "experiential theology" as shorthand terms for White's position, and "neoscholasticism" or conservative Thomism for the position Gilby embraces here. For my purposes this simple distinction between two schools of Thomistic thought is sufficient; it will help to explain at least some of the theological conflicts White experienced in his Order and within himself concerning his collaboration with Jung.[7]

2. *Blackfriars, Oxford*

The atmosphere in which White worked was colored by the history of the Dominican college called Blackfriars. Speaking as a historian and a former resident of that college, Aelred Squire recounts the relevant history as follows:

The modern Blackfriars, Oxford, was founded in 1921 by
the young provincial, Bede Jarrett, the first modern English
Dominican to take a degree at Oxford. (Remember that the
universities had been banned to Catholics until the 19th
century.) And although this is not mentioned either by Seb
Bullough or Gervase Matthew [historians of Blackfriars]
who greatly admired Bede—he is still a cult figure to the
archivist—it is certain that there was substantial opposition
to the founding of a house in Oxford in 1921. Only once did
I meet anyone who could describe the scenes to me. They
feared for the faith and morals of the young men who might
go there. In this they were not of course very unusual
among loyal Catholics.

(A.S., 3 Aug. 1987)

Bede Jarrett's intention was to found a school that could
provide an intellectually challenging theological education for
young Dominicans. His opponents at the time—it was, after all,
the Jazz Age—suspected Oxford as a morally treacherous setting. Although these anxieties had been largely forgotten by the
1940s, the community at Blackfriars, Oxford, still tended to
lean toward theological conservatism, perhaps partly to reassure anyone who may still have doubted the school's orthodoxy.

What survived was the double feeling of loyalty to some
kind of official Church Thomism, created by the fact that St.
Thomas had of course been a Dominican. No one worried
that not all the tenets of modern neo-Thomism would necessarily have been held or even understood by St. Thomas. It
is important to see that most of these problematic things
were not strictly-speaking *dogmatic*; they were mostly philosophical, and very few people take *all* of them seriously
nowadays.

(A.S., 3 Aug. 1987)

As a residual echo of its beginnings in such shady circumstances, the school was not fully endorsed by the English Province until after Vatican II. In the forties and fifties it still could
not independently grant a theological diploma (A.S., 15 July
1987).

Victor White was a brilliant and respected scholar, but even his strongest admirer would not claim for him a place with the church's greatest writers. His prose does not rank with Teilhard's, for example; and his obituary writer in the July 1960 *Blackfriars* comments accurately that White's writing, though theologically profound, has the stylistic defect of being unvaryingly serious.[8] Still, his present obscurity is not a fair measure of his calibre as a theologian. It probably reflects, rather, the somewhat truncated quality of his life and work. Had he lived to enjoy the fruits of the second Vatican Council instead of dying shortly before it, he would now very likely be numbered among the important Catholic theologians whose careers and lives revived in that new atmosphere of openness.

To date Victor White has no biographer,[9] and unlike Jung, he left no autobiography. This fact is not surprising for several reasons. White was laconic, especially about his inner life and feelings. Although he had a circle of friends, both men and women, in the Jungian community and in wider church circles, he cultivated a habit of silence that kept the closest of his Dominican colleagues at something of a distance.[10] Aelred Squire, who knew and cared about Victor White from the early 1940s until the latter's death, recalls—in poignant hyperbole—"I had to batter my way into his life in order to know him at all" (A.S., 15 July 87).

According to Squire, White may have achieved what was for him a uniquely deep level of friendship with C. G. Jung. Yet a careful reading of their correspondence shows that, even in this relationship, White was emotionally self-disclosing only rarely. His letters of 8 November 53 and 4 March 54 are exceptions; afterward he retreated into his core of self-containment and, where personal and emotional matters are concerned, virtual silence.

Clues to his secular education and experience before entering the Dominican Order are sparse. White was born on the outskirts of London in Croydon (VW to CGJ, 10 Aug. 52), on 21 October 1902. His father was an Anglican clergyman, who preached sermons that were apparently stern to the point of fierceness (A.S., 17 Oct. 91). White must have converted to Roman Catholicism by the time he was nineteen; for he went to

Valladolid at that age to study for the secular priesthood (A.C., 25 Aug. 91). Aside from these sparse facts and his baptismal name, Gordon Henry White, it is hard to glean much information about White's youth.

As to his relation with the Order of Preachers, the Subprior at Blackfriars, Oxford, Fr. Paul Parvis, kindly provided the following dates from the *Catalogus Conventuum Provinciae Angliae necnon Fratrum et Monalium Ordinis Praedicatorum in iis commorantium anno MCMLX*. Victor White entered the Dominican novitiate 29 September 1923 at the age of twenty-one, took his simple vows 30 September 1924, and was ordained to the priesthood 2 June 1928. He was then assigned to Blackfriars, Cambridge. In 1930, according to the *Catalogus* he was a student at Blackfriars, Oxford. He lived and studied in Louvain, Belgium, in 1931. White's writing shows his mastery of French and German. He wrote to Jung that he could "read fairly easily French, German, Spanish, Italian and Latin" (VW to CGJ, 9 Oct. 45). He received his STLr degree (Theological Lectorate) in 1930 at Blackfriars, Oxford, and his STM (Master of Sacred Theology—the Dominican Order's highest theological degree, awarded since medieval times as a sign of exceptional merit as a scholar and teacher of theology.) 28 May 1954.

White died of cancer in 1960 at 57, never having produced a sustained book-length work. There were both interior and exterior reasons for this fact, according to White himself.[11] His first two books, *God and the Unconscious* and *God the Unknown*,[12] are compilations of essays written for journals. His last, *Soul and Psyche*, is based on the Edward Cadbury Lectures at the University of Birmingham, which he gave in 1958–59 (*Soul and Psyche*, p.9). White's thirty years as a scholar and lecturer yielded scores of articles, however, on the topics that interested him. Many of these were published in the journal *Blackfriars*, on whose editorial board he served for many years.[13] He wrote on many subjects, including schism and ecumenism, just war theory and Christian pacifism; also reviews of Kierkegaard's *Journals*, modern novels, and books on sexual ethics. Beginning in 1942 he primarily wrote essays and reviews on Jungian psychology (*Letters II*, p.213n).

Although *Blackfriars* was a serious theological journal, it had acquired a reputation in the 1920s and early 1930s for being frivolous and worldly.[14] In 1947 White helped to found a quarterly, *Dominican Studies*, for serious scholarly writing. In the United States he published in *Commonweal* and *National Review*. Articles of his appeared also in Jungian publications on both sides of the Atlantic, including *The Journal of Analytical Psychology* and *Harvest*. A lecture appears in *Eranos-Jahrbuch 1947*, and an important paper, "Kinds of Opposites," in the 1955 C. G. Jung *Festschrift*. He lectured over the BBC and during a trip to the United States in 1954 appeared on television and radio to talk about Jungian psychology (*Letters II*, p.213n).

Evidence of White's style as a classroom teacher is of course only anecdotal. Father Aelred remembers that "Vicky" was cryptic and indirect, offering hints and understatements for students to piece together. Rather than directly contradict the current neoscholastic orthodoxy, White would raise linguistic and historical questions about the text, drawing attention to what St. Thomas had actually said. "It was in this area that there was sometimes a contrast with what might have been expected" (A.S., 3 Aug. 1987). Alert students could compare for themselves and draw their own conclusions about points of doctrine.

White would have been unlikely to air his personal convictions in a lecture in dogmatics. Nonetheless, as a student of his recalls, he slipped occasional psychological interpretations into his lectures under cover of a hypothetical case. His students became aware that he disagreed with at least one common Thomistic interpretation. The officially endorsed doctrine of God included a notion of God as "Prime Mover" (based on Aquinas, *ST* 1a.Q2,3) which White did not consider either theologically adequate or faithful to Aquinas' theology in a broader sense. In the classroom and elsewhere, White showed his opinion by referring to the doctrine as "First Shove" (A.S., 15 July 1987).[15]

Given circumstances at Blackfriars and White's theological focus, his position as a Dominican teacher of dogmatics was undoubtedly isolated and a bit difficult even before he joined forces with Jung. He clearly identified himself with the Dominican Order and felt keenly responsible, in his published writing and teaching, to represent what was then considered orthodox doctrine. Yet his attraction to Jung's psychology was based, in part, on a reading of Aquinas which differed from the "official" Thomism that predominated among his colleagues. White's effort to validate Jung from a Thomistic perspective was therefore also a process of vindicating and clarifying his own theological proposals. His investment in that endeavor, once he committed himself to it, entailed fateful consequences for his life and work.

B. WHITE'S THEOLOGICAL POSITION

A first step toward understanding the issues which arose between White and Jung is to study their commitments to a few basic presuppositions. Some of White's theological writings, especially those predating his work with Jung, clearly show the basic cast and direction of his thought. One of his fundamental assumptions is that faith can be communicated, i.e., that human understanding is capable of grasping and being grasped by God's reality and God's Word. Following from this relatively optimistic conviction, White was especially interested in the questions raised by Christian apologetics and pedagogy. For example, granted that the faith *can* be communicated, how is it *best* communicated? What language and teaching methods will be both faithful to the material and consistent with the capacities of the learners?

White was committed to working toward a new synthesis of revelation and science. He believed such a synthesis possible because God is the source and end of all truth, and desirable because it promises to make the church's message understandable to modern hearers. If all true learning comes from God and leads the soul to God, as White maintained, then serious damage is done by thinkers in any century who open a split between religious and rational kinds of truth. A theologian may study a science, such as psychology, as an extension of interest in all forms of knowledge; and psychological wisdom can properly be integrated into the theologian's work.

Another crucial presupposition for White was his two-fold epistemology. He was convinced—and called upon St. Thomas for corroboration—that human beings know God both through discursive reason and through the intuitive and affective (loving) response of the soul. Whether knowledge of God is by reason or by loving intuition, then, the same God is known; there is no conflict in principle between affect and intellect, or between subjectivity and dogma. Some of White's eventual frustration with Jung arose from his failure to convince Jung of this two-fold, self-consistent, and (for White) indispensable epistemological assumption.

Based on important writings by Victor White, we can identify specific aspects of these two major theological commitments: a complementary relationship between revelation and science, and a knowledge of God deriving equally from reason and affect. It will be helpful to take the time here to explore five essays that lay out these convictions. At the same time, we can discern in a preliminary way the relevance of these theological commitments to White's conversation with Jung.

1. "Scholasticism": A Single Kind of Truth

Victor White's interest in the implicitly psychological dimension of Thomistic theology is already present in an essay predating his first contact with Jungian psychology. In 1934 the Catholic Truth Society in London published an historical and conceptual overview by White, titled *Scholasticism*.[16] Because this essay predates White's encounter with Jungian thought and states his theological convictions so fully, it will be useful to us as a baseline from which to measure both the distance he later traveled and the ways in which he remained consistent with his early convictions.

In this essay White delineates the rise of Western theology out of the relative intellectual stagnation of the Dark Ages, showing its continuity and discontinuity with the obedience to authority that characterized much of medieval thought. He describes Anselm's "revolutionary but not rebellious" treatment of canonical and patristic authority (*Scholasticism*, p.7), and the positive and negative effects of Abelard's rationalism. He is especially concerned with the nearly devastating impact on theological thought that was felt when Aristotle, read through Arab lenses, became "the fashion of the day" (*Scholasticism*, p.17).

Under that impact, he says, theology lost its own internal consistency, because it permitted a conceptual split to be opened between rationality and religion.

A crucial theme in White's early work, one which continued to occupy him in his collaboration and dispute with Jung, is the single standard of truth, i.e., the conviction that all truth comes from a single source, God, who is the source of all reality. Discussing the crisis of Christian thought in the thirteenth century under the full impact of the new Aristotelian science, White describes the error of a Christian academy which sorted truth into two categories, truths of faith and truths of knowledge. The champions of this error, he says, were some of the leading Aristotelian-Christian philosophers at the University of Paris, for whom the deposit of revelation could now only be understood separate from the discoveries of empirical knowledge.

> The creation of the world in time, the divine government and Fatherhood, the individuality and immortality of the soul, free will and moral responsibility gave place to an eternal world, an abstract God cut off from communication with creatures, a unique Intellect for all men which alone was immortal, a strict determinism, physical and psychological, which ruled out all responsible actions. That was Knowledge. . . . "We have no doubt," they would say, "that Faith is true, but we are speaking as philosophers."
>
> (*Scholasticism*, p.17)

White concludes that the inevitable result of the split between faith and philosophy, given both the persuasive power of the new science and the inequality inherent in a double standard of truth, was the scientific devaluation of biblical belief.

Some thirteenth-century theologians, White goes on, proposed two pseudo-solutions. The first was total capitulation to the interpretation of Aristotle mediated through Arabian philosophers (Latin Averroists). The second, "that of the majority of theologians who rejected the new learning with equal discrimination" (*Scholasticism*, p.18), was isolation in a Christian intellectual ghetto.

Both solutions spelt capitulation, the final divorce of faith and reason, the end of all that Scholasticism had stood for. . . . It was the old false alternative of submitting to the forces of paganism or escaping to the catacombs of intellectual obscurantism.

(Scholasticism, p.18)

White argues that the great achievement of Albert of Cologne and his pupil, Thomas Aquinas, was that they showed the way to a synthesis making Aristotelian philosophy compatible with Christian revelation. These two demonstrated that—in the context of the powerful new learning—there was still only one standard of truth for Christians, governing science equally with faith. It was therefore necessary neither to reject the "dynamic ideas which swayed the world in which they lived" *(Scholasticism,* p.18), nor to submit to them in their pagan form. White himself, convinced by a Thomistic tradition which assured the value of science as a help to faith, took the synthesis of science with faith as central to his scholarly vocation. His embrace of Jung's psychology was thus a reflection of his foundational commitment to the belief of Albert and Thomas that truth is one.

To show how deeply rooted this principle was in the history of Christian thought, White turned his attention to the neo-Platonism of Augustine. Epistemology for Augustine, as for Aquinas after him, is founded on the ontological premise that God, being, truth, and goodness are one and the same: *Bonum et esse convertuntur.* In this early essay White showed the continuity of Augustine's epistemological premise with that of Albert and Thomas, and stated the principle in language that made it virtually a battle-cry for White himself:

[St. Thomas] knew that all truth comes from God and leads to God, and that to close one's eyes to the new learning was to repudiate a Catholic's birthright.

(Scholasticism, p.19)

Continuing, White describes Thomas' epistemology in terms of "a two-fold conviction, philosophical and theological"

(*Scholasticism*, p.24). The philosophical side states that humans are able to know metaphysical Being, and thence to come to the very threshold of knowing God's reality itself. The theological side is the conviction that God, infinite and uncontingent, is *freely related to* the finite, contingent world.

In making these statements about the deepest philosophical and theological convictions of Thomas Aquinas, White was staking out a territory that would inevitably place him, in differing ways, in a confrontation with many of his Catholic fellow scholars and eventually also with Jung. White here declared his own conviction that human *perceptions* of God are ultimately consistent with God's objectively *real relationship* with humanity. That is to say, the truth of experience is also the truth of reason; they do not conflict.

White elaborates these ideas in a terse statement, which he says gives not even "the barest outlines of the Thomist Synthesis" (*Scholasticism*, p.23). For clarity, his statement is broken here into numbered paragraphs:

1. [Thomas'] philosophical conviction . . . is that our thought can know Being: the metaphysical world of essences, causes, purposes, and laws, which lies beyond the world of appearances; that it can attain the inmost structure of finite reality and from it can argue to the existence and attributes of infinite God, transcendent and immanent.

2. [His] theological foundation is the conviction, guaranteed by God Himself, that over and above the suprasensible and the metaphysical realm there is a boundless Supernature, the Triune God revealed to man in Christ, to the sharing of whose life, through Grace here, in Glory hereafter, man is called and destined.

3. Over and above this [theological foundation] is the conviction that these two orders of nature and supernature—the first the object of reason, the other of Faith—are in reality one, owing their unity and cohesion to the one God from whom all proceeds and to whom all tends. . . . Hence all St. Thomas' thought centres in God,

and all science, however "secular," receives a religious
significance.

(Scholasticism, p.24)

These ontological presuppositions in White's theology allow,
even encourage, him to treat an empirical and contingent science
like psychology as an avenue to understanding his own faith. In a
systematic sense, these observations about St. Thomas should be
read as defining White's own philosophical and theological commitments, both as a professor of dogmatics at Blackfriars and as a
collaborator with Jung.

2. "Exemplarism": A Platonic Reading of St. Thomas

Although at first glance, systematic Thomism would seem to
lock one into an Aristotelian perspective, White believes that he
can demonstrate an important Platonic thrust in the thought of
St. Thomas. A full picture of these Platonic tendencies is provided when White examines Thomas' doctrine of "exemplarism"
or participation, i.e., the notion that material reality is analogous
to and a participation in transcendent, eternal reality. Precisely
how White understands this element in Aquinas can be seen in
Chapter V of his book *God the Unknown*. This chapter, titled "The
Platonic Tradition in St. Thomas Aquinas,"[17] was originally written in 1941 as an essay contributing to theological dialogue with
the Eastern Orthodox Church.

The argument of the chapter is that Plato's philosophy, far
from being "acosmic" and antimaterialistic, actually teaches a
sacramental, symbolic view of the world:

> The Platonic world-view consists essentially in its interpreta-
> tion of this world as an imitation, a participation, a shadow,
> and thus as a symbol, a sign, a sacrament, of a transcenden-
> tal world of pure intelligibility and immateriality.
>
> (God the Unknown, p.63)

Consistent with this argument, White sees in Thomism not the
overthrow of Plato by Aristotle, but rather the synthesis of the
two. The great, insufficiently appreciated gift of St. Thomas to

the West, White says, was "his painstaking synthesis of Plato and Aristotle" (*God the Unknown*, p.66). Such a synthesis would be impossible if the two philosophies were inherently inconsistent; but White argues that they are not. Plato's relative disinterest in materiality, he says, only superficially contradicts Aristotle's empiricism; and Aristotle's focus on this world and our experience of it only superficially contradicts Plato's theory of Ideas.

What may seem an outright negation of materiality in the early Plato, White explains, is only a provisional negation for the sake of "a positive 'call to' the contemplation of a reality beyond, behind and above the merely material" (*God the Unknown*, p.64). The world itself has real importance as a sacrament: it symbolizes and participates in something far more important beyond it. And because Platonism does not despise materiality but only looks beyond it, there is nothing implicitly contradictory, White declares, about a Christian Platonism. "St. Augustine was surely right in seeing the Incarnation as the completion and correction of the Platonic world-view rather than as its negation" (*God the Unknown*, p.65).

The synthesis of Christian revelation with Platonic philosophy, White says, opened

> ... the possibility of an attitude towards this world which would acknowledge it as of interest and value in itself without prejudice to its significance as a symbol of eternal Truth, Goodness and Beauty.
>
> (*God the Unknown*, p.67)

Thus, Thomas has a sacramental, symbolic doctrine of matter, a doctrine according to which material reality exemplifies, anticipates and participates in a reality transcending the material. Moreover, White argues that such an appropriation of Plato is fully consistent with Aquinas' appropriation of Aristotle's hylemorphism. Plato, properly understood, is not antimaterialist. In fact, according to White, St. Thomas himself sees Aristotle's attack on Plato's "antimaterialism" as arising out of and depending on the "exemplarism" which was originally Plato's idea (*God the Unknown*, p.68). On White's reading, then, Aquinas is basically in sympathy with Augustine, so that he does not reverse but fulfills the Platonist tradition of the earliest church. In particular, this reading of Aquinas leaves room to unify the theologies of Eastern Orthodox and Roman Catholic tradition.

It may be worth noting that "The Platonic Tradition in St. Thomas Aquinas" was written about the time that White entered Jungian analysis and began his study of Jungian psychology. Almost at once, when he became seriously engaged with Jung's theory and practice, White began to build what he hoped would be a solid conceptual bridge between Jung's psychology and Thomism. The optimism of that early effort, which is discussed at some length in the following chapter, is well mirrored here by his easy approximation of Aquinas and Augustine, Aristotle and Plato.

Two questions about White's argument can be raised at this point, pointing toward possible complications in his conversation with Jung. First, it might be said that the agreement White finds between Plato's and Aristotle's views of matter is not as positive as he thinks it is. To "look beyond" matter may still be in some sense to negate it; it suggests at least that the physical world is not where real meaning resides. If this is truly an implication of White's (or Thomas') "exemplarism," White is vulnerable to a suspicion of preferring the metaphysical realm to the empirical. In Jung's terms, such a preference contributes to the "medieval" mentality of many theologians, which makes the dialogue between theology and psychology so difficult.

Second, White may be underestimating the epistemological differences between Augustine and Aquinas, or between Plato and Aristotle. Not every reader would take the view that Augustine saw the Incarnation as "the completion and correction of the Platonic world-view," as White puts it. Some modern scholars, such as Eugene TeSelle, see Augustine's treatment of the Incarnation as dealing Plato a fatal blow.[18]

White's argument in the essay is generous and reconciling; but as he seeks conceptual grounds for agreement, it may be that he minimizes basic tensions between Aristotle and Plato, and between Thomas and Augustine. If so, it may herald a weakness in his systematic thought-pattern which comes back to haunt him. We will see a parallel in his initial naïve embrace of Jung's psychology, the implications of whose epistemology did not strike White with full force until they had worked together for about five years.

To say that the essay downplays important epistemological differences, however, is not necessarily to discount its positive contribution. George Lindbeck makes the case that, even if one distinguishes clearly between the Platonic-Augustinian and the Aristotelian-Thomistic epistemologies, it is possible to maintain that St. Thomas permits a version of existentialist or Kantian epistemology.[19] The doctrine of participation may be related more to Aristotle than to Plato, as Lindbeck maintains. But it is still a powerful aspect of St. Thomas' theology.

By proposing that this dimension of Thomism be given its due weight, whether or not he correctly evaluates its philosophical antecedents, White tried to correct what he sees as a blindness in neoscholasticism and began to build a bridge between his revised Thomism and the Jungian universe. As we will see, the doctrine of participation he develops here was essential to White's own theology. It helped him to connect Aquinas' and Jung's epistemologies. Then, as he grew more aware of the starkly Protestant cast of Jung's religious world, sacramental implications of the doctrine informed White's concerned response.[20]

3. "Affective Knowledge": Truth and the Human Subject

What White understood theologically by the term "experience," and the evidence he found of an implicit appeal to experience in St. Thomas' theology, are explored in a major three-part essay, "Thomism and 'Affective Knowledge,' "[21] published by *Blackfriars* in January and April 1943 and September 1944. Despite its conceptual density this essay has an unfinished, tantalizing quality, as if it were the proposal for a longer work. A great amount of material is presented; not a word is wasted. But the bulk of the argument is left, it seems, for development elsewhere. Reading the three parts of this essay leaves an impression that, if White had ever written a sustained book-length work, "affective knowledge" might well have been its theme.

A detailed examination of all three parts of this essay may clarify the function for White of his Platonic reading of Aquinas.

Whatever Platonism may imply in another context, White's view of it is neither static nor abstract. His interpretation of Aquinas' thought stresses dynamic movement more than form, focuses on human subjectivity, and allows for a knowledge of God based on the direct experience of the soul. He sees "affective knowledge" as a neglected aspect of Thomism vital for modern apologetics, and proposes this important missing ingredient for his church's approval.

Insofar as he tries to supply a perspective that has been missing from the collective dialogue, White's purpose here has formal similarities to Jung's in his context. They both work on the principle that scholars have a moral duty to provide, by making them conscious, hidden aspects of the collective reality needed for wholeness.[22] They differ, however, on the question of *what* aspects of reality ought to be present. White's emphasis in this essay is on the legitimacy of subjective experience as a source of human knowledge; but he recommends this dimension without forsaking the dimension of discursive intellect. His double epistemology—the theory that knowledge of God is both intellective and affective—gives his thought great potential breadth, by attempting to join the metaphysical and the empirical realms of discourse.

PART I.

The first part of White's essay (Jan. 1943) makes it plain that his theological concern is with apologetics and theological teaching in the broadest sense. He raises the issue of human subjectivity in theological discourse, by asking whether there can be any real "*rapprochement* between Thomist and much 'modern thought'." In an obvious rebuke to his more conservative neo-Thomistic colleagues, he cites "the widespread misgiving about Thomism, that it ignores or rejects 'value-perception' and 'value-experience'." Is the layperson right, he asks, who attributes to the "frigidly rational" and "rigidly scientific" system of Thomism "denial of the validity of one's most cherished and intimate personal experience"? ("Affective Knowledge" I, p.8).

The question is important, White says, not only to the practice of Christian apologetics, but also to dogmatic theology itself. If "experience" be divorced from "thought," he argues, what follows is a dichotomy in the nature of God: we have one God known rationally ("the God of thought, First Mover, Metaphysical Absolute") and another ("the God of 'religious experience' ") known, as it were, by the heart (Ibid, p.8).

As we have seen, for White it is essential that "truth" be recognized to be ultimately one in God. It is conceptually absurd that there should be two kinds of truth; if two kinds of knowledge exist, they must both point to the same thing in the end. Furthermore, neither kind may reject the warrants of the other; as hard as it may be to exercise two modes of knowledge at once, faith requires it. The history of ideas, however, shows that Western thought has swung between these two kinds of knowledge, from reason to feeling, from Enlightenment to Romanticism, and thence back to the "hard science" of materialism. Always in the past, one side has been unfairly disqualified, until it exerts its power equally unfairly and misleadingly, to disqualify the other.

Not wanting to become one-sided in his adherence to the knowledge born of intimate experience, White acknowledges the danger of anti-intellectual romantic subjectivity. He briefly bows to Kierkegaard, who, in his characteristic emphasis on subjectivity, still avoids (in White's view) the danger of being swept away by it (Ibid, p.9). But the point he most stresses is that no true philosophy exists without a connection to affective experience. Intellectual knowledge must be prepared to "account for the most vital and intimate forms of personal experience" or "forfeit the claim to be either truly intellectualist or truly philosophical" (Ibid).

Philosophy thus becomes futile when it severs its tie with human subjectivity. But then, how do things stand with St. Thomas? "At least," White asks, "is there room in his synthesis for this method of approach to reality?" If not, then serious doubts are cast on the whole project of Thomistic apologetics, for the teachings of Aquinas will not commend themselves to real human beings, "living under the influence of contemporary culture and beset by present-day problems" (Ibid, p.10). White answers his rhetorical question with an exposition of what he takes to be St. Thomas' theory of two kinds of knowledge: first, the knowledge *per usum rationis* (which has several

other shades of meaning), and second, *cognitio affectiva* (Ibid).
The bulk of the first part of the essay consists of documentation
supporting the claim that Aquinas recognizes human affectivity,
the natural closeness of relationship, as a way to the knowledge
of God.

A Thomism which overlooks affective knowledge, White
writes, makes the mistake of treating the discursive method of
the *Summa Theologiae* as though it exhausted St. Thomas' epistemology. The First Part of the *Summa Theologiae* supplies the
evidence which could prevent such a misunderstanding, for it
expressly denies that the *Summa* demonstrates all possible ways
to know God.[23] There are two kinds of knowledge, affective
and discursive, and the *Summa* demonstrates only the discursive
kind.

These two kinds of knowledge, White explains, are distinct
in Aquinas but not in conflict; indeed, they cannot conflict, for
they both lead the soul to God in whom all truth is one. According to St. Thomas, affective knowledge connects the soul to God
as well as or better than rational knowledge, because it involves
the whole person through love. The *Summa*, White acknowledges, treats God like an object of mathematics; but "unlike the
object of mathematics, the Object of Divinity is *lovable*" (Ibid,
p.12). One knows propositions about God; but one also knows
God directly and affectively. In his discussion of the role of love
in knowledge, White quotes one of the passages that persuades
him Aquinas is influenced by Augustine.

> [Christ is] no sterile Concept of the Divine Mind, but the
> Logos who breathes forth Love in the Person of the Holy
> Ghost. *Verbum spirans Amorem*: "The Son is the Word, not any
> sort of word, but the Word Who breathes forth Love. Hence
> Augustine says: 'The Word we speak of is Knowledge with
> Love'."
>
> (Ibid, p.13)[24]

The practical significance of this distinction between discursive and affective knowledge is made clearer in a statement
White quotes from the *Secunda Secundae*, concerning moral
judgments. In White's translation, St. Thomas writes:

> Correctness of judgment can come about in two ways: in one
> way by the right use of *reason*, in another way by a certain
> *connaturality* with those things concerning which judgment is
> made. Thus, he who has learned Moral Philosophy can, by
> the research of reason, form a right judgment concerning
> those things which belong to the virtue of chastity. But he
> who *has* the virtue of chastity can judge rightly of those
> things by reason of a certain connaturality with them.
>
> (Ibid, p.14).[25]

White adds a crucial piece to his discussion when he corrects
the mistaken notion that Aquinas sees affective knowledge of
God strictly as a supernatural gift. It is a gift of grace, St. Thomas
says, but it is *also* a natural possibility (Ibid, p.15), and therefore it
can and should be understood psychologically, not only sacramentally. The knowledge of God is acquired not only rationally
(though intellect is one way), and not only supernaturally
(though grace is another way), but also—and very effectively—
through ordinary personal experience.

To sum up, according to White, St. Thomas believes that
direct knowledge of God comes to the soul by love, and that the
union of love surpasses the indirect knowledge conveyed by
concepts. Concepts necessarily fall short of the reality they
name. This idea, that the soul can have a "direct experience of
God," constitutes an important point of contact between Jung's
psychology and Thomistic theology.

PART II.

The second part of the essay (April 1943) begins by defending St. Thomas once again against narrow rationalistic interpretations. It is crucial to White that St. Thomas makes no
"unwarranted assumptions based on illegitimate abstractions"
("Affective Knowledge" II, p.126). Knowledge for Thomas is an
event that occurs *between* the knower and what is known. Carte-
sian theory stands here under indictment: it misses the dialectical
and relational aspect of the *cogito*.

> To think is not an intransitive verb; it must always (at least
> tacitly) have an *object*. . . . St. Thomas was as emphatic as any

of the modern Existentialists that there can be . . . no consciousness of a subject except in and through the consciousness of an object.

(Ibid, pp.126f)

Here as in the first part, White cautiously affirms the perspective of Kierkegaardian existentialism:[26]

Thomism and Existentialism are in agreement at least as to this: that the given fact of knowledge must be viewed in its *wholeness* as we experience it, if we are to construct a valid theory of knowledge.

(Ibid, p.127)

At this point, however, he inserts a footnoted excursus which, like many footnotes of its kind, tells the direction of the writer's thought in a vitally important area. White's approval of phenomenology and existentialism is limited; he does not accept their complete repudiation of metaphysics.

We do not of course intend to endorse all the *developments* of Existentialism and Phenomenology, which have tended to degenerate into an anti-metaphysical phenomenalism. . . . Marcel de Corte in his *La Philosophie de Gabriel Marcel* has shown convincingly how the preoccupation with Idealism has inhibited the full development of the Existentialist trend since Kierkegaard, and how its principles in effect demand the complement of a metaphysic such as Aristotle and St. Thomas have elaborated.

(Ibid, p.127n)

It should be kept in mind that White's commitment to both sides of the Thomistic epistemology, his refusal to abandon metaphysics as a corollary of bringing phenomenology and existentialism into play, would put him fundamentally at odds with Jung. White affirms two ways of knowing, but a single source of truth. Jung affirms a single way of knowing, but finds the source of truth equivocal or at least ambivalent.

White's affirmation of rational as well as experiential knowledge has profound implications for a cognitive psychology. He

describes what it means to "know an object" in terms of participation and self-transcendence. St. Thomas says, " 'It is of the
nature of a thing-which-knows to possess also the specific reality
of the *other*' [*Summa* I,xiv,1]" (Ibid, p.128). The knower's partici-
patory "possession of the reality of the other" constitutes an
experience of self-transcendence with overtones of intimacy.
We know the other best of all through a closeness which cannot
be matched by rational constructs. Human cognition (of God,
an idea, or another person) is here recognized not only as a
function of intimacy, but also as part of the psychology of intimacy, part of what makes intimacy possible.

On the other hand, a limit is set to the meaning of participation. Human knowing, unlike God's, must always submit itself to
the objective, rational test of truth. We cannot simply become en-
gulfed in knowledge-as-participation; we are required to distinguish between ourselves and what we know. White also shows how
Aquinas relates the analogical participation between knower and
known to the doctrine of God's omniscience (Ibid, pp.128f):

> The awareness of Subject-Object *distinction* is inseparable
> from the creaturely apprehension of truth. For here the
> Knower is *not* the Known. . . . This leads to a further point
> which is central in St. Thomas's epistemology, and which
> will be found to be of the greatest importance in apprais-
> ing his conception of affective knowledge. . . . [T]o possess
> a thought which is conformed to a thing is not to possess
> truth about that thing. I must also *know* that my thought is
> conformed to a thing if I am to know truth.
>
> (Ibid, p.129)

Rational judgment, then, is still essential to knowledge, since it
allows us to differentiate between truth and falsehood. A relevant concept for White (although he does not use the word) is
"falsifiability": not everything that is affectively known is *true*.
There must be some means of knowing when things are false, or
else "true" has no meaning. The truth of all knowledge, including affective, must be tested; it cannot be simply perceived. The
knower, who participates with the object, yet remains a separate
subject who can discriminate truth from falsehood:

> Perception or apprehension is the indispensable beginning
> of knowledge, but there is no true knowledge unless there
> be affirmation or negation, or their equivalent.
>
> (Ibid, p.129)

Without the use of discriminating judgment, the self-transcendence that comes from knowing is likely to prove a self-deception. God, on the other hand, does not and cannot "self-transcend" or judge the truth of God's knowledge; because unlike human nature the nature of God is already fully realized (i.e., in God is no possibility of ignorance). In Aquinas' terms, God is not *in potentia* but completely *in actu*. "He *is* of His Nature All" (Ibid, p.128). This presupposition will become important when we compare it to Jung's skeptical treatment of God's "omniscience" in *Answer to Job*. For Victor White, whose standard is St. Thomas, there is no sense—literally, no way to construe Jung's sense—in attributing "deficient" self-knowledge to God as Jung does. The concept simply does not cohere with White's Thomistic universe.

White's final argument in Part II defends St. Thomas against anyone who might consider him a "naïve realist." Aquinas does not see human intellect as "a mere passivity which merely reflects the 'outside' object." It cannot be so, he explains,

> For the "outside" world with which the human mind is con-
> fronted is a world of sense-phenomena, which is not actually
> but only potentially intelligible. . . . This means that the
> world around us is *intrinsically* non-intelligible, and must be
> *made* intelligible by the activity of mind itself.
>
> (Ibid, p.131)

In this statement White does not go as far as Jung's Kantian subjectivity. But the theory of cognition implied here at least allows him to take Jung's position seriously.

PART III.

In the last third of the essay (Sept. 1944). White continues to build his argument that human subjectivity is essential to knowledge. Here he brings the focus back to the nature of theology, arguing that theology must be faithful both to the thought-process and to its object. The object of theology is not a conceptual formula but the God whose very being is love.

In a slanting reference to the prevailing neoscholastic school, White warns that the intellect must not become "an instrument which stifles its possessor" ("Affective Knowledge" III, p.322). What is needed, he implies, is a degree of epistemological balance. Focusing overmuch on the intellectual aspects of theology, White points out, invites an equal and opposite reaction. One-sided devotion to discursive theology which undervalues affective knowledge can lead in time to an equally one-sided flight from abstract thought:

> The Renascence contempt for the later Schoolmen, Kierkegaard's revolt against Hegel, Bergson's revolt against reason, were so many protests against this disastrous substitution of thought for thing—protests which, unhappily, too often threw out the baby with the bathwater. But a *Summa* should help us to know God and His world; we shall misuse it, and it will suffocate us, if we study it *instead of* God and His world.
>
> (Ibid, p.322)

Thoughts, White goes on, are "signs of signs"; they do not give life. No responsible theologian confuses concepts with reality, or substitutes a conceptual formulation for the personal immediacy of faith. White adds that Thomists, of all people, should know better than to mistake static signs for the motion of life. St. Thomas begins his theology inspired by awareness of life's perpetual state of motion:

> The fact of Movement, Change, Becoming is for him the most fundamental and unquestionable of the facts of our experience. . . . The fact of Becoming (*motus*) is the basic datum of experience from the analysis of which his whole philosophy is inferred.
>
> (Ibid, p.323)

In this passage we may hear echoes of Heraclitus, a philosopher Jung favored.[27] But White clearly has Augustine in mind, more than Heraclitus or Jung, when he adds:

The world in which we live, as St. Thomas sees it, is beyond all doubt a world of change and movement; impregnated, it would seem, with some deep discontent in which nothing can rest satisfied with remaining as it is. . . .

(Ibid, p.323)

4. "Holy Teaching": Inclusive Pedagogy

In a paper published late in his life, "Holy Teaching,"[28] White argues that St. Thomas intended the whole *Summa Theologiae* explicitly as a manual for teachers of theology:

It is usually assumed, even by Père Chenu, that the "beginners" [in the First Question] are to be understood as the readers of the *Summa*, and the *doctor* as the author. But I suggest that this reading is unwarranted, though hard to disprove except by showing that the contents of the *Summa* as a whole disprove it. Rather, I suggest, the *doctor* or teacher is the reader for whom the book is designed and intended, the *incipientes* are among those whom he has to teach; for in fact there is nobody whom the teacher of Catholic truth can exclude from his teaching.

("Holy Teaching," p.6)

White sees Thomas' whole notion of theology as predominantly "*kerygmatic, evangelistic* or *pastoral*—as distinct from the *academic, speculative* or *scholarly*" ("Holy Teaching," p.4). *Sacra doctrina* is thus concerned with both objective, thematic content and pedagogical process, as both are necessary for the communication of salvation. If there is nobody whom the teacher can exclude, then the whole range of human condition and experience is of immediate and practical interest to the theologian. Because of the importance of caring for human souls, both within and outside the church, one test of a theology is its communicability.

Furthermore, although White understands the objective content of Christian theology—the Word of salvation in Christ—as a constant, he recognizes that its interpretation and the manner of its teaching must develop over time. Because faith must be communicated to human hearers, certain variables in the human soul—involving the speaker's ability to communicate and the listener's ability to understand—must be allowed to color the conversation. The preacher and teacher must understand both the constant message and the changing context of their listeners.

White's theological bridge-building with psychology was, as we have seen, consistent with the way he read St. Thomas. Like Thomas, he wanted to synthesize for the sake of truth. He considered psychology the most important "new science" of the twentieth century and presented this new learning as a challenge to theology. The church must become more cogent in its teaching, lest the unity of the truth again be lost. In addition to identifying psychology as the best new science, White saw it as a practical means to open the door of the heart in two directions. First, psychology could teach the preacher to understand the language of the human soul, so that the questions and claims of ordinary experience would be correctly perceived. Then the reverse: the teacher or preacher could begin to address the soul in language modern people would understand, to mediate the *salus* of Christ in a form the heart could take in.

5. "Religious Tolerance": The Demands of Pluralism

This dialectical process of learning in order that one may teach is a theme White had begun to develop five years earlier in a 1953 BBC address, "Religious Tolerance,"[29] which was published in the United States. The gist of the essay is that theology must not only speak but also listen, not just for the purpose of overcoming opposition through polemics, but rather for the sake of genuine dialogue in which the other partner in the dialogue has equal standing. The final goal of dialogue is the unity of the body of Christ; but that goal requires a toleration of differences. Only in toleration can the other be addressed and taught.

The 1950s were a tense decade for a Catholic teacher to defend theological freedom in print. The encyclical *Humani generis* had recently closed theological options for many prominent Catholic teachers. This disciplinary intervention seemed to express the official church's profound distrust of its theologians' intellectual freedom and its anxious resistance to doctrinal development. White recognizes the problem with a dry remark:

> We know now that our era of liberal toleration is not so secure as we liked to suppose a few decades ago.
>
> ("Tolerance," p.531)

But, White continues, the alternative to respecting individuals and their experience of divine mystery is for the church to fall into "idolatry of the dogma: the substitution of the formula for the infinite mystery which it should communicate" ("Tolerance," p.533). White here picks up the same theme he began to enunciate nearly a decade earlier, in Part III of his essay on affective knowledge. To illustrate how much is at stake, in the "idolatry of the dogma," White points to the damage done by Christian missionaries:

> The ruins of countless tribal organizations and cultures are there to tell us what happens when, by force or craft, an alien religion or *Weltanschauung* or ethic is superimposed on, and destroys, the inherited native pattern.
>
> ("Tolerance," p.532)

In this courageous essay, White expresses sympathy with the teaching of several contemporary theologians, including John Courtney Murray,[30] on "the character and grounds of tolerance" ("Tolerance," p.531). He protests against theological Acts of Uniformity and, citing the authority of C. G. Jung and Suzanne Langer, compares religious intolerance to "spiritual murder" ("Tolerance," p.532). He urges that the church not exclude or silence individuals for the diversity of their religious convictions. Those who are supposed to be "preachers of Divine love" should not find themselves "acting as judges of religious orthodoxy" as they did in the Inquisition ("Tolerance," p.532).[31]

White thus takes Jung's side against what Jung calls the "totalitarian" truth claims of the Catholic Church.[32] Indeed White rejects, as an anomaly of history, the medieval notion of a sacral society, i.e., one which claims the right to enforce religious truths by political means.

> Invaluable, too, is the distinction some French thinkers have made between what they call sacral and pluralist soci-

eties. . . . In such a [sacral] society, so-called metaphysical beliefs and religious practices cannot be a matter of private choice or individual opinion.

("Tolerance," p.531)

White pleads for the pluralism of a desacralized state. Religious differences must be allowed, he insists, even at the cost of error. The way to deal with error is to engage it in dialogue, not to silence it by "*force majeur*" ("Tolerance," p.534). A theologian, he says, never deals in the sort of "truth" that can be catalogued or have its boundaries set. The warrants for theological freedom are located both within the Gospel, whose truth is hidden in the mystery of God, and within the psyche, which can respond truly only if it responds freely.

His [the theologian's] professional concern is not with any sort of truth, neither mathematical, nor scientific, nor philosophical, nor social, nor even ethical truth, but with the *verbum salutis*, the message of human healing and salvation, the Gospel, the good news of the Divine offer of human deliverance and the means for its attainment. . . . It is of the very essence of that message itself that its acceptance means free, individual response and decision, and that discipleship means personal willingness to take up a cross and to follow.

("Tolerance," p.533)

In thus combining theological orthodoxy with a commitment to religious pluralism, White occupies a position ahead of many Roman Catholic theologians of his time and anticipates the direction which many in the church have tried to follow since Vatican II.

A pluralist society is one in which a Christian must be a Christian indeed; in which even the theologian can breathe more freely. . . . Now he is better able to get on with his own job: the job which Aquinas described as the "greater clarification of the content of Divine Teaching" to human minds. . . . For toleration brings intercommunication; wider and deeper knowledge of the variety of the needs of the human soul, and of the mysterious and manifold ways of God with man. . . .

> Idols must still be destroyed; but now men must freely de-
> stroy their own idols rather than have them destroyed by *force
> majeur.* . . . To all this the theologian should have much to
> contribute. Perhaps he may even contribute to laying a firmer
> foundation for the Western world's precarious experiment in
> toleration itself.
>
> ("Tolerance," p.534)

When White wrote this passage, he was balancing the decision
to stay in the Dominican Order or leave it. A church where
teachers, representing different perspectives within an orthodox spectrum, could be trusted to destroy their own idols without being forcibly silenced must have been the church he
wished for at this moment.

Despite his dramatic disclaimer of any interest in "the
truth," theological freedom, for White, is associated with an
objective process of testing truth claims. He maintains that theologians should carry on a dialogue about religious texts, experiences, concepts and theories unhindered by an Inquisition, but
without abandoning philosophical rigor. His defense of religious freedom by no means supports the idea that what is
wrong with the church is "dogma." On the contrary, he says, the
church needs better dogma, i.e., teaching, since only good theology can combat bad practice.

White's defense of the relationship between God and the
individual soul owes something to Jung as well as to White's
own study of "affective knowledge" in Aquinas. Whether Jung
would agree or not, White invokes him in support of his plea
for more adequate theology, proven in more adequate practice.
Reflecting on Aldous Huxley's book about officially sanctioned
religious persecution, *The Devils of Loudun*, White writes:

> Behind the monstrous atrocities at Loudun was not too
> much, but too little, dogma and theology; and Jung also,
> from his purely empirical standpoint, has helped us to un-
> derstand how great was the issue, even for the history of our
> European consciousness, in the old, passionate controver-
> sies about the Trinity and the Incarnation.
>
> ("Tolerance," p.533)

The point comes to this: Ideas influence practice, and practice proves out ideas. Dogmas bear fruit. The truth of a concept is visible in its application. This observation is borne out, he says, by the findings of psychology as well as by theology. He implicitly reminds Jung, and perhaps also himself, that abstractions—even metaphysical ones—are important because they have concrete psychological effects. An irony, if one chooses to look at it that way, is that a major agreement between the two men was their shared conviction that ideas are "real" because they have effects. This agreement in principle is precisely what gave their disagreements such moral weight.

To my knowledge, Victor White published no other essay except "Religious Tolerance" defending the freedom of the individual conscience to express its religious convictions over against the claims of the magisterium. The timing of this BBC lecture, which came when White was already disputing with Jung about *Answer to Job*, makes its content all the more interesting. White's defense of intellectual freedom and his willingness to challenge the claim that uniformity of doctrine must be enforced show where a piece of common ground still existed in principle between the two men.

No such agreement in principle would have sufficed, obviously, to bridge all their substantive differences. But one is tempted to speculate what White might have been able to do if his relationships within his Order had been more secure and the ecclesial politics in his day more open to religious pluralism. It is possible that, had he himself been less constrained by circumstances, his communications with Jung would have been less thorny. Perhaps White could have pursued this crucial topic with Jung's help farther than he did, if his church had been more ready to contemplate the religious pluralism he pleads for in this essay. The disagreements with Jung would have presented themselves with less urgency, and the personal tensions between them would also have been slower to arise, since their ongoing collaboration would not so seriously have threatened White's standing as a theologian.

Chapter Three

At the Wind's Mercy

A. WHITE'S SYNTHESIS

1. *Faith in Search of Science*

We are beginning to be in a position to address aspects of convergence and divergence between Jung's psychology and White's theology, as viewed from the theological side. Even before he encountered Jung's psychology White hoped to construct a theological synthesis similar in spirit to the one constructed by Aquinas, but suited to the modern era. As we have seen, in 1932 he claimed this challenging task:

> It is the aim of the modern Thomist to integrate all modern discoveries and scientific achievements, all that is truly valuable and permanent in post-mediaeval thought, into the Thomist synthesis, for the good of man and the glory of God: in short, to do for our own age what St. Thomas did for his.
>
> (*Scholasticism*, p.31)

White's passion for Christian apologetics was part of the reason why he gravitated to the thought of a scientist outside the Catholic fold. Deploring the tendency of theology to insulate itself from secular knowledge, he blamed the ghettoizing of theology for the paganizing of society. He welcomed the avenue back toward religious faith that Jung seemed to open to "modern" people. Jung could address such people with the authority of a scientist who had found—as he claimed—*empirical* reasons to take religion seriously.

In addition, White saw Jungian psychology as a pedagogical tool for the church and its clergy. He hoped that an assimilation of Jung's insights would enable Christian leaders and institutions to resume their traditional leadership roles in addressing the world credibly on matters of ultimate importance. If scientific wisdom were taken up into a new Thomistic synthesis, he hoped, the unity of truth could be perceived once more; the church need no longer be seen as an inferior teacher by scientific standards.

White's yearning for the unity of faith and science was coupled with a far-reaching vision. He believed that a deeply worked-out synthesis of Thomism and modern learning could change the course of intellectual and religious history for centuries to come. For himself, as a Catholic theologian and a faithful teacher in the church, his chief hope seems to have been to further this change as far possible. This mission, however, entailed a strong critical stance toward any kind of Catholic theology that opposed the needed synthesis.

In White's 1932 essay he identified a dangerous parallel between the late medieval scholasticism that grew up after St. Thomas and the neoscholastic Thomism of his own era.

> Had the Thomists left their wranglings with the Nominalists and their purely theological preoccupations to lead the new learning and show how its humanist aspirations found within the Thomist system a fulfilment they could never find outside, the history of the neo-pagan Renascence would have been very different.
>
> (*Scholasticism*, p.26)

Implicit in this interpretation of history is a warning to modern church leaders not to make the same mistake as their predecessors. For the sake of modern civilization and the health of the church, White implies, Catholic theology must not be cut off from "the new learning."

Another dimension basic to White's adoption of Jung's psychology was his concern for pastoral care, a concern grounded in his practice as a confessor and spiritual director. When he began studying Jung's work he found several writings where Jung pointed to similarities between analytical psychology and the traditional Catholic "cure of souls." For example, the 1932 lecture, "Psychotherapists or the Clergy," which White read in the small collection *Modern Man in Search of a Soul*,[1] suggests that much of the work done by psychotherapists could be done as well by clergy, if only more clergy would acknowledge the reality of the soul, and more people would trust the clergy with their inner lives (*Modern Man*, pp.227f).

White also knew Jung's 1928 article, "Psychoanalysis and the Cure of Souls,"[2] which calls religious ritual and dogma implicitly therapeutic: "Any sacral action, in whatever form, works like a vessel for receiving the contents of the unconscious" (*CW 11* §543). In this and other writings, Jung praised the Catholic tradition on therapeutic grounds, because it is richer than Protestantism in these sacral actions:

> The Catholic Church has at her disposal ways and means which have served since olden times to gather the lower, instinctual forces of the psyche into symbols and in this way integrate them into a hierarchy of the spirit.
>
> (Ibid §547)

In this and many other ways White found that Jung's psychology yielded, as Jung claimed, a picture of the human soul consistent with the Catholic Church's age-old wisdom.

The first piece of writing in which White publicly laid out his discovery of the many affinities and connections between analytical psychology and Thomistic theology is titled "The Frontiers of Theology and Psychology."[3] In 1942 he presented it as a lecture to "a group of psychologists, clergy and others" led by the Jungian analyst who was, in fact, White's own analyst at the time, John Layard.[4]

An important Jungian concept that White valued and found consonant with traditional Christian teaching was what Jung called the personal shadow—referring to the parts of the personality disliked and denied by the conscious ego. White found in Jung's treatment of the shadow a perfect reflection, in psychological terms, of the way Christian theology deals with the fact of sin. White's ongoing study of the English mystic Walter Hilton[5] equipped him to draw the comparison:

Jung only echoes the teaching of the Christian ascetical writers (such as Walter Hilton) when he insists that the first step
in the way to integration, which the Christian understands
as conformation to the image of Christ, is by recognition
and acceptance of the "Shadow."

("Frontiers," p.22)

So far toward synthesis, so good. But did Jung's psychology
threaten the church's authority by trying to supersede and replace the tradition of ascetical theology with a new religion?
White was not afraid of such a usurpation, because he saw that
while Jung's psychology aspired toward spiritual wholeness, it
had to halt at the limits of finitude:

When [Jung] writes that "The Personality as a full realisation
of wholeness of our being is an unattainable ideal"[6] he
confirms—though necessarily only negatively—the Christian teaching that the fulfilment of this process awaits an
eschatalogical realisation, and is consequently beyond the
sphere observable by this-worldly psychology.

(Ibid, p.22)

This meant to White that a final realization of the promise implicit in Jung's psychology—a promise of psychological wholeness and not merely of symptomatic relief or "cure"—required
an appeal to grace. So Jung's psychology pointed toward the
salvation mediated by Christian faith:

Such a psychology leads beyond itself into a realm where it
alone is insufficient. It brings us to that point where, according to Christian teaching, "nature" itself is impotent to
realise the fulfilment of its own innate tendencies.

(Ibid, p.23)

By arguing that psychology, consistent with the natural
good of creation, is in no conflict with the supernatural good,
White hoped to convince his audience that a "this-worldly" empiricism could be happily married to Catholic metaphysics. In
the process he hoped to create an experiential Thomism—

entirely faithful to Aquinas, though not as read through the lenses of conservative neoscholasticism—in which the authentic psychological insights of Catholic tradition could once again play their rightful part.

2. *Teleology in Jung and Aquinas*

White's discussions of Jungian thought in the 1940s circled around a relatively basic philosophical observation with potent ramifications. He looked at Jung's methodological leanings and saw in them a teleological system. Jung's rejection of determinism and materialism were promising features of his thought; but most important, White said, was Jung's willingness to see the instinctual drives (including the sexual), not as reductive etiological facts, but as symbols of spiritual forces conducive to health. Jung's break with Freud had been necessary, White explained ("Frontiers," pp.6ff), because Jung treats the spiritual dimension as an irreducible part of the psyche. Consistent with Jung's radical divergence from Freudian theory, he went so far (White summarized) as to treat "the *absence* of religion as the root cause of all adult psychological disease" (Ibid, p.4).[7]

White's emphasis on teleology revealed an accurate reading of Jung's thought. One of the reasons Jung himself gave for his break with Freud was the difference between his prospective (goal-oriented) interpretation of psychological processes and Freud's reductive (materially causal) theory that every psychological process had its genesis in infantile sexuality. Jung criticized Freud's sexual theory as negatively one-sided, depending too much on the search for pathology.[8] His own, meanwhile, was grounded in the observation that the unconscious compensates for what consciousness lacks; the personality is intrinsically healthy and tends towards wholeness.

Metapsychological differences between Jung and Freud were essential to the argument White made for relating Jung and Aquinas. Jung's hermeneutics, he commented, reverse Freud's order of the signifier and the signified: Jung sees the primary human drives as reflecting the existence of an *a priori* transcendent reality. Freud, on the contrary, finds any so-called "transcendent" reality an illusion generated unconsciously from unmet infantile desires.[9] Jung also reverses Freud's valuations of culture and symbol: Freud sees language, art and religion as "disguises" for the repressed incestuous instinct, whereas Jung sees these symbolic expressions as generated by a spiritual drive. The spirit is a primary "instinctive" reality of human existence, Jung says, equal in power to sexuality.

In delineating these major differences between Jung and Freud, White shows that Jung subscribes to a version of "final cause": he envisions the unconscious as a prospective force, pulling the personality toward its wholeness. In 1942 White is certain that Jung and St. Thomas can accommodate each other's views of reality, even if they do not agree in detail.[10] Jung's view that psychic processes—individual and collective—tend toward wholeness means that "wholeness" is the end point of the soul and of the world. The parallel theme in Thomas, meanwhile, is that God is the divine *telos*, the final cause toward which all creation moves.

As a spiritual director White was delighted to see that Jung, through his theory of the archetypes, attributes to people's emotional and sexual lives a spiritual meaning. He perceived that in Jung's psychology, as in St. Thomas' doctrine of participation, finite acts and feelings partake of the infinite. White is not disturbed by the mythic terms in which Jung describes this relationship between finitude and infinity; it is enough that for Jung an inevitable participation exists between the particular and the universal:

> Behind the particularized mother's womb lies the archetypal womb of the Great Mother of all living; behind the physical father the archetypal Father, behind the child the "puer eternus"; behind the particular procreative sexual libido lies the universal creative and recreative Spirit. The second of these pairs appear now, not as phantasy-substitutes for the first; but rather do the first appear as particularized manifestations and symbols of the second. . . . The way is now open to us . . . no longer to conceive of God as a substitute for the physical father, but rather the physical father as the infant's first substitute for God, the genetically prior bearer of the image of the All-Father.
>
> ("Frontiers," p.13)

In Jung's psychology as in St. Thomas, the instinctual or sexual level of human reality is neither self-causing nor materially determined; it manifests itself because of, and derives its ultimate meaning from, its relationship to the eternal spiritual reality: God, or the image of wholeness. Jung's teleology, as White reads it, thus coincides nicely with St. Thomas' picture of God as *causa causarum*.

A large piece of White's correlation between Jung and St. Thomas is outlined in a section titled "Sexuality or 'Libido'" ("Frontiers," pp.6ff).[11] Here, however, he runs into a possible difficulty. White summarizes Jung's anti-Freudian view of "undifferentiated libido" as an "abstract (and indeed strictly inconceivable) conception" ("Frontiers," p.6).[12] With this much Jung might agree. But White then presses further, admitting that he is taking Jung into a philosophical territory which Jung himself would not hurry to enter:

> He has always been very sensitive to the charge of being a metaphysician; but it can hardly be denied that in positing an undifferentiated *libido* he was, in spite of himself, asserting that the psychological data were unaccountable except on a postulate which was as metaphysical as could be.
>
> ("Frontiers," p.7)

The implications, for White, seem clear. Having asserted Jung's metaphysical investment, he draws a direct parallel between Jung's "libido" and Aquinas' concept of God:

> Yet the fact remains that formless energy is synonymous with *actus purus*, and *actus purus* (under one name or another) is, as natural theologians have pointed out, what men call God.
>
> ("Frontiers," p.7)

The correspondence is attractive on the surface. But White rushes too quickly here to establish an equation between Jung's concept of libido and Aquinas' of pure act. It was perhaps typical of White's early optimism about Jung's work to think he had found a metaphysical bridge ready-made. A footnote at the end of the discussion shows that White, enjoying his sure-footedness on the theological parquet, relished this insight into Jung's "undifferentiated libido":

> Jung's "undifferentiated *libido*" is confessedly no more than an abstraction from differentiated forms of *libido*. It stands in a similar relationship to *actus purus* as does *ens communissimum* to *ens realissimum*.
>
> ("Frontiers," p. 25, note 6)

Nontheologians in White's original audience probably could not garner much from his analogy; nor does it help us toward understanding the equivalence he wanted to establish between "undifferentiated libido" and a natural theologian's concept of God. White knew that Aquinas' "pure act" contains nothing merely potential, nothing still to be realized, changed or developed. If the correlation with Jung's "libido" was to carry theological or psychological freight, a perpetually moving, changing and developing energy had to be identified with a divine actuality in which there is no potentiality, and therefore no change, movement, or becoming. We will return below to the implications of St. Thomas' *actus purus*, and White's complicated response to it.

B. OBSTACLES

1. *Theoretical Barriers*

As the above suggests, obstacles still stood in the way of White's synthesis. In the first period of his work with Jungian psychology, when he wrote "The Frontiers of Theology and Psychology" and his other early essays, White apparently did not calculate the true seriousness of difficulties that were already in view. For example, he wrote that Jung's teleology seemed to promise

> a revaluation of religion, and particularly of Christianity, far more radical than Jung could then see—perhaps more radical than he has yet seen.
>
> ("Frontiers," p.10)

The statement may pose a dramatic irony for later readers, when we recall that Jung's revaluation of religion was finally more radical than White himself had yet seen, or would be able to bear.

What White meant at the time by this approving statement probably did not take Jung's understanding of religious symbols into account. To the degree that "Christianity" refers to the Western world's major symbolic expression of a universal religious impulse, White could agree to a radical psychological revaluation of its symbols. But to the degree that it refers to a credal and theological language system, distinct from other such systems, White eventually found himself in a quandary, since Jung challenged the received definitions of key elements within that system.

At this early point, White seems not to have been fully aware of Jung's insistence that his psychology applies to religion in general and not only to Christianity. In this, his first essay on the subject, he quotes Jung's famous statement attributing adult psychopathology to a lack of religious outlook. But he omits the qualifying clause on the next line, where Jung carefully explains that what *he* means by "a religious outlook" has "nothing whatever to do with a particular creed or membership of a church" ("Psychotherapists or the Clergy," *CW 11* §509).

White also made a major miscalculation when he blithely brushed aside Jung's "mistake" about the transcendent nature of God:

> One basic issue which needs to be cleared up concerns his objections to an absolute God, an idea which he has palpably very imperfectly understood and consequently totally rejected. . . .
>
> ("Frontiers," p.17)

Jung's ambivalent God-image was to prove the basis of a disagreement whose roots lay far too deep for such easy "clearing up." Much of White's early writing about Jung's work has this same quality of gentle donnish scolding, combined with an optimistic reasonableness which assumes that when the student—in this case Jung—has read his lesson better, the problem will be solved.

Some very complex causes may have underlain White's initial miscalculation. As suggested above, a conceptual incoherence was at the heart of his equation between Jung's definition of libido and Aquinas' *actus purus*. But was the incoherence simply a result of his naïve reading of Jung? Or did White also adapt Aquinas' teaching in an eccentric way, which invited the deceptive equation of natural theologies in Aquinas and Jung? Looking at how White appropriated Aquinas' basic ways of describing God's being, we may discover a clue to the way he applied these concepts to Jung.

In the second question of the *Summa Theologiae*, Aquinas begins his proof of God's existence by discussing the phenomenon of motion. Created things can and do experience motion, he says, because they are *not* in a perfect state of actuality. Things are moved (by a "mover" outside themselves) from potentiality to actuality (*ST* I. Q.2, a.3). In fact, the change from potentiality to actuality is, according to Aquinas, what the phenomenon of motion is all about.

White was quite familiar with this article of the Summa. He saw Aquinas' treatment of motion as basic to his own project, because it allowed him to bring psychological and empirical information to bear on theology. In the third part of "Thomism and 'Affective Knowledge' " White recalls that Aquinas made "the fact of Becoming (*motus*) . . . the basic datum of experience from the analysis of which his whole philosophy is inferred" ("Affective Knowledge" III, p.323). From this observation, he goes on to argue that Aquinas' entire system of thought—anthropology, ethics, and metaphysics— "is constructed by the analogical application of concepts derived from the world of change and movement" (Ibid). White claims that Thomas Aquinas was, if nothing else, a good phenomenologist.

Aquinas' argument from motion, however, also makes God the unmoved mover, the origin of motion who moves all things (*ST* I. Q.2, a.3). So the doctrine of Prime Mover, which White did not like, is closely associated with the doctrine of God's absolute undivided goodness, with which he agreed. Thus there may be a split, an incoherence or paradox, at this point in White's appropriation of St. Thomas' thought. Both the immobility and the perfect goodness of God make sense, for Aquinas, only if there is nothing potential, undeveloped or unfinished in God's being. Aquinas' God is utterly simple, unified, and perfect (*ST* I. Q.3; Q.4; Q.7; Q.9; Q.11). White agrees with this description of God, which is expressed in Aquinas' teaching that, unlike created beings (which are always to some degree or in some respect *in potentia*) God is the only being perfectly *in actu*. These claims about God are implications of the concept of *actus purus* that White approximates (formally at least) to Jung's "undifferentiated libido."

Perhaps what appears to be a logical discrepancy in White's treatment of Aquinas is only a matter of emphasis: White stresses as much as possible the aspects of Thomas' thought that support a phenomenological starting place, and as little as possible the aspects that support a hyperintellectualist, authoritarian or static theology. But the problems with Jung go deeper. As we shall discuss in Chapter Five, Jung flatly disagrees with the orthodox depiction of God as a perfectly good, unchanging, unified being. His God-image includes unfinished work, change, development, unconsciousness and even moral contradictions. His concept of "libido," too, is necessarily a dynamic, imperfect mass of potentialities.

Indeed, Jung's mature cosmology regards both "libido" and "the God-image," in fact every archetype, as a *complexio oppositorum*—complex of opposites—since "there can be no reality without polarity" (*Aion, CW 9ii* §423). Jung's writing of *Aion* and *Answer to Job* would later reveal that, all through the period of his collaboration with White, he grew only more convinced that the Judeo-Christian God (the God-image native to Western Europe) has both a dark side and a potential for transformation. His position on this issue was not, as White for a long time assumed, a sign of curable confusion but a deep, epistemologically rooted commitment.

In theory, even at the outset White could have known the theological tensions he risked by involving himself in collaboration with Jung. Predating their first correspondence in 1945, Jung had already begun to publish writings that clearly reflect a view of God foreign to Catholic orthodoxy. In his Terry Lectures at Yale, which appeared in English in 1938,[13] Jung's images of God and the institutional church are highly ambivalent. Unfortunately, however, when White published "The Frontiers of Theology and Psychology" and "Thomism and 'Affective Knowledge,' " he seems not to have read Jung's Terry Lectures. No mention of this seminal work on the relationship of psychology and religion appears in his writing until 1948.[14]

It may prove instructive for us, who are trying at a remove of more than four decades to understand how the two men viewed their collaboration and what was at stake for them, to compare two nearly contemporaneous writings by White and Jung, even if neither of them ever made a systematic comparison between these writings. The third essay in White's "Thomism and 'Affective Knowledge' " and the second lecture in Jung's *Psychology and Religion* illustrate how differently the theologian and the psychologist tended to construe the relationship between formal doctrinal theology and the more subjective data of religious experience.

In Jung's second Terry Lecture, "Dogma and Natural Symbols," he contrasts "experience" and "religion" in a way which is formally equivalent to White's contrast of "thing" and "thought" in Part III of "Thomism and 'Affective Knowledge.' " A feature of Jung's argument that could have lent strength to White's conclusions, if he had known about it, is the observation that when a collective form of religion is substituted for direct individual experience of God, the result can be a serious neurosis. Jung and White agree, then, that an overintellectualized theology soon loses sight of the soul's direct encounter with God.

Jung's support for White's argument grows complicated, however, when he adds his pragmatic hypothesis that the substitution of "religion" for "immediate experience" may serve a valid psychological purpose for individuals and societies:

> What is usually and generally called "religion" is to such an amazing degree a substitute that I ask myself seriously whether this kind of "religion," which I prefer to call a creed, has not after all an important function in human society. The substitution has the obvious purpose of replac-

ing immediate experience by a choice of suitable symbols
invested in a solidly organized dogma and ritual.

(Psychology and Religion, CW 11 §75)

Institutionalized and intellectualized religion, Jung observes, may have the protective value of a defense mechanism.
Jung's therapeutic approach takes precedence here, for he
maintains that a direct encounter with the unconscious (he approximates "direct experience of the unconscious" to "direct
experience of God" without completely equating them—§75ff)
is never a safe or simple event for the soul. Contact with the
unconscious is essential and life-giving. Yet it is also terrifying
and dangerous, and all the more so if one cannot wholeheartedly take shelter in the symbols and rituals of a religious system.
One function of religious symbols and rituals, Jung theorizes, is
to shield the soul against the "terrible double aspect" of direct
contact with the God within. "Solidly organized dogma and
ritual" function like lightning rods for the vulnerable human
psyche.

Thus, as protection against the terrors of immediate experience, dogmas and creeds can be either stultifying or support-
ive. Their usefulness varies with the ability of the soul to tolerate the reality of the unconscious in a direct onslaught. It
may be more valuable—humanizing, empowering— to tolerate that experience in its nakedness, as Jung himself was wont
to do.[15] But he warns that when religious symbols and rituals
lose their credibility, people are thrown unprepared into "the
zone of world-destroying and world-creating fire" (Ibid §84).
To be sure, some can encounter God in the psyche and survive
the experience without needing to substitute creed for reality;
but not everyone can withstand the fire. For many, it would be
better to remain within the "substituted" reality of collective
dogma.

In contrast, White's proposals for "affective knowledge"
presuppose that the God of love is eminently reasonable and
benign. The soul may embrace without peril a God without
shadow. For White, the function of doctrinal propositions as
defense mechanisms before the onslaught of God's "terrible
double aspect" has no persuasive power. As far as one can dis-

cern from his writings at this stage, White was as yet hardly aware of the crucial place Jung assigns in his psychology to God's terrifying side.

Years later it became evident that White had read Jung's Terry Lectures and other writings that interpret dogma and ritual as therapeutic defenses. He agreed with this much of Jung's view. Yet, unsurprisingly, he never adopted the idea that the soul is endangered precisely by its encounter with God. In his 1953 essay, "Religious Tolerance," White wrote:

> According to Jung, the psychological function of the *mythos*, the ritual or the dogma, is that of protecting the ego from dissolution in the unconscious, while at the same time they mediate its contents in digestible and beneficial form. The ego is at once protected by them from meaninglessness and insanity, which men fear more than death; and they are mediums of meaningfulness and health to the human psyche.
>
> ("Tolerance," p.532)

White attributed usefulness to certain kinds of religious "substitute." Unmediated contact with the forces of the unconscious, he agreed, is dangerous. But he rejected Jung's equation between the danger of a direct encounter with *the unconscious* and the danger of a direct encounter with *God*.

Like White, Jung began the collaboration at a disadvantage. Each of them was unprepared at first to construe certain ideas basic to the other's thinking. So White could propose Jung's "libido" as a match for Aquinas' "pure act," not realizing how Heraclitean a part of nature Jung's idea of libido-energy was or how negative his God-image. And Jung overlooked this and other ill-fitting connections within White's synthesis when he first saw them, because, unversed in Thomistic metaphysics as he was, he did not grasp all the implications of Thomas' "pure act" or anticipate how absolutely—based on his loyalty to metaphysical epistemology and ecclesial hermeneutics—White would continue to insist on a perfectly good God.

Their collaboration suffered in part because of honest failures to engage each other's terms. Yet it is clear that they both did all they could to clear up mistakes and misunderstandings when they recognized them as such. They tried to educate each other in their respective fields. When Jung noticed a problem in White's use of psychological terms, he promptly corrected it (*Letters I*, p.413). Jung requested help with theological language, and received it. White sent Jung copies of his papers and extracts from St. Thomas. Jung invited White to Bollingen and included him at Eranos conferences, making him a full part of the Jungian intellectual circle.[16]

Nevertheless, Jung grasped the ramifications of White's metaphysical categories only slowly, and White held off as long as he could the realization that some of Jung's theological ideas diverged irreducibly from Catholic orthodoxy. Indeed, it was only in the process of collaborating that each of them found it necessary or possible to write some of the lectures and books which exposed the differences between what he was saying and what—as he came gradually to understand—the other wanted him to say.

On his side, White's later works showed the results of his struggles to understand Jung and to be understood. Some of his theological essays were written as much for Jung's benefit, it seems, as for the theological audience. "Kinds of Opposites" is one of these: White almost certainly would not have written this monograph, if the definition of evil as "privation" had not become such a sticking point between himself and Jung. He submitted the work for Jung's 80th birthday Festschrift; but it is doubtful that Jung found it instructive. The greatest value of the piece was, finally, to the editors of the Blackfriars edition of the *Summa Theologiae*, where it appears in digested form as a footnote to St. Thomas' discussion of evil.[17]

2. *Contrasts in Piety*

Not all of the differences between White and Jung found expression in the two men's published writings. Some of the most important can be seen only in the context of their personal relationship, where the outlines of the difference are often only hinted on one side or the other, not filled in by a systematic exchange.

In January 1948, about two-and-a-half years after he first

contacted Jung, White wrote to him with affectionate concern, offering a spontaneous commentary on an aspect of Jung's religious psychology, and in the process delineating one of the fundamental differences between them. White was then in the middle of a year-long visit to the United States, staying with a family in Stone Ridge, New York. Perhaps his comfort in that setting accounts for his having time to reflect so deeply and write so expansively.

White reflected on a dream Jung had sent to him a month before, and sympathized with the insomnia that had been plaguing the earliest stages of Jung's work on a piece that would develop into *Aion* (*Letters I*, p.481). As he considered aspects of Jung's situation, he intuitively connected his friend's inner tension with the Protestant "Stoicism" expressed in the Terry Lectures. Evidently Jung had sent him the lectures in their German language revision; for although White's letter is in English, he quotes in German:

> There is one thing you have written which has rather worried me; and more so since I have come to know and love you personally. (Permit me to be quite frank about it.) It is where you write of the "Demut" of the Protestant; and how "Der Protestant ist Gott allein anheimgegeben. Es gibt für ihn keine Beichte, keine Absolution, usw. Er muss seine Sünde allein verdauen . . ."[18] Oh, it is splendid, magnificent; I too still feel deeply and intensely the fascination of it—whether we call it Protestant, or just Stoic—to live like that, and to die like that. But is it really Demut—or Armut?[19] Is it even truly human? (I recall Aristotle's "The solitary man is either a Beast or a God.")
>
> (VW to CGJ, 3 Jan. 48)[20]

Among all of White's letters to Jung, perhaps none better reflects the friendship that had grown up between him and his "dear C.G." than this one. White here speaks to Jung in the voice of a moral equal, a spiritual friend. His assurance in the letter is remarkable, as other letters reveal a rather self-effacing mood. In his previous letter, for example (27 Dec. 1947), he had said he would "not dare to comment" on the dream Jung had sent him, although (as he later admitted) he had rather clear thoughts about it at the time.

A vision, he explains, made him think again about his refusal to comment. The content of the vision tells us of the depth of White's sympathy with Jung, and suggests that he needed (or had already begun) to address, in more conscious ways, the implications of the encounter between his Catholicism and Jung's Protestantism. In White's vision he denied a meal of fish to Jung, because Jung was not Catholic and need not fast as White did. "You asked me to pass you the fish (the IXθUS!). I said: 'Hell: YOU don't have to eat fish today'. . . ." But Jung (in the vision) only looked at White "reproachfully and disappointed and ill" (VW to CGJ, 3 Jan. 48). White drew the moral: he should not deny his Protestant friend the benefits of what a Catholic thinks.

White's tone of confidence extends into the next paragraph of his letter. Not as an academic theologian, but as an experienced spiritual guide whose practice undergirds his teaching, White gently questions the heroism implicit in Jung's solitary piety, and tries to convey to him a more sacramental view of human life and death:

> It took me a long time to see and to accept it, but I think there is a terrible hidden HYBRIS in "seine Sünde allein verdauen." "Beichte, Absolution, Ritual" and the rest, I see not just as a matter of "consolation." The Catholic must acknowledge and accept to the very end, especially at the very end, his dependence on the Earth which to the very end supports him—even physically: there is always gravitation! To the end he must submit to the Spirit THROUGH matter: the oil, the bread, the wine, the hands and forgiveness and well-wishing of his fellow men, representing earthly society. . . .
>
> (Ibid)

A familiar theme appears in this paragraph, the doctrine of participation, which White had explored earlier in a Thomistic context. Here it appears more quietly as the harmonic accompaniment to his personal concern for his friend. Jung's previous letter had alluded to the work he was beginning to write (with anxiety) about "Christ—not the man but the divine being" (*Letters I*, p. 480).[21] By writing from the heart about a basic principle of his own piety, White's letter ventured into the realm of spiritual counsel to the older man.

As sometimes happened when profound religious or philosophical differences opened between them, White's message on this occasion seems to have had no immediate response. Jung's next letter, dated 21 May 48, began, "Finally I am able to write to you" (*Letters I*, p.501). In it, however, he did not refer to White's sacramental piety. He praised his friend's "excellent lecture on Gnosticism" and explored the question the essay had raised for him: "*Have I faith or a faith or not?*" (Ibid).

In this letter Jung reflects that faith means, for him, the involuntary "respect" he feels for most of the world's religions, including but not limited to Christianity (Ibid, p.502). Only if symbols possess "vitality" and "motive-power," he explains, can they elicit this feeling of respect from him. The process is not intellective but irrational, immediate, a function of emotion and intuition.

> There must be—so I conclude—a rather strong motive-power connected with the Christian Truth, otherwise it would not be explicable why it influences me to such an extent. My respect is—mind you—involuntary; it is a "datum" of irrational nature. This *is* the nearest I can get to what appears to me as "faith." There is however nothing specific in it, since I feel the same kind of respect for the basic teachings of Buddhism and the fundamental Taoist ideas.
>
> (Ibid)

White has invited him to consider a communally and sacramentally mediated religion, a humble "dependence on the earth." Jung replies, in effect, that he respects the sheer power and vitality of religious symbols, wherever and however they impress themselves upon him. Symbolic truths worthy of his respect mediate their power to him directly, and he is left to interpret this " 'datum' of irrational nature." In defining his personal faith this way, Jung repeats to White the message of the Terry Lectures as it applies to himself. By conviction he is and must remain naked and solitary before the holy.

C. WHITE'S DISLOCATED CAREER

1. Sailing Close to the Wind

It is no easier accurately to depict the England that Victor White inhabited in the 1940s and 1950s, than to write about the Middle Ages. In some ways it is harder, because we see a society that existed in our youth, or in our parents' youth, as being close to us. But the feeling of familiarity is deceptive. The English Catholic world has always been a special environment unto itself. And the urban England that existed before the 1960s—a post-World War society in many ways—was as different from the one we see today as the Catholic Church prior to Vatican II was, in many respects, from the one that has emerged since.

A younger contemporary who lived through events at Blackfriars with White, and a son who witnessed White's visits to Bollingen—Aelred Squire and Franz Jung—these eyewitnesses, too, have trouble recalling accurately and describing credibly the mental and social world in which Victor White and C.G. Jung lived and did their work. It follows that anyone evaluating the story of White and his failed synthesis from a present-day perspective must admit to a degree of hermeneutical distance. It is best to approach the story mindful of a residual ignorance, bridged only imperfectly by sympathetic imagination, concerning the meaning these events had for those who lived them.

In the years following their initial meeting, White's enthusiasm for "Jung's metaphysics" and Jung's delight in "White's empiricism" gradually yielded on both sides to a more sober and realistic evaluation of the issues which separated their respective positions. Later chapters explore these problematic issues from the theoretical perspective. But a purely theoretical understanding cannot exhaust the meaning of what White and Jung attempted or fully show the costs of failure. We need also to try to grasp the personal dimensions of the work they undertook together, beginning with the circumstances of White's proposed synthesis. It was a synthesis he proposed not only to write about but also, in his collaboration with Jung, to live.

White was an intense, introverted thinker to whom the world of ideas was a source of both ecstasy and torment. An unresolved intellectual problem could reduce him to physical illness. As one Dominican contemporary recalls,[22] on these occasions he would be literally sick and take to his room, sometimes for days. He was also, for temperamental as well as professional reasons, lonely much of the time among his fellows at Blackfriars. After his 1947–48 trip to the United States, White apparently complained to Jung in a letter (now lost) that he was feeling lonely on his return to England. Jung, responding, advised him to create a small congenial subcommunity for himself at Blackfriars, as Jung had done years before in Zurich: "If you feel isolated in England, why don't you make one of your *fratres* into a real brother in the spirit?" (*Letters I,* p.517).

Whether White succeeded fully in doing so, in the sense Jung intended, is uncertain. Annotations in White's calendar suggest that his contemporary Gerald Vann, a respected religious popularizer, was his trusted confidant. He and Vann were professed as novices together in 1924. Among White's surviving personal papers is Vann's private ordination announcement from 1929, a card bearing a small engraving by Eric Gill, titled "The Nuptuals of God," which depicts Christ and the Church in erotic symbolism.[23]

White's contemporaries also included Mark Brocklehurst, Conrad Pepler, and Gervase Matthew. A younger man, Richard Kehoe, a brilliant biblical scholar, shared White's psychological orientation. White praised him warmly to Jung and recommended him as a possible lecturer at Eranos.[24] Because of their shared interest in Jung's psychology, it seems possible that Kehoe became—until his quiet departure from Blackfriars in the early 1950s—the nearest thing to what Jung meant by White's "brother in the spirit." Kehoe was also among the few friends who visited White at Cambridge Blackfriars in 1960 when White was dying.

White's friendship with Jung and the fellowship he enjoyed with Jungians in England, Switzerland, Scandinavia and the

United States seem to have provided him another kind of much-desired companionship. Many of his letters to Jung, even in the bad years, express keen anticipation of or nostalgia about a visit to Bollingen. It seems clear that he found in settings apart from Blackfriars an intimacy and warmth that compensated, at least in part, for a certain loneliness that characterized his life as a Dominican.

It must be added that Victor White was a very private man. There are hidden things in his personal realm that we may never know. From indirect or circumstantial evidence,[25] and from themes that recur in his theological writing—such as "experience" and "affective knowledge"—we may hope and guess that somewhere in his life he found wells of sweetness which otherwise seem, on balance, sadly lacking.

In his professional life White soon became thoroughly identified with Jung and the Jungian community.[26] After 1945, virtually all his major writings were on Jungian subjects (reviews of Jung's books, and so forth), as was his collection of essays published in 1952, *God and the Unconscious*. This professional identification meant that White was vulnerable, in a certain sense, to Jung's independent decisions. For better or worse, the hand on the tiller of White's sailboat was Jung's, even if the wind propelling the boat was the Holy Spirit.[27] The image in White's dream included dangerous rocks through which the boat was driven; the rocks were present in life, as well.

2. The Impact of Job

In 1950 Jung wrote *Aion*, his first effort to deal with the psychological meaning of Christ as a divine figure. The following year he produced *Answer to Job*, a far more personal and intense work that went further on the same subject and took up the nature of the God-image mediated through Judeo-Christian revelation. These two books by Jung, but especially the second, cast into high relief certain aspects of his thought that up to now White had ignored, rationalized, or expected to clear up in time.

Meanwhile, the pressures for theological conformity had intensified in 1950 when the promulgation of *Humani generis* silenced some Catholic scholars and began to exercise its chilling effect on many more. White gradually realized that he had a new kind of problem on his hands: *Answer to Job* contained a great deal that, taken at face value, diverged sharply from official Catholic doctrine. Because of his public identification with Jung, he knew he would soon have to produce a public response to this very challenging book.

It is most probable that White first heard about Jung's work on Job and saw it in typescript during his visit to Bollingen in the summer of 1951.[28] The next spring he wrote to Jung asking for permission to read the published version, saying that Jung had promised he could read it when it came out (VW to CGJ, 30 March 52). White was delighted when a copy of the book arrived. His response to his first full reading of *Antwort auf Hiob* was a long letter, in which he called it

> the most exciting and moving book I have read in years: and somehow it arouses tremendous bonds of sympathy between us and lights up all sorts of dark places both in the Scriptures and in my own psyche.
>
> (5 April 1952)

Apart from this glowing affirmation, White mentioned a few serious theoretical problems the book raised for him as a theologian, especially the need to resolve "this deadlock about *privatio boni*"[29] (Ibid). He cautiously suggested ways for Jung to look at the matter of evil, phenomenologically and metaphysically; and he attempted to correct Jung's use of technical theological terms, such as *ouk on* (negation) and *me on* (absence). But this letter ended in the same vein as it had started, rejoicing in the fact that *Antwort auf Hiob* ("a fascinating book—and an encouraging one too in these grim, deluded times") had in fact been published.

In the years that followed his first reading of the book, White's original positive response was practically lost to view. He struggled to make Jung understand the difficulties the book raised for the Thomistic theological system, for believing Christians, and for White personally in his Order. Finally he came to believe that, by publishing the book at all, Jung had inexplicably betrayed not only his Catholic collaborator but also the Christians for whose psychological welfare he had formerly seemed to care.

As long as Jung's *Job* did not appear in English translation, White could feel that it did not directly threaten his position within his Order. At least its impact would not be felt by most of the English-speaking Catholics who supported his work as a theologian. White was acutely conscious that his livelihood, and the security of Blackfriars, depended on the support of good souls in the Catholic lay community. If he believed or approved of what Jung said in *Answer to Job* (which, as his letters show, he partly did), he was beyond the pale of the lay Catholic community that was his primary means of support. In his own eyes he was false to them, his "very clerical clothes . . . a lie" (VW to CGJ, 8 Nov. 53).

A shadow must have fallen over White's work from 1952 on, cast by the approaching English translation of Jung's *Job*. White increasingly confronted the pressure of his own ambivalence, aggravated by the reaction he knew he could anticipate from colleagues and superiors at Blackfriars. The translation of *Antwort auf Hiob* appeared in England in 1954.[30] In January 1955 White wrote (from California):

> I am frankly rather relieved that "Answer to Job" has not yet appeared in USA! It would queer my pitch rather badly among these mostly very naïve, but very well meaning, Catholics. Already of course I am getting perplexed and indignant letters from England asking "What the hell . . ."
> (VW to CGJ, 8 Jan. 55)

During the years after 1951, for all these reasons, White's bridge-building task thus became more a torment than a joy, and his friendship with Jung—which was by now a component of his basic well-being—increasingly strained. White began to see himself as caught between the commitments of his work with Jung and the very different commitments of his ongoing life and work in the Dominican Order.

3. Riding Out the Storm

The letters Jung wrote to and about White at this period show clearly—corroborated by White's own letters—that in the mid-1950s White was on the horns of a personal dilemma. Jung perceived the problem, from his own point of view, acutely and with sympathy:

> Analytical psychology unfortunately just touches the vulnerable spot of the church, viz. the untenable concretism of its beliefs, and the syllogistic character of Thomistic philosophy. . . . Father White, however, is by no means unconscious of those clashes; it is a very serious personal problem to him.
>
> (*Letters II*, p.228)[31]

By late 1953 White found himself at an exquisitely painful crossroads. He felt forced to choose definitively between his collaboration and friendship with Jung and his professional role as a theologian. For a time, he seemed about to leave the Order. He wrote to Jung that he dreaded starting over again in the world at 51; but he felt morally bound to end the "lie" he was living (VW to CGJ, 8 Nov. 53).

Two of White's letters, dated 8 Nov. 53 and 4 March 54, expose the depth of his suffering over this question. In the first he states his conflict in the starkest possible terms:

> If Christ is no longer an adequate and valid symbol of the Self, . . . then must one not choose—at whatever the cost? . . . One has lost any sense of oneness that one ever had with one's community, with the Church. . . . Their God simply isn't my God any more: my very clerical clothes have become a lie.
>
> (VW to CGJ, 8 Nov. 53)

He writes that he now wishes intensely to quit the Order; but when he yields to that wish in his imagination, he immediately starts to suffer from nightmares and physical illness.

At the end of his letter White regrets that he cannot be with Jung in Zurich at present, to see Jung presented with the Gnostic papyri that would receive his name. But immediately after that, White's final sentence discloses the ultimatum to which his inner conflict is driving him. If he cannot integrate his professional role with the insights of Jungian psychology but dares not leave his Order, only one way remains to end the tension. But it is an alternative that White approaches with intense ambivalence:

> I must confess that there are times when I wish to heaven I had never heard of your psychology (and some of your disciples!); and yet I tremble to think what would have happened if I hadn't!
>
> (Ibid)

White's next letter on the subject reflects a less desperate mood. At base, however, it poses the same problem, a sharply unsettling vocational dilemma:

> I feel this question of "Can I stay where I am?" as a *moral* issue; and not just one of suffering, loneliness and discomfort. Is it *honest* to go on wearing a persona with which my inner thoughts and much of my outer conduct is in such violent contradiction? In particular, can I again take an oath . . . that I believe all the Nicene Creed, the Creed of Pius IV, the anti-modernist oath . . . , and not to teach otherwise than the SOLID doctrine of St. Thomas Aquinas and his school? Ugh. . . .
>
> (VW to CGJ, 4 March 54)

Jung responded to his friend's crisis with two very long letters, in which he marshalled every conceivable argument from both psychology and theology.[32] The direction of both letters was to urge White to consider how he might in good conscience remain a Dominican, while holding faithfully to his psychological convictions. In the end White did find his way clear to staying in the Order, and he thanked Jung for showing him another way to think of his situation. "Anyhow," he wrote, "the practical upshot is that here I stay; and I hope a new attitude and perspective is forming. . . ." (VW to CGJ, 15 May 54).

As White had complained in his March letter, if he was to remain at Blackfriars as a theologian he must swear an oath required of Dominicans at this period, combining the Vatican Oath Against Modernism with endorsement of an officially approved reading of Aquinas. In good conscience White could and did disavow what the Vatican called modernism (as we have seen, he carefully defined "experience" in language excluding known modernist ideas[33]). But it repelled him to promise not to teach "otherwise than the solid doctrine of St. Thomas Aquinas and his school"—an encoded reference to neoscholasticism. With Jung's support, however, he finally decided to stay where he was and take the oath.

After he received White's rather desperate letter in November 1953, Jung tried to help him look pragmatically and therepeutically at his function in the church. He argued that for the sake of a spiritually needy human race, the church must continue to teach the imitation of Christ,

> until it is clearly understood what assimilation of the shadow means. Those that foresee must—as it were—stay behind their vision in order to help and to teach, particularly so if they belong to the church as her appointed servants.
>
> (*Letters II*, p.136)

He also addressed White's own vocational dilemma directly, adding,

> Whatever your ultimate decision will be, you ought to realize beforehand that staying in the church makes sense as it is important to make people understand what the symbol of Christ means, and such understanding is indispensable to any further development.
>
> (*Letters II*, p.137)

In short, Jung advised White to stay where he was for the sake of humanity, to help the necessarily slow process of transformation in collective consciousness. In this light he interpreted White's teaching role, so as to ethically justify, or even require, White's decision to stay:

> It would be a lack of responsibility and a rather autoerotic attitude if we were to deprive our fellow beings of a vitally necessary symbol before they had a reasonable chance to understand it thoroughly.
>
> (Ibid)

Suffering will be unavoidable in White's situation, Jung admits; but it can become bearable when it has meaning. The ultimate meaning of White's struggle lies, he suggests, in the hope that the church will someday radically change its perspective.[34] This is the distant future, the *telos*, to which White may dedicate his present sufferings, if he decides to stay where he is.

In this complicated letter, Jung offers White two apparently conflicting kinds of advice: both to see his troubles eschatalogically, and to avoid eschatalogical escapism. On the second theme he writes,

> An anticipation of a faraway future is no way out of the actual situation. It is a mere *consolamentum* for those despairing of the atrocious possibilities of the present time.
>
> (*Letters II*, p.138)

White apparently seized on aspects of both alternatives, for he confessed, "the points that 'ring the bell' most immediately are those about the 'autoerotic attitude' and about 'an anticipation of a faraway future is no way out' " (VW to CGJ, 4 March 54). A month later Jung reported in a note to Aniela Jaffé: "I am writing a long letter to Pater White. He has—thanks be to God—chosen the better course of facing his difficulties with complete honesty" (*Letters II*, p.163). By this time White was no longer ready to leave the Order. Although the conflict within him was not yet resolved, he was trying to bear it consciously.

To bear internal conflict consciously, however, has a double edge. After urging White to continue where he was, Jung admonished him not to abandon his private convictions. Jung's massive letter of 10 April 1954 reminds White that if personal, individual autonomy is lost, God is not served. The ultimate appeal, he says, is always to one's private conscience, and not to the orders of the magisterium. This thought is consistent with elements of White's own Thomistic tradition; but Jung gives it a relentless edge:

> The old trick of law obedience is still going strong, but the original Christian teaching is a reminder. The man who allows the institution to swallow him is not a good servant.
> (*Letters II*, p.170)

How much does the service of God, who is truly served only in congruence with a person's inner truth, require of a theologian like Victor White, who experiences an inner truth that he dares not articulate—at least not in the hearing of his wider community, the church? White decided that he would try to keep his personal autonomy intact while performing in as good faith as possible the public role in which he still hoped to achieve some measure of institutional success.

D. SACRIFICE: VOLUNTARY AND INVOLUNTARY

1. STM and Regent of Studies

As Jung perceived White's situation—crucified on the opposites—the only possible resolution would have been to remain both in the institutional church and therapeutically above it. To keep one's soul in White's circumstances, one must be outwardly compliant, yet conscious of private contradictions. Many people tolerate such a conflict between their inner orientation and their public role by cultivating a mild sociopathy, a conscious split in their thinking ("mental reservations"). Others avoid the demands of too-literal authenticity by invoking the symbolic nature of all religious ideas. It seems unlikely that Victor White could have borne his ambiguous position in either of these ways.

As the date neared for publication of the English translation of *Job*, White was also nearing a turning point in his career. The STM degree, and the oath against Modernism that would be administered with it over which White had struggled so hard with Jung's help, were the prerequisites to an important promotion. By all academic standards, White was the obvious candidate to be appointed regent of studies at Blackfriars. As it turned out, however, after receiving the STM degree he was not only passed over for the regency, but also asked by his Provincial to leave Oxford and England for a period of unknown duration (VW to CGJ, 25 Sept. 54).

Events in the summer of 1954 had all the more impact on Victor White and his community at Blackfriars[35] because they reversed expectations and plans that had been years in the making. White had been preparing to receive the degree of Master of Theology for four years or more. In February 1950 he wrote to Jung that he would need to visit Rome at some point in the coming year to take the required examination, which he regarded as pro forma, and something of a nuisance (VW to CGJ, 10 Feb. 50). As it turned out, he was called to Rome for three weeks that fall, starting in late October. There he took and passed what he called "this ridiculous examination" (VW to CGJ, 3 Dec. 50). Noting his success, he concluded wryly, "My peculiar 'heresies'—which I did not disguise—are tolerable even there" (Ibid).

At this time the Dominican STM degree was normally not given until its recipient was ready to take on a leadership position, such as the regency White was to assume (A.C., 26 Feb. 92). A delay of months or years between examination and award was therefore not unusual. The document granting White his STM degree was issued in Rome on 28 May 1954,[36] and the degree was actually awarded at a ceremony in Oxford in June. To the surprise of some who attended the ceremony, the degree was awarded to two men at once. When a few months later the appointment of the new regent of studies was announced, the appointment went not to Victor White, but to the other STM recipient.

White's fortunes, it appears, were reversed after the STM ceremony by an unexpected event at a high level of the Catholic hierarchy: the death of the Master General of the Dominican Order and the appointment of his successor. The new Master General ruled in July that White could not become regent.[37] White's friends in Rome were evidently as shocked by this reversal as those in Oxford (A.C., private correspondence,

5 June 92). In early August, as White reported to Jung six weeks later, he received a letter from his Provincial informing him that he was not to be regent of studies and asking him to consider going to California (VW to CGJ, 25 Sept. 54). The Provincial's letter breaking this news clearly came as a grievous surprise to White.

White wrote to Jung in late September. Judging from this letter and later events, he felt a keen sense of rejection when he was passed over. The nature of the humiliation, however, made it likely that he would conceal his private feelings. White's practiced persona also seems to have protected him well in this crisis. Many of his Dominican colleagues saw no sign of struggle.[38] His letter to Jung is only slightly more revealing.

He alludes with bitter irony to the STM ceremony and the complicated loyalty oath, over which he and Jung had labored for so long. It is clear to him that he has been passed over for political reasons. The new regent he calls, parenthetically, "a complete incompetent" (VW to CGJ, 25 Sept. 54).[39] The degree and the oath appear to him a wasted sacrifice and an embarrassment, since now it is plain he will never reach the goal that justified his compliance:

> So all my fuss about the oath, the degree, and my beautiful self-sacrifice pro bono publico has been a sort of sacrifice of Isaac—or maybe something a great deal more comic.
>
> (Ibid)

In the same letter White informs Jung of his approaching travels. Arrangements are complete: he is about to depart for California. The decision was made easier, he says, "since, at least to start with, it will be only for about five months." He adds that his duties to the Order will take him to Rome in April; but whether he will ever live and teach at Blackfriars again is unclear.

> I am no longer "indispensable" at Oxford: indeed, it seems definitely "not wanted." I am still left guessing the reasons: there could be several. But in many ways it is of course a huge relief.
>
> (Ibid)

In a real sense, these events marked the end of White's career as a professor of dogmatics. He would never teach at Blackfriars again. Although no official reasons for his demotion were offered, probable causes were not far to seek. White could guess that he had been judged after all on the basis of his "peculiar 'heresies,' " specifically his longstanding collaboration with the author of *Answer to Job*.

2. White's Review of Answer to Job

As we read about White's break with Jung and the other sufferings of his final years, we need to remember the impact of this loss in 1954. After this blow, a confluence of inner and outer forces led to his eventual estrangement from both his Order and his collaborator. In particular, White's review of *Answer to Job*, with its disastrous results for his friendship with Jung, must be seen against this background of professional rejection by his Order. Otherwise the vehemence of the damaging essay will be only poorly understood.

It should perhaps be made explicit that White was never threatened with expulsion from his Order if he did not abandon his work with the psychologist. On the contrary, he was elected to represent the English Province in 1954, and given positions of responsibility in his Chapter following that year. Yet, as he finally concluded (VW to CGJ, 18 Oct. 59), on account of his collaboration with Jung his work as a Dominican theologian was put under a cloud; he was no longer trusted as a teacher of dogmatics for his Order.

White thus set off to California in October 1954 without any specific assignment. Professional exclusion must have been especially difficult for someone isolated by temperament, who laid great store by his career. Suspecting that his work with Jung had been his nemesis, he was furious as well as profoundly hurt. We can believe he was, as Jung wrote to him in 1955 at the peak of their quarrel, "in a hell of suffering" (*Letters II*, p.241).

As becomes clear when we look at events in the months that followed, at a conscious level White directed his anger at Jung rather than his superiors in the Order. Before he returned to England, on his way to Rome for the General Chapter meeting in spring 1955, he wrote his review of Jung's *Job*. Crossing the Atlantic, on stationery bearing the Queen Mary letterhead, he both begged Jung's forgiveness for the excesses of his review and defended himself for writing it (VW to CGJ, 17 March 55). By this time, however, the damning essay was in print. The two men's ensuing correspondence only aggravated the damage.

It is not too much to say that in parting irrevocably from Jung in 1955, White separated from a part of himself he could scarcely bear to lose. Although he meant to make this self-sacrifice consciously, in a state of moral awareness, in fact it seems that he cut off his relationship to Jung without fully knowing what he was doing. This sad surmise is supported by several kinds of evidence. The final paragraph of his important essay, "Kinds of Opposites," written for Jung's 80th birthday Festschrift in 1955, suggests the dimensions of White's struggle and the degree to which he felt himself forced to choose between irreconcilable paths.

In the conclusion to this essay White reflects on the agony of Christ at Gethsemane, confronting his contradictory opposites. Christ was forced to choose, White says (citing Aquinas), between the objects of his divine and his human will. This choice, he goes on, involved "agony" but not inner "conflict," because Jesus had faced the inexorable contradiction between God's will and his own and consciously accepted the necessity of sacrificing one to the other. A decision made in total consciousness may be excruciatingly painful; it is not psychologically conflictual. White's essay concludes:

> The consideration is perhaps not entirely irrelevant to those who, with or without aid from analytical psychology, find themselves tormented between the opposites.
>
> > ("Opposites," p.150)

When we remember the sequence of his responses to Jung's *Answer to Job*, it becomes plain that an internal contradiction tormented White himself. He presumably tried to resolve that contradiction as consciously as possible by sacrificing the "human object" of his will to the "divine." But in cutting himself off from Jung, White suffered under a profound psychological conflict. Publication of his review of *Job* was the act which pre-cipitated the end of his collaboration with Jung. Features of that review and White's letters regretting and justifying it support the theory that he only half-consciously consigned a part of himself to oblivion.

The causes for White's vehement public attack on Jung are not self-evident, unless we take his internal turmoil into account. External conditions did not require such a broadside. Indeed, a far more sympathetic review had been published in 1952 when *Antwort auf Hiob* came out in German, by another psycho-logically-minded scholar at Blackfriars, Richard Kehoe.[40] In his brief article, Kehoe warns that Jung's new book will be "more of a liability than a comfort" to some who read it, and that

> . . . an ordinary Christian, unless he were already well pre-pared to grasp at what level the Jungian psychology operates and the form of truth to which it is attuned, may think this to be a positively blasphemous contribution to the great debate.
>
> (Kehoe, p.228)

But with this warning, Kehoe tries to help readers past any initial misunderstanding of Jung's intentions, putting them on notice that the "form of truth" appropriate to a psychological hermeneutics is different from the form appropriate to the church's usual discourse. He calls Jung's *Hiob* "a generous book, abounding in magnificent insight," and his review concludes:

> If it falls short of, and in many ways fantastically obscures, the biblical truth, in many ways also it will contribute to its better understanding, somewhat as Job's wildest outbursts even were constructive, because prompted by honesty and love.
>
> (Kehoe, p.231)

Victor White's review of *Answer to Job*, in contrast, is a per-sonal attack on the author. In the March 1955 issue of *Blackfri-ars*, this is the treatment White gives to Jung and his book:

> It is not surprising that some of Jung's friends, jealous for his honour in his old age, . . . have regretted the publication of

this document. . . . Is he, after the manner of his own "Yahweh," duped by some satanic trickster into purposely tor-
menting his friends and devotees? Or is he, more rationally,
purposely putting them to the test to discover how much they
will stand rather than admit the fallibility of their master—or
how many, more Job-like, will venture to observe that the
Emperor has appeared in public without his clothes?

("Jung on Job," pp.55ff)[41]

Such a passage reveals White's sense of outrage and personal
betrayal by his teacher and friend. Its fury arises in part from
his conviction that he and all Jung's Christian followers have
been "publicly guyed" by the master, as his next letter to Jung
would complain (VW to CGJ, 17 March 55).

White's review also attempts to do justice to Jung's motives
by acknowledging human suffering, which arouses Jung's anger at God. But instead of recognizing parallels between Jung's
anger and Job's, and thus supporting Jung in principle (which
he could have done with perfect Christian orthodoxy), White
suggests that inferior teachers, the equivalent of Job's friends,
are the only right targets for anger.

[*Job*] is an angry book, but it is an anger born of experience
and compassion for mankind in its contemporary quandary,
and in the disastrous inadequacy of its supposed Christian
education to enable it to come to terms with contemporary
realities.

("Jung on Job," p.58)

In the very next paragraph he cuts Jung off at the knees. Far
from being a modern Job, the great doctor is only a self-
centered child with a child's grasp of religion:

Even an instructed Christian may expect an explosion when
an adult, whose religious development has become fixated
at the kindergarten level . . . becomes confronted with the
realities of life, of the ways of God both in the Bible and in
contemporary events. . . . the only reaction is that of the
spoiled child.

("Jung on Job," p.58)

Finally, White accuses Jung of being in a state of paranoia, utterly unconscious of himself and his motives:

> [*Answer to Job*] has—and this is its most distressing feature— the ingenuity and power, the plausibility and improbability, the clear-sightedness and blindness of the typical paranoid system which rationalizes and conceals an even more unbearable grief and resentment.[42]
>
> ("Jung on Job," p.59)

The question whether White felt under pressure to condemn Jung's work publicly in this way, or hoped to earn back official approval from his Order, is really beside the point. No amount of pressure from colleagues or superiors could have forced a practiced writer to abandon his usual rhetorical control for this degree of critical overkill. Perhaps White did hope to win back some of his lost support in Rome; but a personal attack on Jung did not strengthen the theological orthodoxy and effectiveness of the piece. White's language was dictated almost entirely by rage.

Significantly, White himself recognized at a later point in his life that this review had gone farther than argument required, farther than, in a calm moment, he wanted to go. The version he included as Appendix VI in *Soul and Psyche* is purged of the most offensive phrases and passages of the original, including one that calls Jung "very—we might say blindly— angry" ("Jung on Job," p.54). This more moderate revision avoids saying that Jung has been "duped by some satanic trickster" and omits the passages calling him an emperor without clothes and comparing his argument to a paranoid system. Publication of the milder version came too late, of course, to mend the damage of the original.

3. The Final Quarrel

In the spring of 1955, after the General Chapter meeting ended in Rome, White went to Zurich. Once there he wrote to Jung several times but was not able to see him. This must have been a painful disappointment, for he had written to Jung that he hoped to "stay around quite a while," making himself useful

if possible at the Jung Institute (VW to CGJ, 25 Sept. 54). White
had little to look forward to back in Oxford. While in Zurich he
received orders to go on to California directly, rather than return to England (VW to CGJ, 21 May 55). So he had every
reason to try to make his visit to Zurich fruitful.

His three letters to Jung during the visit make complex and
poignant reading. Attached to the first (9 May 55) is a handwritten "agenda" for a discussion that never took place, a series of
long numbered paragraphs titled "Problems Arising from Publication of Answer to Job." White's account of these "problems"
contains much that is false to Jung's psychology. It also reveals an
exaggerated sense of Jung's authority, and it fiercely questions
Jung's judgment and motives. From this document it becomes
clear that White tended to view Jung as a quasi-hierarchical figure like an archbishop; if so, it is easier to understand his conviction, expressed here and in other letters, that *Answer to Job* should
have been reserved for Jung's private circle.

White's next letter (10 May 55) was a reply to Jung's of 2
April (*Letters II*, pp.238ff), which had only just reached him. It
was thus the third in the contentious series beginning with
White's of 17 March. The March letter, written on board the
Queen Mary as White returned from the United States, had
anticipated his forthcoming review of *Answer to Job*, calling the
book "a public parade of splenetic shadow" and accusing Jung
of "guying publicly the Christian beliefs, symbols, myths, virtues. . . ." Jung's answer (2 April 55) rebuked White for unfairly
impugning his motives. In reply (10 May 55) White expressed
regrets, but denied that his accusations had been unjust.

White's final letter from his Zurich hotel (21 May 55) is a
farewell, full of good wishes. In it he apologizes for disturbing
Jung during his wife's illness,[43] and says that he himself is about
to return to California, against his own preference, as "a very
independent Catholic priest." It ends in a strange postscript,
whose combination of commiseration and thinly veiled rage
undercuts the friendliness of the rest and leaves a bitter taste:

> I hope you do not doubt my friendship, wrong-headed &
> heartless though it sometimes is. Poor Job at least had
> friends—however stupid. The horrible impression has come

upon me in Zürich (I hope it is wrong) that my dear C.G. has
around him only sycophants & flatterers: or people requiring
audiences or transferences which no mortal can carry. I *hope* I
am wrong: such a situation is *too* inhuman.

(VW to CGJ, 21 May 55)

In connection with his review of Jung's book and the exchanges that followed one notes signs of White's conflict. One
indication that he suffered during this traumatic period from
profoundly mixed feelings and self-contradictory intentions is
that at the end of his life he experienced a kind of amnesia
about his own actions during this period. Even though his revisions of "Jung on Job" for *Soul and Psyche* show that at some
point he recognized the excesses in his review, he seems to have
lost all awareness, judging from his final letters to Jung, of
having published a personal attack on his friend.

This fact is especially curious because at the time of the
original review, White knew he owed Jung some sort of an apology. At one moment, amid the attacks and defenses that burdened the two men's correspondence in 1955, White confessed
that in publishing his review of *Job* he had treated his friend
ruthlessly.

I do indeed deeply regret having published that article without any regard for your feelings or my own feelings for you.

(VW to CGJ, 19 May 55)

This statement stands out as a brave confession. It is almost
buried, however, in White's reiterated accusations and arguments in self-defense.

White defended himself and accused Jung partly on the
ground that Jung had broken a promise by publishing *Answer to
Job* in the first place. This theme, emerging in White's letters of
1955, is quite mysterious. His earlier letters show that when he
first saw the book he expected Jung to publish and approved
the plan himself. He wrote in 1951,

I am thrilled to hear that "Hiob"—especially—has gone to
the press. I cannot say how much I am looking forward to
being able to read and ponder it again. I am curious to know

what the biblical pundits—let alone the "psychologists"—
will have to say

(VW to CGJ, 23 Oct. 51).

Six months later, learning that the German edition was out, he
wrote simply, "I am very excited to hear today from Michael
Fordham that *Das Buch Hiob* . . . has appeared" (VW to CGJ, 30
Mar. 52), and requested a copy for himself.

In neither letter does White express dismay at the book's
publication or demand—as he did later—to know why Jung
had decided to make it public. It is hard to tell exactly how or
when he became persuaded that Jung had broken a promise by
publishing it. No evidence exists that such a promise ever was or
could have been made.[44] Yet, beginning in 1955, White insists
that Jung had originally promised to show this very personal
work to no one except a circle of close friends.

In a defined community such as a religious order, whose
members may practice a considerable degree of social and intellectual conformity, it sometimes happens that symbols and writings reflecting unorthodox but powerful personal feelings are
shared within a small group of friends. Gerald Vann's circula-
tion of a private ordination announcement may serve as an
example. Such sharing can define a meaningful sphere of intimacy and trust within the larger community; it also commonly
requires discretion by the privileged few, to make sure the
larger community is not exposed to scandal.

We do not know exactly how White came to believe that
Jung originally intended to keep *Job* secret; but the belief appar-
ently supported a sense of righteous indignation. Aware in
March 1955 that his review of the book could offend its author,
White justified himself by complaining that Jung had created
the circumstances that led to the attack upon him:

> I wonder what induced you to publish it: when you gave me
> the MS to read you were so emphatic that you would not! . . .
> I can see only harm coming of it, not least to my own efforts to
> make analytical psychology acceptable to and respected by
> the Catholics and other Christians who need it so badly.
>
> (VW to CGJ, 17 March 55)[45]

At this time of his personal crisis, White perhaps forgot how different from his own was the social and intellectual world in which Jung lived. He certainly ignored the public significance that *Answer to Job* had for its author. At any rate, it now seemed to him his friend had broken faith with him and betrayed their common vision by loosing the scandal of *Job* on an unsuspecting world.

The fact that White accused Jung of bad faith, both in print and in private correspondence, was the lethal blow to their collaboration. Theoretical differences between them had been clear before this; a personal attack was something new. White wrote to Jung only a few times between 1955 and 1959 and received no direct answer. In 1956 he sent Jung a copy of *God the Unknown*, for which Jung's secretary thanked him. In June 1958 White visited Jung briefly in Küsnacht (VW to CGJ, 26 July 58); it was the last time they met.

4. Reconciliation

The good will fundamental to the relationship reasserted itself more fully, however, in the letters and messages exchanged before White's death. On hearing in 1959 through a mutual friend[46] that in April, White had been seriously injured in an accident on his motor-scooter (*Letters II*, p.516n),[47] Jung contacted him for the first time since their falling out. White replied with an appreciative letter. Jung's answer in October 1959 broached the subject that still needed to be explored between them if their friendship was to be restored. Alluding to White's review of *Job*, he complained,

> You expressed yourself publicly in such a negative way about my work that I really did not know what your real attitude would be.
>
> (*Letters II*, p.518)

To Jung's great surprise, White simply did not understand this rebuke. His bafflement is expressed in the long letter he wrote to Jung the following March, after he had undergone surgery and received a diagnosis of cancer:

I have been, and still am, sorely perplexed to understand *when* and *where* I am supposed to have done this—and not a little distressed that you should think this.

(VW to CGJ, 18 March 60)

White goes on to wonder whether perhaps his review of Volume 7 of the *Collected Works* (*Two Essays on Analytical Psychology*) was the source of Jung's doubts.[48] This wild guess, so wide of the mark, suggests that by now he had lost all awareness of the hostility conveyed by his review of *Job* and his letters of 1955. We cannot attribute White's forgetfulness to illness, since his mind was reportedly clear and lively in his final days.[49]

Jung in turn found White's confusion strange and, no doubt, psychologically revealing. His private response is recorded directly on the page of White's letter, where a marginal note in Jung's own hand[50] reads: "cf. Victor's Brief 10.V.55 pag. 2/3." In White's letter of 10 May 55, at the turn of page three, we find White's statement of regret that, in publishing his review of *Job*, he had considered neither Jung's feelings nor his own. Beside this statement a line in the margin, presumably drawn by Jung himself, marks the crucial words.

Without imposing psychological interpretations where they do not belong, it seems fair to speculate that a large part of White's hostility toward Jung in 1955 was displaced from a target closer to home. If the destructive force of his attack in 1955 was, as appears, less than fully intentional, the explanation probably lies in the blow he had recently endured at the hands of his superiors.

Being passed over as regent of studies was not White's only professional disappointment, but it was the one that hit the hardest. Early in his career, in 1940, he had been shaken when he was suddenly asked to step down as acting editor of *Blackfriars*, replaced by Conrad Pepler after only a few months (A.C., 5 June 92). Another shock was to come in early 1959, timed with awful synchronicity for the occurrence of White's near-fatal accident, when the Roman Curia moved to suppress his book *God and the Unconscious* (A.C., 25 Aug. 91). As it turned out, this early book of essays was not finally suppressed; but the fact that it was called in question once again put White's Jungian work—in fact, all the work of his maturity—under a cloud.

He wrote to Jung in October of that year, answering the messages of concern that Jung had sent to him after hearing of the motor-scooter accident:

> I smiled, somewhat cynically, at your remark that I did not wholly disapprove of your work. (How could I?) It seems that I am in quite serious trouble (and in Rome itself!) for (apparently) my approval of it; so much so that my future is quite uncertain!
>
> (VW to CGJ, 18 Oct. 59)

White did not live long enough after this to experience more professional disappointments. Emergency surgery revealed his intestinal cancer soon after this letter, and his death followed some months later, on May 22, 1960.

Although their philosophical differences remained unresolved and their final quarrel ended inconclusively, White and Jung each asked for and received the other's forgiveness and blessing at the end. Jung wrote to say he would come to England to see White if only his own health allowed. He assured White of his friendship, apologized for being a *"petra scandali,"* and expressed gratitude for all he had learned (*Letters II*, pp.554f). In his last letter White replied,

> I do not know if it is true that you have been a "petrus (*sic*) scandali"[51] to me . . . but to the extent that you may have been, I think that I can honestly say that I am grateful for it.
>
> (VW to CGJ, 8 May 60)

He concluded the letter saying he prayed for Jung's "well-being, whatever that may be in the eyes of God" (Ibid).

As we have seen, White's work as a theologian was tied to Jungian psychology for over a decade; but for much longer than that he worked with and was supported by his Order at Blackfriars, Oxford. In this place he had been professionally and personally at home since his early twenties. Though he liked to think of himself as a Jungian, and even sometimes as an analyst, in the end he had no other way of life than as a Dominican theologian. When his contribution in that role was suddenly unwanted, the experience of loss and failure must have been crushing, all the more because he had struggled so hard over the decision to stay.

The inner process that led White to turn his anger in Jung's direction, obviating further work and communication between them, wounded White himself deeply; we will never know how much. But we know that this choice answered to one side of his conflict. We can figure its symmetry, if not its reason. Finding himself cut off by his religious superiors because of his work with Jung, in his rage he cut himself off from Jung, who was his chief alternative source of emotional and intellectual support. The ensuing sense of isolation must have been nearly unbearable. Yet Victor White persisted faithfully in his work as a theologian and scholar, and waited for the day when his work would be rehabilitated by his church. It is not an exaggeration to say that if he had lived a few more years into the 1960s, that day would almost certainly have come.

If in his latter years White achieved a costly degree of resignation, this does not mean he never wondered how things would have worked out if he had chosen another path. To the end of his life he continued to reflect on the issue, as one of Aelred Squire's recollections from that time suggests. When White was sick with cancer, he was moved to the Blackfriars house in Cambridge. A few friends sometimes visited him there, among them Richard Kehoe, who by then had left Blackfriars. Some time after Kehoe's visit, Doris Layard also visited White in Cambridge, bringing Aelred Squire with her. Each spoke with him separately. After her conversation with the dying man, Mrs. Layard reported that he had said, "Richard was lucky. He got out in time" (A.S., 3 Aug. 87).

It would be mistaken to attach more weight to such a remark than it deserves, for it is very unlikely that Victor White would ever have taken another path than the one he took. It was also not true in a literal sense (as White himself knew) to call Richard Kehoe's departure a function of luck. That event occurred in the context of Kehoe's native independence, and in light of personal reasons rather different from those which prompted White at various times to wish he could leave the Order.

A major distinction must be made, also, between White's struggle with his vocation as a religious, and his orthodoxy and loyalty as a Roman Catholic. Although at one point White confessed to Jung his "lost . . . sense of oneness . . . with the Church" and referred anxiously to the "friends and 'analysands' I have positively helped to get out of the Church" (VW to CGJ, 8 Nov. 53),[52] we can be sure he entertained no thoughts of leaving the church himself. All of White's mature work, including *Soul and Psyche*, his most thorough and thoughtful response to Jung, indicates that he remained deeply rooted in Catholic tradition. The moment of his death, too, is recalled by friends with the hagiographical detail the church reserves for its faithful:

> Whatever his human anguish about the difficulties of his position, he appears to have died without bitterness, his last words being "Dear God, take me," as widely reported to her friends by Mother Michael of the Blessed Trinity, on the authority of Mrs. Ginsberg, who was present.
>
> (A.S., 3 August 87)

Chapter Four

Jung's Relationship to Christian Thought

A. JUNG'S THEORY OF KNOWLEDGE

1. The Priority of Experience

Victor White was not alone in attributing a philosophical, even a metaphysical, basis to Jung's psychology; such attributions were made by many in Jung's lifetime and have been made since. As discussed above, Marilyn Nagy's *Philosophical Issues in the Psychology of C. G. Jung*[1] offers a uniquely penetrating historical and theoretical analysis of Jung's philosophical heritage. Approaching Jung's work as a practicing Jungian analyst, but using also the tools of a historical philosopher, Nagy concludes that Jung's basic presuppositions—his Platonic idealism and Aristotelian teleology—are identical with the philosophical structures of most Western religious thought (Nagy, p.267). For this reason, too, certain parts of Jung's work invite attack by scientific materialists, who emphatically reject his "idealist and metaphysical view of reality" (p.265).

The implications of Jung's epistemology need to be described more fully now, so that basic assumptions governing his collaboration with White, and some of the deeper philosophical grounds for conflict between the collaborators, can be understood more clearly. Jung protested often that his work rested on purely empirical observations, uninfluenced by metaphysics. For example, he wrote in March 1955 to a theological student:

> Your question is difficult to answer, since Thomistic theology is on a metaphysical basis, and the psychology of the unconscious on an empirical foundation. Through many

114

> talks with theologians, I have learnt that the greatest diffi-
> culty . . . consists in the difference of the *point de départ*. The
> theologian starts with philosophical concepts which have
> practically nothing to do with the merely nominalistic con-
> cepts of the empiricist.
>
> > (*Letters II*, p.234)

Jung and White were approaching estrangement when this letter was written. There is therefore some poignancy in Jung's
suggestion that the student come to Zurich in May to meet
Father White, who will be giving a course at the Jung Institute.
About his theological colleague he adds only:

> I have done a number of comparisons with him, and he has
> a fair knowledge of my psychology, so that if you have a
> chance to talk with him it might be of considerable impor-
> tance to you.
>
> > (Ibid, p.235)

Jung's own knowledge of Thomistic thought, he stresses once
again in conclusion, "is almost nil, since I have devoted all my
available time to the study of facts and not of opinions."

Similar protestations against any presumed entanglement
of his psychology with metaphysics appear in Jung's correspondence in every era of his life. Yet he finally had to admit the
impact of philosophical ideas upon his thought; for only by
reference to the neo-Kantian philosophy of his youth could he
explain the commitment to "empiricism" that was his epistemic
touchstone, or justify his rejection of what he understood under
the term metaphysics.

Thus, when reflecting on criticisms of his thought by Martin Buber, Jung wrote in 1957 to Bernhard Lang:

> It does not come within the scope of a science like psychol-
> ogy to ascertain the truth or untruth of metaphysical asser-
> tions. It is a thoroughly outmoded standpoint, and has been
> so ever since the time of Immanuel Kant, to think that it lies
> within the power of man to assert a metaphysical truth.
>
> > (Ibid, p.368)

In his next letter to Lang, in June 1957, Jung spelled out in detail the implications of his philosophical presuppositions. He summarized this letter as "Kantian epistemology expressed in everyday psychological language" (Ibid, p.379).

Toward the end of his life Jung confessed, both privately and in print (*Letters II*, p.500; *Man and his Symbols*, p.56), that he had been deeply influenced in university days by the ideas of Plato, Kant, Schopenhauer and others. Predominantly, always, he stressed the debt he owed to Kant. Embracing Kant's philosophy, Jung declared, he turned his back on the alternative epistmology of his day, materialism with its "ridiculous mythology" (Ibid, p.501). From Kant he learned to see all knowledge as mediated and limited by human subjectivity.

Systematic commitment to this neo-Kantian subjectivism undergirds all of Jung's arguments with theologians, whether Protestant or Catholic. His epistemological starting point forbids to him the metaphysical certainties claimed by many theologians, especially claims to know the nature of God as an "objective" being apart from the human psyche. Equally, on the other hand, Jung's Kantian starting place renounces the quantitative certainties sought by positivism, since his neo-Kantian subjectivism limits what can be said about the ultimate "reality" of matter.

The truth of Jung's claims is appropriately tested, not as philosophers test the content of propositions, but as one tests the truths of art and literature—that is, through a method of interpretation, dependent on personal perception and contextual appropriation. Claims of truth, for Jung, are also relative to the practical implications of the ideas in question, as viewed by those who live and suffer with them. Logical coherence and propositional content are less persuasive than individual and collective experience. To borrow from the language of theology, he is interested in changeable truths, experienced *pro me* or *pro nobis*, and not with putative unchanging, absolute truth *in se*.

Sometimes when Jung calls himself an empiricist, he might better say he is a phenomenologist. His "empiricism" refers to his examination of the perceived phenomena of individual and collective experience,[2] rather than to the quantifiable results and repeatable tests of "hard-data" experimental sciences. Jung's method attends to the observer's participation in the event and assumes that personal factors contribute in a major way to the accumulation of knowledge. An empiricism of this sort does not expect to confirm the outcome of its investigations by controlling for variables and predicting the outcome of repeated trials.[3] It is not, in the rigorous sense, experimental.

Occasionally, however, Jung claimed that his findings were consistent with the repeatable experiments of hard science. He wanted his psychology judged quantitatively, like any other empirical science, rather than by the canons of aesthetics. Those who could not see his experimental results were merely refusing to look. For example, he wrote:

> Wherever my methods were really applied the facts I gave have been confirmed. One could see the moons of Jupiter even in Galileo's day if one took the trouble to use his telescope.
>
> (*Aion*, *CW 9ii*, §63)

In fact, however, Jung's methods are not as repeatable as the use of Galileo's telescope. It is difficult to replicate data when the personal characteristics of the experimenter are the lens through which observations are made. In fact, Jung's epistemic starting point anticipated what has come to be known as the Heisenberg uncertainty principle. Celebrating this paradox of modern physics, he writes: "The observing psyche is already included in any formulation of objective reality" ("On the Nature of the Psyche," *CW 8*, §417).[4]

Jung's methods should thus rightly be called "empirical" only in a phenomenological and subjective sense, consistent with his neo-Kantian categories of perception. In his second letter to White he asked the theologian to refer to a footnote in *The Psychology of the Unconscious*, the 1916 English edition of *Wandlungen und Symbole*.[5] The footnote reads:

> Here it is not to be forgotten we are moving entirely in the territory of psychology, which in no way is allied to transcendentalism, either in positive or negative relation. It is a question here of a relentless fulfilment of the stand-point of the

theory of cognition, established by Kant, not merely for the
theory but, what is more important, for the practice. . . .

(*Letters I*, p.384n)

As he emphasizes subjectivity, Jung also respects the claims
of a kind of objectivity; but he understands the word in a particular way. "Objective" in Jung's writing usually applies either
to the generally perceivable effects of an experience, or else to
images and ideas held by a group over time—whatever the
collective culture agrees to call real. In his Terry Lectures he
explains that he calls both an elephant and an imaginary cancer
"real," because each is equally present to the psyche as an image
or idea; and each has real psychological effects.

> Psychology deals with ideas and other mental contents as
> zoology, for instance, deals with the different species of ani-
> mals. An elephant is "true" because it exists. The elephant is
> neither an inference nor a statement of the subjective judg-
> ment of a creator. It is a phenomenon.
>
> (*Psychology and Religion*, CW 11, §5)

In this, the first of his 1937 Terry Lectures, Jung illustrates
the importance of a "merely" psychic or subjective truth, by
referring to a patient suffering from an imaginary cancer. Such
a cancer, Jung allows, is a psychological, not a clinical fact; but
the manifest suffering of the patient shows the real effects of an
imaginary condition. Psychic phenomena, he concludes, may
have serious effects, and must be taken as seriously as physical
ones. The psychic disorders of the twentieth century, he adds,
are "far more dangerous than epidemics or earthquakes" (*Psychology and Religion*, CW 11, §17).

What Jung means by "truth" or "reality," then, is mainly a
practical matter: it is defined in a functional sense as "what has
effects" or "what works." He makes a crucial distinction, however, between inner and outer realities, and between reality and
illusion. A physical cancer may require surgery; an imaginary
one does not. Jung's treatment of "reality" is complicated, moreover, by the fact that he thinks (like Kant) that the human mind
cannot grasp reality in itself, but only the images of a reality

which remains forever hidden. The psychic images are real in one sense; but they are generated by a far deeper reality for which they can only stand as representations.

Jung's 1946 lecture, "On the Nature of the Psyche," is a sustained effort to draw clear distinctions between the levels of reality. Here Jung distinguishes first between instincts and archetypes, and then between archetypes-as-such and the archetypal images present to consciousness. The spectrum of psychic life, Jung writes, goes from the physical instincts at one end (the "infra-red" end of the spectrum) to the spiritual archetypes-as-such at the other (the "ultra-violet" end). Neither of these extremes is available to consciousness, but the extremes—he speculates—touch. Archetypes are the "images" of instincts, and instincts the "roots" of archetypes.

For Jung, the physical-as-such and the spiritual-as-such are thus at bottom equally unknowable. All that is available to consciousness is the world of psychic images. These are "real" (wirklich) in a pragmatic sense, in that they have effects.[6] They are also "real" in the sense that they refer—as Jung hypothesizes—to prior reality, the invisible and unknowable world of instincts and archetypes. Archetypal reality is the "spiritual goal toward which the whole nature of man strives" ("On the Nature of the Psyche," CW 8, §415). We cannot know this goal directly, since the archetypal realm is unconscious and unknowable; but we can hypothesize it, because its effects are seen in human life.

As we have seen, Jung's writings about the spiritual goal of life led White to hail him as a fellow teleologist—one whose thought, like St. Thomas', turned on the assumption of a final cause. A major contrast exists, however, between Jung's use of his teleology and the use White hoped to make of it. Whereas orthodox Christian doctrine describes God's nature with faithful certitude as ultimately good and loving, Jung insists that humanity will always remain uncertain of the precise nature of the wholeness that beckons and compels us. We must treasure Christian images, myths and symbols, and those of other religions; but we know neither how closely revelation corresponds to the archetypal realm nor—from the evidence available—whether the final goal of life is good, bad, or an ambiguous composite. Our images are complex and self-contradictory, both fearful and wondrous, and we cannot get beyond them to touch the ultimate reality. The archetypes-as-such are beyond our knowing.

The truth of archetypal images—including the image of God—is therefore always metaphorical and symbolic for Jung, never univocally, literally, or concretely "true." We do not know how close to the archetype-as-such the image comes.

> Every archetype, when represented to the mind, is already conscious and therefore differs to an indeterminable extent from that which caused the representation.
>
> ("On the Nature of the Psyche," *CW 8*, §417)

We do not grasp the thing in itself, which Jung calls "spirit"; and yet the spirit is for Jung the "most real" level of reality.

> *Although there is no form of existence that is not mediated to us psychically and only psychically, it would hardly do to say that everything is merely psychic.* . . . Since their [the archetypes'] essential being is unconscious to us, and still they are experienced as spontaneous agencies, there is probably no alternative now but to describe their nature, in accordance with their chiefest effect, as "spirit." . . .
>
> ("On the Nature of the Psyche," *CW 8*, §420)

The thought of the cognitive priority of psychic images occurred to Jung at least as early as 1937, for he proposed when lecturing at Yale:

> It is almost an absurd prejudice to suppose that existence can only be physical. As a matter of fact, the only form of existence of which we have immediate knowledge is psychic. We might well say, on the contrary, that physical existence is a mere inference, since we know of matter only in so far as we perceive psychic images mediated by the senses.
>
> (*Psychology and Religion, CW 11*, §16)

2. Addressing the Materialists and Logicians

Jung's "empiricism" has been subject to attack from two angles. First, from the perspective of "hard" science, or materialism, Jung is accused of giving the status of facts to many things which other scientists would call unreal because they cannot be predicted, quantified or objectively verified. Jung's initial line of defense against this materialist attack is practical: he directs attention to the reality of psychogenic suffering, and the cures effected by psychological treatment which takes such "unreal" phenomena seriously (*Psychology and Religion, CW 11*, §14f).

Jung's most frequently used defense against reductive materialism was his explication of the German verb *wirken*, meaning "to work" or "to be effective." From the verb comes the modifier *wirklich*, meaning "real." If something works or has an effect (*wirkt*), he says, it is real (*wirklich*). Imaginary cancers, animal gods, and the symbols of the Mass are all "true" and "real" in this pragmatic sense. Jung's phenomenology calls even a mental delusion like his patient's cancer "psychologically true inasmuch as it exists. . . . Its truth is a fact and not a judgment" (*Psychology and Religion, CW 11*, §4).

Jung's style of empiricism also comes in conflict with logical standards of truth and falsehood. By normal logical standards one would wish to apply a test of falsifiability to Jung's "truths," because things that are not logically falsifiable are also not logically verifiable. In contrast, Jung's pragmatism tests the truth of things by observing their effects. It is difficult to falsify a myth, a dream, or an elephant in the logical sense. These phenomena can have psychological reality regardless of logical coherence.

Of the two classic tests of falsifiability, coherence and correspondence, Jung is more willing to apply the latter than the former. He accepts the correspondence test when he asks whether a notion has an empirical referent. (Did the patient dream this image?) The test of coherence, which looks for logical consistency among ideas, is irrelevant to much of Jung's argument. Incommensurate and even mutually contradictory "truths" coexist happily in Jung's symbolic world.[7] Jung justifies the resulting paradoxes by pointing to a fundamental contradiction or oppositeness intrinsic to the human mind, which is, or has, equally *real*, though mutually contradictory, conscious and unconscious dimensions. Indeed, he insists that these apparent contradictions must be recognized and permitted to coexist: the opposites require each other (*Aion, CW 9ii*, §423). Not surprisingly, Jung is often short-tempered with arguments based on formal logic; and his writings frequently shorten the tempers of logicians.

Knowing that theologians are baffled by his methodology, Jung occasionally tries to explain himself for their benefit. In a 1935 letter to Pastor Ernst Jahn he states the problem in terms of conflicting epistemologies:

> It seems to me that it is difficult for a theologian to put himself in an empiricist's shoes. What the theologian takes for spiritual realities are for the empiricist expressions of psychic life, which at bottom is essentially unknown. The empiricist does not think from above downwards from metaphysical premises, but comes from below upwards from the phenomenal world and . . . must be content with understanding the psychic processes reconstructively.
>
> (*Letters I*, p.196)

If psychology knows things only from below, it must reason humbly and systematically to its ever-tentative conclusions. In contrast, theology, Jung believes, claims to possess eternal truth and pretends to know what it only posits. Disdain for the humble phenomena of human experience is Jung's chief charge against theologians who dispute his findings.

Metaphysical thought seems inimical to Jung's psychology because, as he views it, metaphysics proceeds from concepts known *a priori* and supports its conclusions without observable evidence. Twentieth-century thinkers, Jung states, have no business construing their reality in metaphysical terms. To think metaphysically is to escape backward into a pre-modern mental state (Foreword, *God and the Unconscious*, p.xxvi). Jung identifies as "medieval" the habit of abstract thought that deals in metaphysics at the expense of experience. He calls theologians, for example, "medieval," if they cannot grasp the premises of his epistemology, even if they belong in other respects to the modern world.[8]

The abstractions of metaphysics, according to Jung, are responsible for dangerous blindness and self-deception, for they neither base their arguments on empirical observation nor look at the practical effects of their conclusions. Jung thus goes beyond looking at "medieval" thought as a benign archaism. He objects to it on ethical grounds. It is wrong, he says, to live as if reality were exhausted by definitions and syllogisms, paying no attention to the facts. Such abstractions are false; they either prove useless or do actual harm in practice.

B. JUNG'S RELATION TO THEOLOGY

1. The Experiential Canon

If his bias against metaphysics were not reason enough, many theologians also detest Jung for resorting so freely to subjectivity through his Kantian epistemology. The language of "experience" is seen by many philosophers and theologians as far too various and slippery. While acknowledging this problem, Jung persists in speaking that language as if it were the only reliable pathway to truth. To mention one category of experience dear to Jung's heart, images of God in dreams often resist being systematically lined up with Christian teachings. Scriptural images themselves provide a tremendous variety of possible meanings, unless their interpretation is harnessed by established doctrines.

Jung widens the categories of revelation to take in not only the diversity within scriptures and dreams, but virtually everything that happens. In an interview in 1955 Jung reflected on the nearly universal urge to know God which he observed in people, otherwise not interested in religion, who came to see him for treatment.

> I make my patients understand that all the things which happen to them against their will are a superior force. They can call it God or the devil, and that doesn't matter to me, as long as they realize that it is a superior force. God is nothing more than that superior force in our life. You can experience God every day.
>
> ("Men, Women, and God," *C.G. Jung Speaking*, p.250)

A God-image generated through the "disintegrating and schismatic effect of individual revelation" (*Psychology and Religion, CW 11*, §33) is to be taken with entire seriousness, even though such an image is often complex or contradictory. And (despite the degree of objectivity attained by archetypal amplification) dreams are necessarily subjective—the bane of systematics. Such "truth" as dreams afford is verifiable or falsifiable only by its effects, and always subject to interpretation.

To add to the potential confusion, the subjectivity of individual experience is linked, for Jung, to one of the truly *objective* avenues to understanding. The inner voice that gives authority to a personal vocation is called the "objective psyche" ("Personality," *CW 17*, §313).[9]

Ultimately the experience of the individual is one test of truth—though even this truth is only relative—to which Jung subscribes wholeheartedly (*Psychology and Religion, CW 11*, §88). He accepts the risks of such a canon, acknowledging that doctrines of God generated outside the church involve a high probability of error (*Psychology and Religion, CW 11*, §167f). The errors of genuine individual experience, he implies, are to be preferred to those of a collective authority that silences opposing views.

Beside the kind of objectivity Jung sometimes attributes to individual revelation, he locates another kind in the *consensus gentium* (*Psychology and Religion, CW 11*, §6). The test of common consent owes its best-known formulation to the medieval theologian Vincent of Lerins, who said the church could claim as true what has been believed always, everywhere, by everyone. But Jung immediately crosses the wires of the Vincentian canon. Under the generous phrase "always, everywhere, by everyone" he includes positions that have long been rejected by church orthodoxy. In the shadows of official Christendom, he says, the Gnostics, alchemists, heretics—embattled outsiders of western European history—possess truths which can claim to form a sort of alternative *consensus gentium*. These truths are also "objective," although rejected by the official consensus. Without them, the church's truth is less than whole.

For other reasons, as we have seen (Chapter Three), Jung ascribes very ambiguous weight to the collective truths of dogma. His commitment to a paradoxical union of conscious and unconscious perspectives and his respect for individual revelation are stronger than his adherence to any collective authority. This is why the teachings of those outside the church are a part of what Jung includes in his discussion of the Western image of God. An orthodoxy which rejects the teachings of its dissenters has, he argues, divisive, even brutal effects, and is therefore empirically false. To embrace the whole truth, the church must learn to accept its heretical shadow, which up to now it has refused to do.

Such an inclusive view of truth must be prepared to encompass mutually exclusive propositions, practices and even theories of knowledge. But this logical problem does not deter Jung, who insists that revelation unwittingly already includes all the conflicting views of God. Official doctrines and the competing positions labelled heresies are merely the two sides of a collective faith. The task for theology is thus to become conscious that the opposites compose the whole. So-called heresies and the perspectives of outsiders have been suppressed by the church's official teachers; but as long as these are omitted, the "truth" of Christian doctrine is only partial and may do actual harm.

The moral practice required by this inclusiveness, as Jung sees it, is already implied by the Christian love commandment. Christian love requires that he "not only bear with and understand my schismatic Protestant brother, but also my brothers in Arabia and India" ("Why I am Not a Catholic," *CW 18*, §1472).[10] On a practical level, then, his teaching is in line with that of Christian ethics. If Jung went no further than the injunction to love the heretical brother, and drew no conclusions about the unconsciousness of God, his teaching would obviously chime well enough with theology. The real difficulty arises when Jung attributes two-sided knowledge, ambiguous experience and paradoxical truth to God as well as to humanity. Insisting that we know God only through the psyche,[11] Jung concludes that the shadow of human consciousness reveals an equivalent shadow in the image of God. Following his Kantian approach, which refuses to separate these phenomena from each other, we have no basis for saying that God is different from the God-images in the human psyche. And the images themselves are mixed.

Like Kant, Jung maintains that neither God nor the psyche can be fully known. For that very reason, he concludes, both must be feared. The power of the psyche and the power of God are equally objective—real and transcendent—in relation to our limited ego-consciousness. Both are capable of imposing unwanted and terrifying experiences. In his 1932 essay, "The Development of Personality," Jung accuses the spirit of rationalism for suppressing knowledge of the essential ambiguities of divine and human nature, by confining the accepted definitions of both to what reason and consciousness regard as real. The spirit of the essay owes a great deal to German Romanticism, as when Jung writes:

> The Age of Enlightenment, which stripped nature and human institutions of gods, overlooked the God of Terror who dwells in the human soul. If anywhere, fear of God is justified in face of the overwhelming supremacy of the psychic.
>
> ("Personality," *CW 17*, §302)[12]

To many theologians, it might seem that Jung leans too heavily toward the negative in his depiction of God and the soul. Granted that we cannot stand apart like independent observers to find out whether our images of God and the psyche refer to some reality "outside" these same images. But why does Jung insist—with such certainty, as if he knew what he says in principle *no one can know*—that the nature of the unknown (whether God or the psyche) is terrifying?

The answer must be either that lack of knowledge creates terror indirectly or that the power of the psychic images, arising from the unconscious, is directly and inescapably terrifying to human consciousness. For Jung, I think, the second answer weighs more heavily. We do not know God or the soul directly; but the images that arise, our only source for intimations about God and the soul, are terrifying in their ungoverned and ungovernable power.

> Only the tiniest fraction of the psyche is identical with the
> conscious mind and its box of magic tricks, while for much
> the greater part it is sheer unconscious *fact*, hard and
> immitigable as granite, immovable, inaccessible, yet ready at
> any time to come crashing down upon us at the behest of
> unseen powers.
>
> ("Personality," *CW 17*, §302)

If therefore the tiny ego is not crushed or capsized by a "sheer
unconscious *fact*," one must thank the grace of God. But one
must also acknowledge that the gratitude of the ego is somewhat hollow if God is part of the threat of annihilation, from
which one has inexplicably been spared.

2. Jung's Use of Theological Texts

Given Jung's epistemological commitment, it seems that
anyone who agreed to collaborate with him would be required
to treat both theology and psychology from a Kantian and therapeutic standpoint, refraining from metaphysical arguments.
But Jung was inconsistent about this requirement in one respect. He wanted his theological partner to understand and
apply a Kantian subjectivity, but also (as we shall see) to contribute as much help as possible from the perspective of orthodox
Catholic theology. Jung's stated needs would not have been met
if, instead of an orthodox Catholic theologian, he had worked
with one whose methodology had been in substantial conflict
with Catholic theological tradition.

Yet Roman Catholic theology, to do its work in its own way,
is accustomed to be at least part of the time and at some level a
philosophical and metaphysical discipline. This brings us to a
serious problem concerning Jung's attitude toward theological
authority. Returning to the basic metaphor set forth in the first
chapter of this essay, we may ask whether Jung recognizes theology as a valid language with its own grammar. He answers that
question inconsistently. Sometimes he seeks theological confir-
mation for his psychological formulations, turning to theologians as practitioners of an autonomous discipline. At other
times he dismisses the presuppositions of their discipline as

foreign to modern thought, or quotes their statements merely to amplify his own previously established arguments.

Jung is also sometimes guilty of prooftexting, i.e., of quoting isolated statements to validate his position without considering the larger context from which they are drawn. For example, in 1929 he scathingly dismisses Barth's overemphasis on divine transcendence;[13] but in an essay written about ten years later, without qualifying his dislike of Barth's work, he approvingly cites a statement by Barth that resonates with his own thinking about the Trinity:

> "There is indeed a unity of God and man; God himself creates it. . . . It is no other unity than his own eternal unity as father and son. This unity is the Holy Ghost."
>
> ("Trinity," *CW 11*, §117)[14]

Such an example is petty in itself, but it introduces the larger question: to what degree does Jung use theological statements to authorize his psychological position, and to what degree does he treat statements of theologians merely as symbolic illustrations for his position? To what degree does he believe his position is *self-authorizing*? If the latter, we would expect him to cite theologians like Barth, not to provide warrants for his position, but simply to amplify[15] a point that he has already established.

Jung's reading of Barth's theology cannot have changed much between 1929 and 1940; their basic epistemologies remained radically opposed. Even though the later Barth abandoned his radical early rejection of human experience and culture, he continued to insist on the systematic priority of God's freedom.[16] In what sense, then, does Jung use Barth's statements to support his own discussion of the Trinity? Apparently the value of Barth's formulation to Jung was merely the happy fact that it existed as a text, i.e., that a theologian of repute had found occasion to write it. Jung does not support himself on Barth's authority; he calls on Barth for variation on a theme, to demonstrate its validity in yet another way. Amplification of this kind is not what is usually meant by giving a warrant for one's position. In fact, Jung applies the warrant in reverse. Calling attention to the resonance between his position and Barth's phrase, he generously validates Barth. The quotation, in return, embellishes what Jung has argued on other grounds.

3. The Passion of an Agnostic

Jung claims not to know anything about God directly, and to have no ambition to be a theologian himself. Yet a certain ambivalence is clear if one considers his rhetoric. Despite his declared commitment to empiricism, Jung echoes the bible like a prophet and disputes about the truth of doctrines like a theologian. (At times, some would say, he disputes like an untrained and clumsy theologian; but that is to grant the point.) As we have seen, Jung's denial that God can be known *in se* does not prevent him from engaging passionately and personally with the psychic images of God.

By arguing in psychological essays about how God should be perceived and characterized, Jung appears to be breaking the epistemological rule he has laid down for himself. And so he would be, if he were talking about God-in-God's-self, rather than the God-image. In fact, although his language is not always careful, Jung is faithful to his intention (at least in works written for publication) to talk only about the image of the archetype, and not about the unknowable archetype itself. In Jung's 8 Feb. 41 letter to a Catholic priest, Dr. Josef Goldbrunner, he states:

> You evidently did not know that epistemologically I take my stand on Kant, which means that an assertion doesn't posit its object. So when I say "God" I am speaking exclusively of assertions that don't posit their object. About God himself I have asserted nothing, because according to my premise nothing whatever can be asserted about God himself. All such assertions refer to the psychology of the God-image. Their validity is therefore never metaphysical but only psychological.
>
> (*Letters I*, p.294)

Jung's determination to deal only with the evidence of the psyche is less limiting to him than it might at first appear. His complete devotion to Kantian epistemology, which knows only the images, removes any practical distinction between knowing the *images of* God and knowing God. If images are all we can know, it matters very much that we know them. As Nagy writes,

> The fact is, he thought, that we know nothing of God. What we do know is our inner experience, and the fact of our belief in God. . . . But if subjective experience is all there is, then belief in God may be the most important thing there is.
>
> (Nagy, p.150)

Jung claims insight into the archetype through insight into its images, and thence finds a way to claim insight into the unknowable "God within." These insights are problematical in their interpretations, as Jung is the first to say. Besides, knowledge of God and the soul becomes possible only to the extent that images of both are manifest to consciousness.

Over and over again Jung asserts the importance of a humble and systematic agnosticism. He says he has learned to be humble in the face of unknowable reality from his work as "a man of science" ("Why I am Not a Catholic, *CW 18*, §1469). Recognizing the objectivity of God in the same spirit in which a scientist might "conclude from the disturbance of a planet's course the existence of a yet unknown heavenly body" ("Why I am Not a Catholic," *CW 18*, §1471), Jung can cautiously affirm *that* God is, as a transcendent, objective being "outside" the human psyche. But as a scientist he firmly refuses to say *what* God is. Theologians, he says, ought to recognize that his agnosticism is based on the nature of the evidence: knowledge of God, being available only through the psyche, is never certain.

In an essay of 1940,[17] Jung argues that science cannot prove or disprove the reality of anything transcendent to human awareness. The principle of scientific agnosticism applies first to the psyche, and then by extension to God.

> It does not seem to have occurred to people that when we say "psyche" we are alluding to the densest darkness it is possible to imagine. *The ethics of the researcher require him to*

admit where his knowledge comes to an end. This end is the beginning of true wisdom.

("Mass," CW 11, §448, emphasis added)

The ethics to which Jung refers here has more than one application. He not only exhorts empiricists, i.e., all "modern" people, to recognize the limits of their knowing; he also insists that there is an ethical duty to recognize the "reality" of the unconscious. That is, we are obliged to be agnostic about that which we do not directly observe, and also acknowledge the objective reality of a huge realm beyond observation, which is our not-knowing.

Jung's passion for empirical knowledge forbids him to fall back on the language of belief. In his Terry Lectures he announces, "I believe only what I *know*. Everything else is hypothesis, and beyond that I can leave a lot of things to the Unknown" (*Psychology and Religion, CW 11*, §79). But his obvious desire to say something nevertheless "true" about God, for the sake of helping people deal with their souls, has led interpreters to conclude that Jung ignored his father's admonition to stay out of theology.

The story of Jung and his father gives considerable insight into the relationship of Jung to the church. "Church" was his father's business, and Jung was acutely aware of his father's misery as a cleric. In his school years, as Jung would recall, his father explicitly warned him not to pursue theology. The intensity of the warning is instructive. They were, after all, in a culture and era in which it was assumed that sons followed if possible in their fathers' footsteps. Pastor Jung obviously feared that, left to himself, Carl Gustav would choose theology, either in the path of filial duty or because of his boyhood passion for questions about God. For his son's own good, he warned him not to.

> Several times my father had a serious talk with me. I was free to study anything I liked, he said, but if I wanted his advice I should keep away from theology. "Be anything you like except a theologian," he said emphatically. . . . He had never taken me to task for cutting church as often as possi-

ble and for not going to Communion any more. The farther
away I was from church, the better I felt. . . . I was able to
reassure my father that I had not the slightest desire to be a
theologian.

(Memories, p.75).[18]

Jung had not the slightest desire to be what he took a professional theologian to be. His father's unhappiness in the pastorate
had been an object lesson. He did suffer from a positive urge,
however, to study things that theologians study, and apparently
for some of the same reasons, including a passion to know
about—not merely to believe in—God. That God is ultimately
unknowable in human terms has never stopped a theologian,
nor did it stop C.G. Jung. Even as a boy he had been eager to
study the Trinity and frustrated when his father put him off
(*Memories*, pp.52f). He had a sort of ear for theology—a natural
gift he could not resist exercising all his life. The untrained theo-
logizing that runs through his books and correspondence consequently has all the untowardness and ingenuity—and occasional
genius—of music played for love of music, without formal education or authorization from a guild of professional musicians.

C. JUNG'S PLACE IN CHRISTIAN TRADITION

1. *The Psychological Celebration of Catholicism*

Jung was thirty years old before he fully got over his childhood fear of Catholic priests. As a little boy he was terrified at
the sight of Jesuits in their cassocks and both frightened and
fascinated by his first sight of the interior of a Catholic Church
(*Memories*, pp.11,16). He was at least thirty, he writes, before he
was comfortable with the idea of *Mater Ecclesia* (*Memories*, p.17).
Although he never came close to joining the Roman communion, he was fascinated and drawn by this liturgical and theological tradition, which coincided at many points with his reading of the religious dimension of the human psyche.

Understandably, Jung's discussions of Roman Catholic
dogma and ritual sometimes confused readers who were native

to Catholic tradition.[19] Catholic clergy and scholars, basically approving of Jung's efforts to bring the Christian symbols into modern conversation, would fail to see that he deliberately appropriated those symbols and applied them outside a church context, in the service of his analytical psychology. Jung tried to untangle this confusion by pointing out that his intention was to study Catholic psychological experience scientifically, not to be baptized into the church's self-understanding. *"My interest is scientific, yours evangelical,"* he writes to a critic, who had tried to correct what seemed to him Jung's very eccentric understanding of Catholic ritual and language. "We talk at cross purposes and charge through open doors" (*Letters I*, p.346).[20]

If Jung's interest in Catholicism was not personal but only professional and psychological, on what psychological grounds did it rest? He made no secret of his impatience with aspects of Protestant belief and practice, which he saw as inadequate to the needs of the human psyche. In the Terry Lectures he identified what seemed to him the liturgical and doctrinal "nakedness" of his own tradition. In contrast, he affirmed parts of Catholic sacramental tradition, especially the psychological wisdom associated with Catholic spiritual direction and confession, as being healing and protective to the souls of Western people. On therapeutic grounds he therefore recommended, for anyone who could genuinely accept it, the full wardrobe of Catholic ritual and belief.[21]

In line with these views, Jung was in the habit of saying that only Catholics understood his work on the soul, whereas Protestants opposed it out of ignorance, having lost touch with the basic doctrines that could link psychology with Christian tradition. In his second letter to Victor White, Jung explained that he needed a Catholic theologian to guide his thinking about the Holy Spirit and the Trinity.

I realize that it [theological help] can come only from the Catholic side, as the *sola fide* standpoint of the Protestant has lost the tradition of the doctrine too much to be useful in disentangling the knots in the empirical material.

(*Letters I*, pp.385f)

The second Terry Lecture, "Dogma and Natural Symbols," repeatedly sounds Jung's theme that in dismantling the structure of the church's ancient ritual and dogma, Protestantism has left the soul "naked" before the "terrible immediate experience" of God. In this crucial passage, criticized with such friendly concern by Victor White at an early stage in their collaboration, Jung had written:

> The Protestant is left to God alone. For him there is no confession, no absolution, no possibility of an expiatory *opus divinum* of any kind. He has to digest his sins by himself. . . .
> (*Psychology and Religion, CW 11*, §86)

In contrast, Jung commends "the Catholic 'director of conscience' [who] often has infinitely more psychological skill and insight" than the Protestant parson. Parsons, he says, "share in the common dislike of psychological problems and also, unfortunately, in the common ignorance of psychology" (*Psychology and Religion, CW 11*, §76).

Nevertheless, we must recognize Jung's ambivalence. Although he criticized his own tradition and praised the psychological merits of Catholic ritual and dogma, he himself remained by temperament and conviction in the Reformed communion in which he had his earliest education. In the same lecture that cries with alarm about Protestants "left to God alone" and complains about the psychological ignorance of parsons, he admits that Protestantism is a spiritual challenge to courageous souls. His description makes Catholicism sound like life in a comfortable domesticated landscape, and Protestantism like a terrifying, vivifying journey into the wilderness:

> Protestantism was, and still is, a great risk and at the same time a great opportunity. If it goes on disintegrating as a church, it must have the effect of stripping man of all his spiritual safeguards and means of defence against immediate experience of the forces waiting for liberation in the unconscious. . . . The Protestant has a unique chance to make himself conscious of sin to a degree that is hardly possible for a Catholic mentality, as confession and absolu-

tion are always at hand to ease excess of tension. . . . If a
Protestant survives the complete loss of his church and still
remains a Protestant, that is to say a man who is defenceless
against God and no longer shielded by walls or communities, he has a unique spiritual opportunity for immediate
religious experience.

(Psychology and Religion, CW 11, §85)

Jung's own path was through the wilderness of Protestantism; but for the sake of needful patients he wanted to understand the Catholic map, even if he was not going to venture into
that territory himself. He was versed in the language of the
Reformation and wielded the language of Protestantism with
confidence (if not with subtlety), having been raised in it. But
his religious upbringing had not included symbols and concepts
with which any educated Catholic would be familiar; he needed
a tutor in Catholic idiom. Thus, when he began to look for a
theological collaborator, Jung's idea of what he was looking for
was quite simple and straightforward. He had no intention of
setting his psychology against the wisdom of the church; he
only wanted his errors of theological diction corrected.

On 22 September 1944, a year before White wrote to him,
Jung rebuked one of his Catholic correspondents, named Irminger, for what he considered a misguided effort to help. In
the course of a long letter of self-explication and defense, Jung
comments:

Instead of such purposeless criticism I would far rather
have a scholarly Catholic collaborator who with understanding and goodwill would correct my theologically defective
mode of expression, so that I could avoid everything that
looks even remotely like a criticism, let alone a devaluation,
of Church doctrine.

(Letters I, p.350)

2. *"Why I am Not a Catholic"*

Apparently one of Irminger's suggestions was that, with
some catechetical instruction, Jung could get over his intellectual errors and become a full member of the Church. The

process of correcting this misimpression seems to have impelled Jung to look closely at his personal relation to Catholicism. He concludes that he is connected both to Protestantism and to Catholicism, and cannot abandon either.

Acknowledging the depth of his Protestantism (*Letters I*, p.346), Jung nevertheless claims, "I start from a positive Christianity which is as much Catholic as Protestant" (*Letters I*, p.349). He notes the split in European religious consciousness and claims there is a parallel split in his own spiritual life: "If the Church has suffered a schism, then I must be satisfied with being a Christian who finds himself in the same conflict Christendom is in. I cannot disavow my brother. . . ." (*Letters I*, p.347).

Jung's ruminations on the split in the Christian West and in himself are continued in the unsent portion of this letter to Irminger, to which he later gave the title, "Why I am not a Catholic." He compares the claims of Catholic orthodoxy with his own concept of Christianity, and in doing so reaches far-reaching conclusions whose significance for his eventual collaboration with Victor White will be obvious. In this writing of 1944, on the eve of White's first contact with him, Jung delineates religious principles that define the practical limits of his sympathy with the Church of Rome.

First, Jung objects to the claims of the Catholic Church on ethical grounds. Calling himself "a practical Christian to whom love and justice to his brother mean more than dogmatic speculations," Jung rejects the authoritarianism of Catholic orthodoxy. The absolute truth-claims of orthodoxy are totalitarian, he argues, because—applied as doctrinal shibboleths—they lead to division between believers. The inevitable result of holding to "truth" in this manner is the breakdown of relationships, the loss of community, and eventually violence and warfare. He could have been thinking of violence between Christians, Moslems and Jews in the Middle East, as familiar a tragedy in Jung's day as in our own, or of the Thirty Years' War, or of internecine religious conflicts in a dozen times and locations.

> Every totalitarian claim gradually isolates itself because it excludes so many people as "defectors, lost, fallen, apostate,

heretic," and so forth. [For this reason, he concludes] I hold
all confessionalism to be completely unchristian.

("Why I am Not a Catholic," *CW 18*, §1466)

Jung's condemnation of "confessionalism" might itself be
called a confession; for in rejecting uniformity of belief he goes
some way toward defining his own position, though his religious stance is individualistic and relativistic, unlike the confessionalism he criticizes. As we have seen, Jung's test of truth is
practice. As a sign of their belief, therefore, he enjoins Christians to embrace religious diversity to the point of pluralism.
Jung's interpretation of the love command challenges the existence of doctrinal barriers. The otherness of religions different
from one's own becomes an invitation to, and a test of, the duty
of neighbor-love.[22]

Citing his experience in caring for souls, Jung also maintains
that the duty of a Christian is to find ways to speak to those for
whom traditional formulas have lost their power to convince.
Faced with modern ignorance and unbelief, he says, Christians
must communicate the good news in a way the particular listener
can understand, and not insist on classical doctrines that have no
common ground with the language or experience of the one
before them.

A Christian has to concern himself, especially if he is a physi-
cian of souls, with the spirituality of the reputedly unspiritual . . . and he can do this only if he speaks their language
and certainly not if, in the deterrent way of confessionalism,
he sounds the kerygmatic trumpet, hoarse with age.

("Why I am Not a Catholic," *CW 18*, §1468)

This injunction to enter into the religious experience of
"the reputedly unspiritual" flows naturally from Jung's understanding, which he owes in part to William James, that there
are varieties of religious experience. God's self-revelation, he
maintains, is not limited to the Christian form. Indeed, for
Jung, the Christian "good news" can never claim to be tran-
scendently absolute, but always comes in forms relative to human experience.

Christianity possesses an *euangelion*, good tidings from God, but no textbook of a dogma with claim to totality. Therefore it is hard to understand why God should never have sent more than one message. Christian modesty in any case strictly forbids assuming that God did not send *euangelia* in other languages, not just in Greek, to other nations.

("Why I am Not a Catholic," *CW 18*, §1468)

In a letter written years later to Bernhard Lang, Jung took up the same theme, again marking the disjunction between "absolutist" beliefs which produce religious intolerance, and the requirements of neighbor-love: "How could I have any communication at all with a person if I approached him with the absolutist claims of the believer?" (*Letters II*, p.376).

3. The Conscience of a Protestant

In 1956, after his collaboration with Victor White had ended, Jung described himself to Howard Philp as a "left-wing" Protestant. The letter continues:

I am definitely inside Christianity and, as far as I am capable of judging about myself, on the direct line of historical development. . . . If the Reformation is a heresy, I am certainly a heretic too.

(*Letters II*, p.334)

Just in case any doubt remains, Jung ends the single long paragraph of the letter by saying, in some bitterness:

Thus far I am a Protestant in my soul and body, even if most of the Protestant theologians are just as childishly prejudiced as the Catholic priests.

(*Letters II*, p.335)

Jung's confidence in his Protestant roots is evident from the fact that he never called for a collaborator from that side. There was no need; he had learned the catechism at home, and at age twelve amused himself by reading theological books in his father's study (*Memories*, pp.56ff). Jung was thus genuinely a Protestant, not in the sense that he regularly went to church (though the Reformed Church in Küsnacht was the location of his funeral),[23] but by temperament and ingrained intellectual habit.

Indeed, Jung's refusal to conform to external collective authority and his insistence on the essentially private nature of religious freedom are hallmarks of the Swiss, and specifically of the Swiss Reformed Church.[24] Jung came close to the radical Protestant faith his father may have yearned for but dared not grasp for himself (*Memories*, p.75), and made up for the latter's timid fideism by undertaking his own momentous search after religious understanding.[25]

We have seen how troubled was Jung's relation to the authority of the collective church, given his emphasis on individual revelation over against systematic theology. His relation to authority in general was a perplexed affair. His commitment to personal moral autonomy was accompanied by a deep distrust of any heteronomy whatever, including even the assertion of authority by the God-image in the soul.

This distrust of external ("objective") authority is indicated by his comments on a dream, reported and interpreted in Chapter VII of *Memories, Dreams, Reflections*. Jung once dreamed that he was led by his father to a meeting with what his father called "the highest presence." In this place in the dream his father bowed deeply, touching his head to the floor. Jung writes,

> I imitated him, likewise kneeling, with great emotion. For some reason I could not bring my forehead quite down to the floor—there was perhaps a millimeter to spare. But at least I had made the gesture with him.
>
> (*Memories*, p.219)

In his commentary on the dream Jung describes the value of independent conscience, even in the face of God. The fact that in the dream his head does not touch the floor becomes emblematic of human freedom:

> Man always has some mental reservation, even in the face of divine decrees. Otherwise, where would be his freedom? And what would be the use of that freedom if it did not

threaten Him who threatens it? . . . The dream discloses a
thought and a premonition that have long been present in
humanity: the idea of the creature that surpasses its creator
by a small but decisive factor.

(Memories, p.220)[26]

Here it might appear that Jung glorifies autonomy and
overlooks the moral ambiguity of sinful human nature. But he
regards the freedom of independent conscience as a two-edged
sword. Freedom entails a fearful responsibility. In discussing his
dream he connects the dignity of human freedom that with-
holds total obedience even from God, to the terrifying ability to
"extinguish all higher life on earth."

Jung was always conscious, in the years following the second World War, of the possibility of nuclear disaster. For example, on 30 June 1956 he wrote to Elined Kotschnig,

Man has already received so much knowledge that he can
destroy his own planet. Let us hope that God's good spirit
will guide him in his decisions, because it will depend on
man's decision whether God's creation will continue.

(Letters II, p.316)

Most probably his emphasis is on the word "good": "Let us hope
that God's *good* spirit will guide. . . ." In *Answer to Job* Jung describes God's other spirit, the evil, unconscious exercise of sheer
power indifferent to mortal suffering. When God's spirit does
the guiding, human beings must hope it is the good one; otherwise, Jung enjoins, they must exercise their moral prerogative
to disobey.

To the end of his life, therefore, Jung insisted that human
dignity entails a radical and dangerous moral freedom, the freedom to withhold full obedience even from God. It is perhaps
puzzling to juxtapose Jung's idea of a God who threatens or is
threatened by human freedom, with his insistence that this God
is found "within" the soul. How can a God who dwells within
the soul represent a heteronomous authority?

The puzzle is less if we remember that, for Jung, God is

ambiguously both good and evil, and this power of God will always be "other" in relation to consciousness. The human ego is finite and mortal; the image of God within the soul is not. Thus, although God's presence is intrapsychic it is still transcendent to the limited, human consciousness on which moral responsibility rests. To use Jung's language, the Self is not the ego. The Self transcends the ego; but it is the ego, not the Self, that weighs moral choices with a seriousness arising from the perspective of mortality.

Jung's proposal can be summed up in a maxim: morality entails mortality. Moral dignity and responsibility reside ultimately not in the God-image,[27] nor in human collectives which claim to speak with divine authority, but rather in the individual as a conscious, choosing ego. Jung states the principle in many passages, including this one from his 1934 essay "The Relations Between the Ego and the Unconscious":[28]

> The greater the aggregation of individuals, the more the individual factors are blotted out, and with them *morality, which rests entirely on the moral sense of the individual and the freedom necessary for this.*
>
> ("Ego and Unconscious," *CW* 7, §240)

Here again we encounter the epistemological substructure of Jung's thought. His distrust of collective authority, like his denial of "absolute truth," is rooted in his theory of the unconscious, with its complex opacity. If nothing is knowable outside the psyche's categories, and the psyche itself is unknowable in all its complexity, then absolute truth and absolute authority are equally dubious entities.

> The psyche cannot leap beyond itself. It cannot set up any absolute truths, for its own polarity determines the relativity of its statements. Wherever the psyche does announce absolute truths—such as, for example, "God is motion," or "God is One"—it necessarily falls into one or the other of its own antitheses. For the two statements might equally well be: "God is rest" or "God is All." Through one-

sidedness the psyche disintegrates and loses its capacity for cognition.

(Memories, p.351)

So on epistemological as well as moral grounds, Jung rejects the church's magisterial claims. Such claims, he says, are false *prima facie*, because of their one-sidedness. They are also totalitarian, repressive, and morally suspect.

Jung's criticism of Catholicism does not, however, preserve him from attacks by Protestants. He is rejected variously as a *bad* Protestant, as an idolater (an inferior Catholic), or as a pagan prophet of self-worship. Protestant theologians who responded to Jung's work during his lifetime, with a few exceptions, did so with disapproval. Jung commented wryly on this fact in his first letter to White:

> Protestant theologians are rather reticent and they don't know yet whether I should be condemned as a heretic or depreciated as a mystic. . . . So there is not much hope for me left from that side.

(Letters I, p.382)

Nevertheless, Jung kept trying. He exchanged letters with a number of Protestant theologians toward whom, by virtue of his lifelong acquaintance with Reformed Church writings, he assumed the posture of a conversational peer. In his 17 July 1945 letter to Pastor Max Frischknecht, for example, he snaps:

> And how does Luther know that the Holy Ghost is not a *sceptic*? This is theological presumptuousness. The spirit bloweth where *it* listeth and not where Calvin with his *providentia specialis* wants it to blow.

(Letters I, p.373)

Jung gave even the Anglicans a chance to come and be enlightened about the psyche. In the letter to Pastor Frischknecht on the unruliness of the Holy Spirit, Jung adds,

> I once told Archbishop Temple: "Send me an intelligent young theologian. I will lead him into the night of the soul

so that one of them at last may know what he is actually dealing with." But nobody came. Naturally they knew it all already, and much better. That is why the light has gone out.

(*Letters I*, p.373).

In locating Jung on the Protestant side of the Western church, we make him a spiritual descendent of Schleiermacher and, more distantly, of Zwingli.[29] Zwingli's theology has the effect of reinforcing Jung's teaching about the two-sidedness of the God-relation and the priority of individual conscience. Schleiermacher's supports his systematic emphasis on religious subjectivity. Of the two, Schleiermacher has priority. Jung uses the insights of Schleiermacher to criticize the shortcomings of Zwingli, calling Protestant churches to account for offering the soul no effective protection from the terrors of the living God; and he protests that Protestant theologians must "*know* a bit more about the human soul" if the church's message is to do the world any good (*Letters I*, p.373).

Perhaps this combination of Zwingli and Schleiermacher in Jung's theological backround explains why, although Jung was in many ways a true son of the Reformation, the Reformed theologians of his day rejected him. He combines the dark doctrinal themes of Zwingli with the humanistic optimism of Schleiermacher, and so takes his stand against both the over-sanguine humanism of liberal Protestants (von Harnack, Ritschl), and the stern *totaliter aliter* doctrine of Barth's neo-orthodox followers, with its suspicion of religious subjectivity.

As a Protestant critical of and criticized by other Protestants, Jung correctly saw doctrinally-based schism as the chief risk of a theological position like his own.

Protestantism, having pulled down so many walls carefully erected by the Church, immediately began to experience the disintegrating and schismatic effect of individual revelation.

(*Psychology and Religion, CW 11*, §33)

But there was nothing for Jung except to forge ahead toward his own truth. No doubt there would someday be time for the pens of scribes to make order out of the prophet's words.

D. SAVING THE CHRISTIAN WEST

It is clear from Jung's late writings that he felt under an urgent personal obligation to bring the fruits of his psychological discoveries to the aid of a violence-ridden, self-endangered world. In recognition of this sense of vocation he has been called at various times (in a complimentary or uncomplimentary sense) prophet, preacher, doctor and shaman to the Western world. His own view of his public role arguably included all these dimensions.[30] For our purposes, Jung's relationship to Western Christianity will be described under two general headings: moral teacher to Western civilization, and healer of schism in the Western church.

1. Jung as Moral Teacher

Commentators have sometimes overemphasized Jung's introverted character, obscuring the fact that he was also driven by his social conscience (as is clear in his late books, letters, lectures and interpretations of dreams) to stake energy and reputation on the often thankless task of warding off the madness he saw threatening civilization. Moral fervor characterized Jung's writing about Christian symbols and beliefs from the beginning of the second World War until the end of his life. As the industrial West moved into an era of total and totalitarian warfare, and the geopolitical split of East and West brought the Cold War and nuclear insecurity into public consciousness, Jung's attitude toward religion began to shift from his early theoretical treatment of Christian themes to a burning interest in seeing those themes applied for the collective good.

The shift began, as Murray Stein reminds us, in 1938 when Jung was traveling in India (Stein, pp.102ff).[31] There he had a dramatic dream, the final moments of which conveyed to him that it was now his personal task to seek for the Holy Grail (*Memories*, pp.280ff). Over the preceding several years Jung had explored fascinating parallels between his psychological findings and the symbolism of primitive and non-European religions. As war approached in Europe, it seemed to him that

> this essentially European dream . . . swept me back to the too-long-neglected concerns of the Occident . . . [and] reminded me that India was not my task. . . . It was as though the dream were asking me, "What are you doing in India? . . . For your state is perilous; you are all in imminent danger of destroying all that centuries have built up."
>
> (*Memories*, p.283)

In the following years Jung began to write about religious symbols of the Western church—for example, the Trinity and the Mass—with as much urgency as if it were indeed the sacred mission of his old age. The fervor of Jung's tone in late writings such as *Answer to Job*, *The Undiscovered Self*, and *Memories, Dreams, Reflections* is related to his conviction that "the so-called Christian West, far from creating a new world, is moving with giant strides toward the possibility of destroying the world we have" (*Memories*, p.280). He saw himself as being on a transpersonal mission to awaken the soul of the West, before we "civilized" humans unconsciously trip the collective apocalypse.

But Jung came to this social task with a conviction that souls can only be awakened one at a time. Like Reinhold Niebuhr, who as a young man argued dramatically that the morality of collectivities is inferior to that of individuals,[32] Jung emphasizes that hope for the West and the world lies in the first instance not in the social programs of governments, nor in the authority of the churches' teachings, but in the psychological work of individuals who are transformed from the inside. Here Jung articulates a position that he holds in common with Niebuhr's great spiritual mentor, Søren Kierkegaard: by being oneself, and not a mirror or clone of one's society, one does the work of salt or leaven in the collective social mass. This is all anyone can do in a moral sense to help society. It is such a difficult task that one can barely do it, even in part; and then only by grace.[33] The Holy Grail of Jung's dream turns out to be a spiritual vision of wholeness, an invitation to a difficult journey toward psychological unity and self-knowledge. The Grail, the never completely attainable goal of this journey, he calls individuation.

Individuation can be undertaken—by definition—only by

individuals. And yet the ongoing practice of or striving toward individuation is not for the good of the single individual, but for the welfare of all. In ascribing priority to the moral development of the individual, Jung wants nothing to do with a solipsistic "ethics of self-realization." On the contrary, although the theory and practice of analytical psychology are largely private and intrapsychic, their ethical fruit and *telos* are communal and relational.

Jung's conviction concerning the social and moral value of individuation is obvious from his earliest to his latest writings. One of the major points in his 1916 essay, "The Structure of the Unconscious,"[34] is that the moral condition of society depends primarily on the individuation of its members. In a summary of this essay, written some years later, Jung explains that "individuality" denotes an autonomous, self-regulating self-consciousness. The private, independent conscience, not over-identified with the ideals of society, is the only guarantor of collective morality. Jung summarizes, with an aphoristic brevity unlike his usual style:

> Development of individuality is simultaneously a development of society. Suppression of individuality through the predominance of collective ideals and organizations is a moral defeat for society.
>
> ("Ego and Unconscious," *CW* 7, §519)

He expresses the same thought more fully in the body of this long monograph (revised in 1928 under the title, "The Relations Between the Ego and the Unconscious," *CW* 7, §202ff). Here Jung specifically distinguishes between "individuation," which means "becoming one's own self" ("Ego and Unconscious," *CW* 7, §267), and two regressive types of moral misdevelopment which he warns must not be confused with it. To become "individual" in Jung's sense is *not* to identify oneself with one's social role, although identification with social roles is popularly associated with doing one's duty. To become identified with roles, Jung argues, is to succumb to the authority of collective opinion, abdicating one's moral autonomy.

On the other hand, being "individual" must not be understood as dwelling on one's uniqueness at the expense of one's relation to the collective. Individuation in Jung's sense is consistent with an ethics of self-realization, but not in such a way that one ignores the claims of others. Jung insists that particular selfhood is the necessary condition for mutuality and self-giving. His concept of individuation therefore does *not* lead to or derive from a principle of "ethical egoism" that would put service-of-self before all other duties.[35]

> Individuation means precisely the better and more complete fulfilment of the collective qualities of the human being. . . . [I]t is a process by which a man becomes the definite, unique being he in fact is. In so doing he does not become "selfish" in the ordinary sense of the word, but is merely fulfilling the peculiarity of his nature, and this, as we have said, is vastly different from egotism or individualism.
> ("Ego and Unconscious," *CW* 7, §267)

In this essay Jung again stresses the connection between individuation and social responsibility when he writes:

> The idea at the bottom of this ideal is that right action comes from right thinking, and that there is no cure and no improving of the world that does not begin with the individual himself.
> ("Ego and Unconscious," *CW* 7, §373)

Given Jung's low opinion of the morality of collectives, we must ask what it means for him to relate the process of individuation to the general welfare of the world. If one believes in the potential sacredness of collective life—as, for example, many Christians believe in collective rather than private salvation—Jung's ideas might sound like moral condescension. Should individuals differentiate themselves from society for the long-term good of society? And if so, does this rule apply to separating oneself from the society of the church, as well? Jung insists that he tries to send religious believers—of any sort— back to their churches and communities. For psychic health, he is convinced, it is better if one can belong to the religious community in which one naturally has roots. And yet his leaning toward individuals and against collectives suggests that his attitude is divided on the subject. The solitary soul, alone with God, has an almost heroic status.

Here is yet another point where we can see how Jung creates resistance from the churches' spokesmen, whether Protestant or Catholic. He appears to arrogate to himself, or at least to the moral individual whom he represents, a mission that has always been claimed by the churches as their own, news of the salvation of the world. Jung's conviction that individuals are the moral center of the world, responsible for the world's welfare, makes him a preacher willy-nilly. He claims not to prescribe how the world ought to work, but only to describe the way it works in fact: great changes in society can happen only through the changes in individuals (*Psychology and Religion*, *CW 11*, §134ff). And yet when he takes it as his moral task to nudge Christendom toward its next stage of development, his preaching frequently invites incredulity from those in the church who thought that task was theirs.

A letter written near the end of Jung's life makes his mission clear, drawing the by now familiar connection between individuation and the social good, and expressing his hope for an internal transformation of Christian thinking.

> [M]y work deals in the main with the transformation of Christian tenets within the Christian era. . . . Developments on such a scale are only possible when the individual, i.e., many individuals, are transforming themselves in their personal psychological life, a fact which cannot take place without a profound shaking up of one's mental peace.
>
> (*Letters II*, pp.510f)

As we have already seen, Jung was faithful to his convictions in at least one instance. In the closing days of their collaboration he encouraged Victor White to remain at Blackfriars, writing in terms consistent with the ethical principles of individuation. For example, his long letter of early April 1954 encouraged White to stay in his Order, but not to lose himself in the church's collective view of him and his teaching role (*Letters*

II, p.172). At the same time, Jung urged, staying as a Dominican would not serve White's personal good alone. The modern world requires Christian symbols more desperately than ever; White's teaching might help to meet the need. In Jung's words of 24 Nov. 53:

> Our society cannot afford the luxury of cutting itself loose from the *imitatio Christi.* . . . We are still within the Christian aeon and just beginning to realize the age of darkness where we shall need Christian virtues *to the utmost.*
>
> (*Letters II*, pp.136f)

White was thus exhorted to make his life at Blackfriars neither a collectively defined duty nor an exercise in psychological self-centeredness, but rather a true task of individuation. That is, he should live as an autonomous individual, concerning himself for others. This entirely characteristic application of Jung's concept of individuation illustrates how his concern for one soul was inseparable from his ethical focus on history and the collective.

2. *Jung as a Healer of Schism*

Jung's relationship with the major branches of tradition in the Western church was conflicted; yet it was a conflict, an ambivalence, which Jung himself prized and did not wish to resolve. In his letter to Irminger he claimed that his conscience was split between Catholic and Protestant forms of belief.

> Though I know little of Catholic doctrine, that little is enough to make it an inalienable possession for me. And I know so much about Protestantism that I could never give it up. . . . Now with regard to this indecision, I must tell you that I have consciously and deliberately decided for it. . . .
>
> (*Letters I*, pp.346f)

Jung's connection with Catholicism, his desire to be in some sense Catholic as well as Protestant, was strong enough to confuse the unwary, as we have seen. His joining with both sides of the divided Western church may indicate that he looked at the church as a therapist looks at a patient whose soul is torn and conflicted. His essay "On the Nature of the Psyche" describes the desired therapeutic stance:

> The ego keeps its integrity only if it does not identify with one of the opposites, and if it understands how to hold the balance between them. This is possible only if it remains conscious of both at once. . . . Even if it were a question of some great truth, identification with it would still be a catastrophe, as it arrests all further spiritual development.
>
> ("On the Nature of the Psyche," *CW 8*, §425)

Only by considering himself equally related to both parts of the "opposites" in the church, could Jung hope to minister to the schism.

And yet the feeling intensity of much of Jung's writing about the church indicates that he is not only a clinical observer. He is personally engaged in the dispute, as a member of the divided family of the Western church. His letter to Irminger states: "As a doctor I am interested only in one thing: how can the wound be healed?" (*Letters I*, p.347). By ascribing to himself the role of doctor, Jung assumes a caretaking function; but the wound is in himself as much as in Western Christendom. Jung's self-description as doctor to the church reflects only half the truth. The church's tragic division entails not only a therapeutic problem for Jung the scientist and healer, but also a personal problem of divided loyalties for the self-declared son of both sides of the tradition.

Jung's position might be described not only as the doctor of divided Christendom but as the child in a divided family. Attempting to heal the schism between Protestants and Catholics, Jung is attempting to rejoin divided halves within himself. Such a wish is difficult to fulfill, especially when one is emotionally and spiritually contained within the system. Did Jung have the requisite therapeutic objectivity? Could he keep one foot outside the problem for balance?

Murray Stein maintains that Jung does indeed have one foot outside the system he is trying to heal, because as a psychologist he brings a perspective that is different from the church's normal categories of self-understanding. Stein sees Jung's participation in the church as the stance of a shaman, who must suffer the illness he would cure (*Jung's Treatment of Christianity*, pp.164f). In making this claim for Jung, however, Stein fails to comment on two facts that may be relevant. First, the institution of the Western church did not come to Jung asking for help, and so was not truly accessible to his care. Second, Jung could not act as a therapist if he failed in one of the basic conditions he required of himself as a doctor. In his second letter to White, Jung himself had stated the condition:

> I cannot "tell" my patient, I have to seek him and I must learn his language and think his thoughts, until he knows that I understand him correctly. Then only is he ready to understand me and at the same time the strange language of the unconscious. . . .
>
> (*Letters I*, p.387)

If this was Jung's attitude toward his patient, it would have to be his attitude toward his "patient" the church. Yet we have seen that to a great degree he rejected the church's language.[36]

For this reason he is open to a critical argument from the perspective of some who see themselves as definitely inside the church. Doctrinally conscious Christians might say that Jung places himself *completely* "outside" the therapeutic context in an important sense. The healing which he wants to offer the church includes the "missing fourth," the "dark side" of Christ, and so on, not all of which teachings assimilate easily to Christian self-understanding. His therapeutic stance toward Christianity may therefore not be as viable as Murray Stein and others have argued; it may be too biased from the start by his rejection of the conceptual coinage of theology.

Notwithstanding the many difficulties orthodox Christians have had with his doctrinal proposals, Jung would probably ask that the work of his later years—his efforts to be a moral teacher of the West and healer of the Christian schism—be evaluated as he once evaluated the earthly work of Jesus.[37] That is, even though the objective value of his endeavors is hard to determine, and his vocational self-description may have been (in human terms) folly, Jung would ask us to recognize the integrity of his effort. He would appeal to us, too, to grant the value of the practical goal which first appeared to him as the Grail, even if its fulfillment will always be imperfectly realized.

Jung denied having "faith," except in his idiosyncratic sense, as the respect he was bound to give—almost against his will—to religious dogmas and symbols that exercised a certain power over him (*Letters I*, pp.501f). As a rule he would not admit to "belief," preferring instead to talk about knowledge. Yet his devotion to his vision of God and his fidelity to what seemed a transpersonal mission gave his mature life the shape that many Christians would recognize as an enacted faith. And although he would not claim to have faith, or belief, or even certain kinds of knowledge, he admitted—in a letter to Erich Neumann in 1952—that the Western image of God held him, as it were, hostage. Here he privately acknowledged the shadowside of his cool scientific empiricism: the "living thraldom, . . . local, barbaric, infantile and abysmally unscientific" (*Letters II*, p.33) to which he was subjected by the Judeo-Christian God-image. Caught in this state of abject captivity before the primary, most powerful biblical symbol, Jung wrote his *Answer to Job*.

C.G. Jung thus devoted himself at great personal cost to a promised good whose historical fruition—the transformation of Western collective consciousness—could not yet be seen. In this sense the work of his mature life enacted a religious hope and—paradoxical word—faith. And yet, as one compelled to wrestle naked with an interior God of absolute power and only relative moral trustworthiness, Jung bore a superhuman burden. For he felt himself called as a mere mortal to reach into the shadows and relieve the sorrows of the world, while remaining staunchly unwilling to rely on a God of ultimate goodness or to accept the sacramental mediation of a corporately attested faith. He labored always under the principle of spiritual and moral solitariness that once led his friend Victor to rebuke him, gently, for hubris.

In this endeavor, heroically confronting the many kinds of misunderstanding and resistance that came from both the theological and the scientific opposing camps as he obeyed the voices of inner and outer wholeness, Jung exhausted himself.

Did he win through to a resurrected body, as he once urged his followers to do? Although the doctrinal content of his hope and faith would not be affirmed by some Christian believers, the integrity and courage with which he reflected on his vision of Christian symbols and engaged the world in terms of that vision is hard to deny.

Chapter Five

Jung's Revisions of Christian Doctrine

A. THE SELF

The preceding chapters explore central philosophical and historical conditions surrounding the collaboration of Jung and White. They delineate as far as possible the two men's personal and professional stakes in their work together and begin to suggest the location of the obstacles and sources of tension that proved insurmountable for them. Keeping in mind Jung's and White's respective epistemological commitments, we can now discuss the two primary points where their doctrines diverged. Jung's concept of the Self and its psychological and religious ramifications are discussed in the first half of this chapter. The second half deals with his direct challenge to White concerning the definition of evil.

Some especially difficult issues arose in relation to Jung's psychological doctrine of the Self. This piece of Jung's theory about the nature of religious and symbolic experience came to bear directly on both his appreciation and his criticism of central Christian doctrines. He referred to it particularly when interpreting the way Christ relates to the human soul, and the way God's omnipotence relates to human moral choice.

The concept of the Self came into focus for Jung through his study of the Trinity and the symbolic meaning of the Christ-image in Western culture. His criticism of the doctrine that evil is a "privation of good" also emerged in the course of his writing about the Trinity, but only began to engage his full attention when he turned to an analysis of the Western God-image in *Aion* and *Answer to Job*.

Jung quickly saw that his phenomenological approach to the center of human personality, which he called the Self, was in stark contrast with the church's claim that the image of God—whether in the Bible or in the personal experience of believers—is absolutely good. Against the orthodox doctrinal claim of un-mixed divine goodness, Jung declares that neither the God-image nor the Christ-image is an adequate symbol of wholeness, unless the shadow of the archetype is included. Jung's inclusion of evil in the image of God and his argument that Christ and Antichrist are linked in a necessary polarity conflict glaringly with predominant Christian teachings.

Jung operated both as a wrecker and as a builder, tearing down parts of the standing order because he wanted to recon-struct it. His radical revisioning of Christianity went far beyond the territory White had wanted to conquer for Thomism, forc-ing White to adopt mainly the posture of a defender and conservator rather than an innovator. As a theologian, there-fore, Victor White did not break new ground on these issues. For the most part, as the conversation progressed, he affirmed the church's traditional teachings and sought fresh ways to con-vey their logic to Jung. It seems appropriate to explore Jung's revisioning of Trinitarian and Christological doctrines before turning our attention to White's responses.

Up to a point, the conflict that developed between the two men was a source of creativity for both. It is often a blessing to struggle with a stubborn conversation partner whose mind one respects. As we study the issues which finally proved Jung and White incompatible as collaborators, it should be obvious that the intensity of their debate and the mutual hope of being understood induced each one to wrestle with profound ques-tions and to produce works which might otherwise never have been written. This is true especially of Jung's ongoing work on the Trinity, and of White's analysis of Aquinas' understanding of evil.

1. Tackling the Trinity

The positive benefits of the two men's mutual inspiration are most evident in work that Jung produced during the early months and years of the collaboration. His original urge to "save the West" from spiritual death and destruction had led him quickly into discussions of Christian symbols and doctrines for which his education had poorly prepared him. In the Eranos meeting of 1940, for instance, Jung spoke about the doctrine of the Trinity. He did not usually lecture *ex tempore* at Eranos; but on this occasion, carried away by a sudden sense of urgency, he spoke off the cuff. Later he had to reconstruct his lecture, "Zur Psychologie der Trinitätsidee," from the notes of his listeners.[1]

The phenomenon of one-God-in-three had intrigued Jung even in boyhood, all the more so because his father refused to discuss it with him (*Memories*, pp.52f). Conscious of his lack of systematic training in this and other theological doctrines, however, he was a bit worried about the adequacy of his statements. In May 1941 Jung wrote to his friend H.G. Baynes about the new problem he was facing and his consultations with a Catholic theologian, Dr. Gallus Jud.[2] His apparent appreciation of Dr. Jud's contribution is wryly qualified, however; the compliment paid in one line is taken back in the next:

> I seem to be dealing more and more with subjects not just suitable for public discussion (f.i. a lecture on the Trinity at Eranos!). . . . I often have interviews now with a Catholic priest, an intelligent and scholarly man. . . . It is wonderful to see mediaeval mentality still at its best.
>
> (*Letters I*, p.300)

Since the "medieval" tradition of reasoning had fatal drawbacks from Jung's perspective, this phrase "mediaeval mentality" is exquisitely loaded. Seven years later, in his expanded and rewritten essay on the Trinity,[3] Jung describes "a 'medieval psychology'" which spontaneously produces trinitarian, rather than fourfold symbols. To call such a psychology "medieval," he explains with a strenuous and not completely successful attempt at tact, is to attribute no moral defect to the people in question but simply to identify a "special problem":[4]

> In all these cases there is so much unconsciousness, and such a large degree of primitivity to match it, that a spiritualization appears necessary as a compensation. The saving

symbol is then a triad in which the fourth is lacking because
it has to be unconditionally rejected.

("Trinity," *CW 11*, §284)

Jung could not have worked for long with a theologian
whose psychology he found medieval in this sense. Indeed,
wherever he finds a habitual rejection of "the fourth" and all
that it represents, he equates that habit with what he calls a
"neurotic one-sidedness," attributing to it an illegitimate, immoral quality. A medieval mentality can thus become virtually
the same thing to Jung as unconscious sin.[5]

Jung laid his work on the Trinity aside for some time, uncertain whether he would ever be able to expand and correct it as
he wished. It was not until after he had read White's four initial
essays and rejoiced to find evidence in them of a theological
perspective and method which seemed congenial with his own
empiricism that he once again dared to raise the subject of his
unfinished essay on the Trinity. In his October 1945 letter to
White he pleads for special help with that topic:

> You can perhaps imagine my feelings of inadequacy when I
> have to tackle such a problem at short notice. It is usually so,
> that I keep quiet for years about such intricate matters as for
> instance the Trinity. But all of a sudden the subject comes up
> in a discussion or in a lecture and somebody deals with it in a
> really inadequate way, then I feel somebody ought to say
> something more to the point and I am launched utterly
> unprepared, only supported by my experience with practi-
> cally nothing on the other, the theological side. There I
> would need some solid theological help.
>
> (*Letters I*, p.385)

White's "solid theological help" encouraged Jung to try
again, yet he still approached the Trinity with trepidation. His
letter of 6 November 1946, which contains comments on
White's important dream of sailing at great speed among
rocks,[6] seems to present the essay on the Trinity as one of the
perils he and White must soon face on their journey. The letter
concludes: "Presently I must make up my mind to tackle my

dangerous paper about the psychology of the H.Trinity" (*Letters I*, p.449). Five months later he writes in the same vein:

> I have been completely swamped by an article which I had
> to elaborate for a new edition. It is that risky thing about the
> Holy Trinity.
>
> (*Letters I*, p.452)

In 1948, after eighteen months of collaboration, Jung finally produced "A Psychological Approach to the Dogma of the Trinity," revised and immensely expanded from his original Eranos lecture. Leaning heavily and gratefully on White's 1947 Eranos lecture, "St. Thomas' Conception of Revelation,"[7] Jung's revision of the essay refers to the writings of Aquinas and to other conventional Christian teaching about the Trinity. He cites passages from St. Thomas which White has brought to his attention; but his use of Aquinas is—as one might expect—extrinsic to the psychological argument. The most evident benefit of White's consultation about the revision of this lecture is the fact that Jung at last had confidence—supported by White's friendly advice—to publish it after the eight-year delay.

This essay represents Jung's first full effort to expound upon his conviction that, for psychological and ethical reasons, evil should be considered to belong to the Godhead. Jung argues here, as later in *Aion* and *Answer to Job*, that when God is formally described as the *Summum Bonum*, and thus cleared of the attribution of evil, human beings become by default the main or only source of moral evil in the universe. This produces an anthropology, he says, which is not only false but may also be psychologically damaging. Either it makes human beings responsible for more evil than finite souls can bear, or else, calling evil "merely" the privation of good, it encourages believers to trivialize sin.

This reasoning, embryonic in the 1940 Trinity lecture, would grow into Jung's hottest argument with Victor White. His original lecture on the Trinity uses language familiar to anyone who knows his later writings on the topic:

Was sagt nun—psychologisch gesehen—das trinitarische Denken aus? Gott, das summum bonum, entfaltet sich im und durch den Sohn zum Heiligen Geist als dem Dritten, der die Perichoresis zum Einen darstellt. . . . Dieser Prozeß ist in sich rund und vollkommen, insoweit er platonische Idee ist. Aber wo bleibt das Übel? Man kommt zum Schluß, zu dem schon das Mittelalter gekommen ist: "Omne bonum a deo, omne malum a homine." Will man den Teufel nicht anerkennen, so sind wir der Teufel. Wir sind es dann, welche die Harmonie Gottes stören.

("Trinitätsidee," p.44)[8]

A translation of this passage would run:

Now what, seen psychologically, does trinitarian thinking express? God, the highest good, unfolds himself in and through the Son, into the Holy Spirit as the third, who represents perichoresis into the one.[9] . . . This process is rounded and perfect in itself, insofar as it is a Platonic idea. But where is evil to be found? One comes to the conclusion, as already in the Middle Ages: "All good from God, all evil from humankind." If one doesn't want to acknowledge the devil, we are the devil. So we are that which disturbs the harmony of God.

Jung also claims that the classic doctrine of the Trinity over-spiritualizes, over-masculinizes, and over-simplifies the account of God's nature, leaving material, feminine, and negative aspects of human experience out of relationship to the divine. Because not only evil but all these other aspects of universal experience have been cut off from participation in the divine nature, Jung calls the Trinity, the threefold symbol, psychologically incomplete.

This does not mean that Jung denigrates the symbolic value of the Trinity in its historical context; he praises Trinitarian thinking as a crucial psychological advance. The Trinity depicts God as a unity that is internally complex and self-related, a better image of psychological complexity and maturity than either the casual confusion of tritheism or the simple unity of undifferentiated monotheism.

> Denn in der Trinität handelt es sich nicht um ein tritheïs-
> tisches *Nebeneinander*, sondern um eine *reflektierte, durch in-*
> *nere wechselseitige Bezogenheit hervorgebrachte Einheit.*
>
> ("Trinitätsidee," p.39)

> Denn unzweifelhaft ist die Trinität eine höhere Form der
> Gottesvorstellung als die bloße Einheit, indem sie nämlich
> einem reflektierten, d.h. bewußtern Zustand der Men-
> schheit entspricht.
>
> ("Trinitätsidee," p.43)

These two statements might be translated:

> For in the Trinity it is not a matter of tritheistic *juxtaposition*,
> but of a *reflected unity, brought forth through mutual inner rela-*
> *tionship.* . . . For without doubt the Trinity is a higher form
> of the God-image than simple oneness, in that it corre-
> sponds to a reflected, i.e., a more conscious condition of
> humankind.

Threefoldness is thus an advance over monotheism; but it is not Jung's idea of the highest and most desirable degree of psychological and religious consciousness. In place of the three-fold symbol, he recommends the "completeness" of a fourfold symbology. A fourfold symbolic complexity is found, Jung says, in the thought of Pythagoreans, Gnostics, alchemists, Indian philosophers, mystics and great European poets such as Goethe ("Trinity," *CW 11*, §244,246,262,280 and *passim*). If the Christian world could adopt a fourfold image of God, it would be-speak the inclusion of many aspects of reality which have hith-erto been hidden from consciousness in an over-spiritualized and over-masculinized tradition.

To restore the "missing fourth" to the church's account of the nature of God, Jung believes, would salvage all that the Western church has openly or covertly marked inferior: matter, flesh, the feminine, and—Jung insists on this—evil itself.[10] Un-til all of the opposites are raised symbolically to consciousness in the Godhead, there will be no transcendent model of wholeness upon which human beings can consciously and deliberately frame their inner lives.

Just as, in the *Timaeus*, the adversary is the second half of the second pair of opposites, without whom the world-soul would not be whole and complete, so, too, the devil must be added to the *trias* . . . in order to make it a totality. If the Trinity is understood as a *process*, as I have tried to do all along, then, by the addition of the Fourth, this process would culminate in a condition of absolute totality.

("Trinity," *CW 11*, §290)

Many elements or aspects are combined in the "missing fourth," as Jung sees it, because all these aspects of reality are repressed in traditional Christian theology. An implication of Jung's thinking about "the fourth," then, is that these contents which have been dissociated from the Godhead (and thus from the practice of Christian life) exist in the condition of all repressed material. They are combined in an undifferentiated mass as contents of the unconscious which continuously contaminate and color each other. The task of raising such a complex to consciousness promises to be lengthy and painful. Before its confused elements can be treated as conscious parts of the Godhead and of Christian experience, work will have to be done to differentiate the strands of the complex—matter, evil, and the feminine—which are still wretchedly confused in Christian thought.

Jung's notion of what theologians have traditionally said about the Trinity is unsophisticated. There is no need to defend him on that score. But we must understand how his inclusion of "evil" in the nature of God is connected with his psychological concerns. There is a direct relation, Jung perceives, between the image we hold of God and the image we hold of ourselves. So in this essay he deplores the shadowless spirituality of traditional Christianity:

One of the toughest roots of all evil is unconsciousness and I could wish that the saying of Jesus, "Man, if thou knowest what thou doest, thou art blessed, but if thou knowest not, thou art accursed, and a transgressor of the law," were still in the gospels, even though it has only one authentic source.[11] It might well be the motto for a new morality.

("Trinity," *CW 11*, §291)

Just as theologians have split apart the two halves of the divine ambivalence, good and evil, in their image of God, the consciousness of the traditional church has been psychologically split off from its collective shadow. Failing to take its own evil into account, the community of faith frequently projects its negative side onto scapegoats and exercises the prerogatives of moral perfection at the expense of those it condemns. All too often in the history of the world, as Jung reminds us, righteous people become possessed in this way by the inferiority and violence they wish to disavow.

Perhaps humanity could survive for some time with impossibly good images of God and of human nature; but Jung is convinced that the tensions and dangers of the modern age no longer allow the luxury of this self-deception. If the world is not to be torn apart by the violent exercise of mutual projections, human beings must learn to tolerate their moral ambiguity and ambivalence. They need to do this most especially by acknowledging the dark aspects of the God-image that is at the center of their conscious self-identity.

The conclusion of Jung's original address on the Trinity is a passage invoking the Holy Spirit, which he identifies as the very principle of psychic wholeness and the bridge between human experience and the Godhead. The Holy Spirit, he says, is the only help for certain moral dilemmas that we can neither solve nor escape ("Trinitätsidee," p.64). Jung cautions, however, that the crucial role of the Holy Spirit in the modern era also poses a danger. Discernment of the Spirit is always a subjective matter, and opens the door to the possibility that we may once again forget our inner moral ambiguity and that of the Spirit itself, and "twist the indwelling of the Paraclete into a self-deification of man" ("Trinity," *CW 11*, §267).

To Jung this danger is yet one more reason why we dare not think of either God or humanity without shadow. If we forget the moral ambiguity at the very heart of human wholeness, we are likely to make monstrous claims about the divinity that indwells us. The antidote to self-deification is humility, and it is this virtue that Jung recommends above all others. If we "remain conscious that we are no more than the stable in which the Lord is born" ("Trinity," *CW 11*, §267), then the God who inhabits human souls may yet save the world through human actions.

> Even on the highest peak we shall never be "beyond good and evil," and the more we experience of their inextricable entanglement the more uncertain and confused will our moral judgement be. . . . Our knowledge of good and evil has dwindled with our mounting knowledge and experience, and will dwindle still more in the future, without our being able to escape the demands of ethics. In this utmost uncertainty we need the illumination of a holy and whole-making spirit—a spirit that can be anything rather than our reason.
>
> (*CW 11*, "Trinity," §267)

Upon this theological paradox, that good and evil are mixed in the very image of God, Jung bases his cautious assessment of humanity's justifiable hope and trust. If this is their basis, our hope and trust must always be nervous and unstable qualities; and so they are for Jung. He warns that we must never cease our vigilant questioning of God, nor forget the mixed grounds of our own actions.

2. Toward a Jungian Christology

Once Jung returned to theological themes with White's help, his exploration of Christian imagery was almost bound to lead him to the central figure of Christian tradition. Jung began to realize in December 1947 that in writing about the Self he was following a christological thread. In a letter to White (mentioned in Chapter Three above) he remarked:

> After I had written about 25 pages in folio, it began to dawn on me that Christ—not the man but the divine being—was my secret goal.
>
> (*Letters I*, p.480)

If Christ was a "secret goal," it was because Jung's conscious aim had been only to write about the psychological union of opposites at the center of the personality, also known as the "transcendent function" or the Self. This archetypal complex, he now realized, must underlie the concrete historical manifestation of the God-man in Western culture, the image of Jesus Christ.

His 1948 Eranos lecture makes the connection explicit: *"Christus veranschaulicht den Archetypus des Selbst"* ("Über das Selbst," p.304).[12] Jung is quite intentional about the logical priority implied here. The archetype of the Self has priority logically and theoretically, even if at a conscious level the image of Christ is what most people are aware of. In human experience it is always a *particular* Self-symbol, that makes itself known. The underlying archetype can be posited, however, by comparing the symbols that emerge in diverse cultures and periods of history.

The figure of Christ, Jung states, is the presiding Western Self-symbol. Yet even this does not and cannot completely manifest (*veranschaulichen*: "bring to view") the underlying archetype. First of all, no symbol can convey an archetype fully to consciousness. But more importantly, the Christ-image is univocally good, whereas the Self, like all archetypes, is ambivalent in its effect on consciousness.

In order to get an idea of the archetype of the Self in its completeness, one has to look at both Christ and the Antichrist, light and dark together, as a single complex.

> Christ is our nearest analogy of the self and its meaning. . . .
> Yet, although the attributes of Christ (consubstantiality with the Father, co-eternity, filiation, parthenogenesis, crucifixion, Lamb sacrificed between opposites, One divided into Many, etc.) undoubtedly mark him out as an embodiment of the self, looked at from the psychological angle he corresponds to only one half of the archetype. The other half appears in the Antichrist.
>
> ("Über das Selbst," p.308; *Aion, CW 9ii,* §79)

"Über das Selbst" brings two strands of Jung's thought together. Neither the psychological value of the Christ-image nor the concept of the Self is a new theme in Jung's work by 1948. He hypothesized a phenomenon called "the Self" in *Psychological Types,* 1921, where he named it the "transcendent function" because he believed that this complex combined the conscious and unconscious (superior and inferior) functions of personality within the psyche.

Jung's study of the psychological value of the Christ-figure, meanwhile, had begun with *Psychology and Alchemy*, published in 1944.[13] In his 1948 Eranos lecture he joined the two themes, by identifying the phenomenon of the Self as the universal and necessary precondition for the religious symbol of Christ. This lecture, "Über das Selbst," reworked only slightly, would soon become the substance of Chapters IV and V in his 1950 book, *Aion*.

The first four chapters of *Aion*, outlining the basic concepts of the individuation process (a process in which one engages with ego, shadow, anima/animus, and finally with the Self), seem out of place when compared with the abstruse later chapters. Why should Jung preface a dense monograph on the primary religious symbol of psychic wholeness in the Western world with such a simple, concise discursus on the primary concepts of analytical-psychological practice? The answer goes to the heart of Jung's whole project. By introducing his discussion of Self-symbology in this way, he sought to present the concept of the Self not as a feature of a static anthropology or (worse) a Platonic philosophy, but as a feature vital to a universal psychodynamic process, which he calls individuation. Thus, if Jung's *Aion* is conceptually coherent, the key elements in the process of individuation must be relevant to consciousness of the Self.

In both "Über das Selbst" and *Aion*, Jung makes it clear that the Self is known not *a priori*, but in the same way we come to know other unconscious elements of personality. As a psychotherapist he has to recognize the non-ego reality of these interior elements of the psyche, because they confront the ego of a patient like autonomous, separate entities. Shadow, anima or animus, and Self emerge in the form of troublesome, mysterious, or fascinating social encounters, or as images in dreams. The ego either locates them "outside" in the world or meets them as foreign elements "inside" the psyche. In either case, the ego only slowly learns to relate to them as intrapsychic elements that are at once distinct from itself and members of its own household. The Self, then, like the shadow, or anima and animus, is presented as a scientific hypothesis, whose necessity is proven in the course of ordinary analytical practice.

One constant in a psychological individuation process is the painful requirement of recognizing and withdrawing unconscious projections. The end-point of the task is a more conscious relation to the Self; but the only way to approximate to that goal is to withdraw all the sorts of projected contents, admitting that they belong to one's own personality. Especially in relation to projections of the shadow, this process can be felt as a crucifixion or dismemberment; it resembles repentance, as Christians use the term.

As mentioned in an earlier chapter, the concept of "projection" was brought into philosophical discussion by Feuerbach in a way sharply critical of theology. Having linked Jung's views of theology even briefly with those of Feuerbach, it is important to clarify here what Jung means by "projections" and their withdrawal. A brief summary of the chief concepts and stages of individuation, as found in the first four chapters of *Aion*, may help to that end. These concepts refer, however, to overlapping stages in a messy, painful, personal work. To face and accept the meanings of shadow-figures that arise in dreams, to work with the contrasexual figures in one's inner and outer world, and to encounter interior images of divinity and premonitions of wholeness, constitutes a heroic labor "against nature."[14]

In this work of individuation, Jung says, a person who persists long enough to withdraw his or her projections of the Self, raising that psychic image to consciousness, finds it to be both the transcendent center and the untraceable circumference of the personality. A separate center from the ego,[15] it holds in paradoxical union all the psychic opposites which belong to the individual: good and evil, conscious and unconscious, masculine and feminine, newborn and aged. It anticipates a wholeness not yet realized and urges the psyche toward that wholeness. It "revolutionizes the ego-oriented psyche," opposing to the conscious center of personality "another goal or center . . . the antithesis of the subjective ego-psyche" (*Aion, CW 9ii*, §296).

To the superordinate, intrapsychic "final cause" of the Self, however, the Christian's image of Christ corresponds only incompletely; it never fully manifests the archetype of wholeness. This Jungian conviction has implications both for christological relativism and for universalism. The Self, being a universal factor in human psychology, is represented more or less completely in the religious symbology of every culture. Jesus Christ is one local symbol of the universal archetype. The Christ-image in the soul is authentic, powerful and necessary for those (such as Jung himself) who relate to this image as to a "native" Self-symbol. But the Christ-image is not absolute; it is relative to the culture that worships in the context of this divine mythologem.

Our Western image of Christ is also not the only Self-symbol in the history of the world. The Buddha is another (*Aion, CW 9ii*, §304). Nor is it, Jung says, necessarily the most complete Self-symbol the world has ever seen; Gnostic visions come closer (*Aion, CW 9ii*, §104). We cannot even say that Christ is the final and unsurpassable Self-symbol for the West; for we are (or should be) involved in a process of religious evolution which—as Jung wrote in letters as an old man—the practice of analytical psychology may further.

Nevertheless, as Jung wrote to White during the latter's struggle to reaffirm his vocation, for Christians in the present era the image of Christ is irreplaceable. Its unique power for Westerners derives from its "autochthonous" roots in our shared history and culture.[16] Although we can and should appreciate the wealth of religious meaning conveyed in the symbols of the East, we must not expect borrowed symbols to mediate the Self to us as well as native ones:

> Though we can learn a lot from Indian thought, it can never express the past that is stored up within us.
> (*Aion, CW 9ii*, §271)

By analogy, those who have learned from childhood to "speak" Buddhism or Islam will find their irreplaceable Self-symbols rooted in the religious languages native to them.

3. God and the Self: An Epistemological Paradox

Jung may have developed his conviction about the power of autochthonous symbols by observing his own experience. In his 1951 letter to Erich Neumann concerning *Antwort auf Hiob* (*Letters II*, p.33), Jung explained that the emotional force of the book was due to the fact that it dealt not with the abstractions or universals, but with the image of God rooted in Jung's own native ground. In *Aion* Jung expounds the idea of the Self as a universal phenomenon; but *Job* brings the "complex of opposites" home. Its passion gives away the fact that the author is intensely related to this God: one does not write with such emotion about abstractions or express such anger at gods that are not one's own.

Remembering the important place of subjective feeling in Jung's epistemology, a paradoxical conclusion can be drawn. The psychological Self has priority for Jung as a universal human reality. But the God-image he really knows, the one that has epistemological as well as emotional priority *for him,* is the biblical image of God he excoriates in *Job*.

This God-image serves Jung's systematic purposes as well. The story of God's injustice to Job illustrates better than any other canonical source the "terrible double aspect" he had ascribed to the divine archetype in the 1937 Terry Lectures. Negative aspects of the Self find no reflection in orthodox doctrines of the Trinity or the person of Christ; but they are inescapably present in the story of God's deal with Satan. Here, for once, the biblical God-image comes complete with shadow.

As he admits in his foreword "to the benevolent reader," Jung is hardly objective in the way he responds to this God-image (*Answer to Job*, p.xv). He wrote the book in a fever, unburdening himself of these thoughts as if they would save his life (which, in fact, he claimed they helped to do).[17] Had he been writing as a scientist, he might have pointed out with satisfaction—if not with scientific neutrality—that the book of Job provides an unusually complete reflection of the negative aspects of the Self. But Jung's mood is neither satisfaction nor neutrality; it is moral outrage.

An archetype is supposed to be both good and evil; Jung is never angry with the Self for combining unconsciousness with consciousness and darkness with light. But when the biblical God allows evil to be done, Jung yields to fury. The God of Job, as Jung presents him, is primitive and unreflective: a *complexio oppositorum* who refuses to become conscious—to acknowledge his shadow or consult his feminine wisdom. The Self may be an archetype of terrible double aspect; but the God of Job should act justly in love.

Here we begin to see a phenomenological difference between two concepts of evil that Jung used constantly without clearly distinguishing them. The evil of myth properly balances good in the archetype; the evil of history consists in the actual harm done to innocent victims by unconscious powers.

We will consider the impact of this conceptual distinction further below. The importance of the distinction in the present context is that it curiously reverses the order of importance that Jung assigns to the Self and its symbols. The Self is a numinous *a priori* hidden in the psyche, not a personal being capable of relationships. It is thus neither knowable nor lovable; and awe is due, not outrage, if the Self wields power ruthlessly. But the biblical God interacts personally and freely in a divine-and-human drama. When this God appears unjust and merciless, as Jung perceives in the drama of Job, moral outrage is due. Thus, although the Self logically precedes the local God-images, the biblical God is far more potent and immediate to the individual subjectivity that is, as we have seen, Jung's main source of knowledge.

B. JUNG'S CHALLENGE TO THE CHURCH

1. Manicheism and Monotheism

In his review of Jung's essay "Über das Selbst," White accuses Jung of indulging in Manicheism.[18] That is, White fears that by locating evil in the image of God Jung commits the ancient philosophical mistake of positing two gods, one responsible for good and one for evil. In Jung's view, however, the union of good and evil defends against just such an error. Indeed, he argues, the morally ambivalent Self-archetype is more truly monotheistic than the all-good God of Christian dogma.

White's accusation of dualism seems to be based on a psychologically naive reading of the doctrine of the Self.[19] Jung states the principle in *Aion*:

> Provided that one has an anthropomorphic God-image— and every God-image is anthropomorphic in a more or less subtle way . . . the reality of evil does not necessarily lead to Manichaean dualism and so does not endanger the unity of the God-image.
>
> (*Aion, CW 9ii*, §99)

The proviso is important. If one agrees with Jung's premise that all thinking about God is in some sense anthropological and dependent on analogies to human psychology, then defining the God-image as a "complex of opposites" is probably more acceptable to monotheism. To say that God is a complex of opposites no more creates two gods than admitting the complexity of consciousness and unconsciousness splits a single human being into two people.

The real danger of splitting God into a duality, Jung argues, lies in the orthodox Christian account of absolute divine goodness. The church's denial of darkness and evil within the being of God is simultaneously (and logically) a denial that evil is a real part of God's creation. If evil is not real it has no source, so God is exonerated from the charge of creating it.

But human beings *experience* evil as real and reasonably seek to know where it comes from, if not from God. If the all-good God does not create evil, the only possible conclusion is that its source is elsewhere. Thus a second creator is posited, i.e., a source of reality apart from God. We begin with belief in God's absolute goodness, add to that an experience of the terrible reality of evil, and end with the heresy of Manichean dualism.

Jung, on the contrary, begins by declaring evil is real. From this beginning it seems clear to him that, if God is the creator of all that is, God must be the author of evil.

> In a monotheistic religion everything that goes against God
> can only be traced back to God himself.
>
> ("Trinity," *CW 11*, §249)

Such radical monotheism is found only rarely in the Bible, and more rarely still in the writings of biblical theologians. Aside from the book of Job the primary scriptural spokesman for this view of God is the prophet known as Second Isaiah. The Hebrew poet, using a verb resonant of the original act of creation, makes a shocking declaration that links God directly to darkness and evil:

> I form the light and *create darkness*; I make peace and *create evil*: I the Lord do all these things.
>
> (Isaiah 45:7, italics added)[20]

The One Creator of Second Isaiah is author of everything, including evil. Such a God may be welcome and terrifying to human consciousness, by turns; but it must be acknowledged that a God who is beyond human understanding and control is no less holy. The radical monotheism of Isaiah makes God infinitely strange and even dangerous from the viewpoint of human understanding. This vision of terrifying transpersonal power found in the biblical landscape may also be used to illuminate Jung's doctrine of the Self.

2. The Missing Fourth: Perfection and Completeness

Jung's ideas about wholeness and holiness are challenging to many from an orthodox Christian perspective. His idea of the reality of evil is especially so. Chapter V of *Aion* presents Jung's first extensive elaboration of his criticism of the Christian account of evil. Its language echoes the essays of 1940 ("Trinitätsidee") and 1948 ("Über das Selbst").[21]

In 1940 at Eranos Jung began systematically questioning the Christian picture of God, which he described as unrealistically light and bright. Neoplatonic philosophy, he pointed out, is an underlying framework for Christian ideas. If Plato had known (*per impossibile*) about the Christian Trinity, he would have written about it just as the theologians do. But if he had done so, modern readers could protest that his image of God was incomplete, that it lacked a necessary "fourth":

> ... insofern Plato das Dreiseitige für das Schöne und Gute hielte und ihm alle positiven Eigenschaften zuteilte, so hätte er ihm das Böse und Unvollkommene aberkannt. Wo ist dieses dann geblieben? Auf diese Frage hat das Christentum unter anderem die Antwort gegeben, daß das reale Böse eine *privatio boni* sei. Diese klassische Formel beraubt aber das Böse der absoluten Existenz und macht es zu einem Schatten, der nur eine vom Licht abhängige, relative Existenz hat.
>
> ("Trinitätsidee," p.53)

In my own translation, this paragraph from Jung's lecture reads:

> ... insofar as Plato would have regarded the three-sided figure as beautiful and good and attributed all positive characteristics to it, he would have denied to it whatever is bad and imperfect. So what happened to *that*? To this question, one of the answers given by Christianity is that real evil is a *privatio boni* [privation of good]. This classic formula, however, robs evil of its absolute existence and makes it a shadow with only a relative existence, dependent on the light.

"*Wo ist dieses dann geblieben?*" Jung asks. Where has the evil and imperfect "fourth" gone, which ought to complete the spiritual geometry? The classic Christian formula, Jung says, deprives evil of its real existence, making it a mere negation of light. This, in Jung's reading, is the defect of the Augustinian (and Thomistic) proposal that evil, not having been created by God, has no real existence[22] and is to be understood only as a "privation," or lack, of good.

In contrast, Jung prefers what he sees as the church's alternative and more honest answer. Evil, in the person of the devil, is as real and eternal as Christ:

Der Teufel als autonome und ewige Person entspricht wohl
eher seiner Rolle als Widerpart Christi und der psycholog-
ischen Wirklichkeit des Bösen.

("Trinitätsidee," p.53)

The devil, as an autonomous and eternal person, corresponds rather to his role as Christ's counterpart and answers
to the psychological reality of evil.

In his final version of his essay on the Trinity, Jung identifies what seems to him the psychological inferiority of the
Christ-image: "the self is by definition a *complexio oppositorum*,
whereas the Christ figure wholly lacks a dark side" ("Trinity,"
CW 11, §283). Likewise, when praising the Christian version of
the individuation process, because it subordinates the ego to
the Self, Jung cautions his readers that the Christian Self-
image, Christ, is missing the shadow side that belongs to the
archetype.

It is . . . well to examine carefully the psychological aspects
of the individuation process in the light of Christian tradition, which can describe it for us with an exactness and
impressiveness far surpassing our feeble attempts, even
though the Christian image of the self—Christ—lacks the
shadow that properly belongs to it.

(*Aion*, *CW 9ii*, §79)

The aspect of the Self-archetype that differentiates it most
sharply from Christ and the Trinity is its moral ambivalence.
In trying to explain this difference, Jung introduces a crucial
distinction between two attitudes which he calls "completeness"
and "perfection."[23] If the Self were "perfect," a Platonic idea,
it would admit no darkness. But the archetype of wholeness is
complete, not perfect. Perfection, Jung says, is a predominantly masculine attitude. It separates and divides, while the
feminine attitude, "completeness," embraces and includes all
the opposites.

The concept of wholeness for Jung is thus beset with paradoxes. In *Aion* we read Jung's description of the Self as a *com-*

plexio oppositorum, the ultimate union of all the opposites: conscious and unconscious, old and young, small and large, female and male, one and many, good and evil. In *Answer to Job*, whether he intends to write theologically or not, he turns his account of this psychic phenomenon into a theological claim. For now he insists that God, to be truly God, should be as complete as the Self. That is, to be as complete as the Self and true to its own reality, our God-images must include "the fourth."

Is it necessary to include evil, then, to be "complete"? How is this to be done? For Jung, the inclusion of evil and darkness cannot be a blind enactment of the shadow. Rather, it must be a process of becoming *conscious of evil* and bearing one's own share of it. The principle applies to God as much as to human beings: God must also become conscious.

Jung had begun his exploration of these concepts—the shadow, the necessity of completeness, the error of supposing that evil is "merely" a privation—at a much earlier date. In lectures delivered in the 1930s, recently published under the title *The Visions Seminars*,[24] he speaks of these ideas in typically earthy, colloquial images. And in a move that will resurface later when he accuses God of failure to acknowledge consciously both divine shadow and divine relationship to the feminine, Jung here links the denial of evil with an unconscious submission to the anima or animus:

> You see, people who do not possess and are not aware of their inferior shadow side, may appear to be marvelously good people, one can discover no flaw in them, they are white as milk. They tell you themselves that nothing is wrong with them; everyone else is wrong, but never they. Yet because they deny their shadow, such people are absolutely possessed by devils; the women are all eaten up by the animus. . . . When you see your own inferior side you can detach from the anima or animus, but as long as you don't see it, you haven't a chance.
>
> (*Visions I*, 211)

As early as 1932, Jung was already critical, too, of the doctrine of *privatio boni*. He interprets this philosophical idea in a way that makes it appear trivial; but he never understates its damage. Against such inadequate teaching about evil, he offers the facts of history:

> To say the shadow is merely the absence of light is like the famous definition which optimistic people give of evil—that it is nothing but the absence of good, only a mistake. But when one sees how things develop in the world, one sees that the devil is really in there, that there is abysmal evil at work. One cannot explain the destructive tendency in the world as the mere absence of good or as a mistake made in something originally good. . . . And so our shadow really exists.
>
> (Ibid, 213)

The scandal of Yahweh's behavior toward Job, according to Jung, is due mainly to denial of the divine shadow. Yahweh's devotion to an ideal of "perfection" makes him unconscious of the divine relationship to Satan. In addition, and as a natural result of the denial of shadow, God lacks conscious connection to the feminine side of the Godhead, Wisdom or Sophia (*Job*, *CW 11*, §617). Thus Yahweh does not love. Job's suffering begins when God, unaware of the cruelty of his absolute power, pursues a one-sidedly masculine ideal and neglects the feminine side of his nature (Ibid, §620). Justice is not done toward Job until divine unconsciousness itself is mended, not by any act of the intellect (which would not answer Job), but by Christ's suffering on the cross (Ibid, §647).

As our defective God-images support parallel defects in our lives, we must be aware, Jung says, that denial of the "fourth" impoverishes every manifestation of the God-image in Christianity. The Trinity is perfect rather than complete, a one-sidedly masculine image of light and goodness. More dangerously, the "perfection" of the Christian God-image means that Christians have only incompletely faced the complexity of their own nature.

If we dared to "complete" the image of God we worship by admitting all the elements that have been omitted from it, we would risk both our security about God and our confidence in ourselves. But the risk of facing the moral paradox of our own wholeness is one we are bound to take. Moral completeness is a duty that governs not only our construction of God-images (God-as-such not being, after all, subject to inspection) but, more practically, the living of our lives.

The practical and moral thrust of Jung's theological proposal is thus aimed straight at the church. For he argues that anything omitted from the conscious image of God (for example, materiality) becomes subtly drained of importance in human thinking and acting and re-emerges in unconsciously harmful ways. Conscious images of God must begin to include the hitherto neglected elements of life: materiality, the feminine, and the force of evil (Satan). Otherwise, not only is the official God-image incomplete, but these aspects of reality remain unreal to us.

Reflecting our image of God, we tend to live in states of disembodied intellect, denigrating the feminine, forgetting to include in our wisdom the fruits of women's experience. At the same time we deny the inferior or destructive aspects of our lives and become sources of evil in history: the "perfect" and thus unconscious authors of destruction. Jung's criticism of God thus shifts into an attack on "good" people, and finally on all humanity. He sounded the theme of unconsciousness and darkness to the last days of his life, as in his well-known interview with John Freeman in 1959:

> We need more understanding of human nature, because the only real danger that exists is man himself. He is the great danger, and we are pitifully unaware of it. We know nothing of man, far too little. His psyche should be studied, because we are the origin of all coming evil.
>
> ("Face to Face," p.436)

To the "masculine" model of spiritual perfection Jung attributes much mischief performed in and by the church in the name of God: projection, denial, and possession by the reality of repressed evil. What we reject consciously we activate unconsciously, by locating it in others (whom we then despise in good conscience) or giving it domination over us.

As a dramatic illustration of the danger, *Answer to Job* offers the history of the images of Christ and Antichrist. When Christ becomes a "perfect" being disassociated from the imperfection of the ordinary human existence of Jesus, Jung says, his perfection invites the image of Antichrist, the unacknowledged "other half" of the Self-symbol, to spring into existence. This compensating symbol could have been understood as Christ's own shadow, according to Jung, and embraced by the church as a part of the ongoing life of Christ in the world. Instead it has been used as the basis of a hostile projection, identifying as "Antichrist" the church's enemies in the world.

Jung's attitude toward the practice of Christianity is therefore cautious, even when admiring. He observes, for example, that the imitation of Christ, in addition to leading to loving behavior, may easily be an incentive to hatred and division. Hatred between divided Christians, and violence between Christians and outsiders (heathens or heretics), are not merely accidents that accompany any attempt to be spiritually perfect. They are the inevitable shadow side of "perfection" itself.[25] It is because the church is devoted to perfection, Jung asserts, that it condemns those it calls heretics, such as the Gnostics and the medieval alchemists. The way to restore the church's wholeness is to rehabilitate its heterodox minorities. They are, he says, the neglected other side of the collective tradition.

In *Answer to Job* Jung attributes to the biblical God-image a state of internal tension, but also the possibility of change. And the internal oppositions contained in the archetype that underlies the Western God-image, too, are perhaps reconcilable. As in the human process of individuation, God's conscious and unconscious halves may be united.

But Jung warns repeatedly that individuation comes at a cost. Dissolving and reintegrating projections is the most basic and also the most difficult part of the work. In a sense, it *is* the work. To become a morally autonomous individual, he says, is like being crucified (*Aion, CW 9ii*, §79),[26] because carrying one's projections, instead of letting them be carried by others, is painful work. It makes one morally complicated in one's own eyes and according to the canons of conventional goodness. But, as we saw above, Jung claims that through this painful shoulder-ing of the shadow a process of healing and moral integration can begin for the collective.

> If you imagine someone who is brave enough to withdraw all these projections, then you get an individual who is con-scious of a pretty thick shadow. . . . He has become a serious problem to himself, as he is now unable to say that *they* do this or that, *they* are wrong, and *they* must be fought against. . . . Such a man knows that whatever is wrong in the world is in himself, and if he only learns to deal with his own shadow he has done something real for the world. He has succeeded in shouldering at least an infinitesimal part of the gigantic, unsolved social problems of our day. These prob-lems are mostly so difficult because they are poisoned by mutual projections. How can anyone see straight when he does not even see himself and the darkness he uncon-sciously carries with him into all his dealings?
>
> (*CW 11, Psychology and Religion*, §140)

In his criticisms of classic interpretations of Christ, Jung intends to be a reformer but cannot avoid being in some sense a revolutionary. Viewing a transformed image of Christ as essential to the survival and health of the West and ultimately the world, Jung calls religious people to wholeness as John the Baptist called to repentance. Like the prophet, he may not intend to herald a completely new dispensation, but only a return to the deepest truths of the old religion. But he is aware of the radical potential of his message when he accuses the shadowless Christ of obstructing the integration of human experience into our talk about God, and wounding the human capacity for maturity.

According to Jung, the complexity of moral wholeness is a more difficult but also a more practical goal than absolute truth. Absolutes are, by their nature, dangerous to living beings. When "heretics" and "heathens" who resist the domi-nant Christian view of truth are thrown into darkness by the self-appointed guardians of light, the shadow of Christianity becomes darker and the church's blindness to its penchant for violence deeper. If we wish to address the unsolved social problems of our day, we must begin with our own shadow (*Psychology and Religion, CW 11*, §140). If the church wishes to heal the wounds of society, it must repent of its own will to perfection.

Aside from a foray into syllogistic logic where he asserts that *privatio boni* rests on nothing but a reductive fallacy (*Aion, CW 9ii*, §94), Jung's arguments about evil repeat themselves, as he drums away at the same points in publication after publication.[27] His arguments in Chapter V of *Aion* are eclectic, uneven, and to some degree only repeat what earlier lectures have said: Completeness, not perfection, is what the psyche requires; archetypal patterns of wholeness naturally involve quaternity, not trinity; the shadow (the "fourth") must be included in consciousness; all kinds of pairs of opposites are "real"; by denying materiality, evil and the feminine the church leads the faithful to deny their shadow; the church, not Jung, teaches dualism by splitting the opposites.[28]

The psychologically relevant part of Chapter V of *Aion*, the part which best moves the discussion forward, is Jung's observation that people—and Jung identifies especially the Christian faithful—do not take evil seriously enough (*Aion, CW 9ii*, §114). This observation has two levels. First, in the case of individual Christian believers who identify with "the good," the psychological results of disowning the shadow are serious enough. Jung often sees these results in his clinical practice. But at the collective level of the church's authority, Jung sees a moral abdication by official theologians that is far more serious in its results. Jung's outrage on this subject is due to his conviction that the church, through its bishops and theologians, is telling the faithful a lie and undermining the very possibility of individuation that the church ought to support.

Jung's complaint about the *privatio boni* is thus not only that this teaching is false, but that its falsehood should be evident to the church's teachers.[29] They have no business being unconscious; they have only to open their eyes. If they do not, they are guilty of the kind of unconsciousness which is, in Jung's terms, morally wrong.

The *privatio boni* doctrine, he says, fosters just this sort of unconsciousness by causing us to talk about evil frivolously in abstractions, when we should be taking action against it. Considering the horrors of this century alone, we trivialize evil if we talk about it as a privation:

> One could hardly call the things that have happened, and still happen, in the concentration camps of the dictator states an "accidental lack of perfection"—it would sound like a mockery.
>
> *(Aion, CW 9ii, §96)*

3. Evil of Myth, Evil of History

With Jung's moral indignation in mind, it is important that we make a conceptual distinction without which we will never really understand his writings on the problem of evil. We must distinguish in Jung's thought between "evil" in a weak and a strong sense. The first is the evil of myth, the other the evil of outrage. Jung himself never pauses to make this distinction, but his arguments are hopelessly confusing if some such distinction is not made for him.

First, to define the evil of myth: Jung sometimes writes about evil in relation to good as if they were equal and opposite realities. Evil in that sense tends to sound like a benign and interesting presence in the world. Mythically and archetypally, evil and good are in some mysterious sense the left hand and right hand; they need each other like sister and brother in the "syzygy" or the alchemists' "chymical wedding"; they are eternally balanced like yin and yang (*Aion, CW 9ii*, §58,72,104,124). For example, discussing a Gnostic vision, "The Ascension of Isaiah," Jung says:

> It might easily be a description of a genuine yin-yang relationship, a picture that comes closer to the actual truth than the *privatio boni*. Moreover, it does not damage monotheism in any way, since it unites the opposites just as yang and yin are united in Tao. . . .
>
> *(Aion, CW 9ii, §104)*

This is a description of "evil" at the archetypal level. It is the kind of ambiguous "evil" which we meet also in dreams and fairy tales, the "sinister" aspect which seems always to be subjectively present in psychological experience. Jung points out that creative developments emerge when people respect and learn from archetypally evil figures in dreams and visions.[30] Jung holds that the dynamic interplay of the opposites keeps the psychic cosmos in existence. He writes in *Aion:*

> In the end we have to acknowledge that the self is a *complexio oppositorum* precisely because there can be no reality without polarity.
>
> (*Aion, CW 9ii,* §423)

Thus when Jung talks about the "fourth," it is objective, archetypal "evil," evil as a mythical cosmogonic reality, a rightful element which ought to be included in the Trinity, like the feminine principle and the material world.

Evil of myth is not on a par with evil of history. The evil of myth calls forth an intellectual or perhaps an aesthetic response. On the other hand, as one English theologian has observed,[31] a response of outrage, recognizing that the right order of things has been or is about to be violated, is a sign that the subject under discussion must be viewed as genuinely evil, i.e., as an evil of history. Outrage can therefore be taken as a diagnostic sign of historic, as distinct from mythic, evil.

Jung frequently expresses this sort of outrage about events such as bombs, death camps, and other ways humanity works living hell for itself. His alarm in the face of the modern capacity for destruction underlies every word of *Answer to Job.* When he considers these historical events and actions, Jung is no longer talking about evil in its ambiguously creative mythical sense, but rejecting it in its concreteness, with horror, as—in the phrase of another theologian—"that which ought not to be."[32]

This distinction in Jung's writings between mythic and historical kinds of evil has immediate application to the debate with Victor White. White represents an orthodox theology that

Jung criticizes for suppressing "the fourth." What constitutes "the fourth" for Jung may be mythic evil; it may also be the *consciousness of* historical evil. It cannot be the evil of history itself.

Jung does not advocate the acceptance of death camps and other historical evils; he requires that they be taken into conscious awareness and made part of our image of God (from whom all reality rises) and dealt with symbolically and psychologically there. But the way to deal historically with historical evil is to fight against it. Mythic evil must be attended to, so that historical evils may be fought against. Jung blames the ancient doctrine of the privation of good for the tendency in Christians to turn a blind or complacent eye to the moral evil which is present in themselves and in history, and not least in the history of the Christian West. By denying evil its reality (*Wirklichkeit*), we have learned to be complacent about its historical presence.

Perhaps because of this disjunction in his usage of the term "evil," Jung seldom connects his discussions of "the fourth" clearly with his arguments against the *privatio boni*. The arguments occur side by side, but the relation between them is dim. It is useful to draw the connection more clearly than Jung does. The connection in Jung's meaning is conveyed through characteristic Jungian shorthand. As we have seen, Jung's word for a certain kind of theological thought is "medieval," meaning psychologically trinitarian, i.e., lacking the fourth element necessary for completeness.

When Jung calls a person "medieval" he is calling him or her overly spiritual, psychologically primitive and personally unconscious ("Trinity," *CW 11*, §284). With this category in mind, a connection between "the fourth" and "the evil of history" can be drawn. For example, let us look at a cryptic statement in Jung's letter to Irminger, where he uses the loaded word "medieval" while referring to concretely evil acts.

Jung complains about the priest's conversionist tone, and calls Irminger's Catholicism "medieval." He tells him to look at what similarly "medieval" Christians are doing in the world at present:

You want to bring me to the goal and consummation of my life's work, and whither do you lead me? To the very spot from which I started, namely to that still medieval Christianity, which failed not only four hundred years ago but is now more of a failure than ever and in the most terrible way. The German Army is supposed to consist of Christians, and the larger half of it of Catholics at that.

(*Letters I*, p.349)

Jung's allusion to Hitler's army cannot mean that he thinks Catholics are especially to blame for Germany's nationalism; that reading would be an oversimplification. Rather, he is arguing that "medieval" mentality in any form involves overidentification with goodness and thus blinds us—as individuals or groups—to both the ambiguities of history and the dark side of our own complicity. If a lack of self-awareness is characteristic of "trinitarian" persons, unconsciousness only makes them "innocent" accessories to moral wrong.

To be unconscious when one ought to be conscious is a moral defect, Jung teaches. It is wrong to remain cut off from personal shadow, since such innocence avoids self-knowledge and confrontation with personal sin. The shadow ought to be present to consciousness, not as an acted (historical) evil, but in the form of humility, of knowingly bearing one's share of common darkness. When we are out of touch with this "fourth" in our own psyche, we are deprived of the shadow that belongs to us; then we more easily involve ourselves in the evil of history.

Not surprisingly, Jung's strongest argument in Chapter V of *Aion* is based neither on appeals to common sense, nor on logic, but on his experience as a doctor of the psyche. According to Jung, the *privatio boni* includes a lack of realistic self-knowledge in two ways. First, by suggesting to the unwary that evil is "nothing," it helps the spiritually immature to justify "a too optimistic conception of the evil in human nature" (*Aion, CW 9ii*, §113). Second, by denying that God is ultimately responsible for evil, it burdens the morally serious with "a too pessimistic view of the human soul" (*Aion, CW9ii*, §113). He brackets these two together in a way that exposes their internal contradiction, and claims that self-contradiction has been implicit in the doctrine from the beginning:

> As early as Basil we meet with the tendency to attribute evil to the disposition (*diathesis*) of the soul, and at the same time to give it a "non-existent" character. . . . [I]t exists, so to speak, only as a by-product of psychological oversight, and this is such a *quantité négligeable* that evil vanishes altogether in smoke. . . . We *can* act differently if we want to. . . . This prejudice is all the more serious in that it causes the psyche to be suspected of being the birthplace of all evil.
>
> (*Aion, CW9ii*, §114)

According to one erroneous attitude, evil is "nothing," because all things come from God, who is good; so human beings need not worry overmuch about their participation in evil. It is a "mere shadow, a trifling and fleeting diminution of good, like a cloud passing over the sun" as Jung puts it elsewhere (Foreword, *God and the Unconscious*, p.xx). From the other false perspective, evil is a very dreadful "something," but a thing for which human beings must take total responsibility because God—who takes responsibility only for good—has nothing to do with it.

Jung has put his finger on two contradictory but perennially co-existing attitudes toward human life, two false versions of Christian anthropology, either of which a Christian theologian should deplore as strongly as Jung does. As we shall see, Victor White recognizes the seriousness of both problems but denies that the *privatio boni* is to blame.

C. JUNG'S CASE AGAINST GOD

1. "Malum Poenae": *The Scandal of Pain*

The most radical of Jung's revisions of Christian doctrine is his proposal in *Answer to Job* that evil—the evil of history, not just of myth—must be attributed to God as well as to humanity.[33] He views classic Christian theodicy, which defends God's love and goodness against such attribution, as a denial of the kinds of cruelty and injustice that surpass human agency and can only be credited to God. For example, in *Answer to Job* Jung writes:

> We have experienced things so unheard of and so stagger-
> ing that the question of whether such things are in any way
> reconcilable with the idea of a good God has become burn-
> ingly topical. It is no longer a problem for experts in theo-
> logical seminaries, but a universal religious nightmare. . . .
>
> (*Job, CW 11*, §736)

If Jung's language about "completing" the image of God often suggests the inclusion of mythic rather than moral evil, here his attitude of outrage makes it plain that the evil in question is historical. He views God as being intimately involved in, if not solely to blame for, the enormity of human suffering.

As Jung speaks of "evil" in two senses, theologians distin-guish between the evil which is inflicted (*malum culpae*) and the evil which is undergone (*malum poenae*). The former is the fault (*culpa*) of an agent; the latter is the pain (*poena*) of a sufferer. Only the former is properly called "moral evil" or "sin." The latter (e.g., Job's boils, White's cancer) says nothing for or against the sufferer's morality. Innocents, too, are afflicted. Even St. Augustine (whose mature view of human goodness is not sanguine) uses the allegorical names Innocentius and Inno-centia to designate two individuals who suffer severe illnesses (*City of God,* XXII.8).[34]

The question of theodicy is how to retain the doctrine of God's goodness and justice in face of this moral scandal. If one believes in a just and loving ruler of the universe, innocent pain seems an insult to reason. Jung affirms God's responsibility for whatever happens in life; but he denies the compatibility be-tween the historical facts of human suffering and theological claims of divine justice. He grants that God is powerful; he merely denies that God (or the God-image) is all-good, all-just, or all-loving.

Sometimes in his reexaminations of doctrine Jung appeals to classical warrants such as scripture. The closest thing he finds in biblical tradition to an adequate description of the experiences of the two World Wars or nuclear catastrophe is the apocalypse in the book of Revelation. This "terrifying picture," he writes, "makes nonsense of a loving father in heaven and rescuer of mankind. . . ."

> A veritable orgy of hatred, wrath, vindictiveness and blind destructive fury . . . breaks out and with blood and fire overwhelms a world which Christ had just endeavored to restore to the original state of innocence and loving communion with God.
>
> (*Job, CW 11*, §708)

Jung's willingness to call the doctrine of God's love "nonsense" naturally alienates orthodox Christians. It may be, however, that we should not ask Jung to defend *Answer to Job* from a theologically objective viewpoint (propositionally). The ideas it affirms are expressive and subjective, not propositional. Jung himself calls the book "the testimony of the soul" (*Job, CW 11*, §556). He sees himself—and the modern world which is his concern—in the predicament of Job, or of the crucified Christ for whom Job is the prototype. In this situation he understandably speaks with emotion rather than reason and answers "injustice with injustice" (Ibid. §563).

If Jung is taken on his own terms, a case can be made that he is not hostile to things committed Christians—including proficient Thomists—have said. The sympathetic though not uncritical review by Richard Kehoe, written when Jung's *Job* came out in German, is one case in point. Aelred Squire quotes Kehoe in a chapter of his book, *Summer in the Seed*,[35] together with other evidence that Jung's point of view is not entirely hostile to Christian and Jewish theodicy.

In analyzing the book of Job, modern scholars have observed that Job's complaint against God belongs to the Wisdom tradition in Hebrew scripture. Similarly, Jung's treatment of the book is not without its place in Christian tradition. Aelred Squire locates Jung's *Answer to Job* among other modern interpretations of Hebrew Wisdom literature. When placed beside the research of Robert Gordis and Gerhard von

Rad, Squire says, Jung shows an intuitive grasp of a particularly formidable theme in Wisdom literature, "the scandal of God's ways" (*Summer in the Seed*, p.107). Squire quotes von Rad's comment on this theme, the problem of God's involvement in human suffering:

> "It is not suffering, as has so often been said, which has become so utterly problematical, but God."
>
> (*Summer*, p.104)[36]

The notion that the problem of evil is in part dealt with by saying that God justly wills innocent suffering (repellent as this is to reason) is shared by Augustine[37] and Aquinas (*ST* I.49.2). It is condemned, however, by Jung and by some modern theologians who join Jung's outburst against falsely tidy theodicies. Squire points out that theories which pretend to explain "the inherent difficulty of being truly and continuously alive to the world" (*Summer*, p.91) are among the distortions of theology espoused by Job's friends. Thus Squire finds room even in Christian theology for some of Jung's arguments against the *privatio boni*:

> If we can feel some sympathy for the ferocious antipathy Jung felt for the classical theological definition of evil as "the privation of a good that should be present" it will be because, like the psalmist and like Job, we shall recognize that no "explanations," however correct, can ever be a satisfactory answer to life. There are some agonies to which only God can give the answer.
>
> (*Summer*, pp.105f)

This statement demonstrates that when human experience is basic to theology, as Squire treats it here and as White wished to do, Jung's ideas create fewer theological problems. His irate rejection of the *privatio boni* is understood best by theologians who acknowledge the enormity of innocent suffering and recall with Jung (*Job*, *CW 11*, §647), and with Squire (*Summer*, p.104), that even the son of God complained to God that he was forsaken at Golgotha. From the vantage of the cross, so-called explanations of evil are irrelevant and even harmful folly.

Jung calls God to account for God's actions, refusing to consider suffering a meaningless accident or to separate human events from God's doing. In this he reveals a basic theology not much different from that of the Hebrew prophets (Amos, Second Isaiah) who ascribe both good and bad to God, seeing God as the source of all reality (*Summer*, p.105). For Jung as for Job, "only God can answer this desperate cry for meaning. . . . *God himself becomes the answer*" (*Summer*, p.104).

In what may be the central passage of *Answer to Job*, Jung sees the isolation and despair of the crucified Jesus as the first unambiguous sign of God's humanity. In this same moment, however, viewing the cry of dereliction from both sides like any theologian confronting the paradox that Augustine calls the abyss of the cross, Jung sees in Jesus' absolute humanness the sign of his absolute divinity.

> There is no evidence that Christ ever wondered about himself, or that he ever confronted himself. To this rule there is only one significant exception—the despairing cry from the Cross: "My God, my God, why hast thou forsaken me?" Here his human nature attains divinity; at that moment God experiences what it means to be a mortal man and drinks to the dregs what he made his faithful servant Job suffer. Here is given the answer to Job, and, clearly, this supreme moment is as divine as it is human, as "eschatological" as it is "psychological." And at this moment, too, where one can feel the human being so absolutely, the divine myth is present in full force. And both mean one and the same thing.
>
> (*Job, CW 11*, §647)

Jung maintains that in Jesus' cry of dereliction God finally answers, because he finally understands, the suffering of Job. A theologian may acknowledge, then, that Jung's anguish faithfully appeals from God to God. But there is a vital difference between the way most Christians read the resolution to Job's paradoxical law case, and the conclusion Jung draws from it in *Answer to Job*. Christian theologians, treating the Book of Job in its context with other Wisdom literature, usually say that God transcends the humanly conceived opposites of good and evil. Jung sees moral opposition *within* the nature of God.

Jung writes that the speeches of Yahweh depict Yahweh as unconsciously and crudely imposing his perspective on Job by force (*Job, CW 11*, §605f). This depiction proves to Jung that Job's Yahweh is guilty of evil ("evil" not of myth but of history). The Christian reading of the Bible, on the other hand, says that the theophany which concludes the poetic section of the book of Job shows that *human* categories of "good and evil" simply cannot be applied to God in the first place. Job is compelled to fall silent before a mystery which lies beyond the categories of human morality. Squire quotes Richard Kehoe's gentle reproof to Jung:

> "Job is for the moment goaded by the devilish doctrine that God ought to answer to man's conception of good, into maintaining that he answers to man's conception of evil; and it is as though Dr. Jung should intervene, saying, He answers to both; whereas the Bible would say, He answers in himself to neither. And yet to have communion with the absolute transcendent goodness that he is, man must be ready to . . . be himself composed of the two. *None is good but God alone.*"
>
> (*Summer*, p. 106)[38]

One can accept Squire's and Kehoe's reading of the end of Job as a classical Christian interpretation of the human situation. Christians have traditionally recognized that the moral categories of good and evil, as applied to human beings, do not apply to God. We human beings are the ones "crucified on the opposites." But what kind of God must it be who abandons us to that crucifixion? The passionate protest of *Answer to Job* may, and I believe must, be read as Jung's cry of dereliction—a cry that is both vicarious and personal.

2. *The Question of Divine Justice*

To call God good implies (and scriptural revelation also insists) that God is just. Christians claim there is real meaning in these statements. But they also state that God's goodness and justice are not to be interpreted in human terms. The meaning of the words is analogical only; "good" in human terms is not "good" in divine terms.

And yet the two meanings cannot be simply disjunctive; if they were, God's holiness would not be the basis for human holiness. Many theologians (for example, Barth) regard the meanings as related, though not univocally. The subject (God) determines the meaning of the predicate (good, just). So Job recognizes in the end that a mortal may not tell God what divine "justice" is, and lays his hand over his mouth.

Jung's reading, on the other hand, makes humanity the grammatical subject which determines the meaning of these words. Based on Job's experience, God is discovered to be not a "good" personal being, but a *complexio oppositorum*. Human beings know enough about goodness and justice so that they could recognize absolute transcendent goodness if they saw it. They see that God is not absolutely good but a mixture of good and bad. Such a God is by no means less powerful or real. But God (or the God-image) should not be called *summum Bonum*. This is borne out experientially, Jung says, and also therapeutically in the ways discussed: to ascribe unmixed goodness and justice to God is an insult to human suffering and overloads humanity with undeserved blame.

Christian and Jungian perspectives seem to agree that God is powerful, real, and beyond understanding. The issue between Jung and Christian theology is not whether God-as-such can be understood (both say this is not possible), but rather what human beings ought to believe and say about God, and how they shall understand *themselves* in the face of this mysterious power with which, or with whom, they are intimately related.

Jung's letter to White, 30 April 1952, indicates how he sees his relationship to God's undoubted reality and power:

> I don't overlook God's fearful greatness, but I should consider myself a coward and immoral if I allowed myself to be deterred from asking questions.
>
> (*Letters II*, p.61)

Jung and White did not separate, therefore, over matters of conceptual abstraction, but over the question whether people ought to be encouraged to love and trust the ultimate source of reality, which both call God. The implications of each one's teaching on this point could not be avoided or softened by abstractions, neither by theological metaphysics nor by scientific empiricism.

Reading the book of Job against a background of the twentieth century's frightful experience, Jung goes so far in rebuking God for lack of love that finally he reduces God to the image of one of his own primeval beasts, Leviathan or Behemoth.

> The lack of Eros, of relationship to values, is painfully apparent in the Book of Job: the paragon of all creation is not a man but a monster! Yahweh has no Eros . . . .
>
> (*Job*, CW 11, §621)

Similarly, Jung sums up the meaning of Yahweh's speeches to Job, which appear to be saying:

> I, too, am an immoral force of Nature, a purely phenomenal personality that cannot see its own back.
>
> (Ibid., §605)

If we read these statements literally they are simply incoherent to Christian eyes. Even in Jung's context, they are meant to give pause. Jung's outrage seems to reverse the order of creation itself, making God part of Nature and humanity the judge over God.

Jung's tirade at Yahweh makes sense only if he knows God is *not*—and must not be—merely a "phenomenal personality" like Behemoth. If God is, rather, a powerful being who knows the meaning of his acts, but behaves as unconsciously and brutally as if he did not, then Jung (Job's alter-ego) has every right to be angry and to call God to account. Human mortality is minding the store of consciousness, while all around, Yahweh is blowing like a great, amoral gale. This is wrong; it is against the order of the cosmos; it must stop. If God lets his "first son" Satan loose on Job, then God's behavior is not simply "complex" or "natural," but morally bad. God may make excuses for himself and drown out Job's complaints, as Jung believes, by describing himself as a force of nature. But if God were really a Behemoth, neither Job nor Jung would cry out about God's injustice. Jung, like Job, expects God to be just. This expectation fuels his outrage.

3. Teleology and Privation

White tried to make Jung agree that the word for "good" is "wholeness" (*Soul and Psyche*, pp.171f), and that anything which splits or diminishes wholeness is effectively what Jung means by "evil." Jung saw only that White was trying to corral him into the *privatio*, and refused to entertain the notion. Without engaging Jung in a metaphysical argument that would violate the terms in which he presents his case, it may still be possible to show that what he writes in *Answer to Job* and elsewhere provides the basis for a formal agreement with Christian theologians about the "privative" meaning of evil. Such an agreement would be only formal; It turns on the notion of "lack."[39]

Jung's case against God in *Answer to Job* is theologically unorthodox, but its logic is familiar to theology. Jung's Yahweh is cruel to Job because he fails to exercise responsibility for his "first son" Satan, and he lacks Eros, the feminine principle (*Job*, CW 11, §621). He acts like "Behemoth" because he lacks conscious relationship, first to the shadow and second to the anima. Failing to "consult his total knowledge" (*Job*, CW 11, §619), God exhibits a specific kind of privation: God does not love.

It seems to Jung that the poetry of Hebrew Wisdom literature recognizes the urgent need of Yahweh for Sophia, his "companion":

> . . . things simply could not go on as before, the "just" God could not go on committing injustices, and the "Omniscient" could not behave any longer like a clueless and thoughtless human being. Self-reflection becomes an imperative necessity, and for this Wisdom is needed.
>
> (*Job*, CW 11, §617).

Parallels to human psychology are intentional: Jung's Yahweh is a divine psychological being, larger and more powerful than but analogical to human psychological being.

In "Über das Selbst," *Aion, Answer to Job*, and all Jung's writings about the Self, it is clear that his understanding of psychic life is teleological: everything needs to happen in order to wholeness: the "fourth" must be included; completion rather than perfection must be sought; the opposites must be complexly and paradoxically related and kept in tension with each other. This teleological pattern makes it inevitable that Jung should use a logic of "privation," whether he admits it or not. The idea of privation of wholeness, as distinct from movement toward that end, can be located in every aspect of Jung's theory.

For example, in Yahweh as in human beings the psychological wholeness necessary for moral relationship involves the legitimate suffering of self-knowledge. When anyone tries to escape this necessary pain, a situation arises which Jung describes privatively: he calls a neurosis "a substitute for legitimate suffering" (*Psychology and Religion, CW 11*, §129). This unconscious substitution of neurosis for necessary suffering is what Jung elsewhere calls sin. It seems clear that Jung should have allowed White to make his point. Teleology logically implies the possibility of privation or lack—lack of progress, lack of growth, lack of wholeness; and Jung's thought is organized according to the logic of teleology, as White always said it was.

White came to believe that Jung's understanding of evil was "absence of consciousness" (*Soul and Psyche*, pp.296f, note 47). It is difficult to disagree, seeing how important consciousness is to Jung's notion of individuation. Jung writes, for example:

> The moral criterion is *consciousness.* . . . To act unconsciously is evil.
>
> (*Job, CW 11*, §696)

And because the Self is a final cause and an end in itself, there is a natural drive to consciousness. No one can escape this drive, which amounts to a law of nature.

> Nature is not at all lenient with unconscious sinners. She punishes them just as severely as if they had committed a conscious offence.
>
> *(Psychology and Religion, CW 11, §130)*

In *Job* Jung repeats the same warning:

> Before the bar of nature and fate, unconsciousness is never accepted as an excuse; on the contrary, there are very severe penalties for it. Hence all unconscious nature longs for the light of consciousness while frantically struggling against it at the same time.
>
> *(Job, CW 11, §745)*

Dreams compensate for a lack in the psyche; they provide images to correct the dreamer's one-sided consciousness. Jung says of a patient, "The very fact that she can dream such a thing proves that she does not consciously think it" (*Two Essays, CW 7, §21*). To transform a neurosis into the "legitimate suffering" of self-knowledge requires this help from the unconscious, governed and guided by the anticipated wholeness of the Self. Dreams, as gifts from the unconscious to the conscious mind, supply the deficits in the ego's waking orientation; they mediate missing reality and hint at the psyche's potential for wholeness.

Ethical life, however, requires conscious engagement of the ego with the events that meet it—inner or outer. Dreams provide raw material for the ego to confront and assimilate; but confronting their imagery does not automatically create wholeness. Jung thus assigns an ethical value to consciousness, insofar as one is willing humbly to accept the images the psyche sends, attractive or repulsive. But one must go further to assimilate and integrate what is received. Moral consciousness entails more than simply confronting "ego" with "dream"; and unassimilated "acting-out" of psychic images is not the definition of goodness.

Conversely, moral evil is not unconsciousness as such, but the refusal to be responsible for one's own shadow and the fact of incomplete consciousness. In an early lecture by Jung we read this reply to a question about the shadow:

> The whole meaning of sin is that you carry it. What is the use of a sin if you can throw it away? If you are thoroughly aware of your sin, you must carry it, live with it, it is yourself. Otherwise you deny your brother, your shadow, the imperfect being in you.
>
> (*Dream Analysis*, p.76)[40]

If one refuses to "carry one's brother," Jung explains, one shifts the burden to the collective unconscious, making the shadow of one's community more destructive than before.

Psychologically, then, evil may be called a privation of consciousness; but it is specifically the privation of *ethical* consciousness. Full self-consciousness, in Jung's sense, involves responsibility not simply to the demands of personal reality as it affects the ego, but to the demands of transpersonal reality as well. The ego must reckon with others besides itself, both the others in the world and the "others" (shadow, anima/us, Self) within the psyche. In fact, the ego must reckon ethically with as much of the cosmos as it can hold in awareness, given its finitude.

We have seen that Jung speaks of God within the psyche as transcending the finite ego. But whether Jung conceives of God as truly infinite, in the sense that God can outlive the cosmos, is problematic. Part of the burning urgency of Jung's late work seems to arise from his doubt that any reality, including God, can survive the end of human consciousness. This possibility would be the ultimate privation. Absolute historical evil will be the end of history.

So at last the mortal ego takes moral precedence over the internal image of God. It is up to the qualifiedly ethical, moderately conscious, finite human being to save the infinite complex of opposites, which is as likely to do harm as good toward the conscious being on which it depends for its very continuation. In "Late Thoughts" Jung writes:

> . . . with God as a *complexio oppositorum*, all things are possible, in the fullest meaning of the phrase. Truth and delu-

sion, good and evil, are equally possible. . . . We must cling
to the hope that instinct will come to our aid—in which
case God is supporting us against God, as Job long ago
understood.

(Memories, p.341)

Jung has this much hope, but no assurance.

Chapter Six

Theodicy

"The attainment of truth is like
the disentangling of a knot"
Victor White[1]

A. THE METAPHYSICS OF EVIL

Biblical faith has taught from the beginning that there is
only one creator, who is both good and powerful. Thinking
believers in every age have looked around the world and demanded, in that case, where evil comes from and how it en-
dures. Any theology which sees God as the sole creator, perfect
in both goodness and power, eventually feels the need for a
theodicy—an attempt to explain, more or less coherently, why
God's power and goodness should continue to be preached in
the face of evils too serious to ignore. The question poses itself
most forcefully whenever vast numbers of innocents are subjected to torture and death, either through a natural catastrophe like the Black Plague in the fourteenth century, or as a
result of human decision and the silence of witnesses, like the
death camps in our own.

The subject of theodicy is complex and fascinating in itself,
but too broad to explore deeply here. To understand what was
at stake for Jung and White, we need to stay grounded in the
terms of their particular dispute. As we have seen, a classic
teaching of the church, rooted in Greek philosophy, defines evil
as a privation, where "privation" can mean anything from a
mere lessening to a gross distortion. This is the theory that
White finds natural, logical and convincing.

Jung's view of evil in human experience leads him to say,

on the contrary, that if evil has effects and is obviously real (*wirkungsvoll*), then theology should not persist in describing it as a mere "lack." And how, he goes on to ask, can Christians maintain that the nature of God is absolutely good, when evil is such a power in God's world?

While Jung hammered on these questions, Victor White repeatedly tried to demonstrate at least that areas of agreement can exist between classical theodicy and Jung's psychological pragmatism. For example, late in 1954 White sent Jung a long statement from the *Summa Theologiae*, in which Aquinas acknowledges that from a mere human perspective, privations do appear to be real forces, i.e., capable of inflicting real harm. In this passage Aquinas recognizes that from the subjective standpoint evil—though not a "being" (*natura*) in itself—does *seem* as real as a created being. Part of the quotation reads:

> And even a privation, as apprehended, has the aspect of a being, wherefore it is called a being of reason. And in this way evil, being a privation, is regarded as a contrary.
>
> (*ST* I-II.36,1; quoted in *Letters II*, p.213n)[2]

Jung was not enlightened by this contribution to the discussion. He remarked in his next letter to White, "Your quotation from S. Thomas is a marvelous puzzle" (*Letters II*, p.213). Perhaps it is not to be wondered that Jung did not immediately grasp what Aquinas is driving at in this and related texts. White did not attach to this quotation the lexical commentary that would allow Jung to grasp the contrast between "a being" and "a being of reason," or between "a privation" and "a contrary." Such a commentary did not, in fact, exist at the time.

Prompted no doubt by the frustration which both he and Jung were experiencing over these issues, White did his best to sort out some basic concepts for the benefit of nontheologians in his long essay, "Kinds of Opposites," which appeared in the 1955 Jung *Festschrift*. This essay is a sort of lexicon of basic terms, a conceptual overview of the categories of opposition as applied in Aquinas' discussions of evil.[3] Behind White's desire to explain St. Thomas' distinctions was perhaps his hope that Jung might yet be reconciled with Christian orthodoxy. Or, if

Jung could not be persuaded to join him, White on his side would at least have spelled out some reasons why an orthodox Catholic might logically resist Jung's attack on the idea of evil as privation.

White was unsuccessful in persuading Jung to look at the problem of evil through the lens of Aquinas' philosophical categories. In the process of trying, however, he made the categories of opposition in Aquinas more available to modern Thomistic scholarship. A lengthy footnote in the Blackfriars *Summa Theologiae* under I.48.1 (Question 48, "De Malo," the passage where "privation" is first mentioned) seems to be based on White's systematic exploration of Aquinas' system of opposites.[4] With breaks added for clarity, the footnote reads:

> Privation, a key-term. It is not the simple negation of a good, but the absence of one that could and should be present, often, but not necessarily according to a moral judgment. The discussions that follow involve the logic of opposition. Strict opposites are what cannot co-exist in the same thing in the same way at the same times.
>
> The opposition may be of contradictories, namely of a positive and its flat negation, good and not-good; this allows of no half-way position.
>
> Or the opposition may be between the having and the suffering deprivation, this last affecting a subject that should possess the quality in question, thus seeing and blind: this allows of an intermediate term, namely not-seeing, yet we do not say that a stone is blind in any privative sense.
>
> Or the opposition may be of contraries, namely of two positives each of which excludes the other, thus red and blue, presumption and despair; this allows of intermediate conditions.
>
> On relative opposites, e.g., father and son, we need not delay, for the discussion on good and evil will revolve around the second and third type of opposition.
>
> (*ST*, I.48.1, note f, pp.106f)

To these distinctions one could add yet others. In addition to distinguishing between *malum culpae* and *malum poenae*, White follows Aquinas in distinguishing between particular evils and the concept of Evil as an abstraction.

White's essay appeared in the *Festschrift* for Jung's eightieth birthday in 1955. In the preamble White says he will not try to resolve serious deep-seated disagreements "by sweet reasonableness, philosophy, logic, or semantics," but that he hopes to offer "*hermeneutic* assistance in psychological analysis" ("Opposites," p.142). The bulk of the paper discusses the basic categories of opposition which St. Thomas applies in his treatment of good and evil (i.e., contradiction and privation). In the end White turns to the two categories of opposition which St. Thomas does *not* apply to evil, but which implicitly shape Jung's work on the subject (i.e., relative opposites and positive contraries).[5]

To judge by the timing of publication, the essay was probably written while White was in the United States in 1954–1955, or even before he left England. He may well have written it within a few weeks or months of writing the review of Jung's *Job*. The personal tensions he was feeling at the time are suggested by his stress on one category of moral opposition: the absolute either-or choice, in which a person is forced to choose one of two irreconcilable alternatives, sacrificing one to secure the other.

White could have been reflecting on the forced choice that had emerged in his own life between collaboration with the author of *Answer to Job* and work as a Dominican theologian. By publishing "Kinds of Opposites" in Jung's birthday *Festschrift* he directly addressed the blockage in his work with Jung, providing a philosophical vocabulary with which to describe differences between Jung's thought and his own. Internal evidence in the paper suggests, however, that he no longer had much hope of salvaging their collaboration. The article's most important practical contribution may have been to shed new light on the intellectual framework which necessitated his refusal to agree with Jung about evil.

At the very opening of the essay, White reflects that one must distinguish between "reconcilable" and "irreconcilable" opposites. "Not every *Gegensatz*" he remarks, "is a *Gegenteil*" ("Opposites," p.143): not every opposite is a positive contrary. Some things called opposites can coexist comfortably in time and space; others exclude each other in the real world. Such opposites can be held together in the mind as abstractions, but they cannot both be acted upon.

For example, in Jungian psychology there are pairs of "opposites" such as ego and shadow, persona and anima/us, which can and must be reconciled for the sake of wholeness. But these are not the only kinds of opposites Jung recognizes; for Jung himself invokes the psychological necessity of "sacrifice" in cases where duties conflict. Some opposites cannot be brought together. An either-or choice must be made, the ego's desires laid aside, and the resulting pain accepted.[6]

White urges that it is essential to recognize the difference between an opposition within the psyche that allows reconciliation, and one that demands an either-or choice:

> More than one analysis has become "stuck," or issued in agonizing and insoluble conflict, because a pair of opposites has been regarded by the ego . . . as complementary and capable of "adding up" to a totality, when in fact it was of such a sort that the positing of one "content," so far from requiring its complement in the positing of the other, completely destroys it. The reverse process is of course familiar in the rationalizing of repression.
>
> ("Opposites," p.143)

Perception of a situation in terms of opposition is sometimes a way to achieve sufficient clarity to make a realistic moral choice. By a process of inner dialectic one sorts out what is and what is not possible, or true. So the categories of opposition can have important practical implications:

> Choice and decision only *can* be made . . . after the opposites have been interiorly confronted. The point may be trite and obvious; but its consideration may be recommended to those who suppose that they are called to "live the opposites," not only interiorly and in introversion, but also in the extrovert life of external behaviour and moral conduct.
>
> ("Opposites," p.149)

To discuss the issues from White's perspective is challenging, too, because he sometimes lacks clarity about what Jung is
saying. He seems unsure, for example, under which category of
opposition to put Jung's understanding of evil. The term "privation" applies to experienced evil all in its concrete particularity.
What we have called the "evils of history," White must call,
strictly speaking, privations.

Significantly, however, White recognizes nothing that corresponds to Jung's "evil of myth." When Jung says that evil and
good are logically and mutually necessary poles of reality, he
makes evil the relative opposite of good. White agrees with
Aquinas, on the other hand, that relative opposition has nothing to do with the relationship between good and evil. This
means that Jung's "evil of myth" occupies a philosophical category to which White attributes no importance in the context of
the debate about evil.

Also, many of White's doubts about Jung's concepts of the
shadow and the Self are related, it seems, to persistent uncertainty about whether Jung intended to reify evil. If evil is re-
ified, or seen as a concrete reality, it is on a par with good as a
permanent part of creation. Reification of evil seems to be implied in some of Jung's arguments; but White cannot decide
whether Jung fully understands the implications of making evil
a *res*, i.e., a real thing in the real world.

Jung is not much concerned with systematic pigeonholes.
White is much concerned with them, as he addresses his own
intellectual court of appeals in an effort to demonstrate whether
the distance between his thought and Jung's can be bridged. If
not, he is faced with a choice between mutually exclusive claims.
Politically speaking, as it appears, White was punished for having
made a wrong choice between Catholic orthodoxy and Jungian
psychology. His association with Jung had caused him to be dis-
credited as a theologian. But what answer did White's conscience
give? This question gives his analysis of the opposites its peculiar
poignancy.

The formal categories of opposition are spelled out in
more detail below, to show how White's reading of these concepts defined his stakes as a theologian and influenced his
dispute with Jung. The tools of White's trade may cause some

readers serious frustration if they share Jung's preference for immediate experience. We have to follow White here into territory that can be hard going without a philosophical background, remembering that he upholds the usefulness of discursive reason, as well as a personal experiential knowledge base.

1. Contradiction

Definition: Contradictories are mutually exclusive terms, allowing no middle or halfway position. This category has a kind of binary precision, like a switch which can be either on or off. Contradictory opposites consist of a positive and its negation, and "they can in no sense be constituents of a whole, for the opposite is the sheer negation of a positive: it adds nothing whatever to it, it only subtracts it in its own totality, and results in zero" ("Opposites," p.145).

As abstractions, and strictly as abstractions, good and evil are treated as contradictories by Aquinas. This means, as White explains in *Soul and Psyche*, that when St. Thomas uses the word evil abstractly, it is defined as the strict negation of good, having no independent meaning or existence of its own. This is probably the description of evil which makes Jung angriest, because it seems to him that theology makes evil abstract and thereby reduces it to "nothing." To this perception White replies:

> But most Christians—and not only Christians—will protest that Jung has radically misunderstood the very nature of evil. Since the great Greek philosophers, it has generally been understood that evil as such does not and cannot exist. It is not in itself a reality, an *ousia*, a substance or a thing; and badness cannot be a quantitative part of reality. Bad people, things, inclinations and wills are certainly very real and very powerful, and it is at our dire peril that we pretend to ourselves that they are not. But their badness consists, we find on examination, not in some positive entity or reality which they possess, but in the absence from them of some positive entity or reality which we account as good.
>
> (*Soul and Psyche*, pp.152f)

Evil as a "contradiction" of good is never concrete and particular. It is only an abstract negative, corresponding to an abstract positive.

> Good and evil, in the abstract, are indeed opposites, but they prove on reflection to be not two positive contraries—*äquivalente Gegensätze* as Jung calls them—but contradictories.
>
> (*Soul and Psyche*, p.153)

Contradictories permit no compromise. They force a choice (speak or keep silent; stay or leave). When one faces opposites of this kind, one must choose, one must act one way or another. One cannot do both, or compromise by choosing a "third thing" that lies between them. Trying to temporize with such choices is likely only to drag one into a paralysis of self-deception:

> To mistake a contradictory opposite for a complementary one is a delusion, which can in practice only result in confusion and frustration. . . . [T]he delusion is not uncommon when a "middle way" is sought in some dilemma in which the two opposites are utterly irreconcilable in practice, and a situation demands a decision (and all that it entails) which the subject is unable or unwilling to make.
>
> ("Opposites," p.145)

The life-or-death quality of the choice between contradictory opposites is confirmed when White gets to the end of the essay. There he illustrates by saying that Christ in Gethsemane faced a decision between irreconcilable contradictory opposites. When he understood that God would not let the cup of suffering pass from him, Jesus knew he must sacrifice, as St. Thomas puts it, either his divine or his human will.

In his effort to probe the nature of Jesus' Passion, White follows Aquinas, who thinks that in his confrontation with this choice between contradictories, Jesus experienced no inner conflict (*contrarietas*) of wills (*ST* III.18.5,6). An inner conflict would imply that there was some degree of unconsciousness; but Jesus was fully conscious of the decision facing him. Knowing what was at stake on both sides he could make the sacrifice with agony, White writes, but without internal conflict.[7]

> This is so, Aquinas explains, because conflict only arises when opposites are willed or sought from one and the same point of view in every respect; and this in its turn arises only from misunderstanding—or unconsciousness. . . . But, just because the opposites had been interiorly confronted and experienced, the decision to sacrifice one to the other was possible.
>
> ("Opposites," p.150)

After citing the "decisive action and sacrifice" of Christ, who could deal with irreconcilable contraries through the integrity of his interior process and his full consciousness of the choice, White concludes:

> The consideration is perhaps not entirely irrelevant to those who, with or without aid from analytical psychology, find themselves tormented between opposites.
>
> ("Opposites," p.150)

The personal application of White's last statement, referring to the agony of deciding between a divine and a human calling, should not escape the reader.

The agony of such a sacrifice is not viewed by White as a "moral evil" (*malum culpae*) any more than Jesus' decision to undergo crucifixion is attributed to "evil" in his moral choice. But it entails the natural evil of unavoidable suffering (*malum poenae*). If both members of a pair of opposites are "good" and make legitimate claims, as in all cases where duties conflict, one good interferes with and denies another. Suffering (voluntarily undertaken or involuntarily undergone) can then result from the impinging of real goods in the finite universe.

Interestingly, on this point Jung agrees wholeheartedly. There are moral dilemmas that the ego cannot resolve but can only suffer, suspended between conflicting duties as if crucified. Such opposition is the characteristic mark of individuation, the psychic process dominated by the Self:

The realization of the self . . . leads . . . to a real suspension between opposites (reminiscent of the crucified Christ hanging between two thieves). . . . Whenever the archetype of the self predominates, the inevitable consequence is a state of conflict vividly exemplified by the Christian symbol of crucifixion—that acute state of unredeemedness which comes to an end only with the words "consummatum est."

(*Aion, CW 9ii,* §123,125)

2. Privation

Definition: "Privation" is the chief category used in traditional accounts of particular evils. Most of Aquinas' discussions of evil are found under this heading, evil being a more significant theological problem in the concrete than in the abstract. The first member of a privative pair has positive existence or being. Its being signifies its participation in goodness, since "all being is good." The second member is defined by reference to the first, as a loss, defect or distortion. It can be said to "exist" only in its dependence on the thing to which it is compared.

As we have seen, Jung strenuously rejects Aquinas' assertion that "Evil is not a being, whereas good is a being" (*ST* I.48.1). Not only in myth but in history, Jung maintains, evil is terribly real (*Letters I,* 541). On this issue White finds it necessary to speak with equal energy, to defend the classic doctrine.

Following Augustine and Aquinas, White sees the concrete evils of human experience as "real," but only in the sense that they derive from and have power to hurt real beings. As Aquinas knows, evil may be perceived as a real existing force from the human perspective; but it does not share in being in the full philosophical sense. Being is—under the sovereignty of God—coterminous with Good. Good therefore, by definition, cannot be said to include evil, as if evil were a part of it, without incoherence.

In White's 1950 essay, "Devils and Complexes" (*God and the Unconscious,* Chapter X) he draws out the implications of the principle that goodness and being are one and the same.

"*Bonum et ens convertuntur*—the 'real' and the 'good' are interchangeable"—affirmed the ancient philosophers. So far as their natures and beings are concerned, the demons are very good indeed, and St. Thomas favors the view that Lucifer or Satan is by nature the very noblest and highest and most Godlike of all God's creatures. But—*corruptio optimi pessima*—the badness of the best is the worst sort of badness.

(*God and the Unconscious*, p.183)

White cannot adopt Jung's idea of completeness; but he tries to demonstrate that the concept of privation need not induce anyone to ignore the reality and horror of evil, as Jung says it does. Privation can be a corruption of good, as well as a subtraction from it. Its constant feature, however, is that one member of the opposition is defined negatively by reference to the positive character of the other:

It is characteristic of this kind of opposites, that whereas the positive content can be thought of and defined without reference to the privation, the reverse is impossible.

("Opposites," p.147)[8]

Among other passages on the subject, White states his response to Jung on the *privatio boni* in a long footnote in Chapter V of *God and the Unconscious*. He replies to a whole range of points made in Jung's essay on the Trinity and in *Aion*, as well as to questions Jung put to White over the course of their collaboration. White attempts here simply to define terms and set the historical record straight. "Of the position of traditional Catholic thought as formulated by Aquinas," White says, "the following may be briefly noted":

(1)   There is no formal dogma of the Church on the subject.

(2)   But inasmuch as the meaning of basic human words, and those indicative of fundamental human values, is at stake, the matter cannot be lightly dismissed as an academic logomachy.

(3)   As Jung himself shows in *Aion*, the conception of evil as a privation of good is asserted by the Fathers of both the Eastern and Western church.

(4) They do not deny, as might a Christian Scientist, the reality of evil (on the contrary, they vigorously affirm it);[9] their concern is with the further question: In what does that reality consist? Or, what is it that constitutes **x** to be "evil" and not "good"?

(5) Their answer is that it is always the *absence* (the *privatio*, not the negation) of a *real* good from a *real* subject— evil has no positive existence in itself—as blindness is real (but consists in the *absence* of sight from a real man) or darkness is real (but consists in the absence of light).

(6) This *absence* may indeed *result from* a presence (as the presence of a cataract causes the absence of sight—and the "better" the cataract the "worse" the sight) but does not consist in it.[10]

(7) This conception is no *a priori* "metaphysic," but is empirically verifiable by an *analysis of meaning* whenever the words "good" and "evil," or their equivalents are used.

(God and the Unconscious, pp.75f, note)

White explains that the privative opposites are distinct from contradictories, because "here we have, not the sheer negation of an affirmative, but the absence of something positive from something positive" ("Opposites," p.146). The classic example is darkness, which is "simply the absence of light from a subject (the atmosphere) which is capable of being either with or without light. Because the subject is real, the dark is real" ("Opposites," p.146).

White would like Jung to understand that the church (Jung's suspicions to the contrary) did not first invent the idea of privation in order to shore up its doctrine of the goodness of God. Indeed, church thinkers did not originate the idea at all. "Privative opposites play a fundamental role in the natural philosophy of both Plato and Aristotle," he states ("Opposites," p.146). In classical philosophical usage, as in theological, the privative opposites do not together, and simultaneously, add up to anything. The supplying of what had been absent indeed "complements" or fulfils the subject, as when the dark atmosphere becomes light, or the blind man receives sight; but there is not, and cannot be, any reciprocal process. When the light goes out, or a man becomes blind, there is only subtraction, no addition.

("Opposites," p.146)

Thus, when anyone speaks of privative opposites, unlike contradictories, it is not a case of two equally positive and real options. Rather, there is a positive quantity, a thing or characteristic or power which "ought to be present"; and there is a phenomenon of reduction, negation, deformity, or destruction. The evil of privation may be any disorder in or divergence from what is normally needed and wanted. It is always a diminishment, with respect to some norm. Aquinas identifies the basic ingredient of evil as a condition of *lacking* what should be present:

Evil is quite different from being and non-being pure and simple, for it is neither like having a form nor like simply not having it, but like being found wanting.

(*ST* I.48.2)

In Jung's *Letters* we see a somewhat comic example of the tangle that quickly ensued when White and Jung tried to communicate about these issues from their respective philosophical starting places. White wrote to Jung in 1952 that an ordinary example of privation is when "I call an egg 'bad' because it *lacks* what I think an egg ought to have" (*Letters II*, p.59n). Jung answered him that a bad egg is not "less real" than a good egg; it has a character of its own, and even has additional characteristics which the good egg was missing.

Jung's understanding of what White meant by "privation" was "reduction of goodness" in rather a literal sense. His reading of Catholic theology on this point was reductive. If communication between the two collaborators had not become so strained, White might have explained that *privatio* means not only "loss" but also distortion and corruption. It would have been possible for him even to argue that Jung agrees with Aquinas' theory of the defectibility of (finite) good and the derivative quality of evil.

For example, Jung is speaking of what Aquinas calls defectibility, when he writes:

> A bad egg is not characterized by a mere decrease in goodness. . . . It develops among other things H_2S, which is a particularly unpleasant substance in its own right. It derives very definitely from the highly complex albumen of the good egg and thus forms a most obvious evidence for the thesis: Evil derives from Good. . . . In this interpretation Evil is far from being a *me on*.
>
> (*Letters II*, p.59)

Jung does not realize that to call evil derivative from good (provided one means *finite* good, as Jung does here) approximates to the teaching of Aquinas. But he wants to go a great deal further, of course, than saying that finite evil derives from a finite good. He follows that train of thought to its logical extreme, and says that the greatest evil derives from the highest good, i.e., God; thus he concludes that an infinite good, corrupted, produces an infinite evil.

> The "decomposition" theory would lead to the ultimate conclusion that the Summum Bonum can disintegrate and produce H_2S, the characteristic smell of Hell. Good then would be corruptible, i.e., it would possess an inherent possibility of decay. That obviously confirms my heretical views.
>
> (*Letters II*, p.59)

His last phrase sarcastically raises the question whether a faithful Christian is allowed to be logically consistent. It would be hard to deny Jung the right to raise his question; classic theodicies, too, get into logical knots.

Aquinas knows that finite good is corruptible; there are degrees of "defectibility" in the universe (*ST* I.48.2). For him, however, it is clear that the Summum Bonum is not finite, and that infinite being is indefectible—not liable to change, positive or negative. The claim of God's infinite indefectibility is one of the places where Aquinas and White decisively part company with Jung who, concerned with images of God in the psyche, is certain that God undergoes change.

White tried again in *Soul and Psyche* to show Jung that privation has reality as an experience. Referring to *Summa Theologiae* IaIIae.36.1, he wrote:

> Aquinas himself recognizes that to the unreflecting apprehensions of the psyche, the privation which is evil . . . has the character of a certain kind of entity— and is a positive contrary.
>
> (*Soul and Psyche*, p.156)

To grant that evil seems real to the "unreflecting apprehensions of the psyche" does not, however, meet Jung on the epistemic ground where he stands, namely the subjective experience by which we know what is real. Evil seems real, says the pragmatist, because it is. At any rate, the human experience of evil is as real as the human experience of good. Against the frustrating background of these arguments, White tries in his essay "Kinds of Opposites" to clarify the difference between the realities of being and deprivation.

A thing that lacks what it "should have," White explains, is corrupted or distorted. We call such a thing evil and know it as real, since it still has the same reality it started with. Its character may be skewed, but it continues in existence. Becoming evil does not mean it loses its power to be or to move. So a child is born with a congenital defect that causes blindness, an evil that it suffers (*malum poenae*). "Because the subject is real," White says, "the dark is real" ("Opposites," p.146).

We could add, "Because a bad egg is still a real egg, it gives off a real smell." The continuous reality of the subject also makes privation "real" (*wirklich*), in the sense that it has an impact on other beings. The *Wirklichkeit* of evil consists in the fact that privation hurts both the being it infects and others. This argument would seem to provide sufficient grounds for a practical agreement with Jung about the evil of history.

What it fails to address, because it cannot conceive, is Jung's notion of the evil of myth, i.e., the missing fourth which Jung says ought to be present in the God-image. Jung predicates this idea of completeness on the anthropomorphism he attributes to all talk about God. But White's Thomism makes an absolute disjunction between the indefectible Being of God and the beings of creation. The infinite difference between God and the creation rules out any talk of privation in the one unchangeable Being who is the beginning and end of all else that is.

Here we can finally see the chasm of incomprehension that was bound to open, gradually and ineluctably, between the two men. Jung is devoted to and in the grasp of a God whose changeability and humanlike complexity are essential elements of the archetype's power to convince. White cannot be related as a Thomistic theologian to such a familiar, Feuerbachian God.

3. Relative Opposites

Definition: "Relative opposites" are irrelevant to Aquinas' discussion of evil, but central to Jung's, especially to the alchemical metaphor of the marriage of opposites (*Aion*, *CW 9ii*, §116f, etc.). These opposites include pairs like moon-planet and husband-wife, in which each part is equally real and neither can be described independent of the other. White remarks,

> Such pairs are truly and obviously complementary; not only in the sense that together they constitute a whole, but also in the sense that each in the pair is dependent on the other in its very singularity.
>
> ("Opposites," p.147)

The categories "privative" and "relative," however, refer to different kinds of opposites:

> Light, sight and (it has been generally held) the Good are intelligible and can be . . . defined and described without

mention of the dark, blindness or evil. These latter (precisely because not positive) cannot be so treated without reference to the opposites of which they are privations.

(Ibid)

According to White, the traditional view of relative opposites makes them the kind of equivalent pairs "of which each entails the other, and which can neither be thought of nor can exist without the other" ("Opposites," p.147). He cites father-son, husband-wife, lover-beloved. Then he adds,

> This category plays a fundamental role in the elaboration of the theology of the Trinity; and results wherever processes of birth (*generatio*), physical or symbolic, take place.
>
> ("Opposites," p.147)

Jung frequently groups many polarities together—light and dark, heat and cold, high and low, good and bad. He lists these pairs along with left and right, sun and moon, the astrological syzygy, husband and wife, sister and brother, and so on (*Aion, CW 9ii*, §84ff). All these opposites, he says, are "equivalent pairs" (*äquivalente Gegensätze*) which "always predicate each other" (*Aion, CW 9ii*, §84, §98).

Of the three types of opposites discussed so far, only the type known as "relative opposites" involves pairs in which both members must be called good and necessary. The final category is a subset of this one. White suggests that Jung's reification of evil may come under the classification of "contraries."

4. Contraries:

Definition: "Some, but not all, relative opposites are also true *contraries*," White writes ("Opposites," p.147). Positive contraries, also called polar opposites, comprise a wide range of phenomena. "Aristotle restricts the term to extreme opposites in any class" ("Opposites," p.147). "Contrariety" includes such various oppositions as joy-sorrow, one-many, black-white, where both members in the pair participate fully in reality. Unlike relative opposites, the contraries can be defined independent of each other. They also permit of intermediate conditions.

Since Jung sees the cosmos held together by the tension of polar opposition (e.g., *Aion, CW 9ii*, §423) the category of contraries is especially relevant to Jung's writing on good and evil. It is here, according to White, that Jung makes his basic category error. By making good-and-evil into relative opposites, White argues, Jung reifies evil, putting it ontologically on a par with good. Paradoxically, because of this error Jung, according to White, finally cannot differentiate evil from good (*Soul and Psyche*, p.156). This is because if one thinks of evil as one member of an equally-matched pair (husband-wife, brother-sister, sun-moon) one inherently approves of each member of the pair. One wishes both halves of the polarity to continue in existence. But can "evil" be celebrated as a natural and necessary part of creation?

In view of this logical incoherence, White rejects Jung's use of *das Böse* as a concrete noun. From the perspective of Christian faith, he writes, "evil" should be an adjectival noun for a particular bad thing ("this evil," "that evil") or else an abstraction ("badness"). Evil hypostasized becomes, he points out, a kind of "good." Alternatively, it forces one into the Manichaean dualism that attributes part of creation to a malevolent god. Evil is never hypostasized in the ancient texts, White declares. As a result, Jung "easily makes nonsense" of statements from the Greek and Latin Fathers (*Soul and Psyche*, p.297, note 52).

Viewed from another direction, however, the category of contraries illumines a place where White's theological tradition and Jung's psychology share a certain practical wisdom. Aquinas points out that privation can arise precisely because there is equal reality on both sides of a pair of contraries. The privation which occurs when they interfere with each other is a *poena* which involves no *culpa*. A person needs sleep, for example, but works eighteen hours a day on a necessary task. Thus one kind of good (work) interferes with and deprives another (sleep). This innocent privation turns on the fact of finitude: two things cannot occupy one space at the same time. One crowds out the other, as both goods seek their conflicting ends.

For St. Thomas, of course, the *poena* which results from a conflict of duties is far less troublesome than the *culpa* which is an active rebellion against God (*ST* I.48.6). The suffering when two finite goods interfere with each other is nevertheless called "evil" because, Aquinas says, quoting Augustine, it is the general mark of evil to injure (*ST* I.48.5).[11]

One feature of Aquinas' thought here clearly supports Jung's views about God and the soul. Aquinas writes that when the pain of privation is for the sake of an uncreated, higher good (*ST* I.48.6), one may say the pain (which is evil) is God's doing. So for Aquinas the infliction of pain may be consistent with love. Like the hand of a surgeon, he says, "Divine wisdom inflicts pain to prevent fault" (*ST* I.48.6). God can thus be said to "cause evil," but only in this qualified sense.

The divinely necessary suffering that results from facing the conflict between two goods is, as we have seen, an idea not uncongenial to Jung. For Jung the phenomenon of sacrifice represents a meaningful and appropriate suffering, especially when undertaken consciously. Describing the ego's sacrifice of its interests as a response to the Self's call to wholeness ("Transformation Symbolism in the Mass," *CW 11*, §397ff), Jung implies that psychological crucifixion is rightly undergone by the ego for the sake of the Self. Similarly, Aquinas says that sometimes the human will is sacrificed by—and for the sake of—the divine wisdom.

B. WHITE'S ANSWER TO JUNG

1. The Struggle with Shadow

In his paper "Kinds of Opposites," White refers to an earlier, still unpublished paper in which he gives a defense of the *privatio boni* ("Opposites," p.146n). That paper, titled "Good and Evil," had been delivered in 1953 to the Analytical Psychology Club in London.[12] The text of this lecture was informally published in 1966 by *Harvest*, with permission from White's regular publisher. It contains both autobiographical and case material, which probably accounts for its remaining unpublished while White was living.

In "Good and Evil" White challenges Jung's contention that evil and good must be viewed as equally real opposites, i.e. (to use White's term) as positive contraries. White knows he cannot prove to his audience that evil is necessarily to be viewed as a privation of good, nor that it lacks ultimate reality, nor that God is all good and goodness must ultimately be sovereign. But he offers to show that the warrants for such positions are solid. The church's wisdom can bear to be questioned, and can muster the kind of experiential evidence that Jung usually respects.

White's position rests on warrants from a wide range of sources: common sense, the history of Jewish and Christian philosophy, common linguistic usage, and passages from Jung's own writings. In addition he brings psychological evidence of a kind he expects his audience to treat especially seriously, since it arises from the direct experience of an individual. Here White appeals to the authority of a Jungian epistemology, for he recounts the dream of a woman, age thirty, who he says "knew nothing and would have cared less about the *privatio boni*" ("Good and Evil," p.30). The end of the dream, as White received it from the woman, seems overwhelmingly affirming to the theory of the *privatio boni*:

> . . . Then there came a great light which dazzled and yet did not dazzle, a giant light sun of ravishing sweetness and enamouring virtue—purifying by a fire that did not burn; and in this moment or moments, for it may have been seconds or hours, the "struggle between good and evil" became an absolutely meaningless phrase—there was *only* goodness, and of such irresistible attraction that even the slightest resistance or temptation to resistance was inconceivable. . . .
>
> ("Good and Evil," p.30)

As one would guess, White takes the young woman's dream as empirical evidence from the unconscious that

> beyond the *opposites* of good and evil is not evil, nor some combination of good and evil, no ambivalent Self or God in

which evil yet remains evil, but rather, as traditional philosophy and theology has always said, "only goodness": a summum bonum in which, just because evil is an absence of
good, evil does not and cannot exist.

("Good and Evil," p.30)

Although White's reading of the dream is plausible, it need
not compel agreement in a Jungian context. Jungian dream
interpretation would assume that, since the dream image is overwhelmingly positive and spiritual, the conscious attitude of the
dreamer had doubtless been materialistic and negative, resis-
tant toward the good which is—after all—a real part of the Self.
The unconscious naturally compensates for a dreamer's conscious attitude, providing whatever part of the truth the ego has
been missing. So a follower of Jung could agree that the conclusion of the dream represents one aspect of the *complexio oppositorum*; he would not be forced to grant that it reveals the entire
nature of the Self.

At the end of his lecture, White goes beyond the realm of
dream imagery to recall his own personal experience in Jungian
analysis. He explains that his very first encounter with analysis
convinced him that the concept of "privation" had more than
academic relevance. This self-disclosure is so unusual in the
context of the theologian's usual work, and what it reveals is so
important in assessing his reading of Jung's theory, that it may
be useful to quote the concluding passage in full.

When first I came, some twelve years ago, into the world
of analytical psychology, I had no idea of Dr. Jung's views
on good and evil. Certainly I had not myself any strong
attachment to the *privatio boni*. I was, of course, well acquainted with the idea: it had seemed sound, logical commonsense, but my assent to it had been purely intellectual,
or what Newman called notional. It had never struck me
as having any vital, personal importance to myself and to
my problems. It was precisely my own experience of analysis—limited as I know it has been—that taught me
otherwise.

("Good and Evil," p.30)

White's experience, which had been confusing and overwhelming, suddenly made sense to him, precisely because he understood it now in terms of privation. The church's traditional teaching about evil was not only logically coherent but intuitively consistent with events in his inner life:

> I have it on record that at my very first analytical interview, I was told that the *whole* psyche was all right, and so were its several parts and functions, but that my dreams showed (as indeed they did) that these parts and functions were disordered, unbalanced, unintegrated. Whether or not I understood my analyst correctly, the penny dropped: this was exactly what my theological mentors had told me was evil in fallen man—a disorder, a disintegration of the parts and functions of the soul. The Fall had brought it about, not that there was anything wrong with them in themselves, but that they were deprived of harmony, order and integration.
>
> ("Good and Evil," p.31)

White argues that if the Jungian understanding of goodness can be equated with the concept of wholeness (White here calls it "positive integrity"), then there must be a privation corresponding to it, i.e., a lack of wholeness.

> I at once jumped to the conclusion—evidently too hastily—that the old idea that the good of man was a positive integrity, his evil a privation of that good, was a governing principle in analytical psychology also: the basic pattern of the integration process. This seemed confirmed when I learned the Jungian technical jargon, and heard talk of "positive" aspects and "negative" aspects in a sense which seemed indistinguishable from good aspects and bad aspects. . . . All seemed to confirm the same interpretation. The shadow, it soon appeared, was not wholly evil; on the contrary, it was basically good, the holder of the most precious values; what was evil, harmful and dangerous about it sprang not from its positive content, but from its privations, its lack of consciousness, light, attention, love, justice to its rightful claims and function within the life of the whole personality.
>
> ("Good and Evil," p.31)

As late as 1953 White was still thinking of the shadow as being fundamentally available for reclamation. This passage and its internal self-interpretation provide hints about sources of difficulty in White's dialogue with Jung.

White's view of the shadow may be adequate to what Jung calls the personal shadow. As far as the shadow is capable of being brought into relationship to consciousness, Jung says, it is indeed basically good, and its apparent darkness comes from the fact that the ego finds it inferior and undesirable. But for Jung the shadow also includes an impersonal, archetypal core of absolute evil and darkness, which corresponds to the extremes of nature sometimes called "acts of God," such as hurricanes and volcanic eruptions. This level is simply not accessible to integration with consciousness (*Aion, CW 9ii,* §19); it *cannot* be assimilated by the ego. The ego can only fearfully acknowledge the reality of this dark unknowable force, and avoid its outbreaks as well as possible. There is no integration of archetypal shadow. When people ally themselves as moral agents with such extreme powers of destruction, what follows is a historical incarnation of archetypal shadow, or absolute evil. Apparently in 1953 White had not grasped the moral ambiguity of the Self; for he did not realize that the archetype could never be freed of its shadow side.

The magnitude of this misunderstanding seems somewhat odd, for by the time White gave this lecture he had studied "Über das Selbst," *Aion, Answer to Job,* and the essays on the Trinity. He knew Jung's reservations about the image of Christ as "all light." And yet he maintained that the "complete archetypal Self" can be delivered from darkness:

> I do not, you must understand, claim to have integrated my shadow; but I still cannot understand what such integration can mean if it is not its deliverance precisely from its shadowness, its darkness. By this it would surely cease to be shadow, as surely as it does in the complete archetypal Self?
>
> ("Good and Evil," p.31)

White's Thomistic theological categories apparently formed such a powerful interpretive lens that they prevented his absorbing the import of Jung's definition of deep, archetypal shadow, which Jung says forms an ineradicable part of the God-image and shares in the reality of creation. When White fully grasped this facet of Jung's thought he finally abandoned his effort to synthesize Jung's psychology with the theology of St. Thomas.

2. Rejection of the Self

For some time in the collaboration, White thought he could separate two aspects of Jung's "Self" concept and hold one while rejecting the other. The Self as the central symbol of human wholeness, the concept of a paradoxical and morally ambivalent transcendent function in the psyche—this presented no problems. But to say that the Self is psychologically equivalent to God (or the God-image)—this portion of Jung's thought could not be harmonized with White's theology. The problematic issue was before him from 1948 on; its outlines were suggested even in 1932. Full realization of the impasse, however, dawned slowly.

In 1949 White challenged Jung on this subject seriously for the first time in print, when he took the publication of *Eranos-Jahrbuch 1948* as an occasion to discuss "Über das Selbst." His review, "Eranos: 1947, 1948,"[13] singles out Jung's key lecture for judicious praise and pointed criticism. Jung supports the preacher and apologist, White says, by demonstrating the objective psychological value inherent in the Christ-image. Since the modern Western world is so largely indifferent to religious symbols, Catholic theology can only applaud the central thrust of Jung's recent work:

> For modern Western man, whether he "believes" or not, whether he likes it or not, the archetypal image of the Self is inevitably embodied in the figure of Christ. No other embodiment has living power for him, and no scepticism or repudiation on the conscious level can rid modern man of the fact that, psychologically speaking, Christ "is in us and we in him."
>
> ("Eranos: 1947, 1948," p.398)

Theologians, he adds, should be grateful for Jung's

presentation of the relevance of Christianity to the individual and social conflicts of modern man . . . [and for his]
challenging recall to a fundamental Christian truth which
has been too much neglected by theologians and preachers.

(Ibid, p.399)

At this early stage of their collaboration White raises no
objections to Jung's interpretation of the antithetical pair, Christ
and Antichrist. He agrees with Jung's observation that the Self,
as the archetype of human wholeness, includes good and bad,
spirit and matter, masculine and feminine—in short, the whole
complex of opposites. He welcomes Jung's suggestion that the
development of Christology offers an "enormous advance in the
differentiation of the human psyche." When collective consciousness accepts the religious symbol of Jesus Christ as a sinless man,
"all Light, and 'in whom there is no darkness at all' " ("Eranos:
1947, 1948," p.398), it is a step forward for the religious thought
of the culture.

But this very advance embodies "only half the archetype:
the other half appears in Antichrist," which,

being neglected, becomes unconscious and manifests itself,
both in the individual and society, in negative and destructive—even totalitarian—forms. Jung knows, however, that it
is an integral part of the original doctrine of Christianity itself
that the coming of Christ must result in the coming of Antichrist, and even in his at least temporary triumph.

(Ibid.)

So far so good: the Self as archetype of human integration
clearly includes everything Jung says it does; and modern Westerners need to become conscious once again of the centrality of
the Christ image for their spiritual health. With that consciousness it is also essential to recognize that Christ and Antichrist
are linked in cosmic warfare. On all these points White agrees
with Jung's conclusions.

The remainder of the review, however, challenges Jung's
tendency, as White understands it, toward metaphysical dual-

ism. He points out in a dry footnote that Jung's whole discussion of evil is confused:

> Dr. Jung's analogies to his theory that Good and Bad are both definable only as opposites of one another seem singularly unfortunate. . . . The *privatio boni* in St. Augustine and St. Thomas was not of course in answer to Dr. Jung's question (Is Evil a real existing force?—their answer to that of course was Yes) but to the question *What* is evil, i.e., why is this called Bad?—a question Dr. Jung neither asks nor answers.
>
> ("Eranos: 1947, 1948," p.400n)

White prescribes basic corrective passages in St. Thomas, as if he were advising a bright student who had unaccountably missed the point:

> An elementary study of (for instance) St. Thomas's sections in the *Prima Pars* On the Good, On the Goodness of God, On Evil, and On the Cause of Evil, should suffice to dispel Dr. Jung's misunderstandings and misgivings, and to supply a metaphysic which would account for the phenomena which concern him at least as satisfactorily as the quasi-manichaean dualism which he propounds.
>
> (Ibid. p.399)

This criticism stung Jung to heated reply in the text and footnotes of *Aion*. He attacked the language in White's review and averred that the charge of metaphysical dualism was likely to hit White's position, not his own.

> My learned friend Victor White, O.P., . . . thinks he can detect a Manichaean streak in me. I don't go in for metaphysics, but ecclesiastical philosophy undoubtedly does, and for this reason I must ask what are we to make of hell, damnation, and the devil, if these things are eternal? . . . So where is the danger of dualism? In addition to this my critic should know how very much I stress the unity of the self, this cental archetype which is a *complexio oppositorum* par excellence, and that my leanings are therefore towards the very reverse of dualism.
>
> (*Aion*, CW 9ii, note to §112)

Thus, a year or so before the publication of *Answer to Job* in German, the chief issue was aired in public. Jung's polemic about evil constitutes the cutting edge of his attack on Catholic orthodoxy. Later White would declare that this attack by Jung, more than any other factor, drove him to give up the idea of a theoretical bridge between Thomism and Jungian psychology (*Soul and Psyche*, p.156).

In the lectures which became his last book, *Soul and Psyche*, White discusses some of Jung's post-1950 proposals for revisioning Christian doctrine. The proposals on which he especially focuses represent various aspects of Jung's attack on the doctrine of God's absolute goodness. In chapter nine, "The Integration of Evil," White touches on several of these hopelessly unorthodox suggestions, often referring directly to Jung's writings. Jung, he says, has asked Christians to agree with the following:

1. " 'To believe that God is the Summum Bonum is impossible for a reflecting consciousness' " (*Soul and Psyche*, p.149; quoting *Job*, CW 11, §662).

2. "On the principle that things are what they do—*agens agit sibi simile*—God therefore *is* darkness as well as light, evil as well as peace. . . . Some early Christian writers also recognized that God has a left, 'sinister' side, as well as the right side on which his good son is enthroned" (Ibid., p.149; referring to *Aion*, CW 9ii, e.g.,§107).

3. "The Incarnation, the embodiment of God in Jesus Christ, is as yet an incomplete incarnation from which the dark and evil side of God has been excluded. But God remains dark and evil—as well as light and good—nevertheless" (Ibid.).

4. " 'God has a terrible double aspect: a sea of grace is met by a seething lake of fire. . . . That is the eternal, as distinct from the temporal gospel: *one can love God, but must fear him*' " (Ibid., p.150; quoting *Job*, CW 11, §733).

5. "Jesus is not the *only* begotten Son of God. There is another Son who represents the dark side of God, and his name is Satan . . . ." (Ibid., p.151).

Noting that "from most of this an instructed Christian, of any tradition, will recoil" (Ibid), White then rehearses some of the chief reasons why an instructed Christian cannot agree with Jung's views of Christian doctrine.

1. Jung is unduly "impressed by a Gnostic myth" about Jesus and Satan (*Soul and Psyche*, p.150).

2. His view of God is drastically anthropomorphic (Ibid, p.151).

3. Unlike Jung, a Christian places God *beyond* all sorts of "opposites"—good and evil, male and female, etc. (Ibid).

4. God's goodness is only analogically, not univocally, comparable to human goodness (Ibid, cf. *ST* I.6).

5. One cannot argue from evil in the world to evil in God. A good cause may produce bad results by its very perfection (Ibid, cf. *ST* I.49.1,2).

6. Evil is very often perceived as real, but perception alone does not provide grounds for theology. "Aquinas himself recognizes that to the unreflecting apprehensions of the psyche, the privation which is evil . . . has the character of a certain kind of entity—and is a positive contrary" (Ibid, p.156).

Most of White's arguments are based on his assumption that God, not the psyche, has epistemological priority and ultimate authority over the truth of theology. For orthodox Christianity, divine knowledge of and judgment over humanity, not human knowledge of and judgment over God, determine the meaning of the very terms good and evil. As an orthodox theologian, then, White puts the point as follows:

> To judge the infinite and almighty God by the ethical laws which are designed to govern human behavior will seem as preposterous as to subject him [God] to the laws of gravitation or thermodynamics. On the contrary, a Christian will

say, it is we, and our ethical standards and behaviour, which
should be subjected to the judgment of God.

(Ibid, p.151)

When White states his objections to Jung in terms of basic
epistemology and moral authority, it is time to recognize (and
White in this chapter reluctantly does recognize) that the disagreement is too deep for negotiation. Either one is prepared to
base theology, as White does, on the premise that God exists,
acts, and exercises judgment prior to and outside the psyche, or
else one reserves the right, as Jung does, to speak of God (i.e.,
the God-image) on a strictly intra-psychic basis. The latter
method entails an obligation to criticize the God-image from a
position of moral and cognitive superiority, which the former
method has to condemn as both ignorant and arrogant.

In what must have been one of White's last professional
writings, in early 1960 he answered a set of questions for a panel
discussion between Jungians and theologians. Since White was
too ill to attend, his answers were printed in the *Journal of Analytical Psychology* under the title "Theological Reflections."[14] Here he
writes in a sadder vein than in *Soul and Psyche*, but the gist of the
comments is the same.

At the conclusion of his comments, White asks and answers
two central questions about Jung's theory of the Self, questions
which sum up his urgent concerns as a believing Christian and
as a theologian. He demands first whether the Self is a God he
can believe in, and second (failing that) whether the Self is a
God he can know. Both questions he answers in the negative.

> Is the Jungian "self" the one God *I* can believe in or
> worship—"the Maker of all things visible and invisible"? Is
> the Jungian "self" even a God I can rationally acknowledge
> by natural theology, and prescinding from faith? I must
> confess that I doubt it.
>
> ("Theological Reflections," p.154)

Although, as he says in his review of "Über das Selbst,"
White gladly embraces the Self as a symbol of *human* integration, he rejects Jung's equation between the Self and the God of

biblical revelation. His objections have to do with Jung's insistence on the "opposition" within the Self. In contrast, the God whom White knows is beyond internal opposition but full of internal movement and relation. The Self therefore appears to him "a static quaternity," God as "a dynamic Trinity" ("Theological Reflections," p.154). White continues to describe the nature of the contrast:

> One contains good and evil, light and darkness, the other is beyond the *opposites* of good and evil, and (according to St. John) "all light, and in Him there is no darkness at all." One seems to be *only* immanent and relative, the other *both* immanent and transcendent, absolute *and* relative. One is an archetype of human psycho-physical wholeness, the other has been commonly seen, since St. Augustine, as the Creator and Sustainer of All.
>
> (Ibid.)

After thus concluding what was probably his last formal statement of theological commitments, White turns again to the psychological question Jung poses. He confesses that he still does not get the sense of Jung's teaching well enough to tell whether he can agree with it. He ends this writing:

> But perhaps my doubts are due to the fact that I do not rightly understand analytical-psychology language about "the self."
>
> (Ibid.)

Did he really not understand? Knowing how carefully Victor White guarded his feelings, and how much he may have wished for a better understanding with Jung despite everything, one would not expect him to say to Jung more plainly than this, "I reject what you are saying."

Chapter Seven

Hope and Possibility

A. FRAMEWORKS FOR HOPE

As White noted, the overall pattern of Jung's psychology is teleological or goal-oriented. To Jung's phenomenological eye it is clear that the psyche mysteriously moves, in the tension and the ongoing play between ego-consciousness and the unconscious, toward greater consciousness. The psyche seeks, consciously and unconsciously, to develop its potential wholeness. Steeped in the Thomistic thought-world, White, too, forms his theology around the concept of a final cause: God is at once the divine source of being and creation's ultimate goal.

The teleological patterns in these two worlds of belief not only help to define the deepest concerns of each, but also open the door to existential questions. Human life is seen as directional, with a beginning and an end. Attainment of the end, though, is always fraught with uncertainty. And so the human soul needs to maintain hope, in order to live at all. But hope for what? And how are we to sustain hope? What reason is there, given the finality of death and all the other obstacles that block us in the attainment of our deepest desires, to believe that human life is nevertheless destined for its true wholeness and fulfillment?

To discuss these questions in a dialogue between theology and psychology can be confusing, because the objects and warrants for hope may differ. For Christian faith, the object of hope is understood to be the state of salvation, which consists in God's ultimate act, promised but not yet seen. The creature, the community, and creation itself will all be restored to wholeness. Christian hope thus relies on a promise which is rooted in a sacred history of creation, liberation, incarnation and resurrection; and all of these are construed in the context of God's love.

In Jungian psychology, on the other hand, hope cannot look confidently to a divine promise of salvation, nor refer (except ambiguously) to the divine love. Jung says that God (or a god), called or uncalled, will be present to the soul in its struggle; but this being is known to the psyche as a morally mixed power: at once trustworthy and untrustworthy, loving and dangerous. Hope in a Jungian sense points mainly to the satisfaction of a human thirst for meaning, knowledge and wholeness. These are to be gained—to the degree humanly possible—by a risky process of individuation. In that process, help may be looked for from the archetypal realm, in numinous transcendent images that reframe the ego's perspective to awesome, sometimes terrifying, effect.

These two interpretations of hope and its object may overlap to some degree. For White, with his Augustinian concern for an inward relationship with God, the promise of human restoration to wholeness through union with the transcendent God is joined with a promise that in this union the soul will discover its own nature and meaning. Jung, meanwhile, despite his agnostic stance toward the extra-psychic reality of God, invests individuation with an importance relating to the welfare of society, if not to harmony with the cosmos.

Recalling the differences between Jung and White that concerned us in previous chapters, however, we must not expect that their respective language worlds will assign the same objects to hope and meaning, or support them on the same grounds. In his theological world, White's main warrant for hope is the promise of a wholly good and reliable God, existing prior to and outside the psyche. Jung's epistemology makes the possibility of "hope" meaningful only insofar as its grounds are perceived and maintained within the soul. He cannot refer, as White can, to God the transcendent promise-keeper, ensuring the triumph of goodness. To grasp the difference, one recalls Jung's famous statement toward the end of *Memories, Dreams, Reflections*:

> Life is—or has—meaning and meaninglessness. I cherish the anxious hope that meaning will preponderate and win the battle.
>
> (*Memories*, p.359)

Jung's neo-Kantian framework permits only his "anxious hope" that meaning may prevail. The psychological evidence is equally persuasive for and against such a prediction, since the inner God desires wholeness and yet is laden with shadow. When Jung crosses over into theological statements that his Kantian bias, if applied consistently, should rule out, he tends to emphasize the negative rather than the positive side of the divine image. This occurs both in *Answer to Job* and in his private correspondence, where he calls God a "morally dubious creator" (*Letters II*, p.60), casting serious doubt on the future of creation.

In contrast to Jung's subjective psychological warrants, White's faith claims, with St. Paul, a "sure and certain hope" based on the incarnation, crucifixion and resurrection of Christ, which reveal God's love toward the creation and all its creatures. The ultimacy of good is also an implication of St. Thomas' concept the divine *actus purus*, i.e., the absolute changeless God whose Being is identical with Goodness. White's warrants are thus offered not as mere possibilities but as objective facts, signaling the transcendence of order and life over the pseudo-powers of chaos and death.

Notwithstanding these doctrinal differences, Jung and White both wish to answer human fear by nurturing the confidence that real meaning (or at least its horizon of possibility) is an essential part of life. At the existential level, they share a concern in questions such as these: Given the evidence of evil in human history up to now, and the potential for new destruction on a scale before unknown, what degree of affirmation is responsible and realistic? On what grounds and by what means can human beings individually and collectively direct themselves toward goodness and wholeness rather than destruction?

1. White on the Ultimacy of Good

As we have seen, White tried to convey to Jung the Thomistic idea of the discrepancy between the *apparent* reality of evil as humans experience it, and the *absolute* reality of the goodness which flows from God. In the ninth chapter of his final work, *Soul and Psyche*, titled "The Integration of Evil,"

White returned to this distinction between the subjective and the objective knowledge of what evil means. Here he repeats what he once wrote to Jung:

> Aquinas himself recognizes that to the unreflecting apprehensions of the psyche, the privation which is evil "habet rationem cuiusdam entis"—has the character of a certain kind of entity—and is a positive contrary.
>
> (*Soul and Psyche*, p.156)

As White knows, "the unreflecting apprehensions of the psyche" are real in a psychological sense; but this kind of reality is not sufficient for one trained as White was in Christian philosophy. Human beings have the power of reflection and have been given the light of faith. To a reflective mind working in the light of faith, awareness of the absolute reality of God's goodness overcomes the naive perception that behind those events and people we call evil, the entity of "evil as such" has its own separate reality.

This conclusion is also implicit in Aquinas' idea of God as *actus purus*. God's energy alone gives all created beings their energy to intend and to act. Thus in the strict sense—St. Thomas writes and White affirms—"evil cannot be an agent" (*SCG* III.7.4). "Nobody can act on account of pure evil" (*Soul and Psyche*, p.160). Rather, "every action and motion are for the sake of a good" (*SCG* III.3.3), even when, due to human ignorance, finitude and sin, the results are evil. Power and intentionality belong only to real beings, and not to the distortions of being that we reify under the name "Evil."

St. Thomas' phrase, "evil does not exist save seated in a good" (*ST* I.49) suggests that the best image for the power of evil may be that of a parasite attacking its host. If we must reify the distortion of good, we would do well to conceive of it as a mouth brainlessly devouring. One can go so far as to imagine the parasite completely devouring its host; but in so doing it would also annihilate itself:

> Evil may indefinitely diminish good, [but] it cannot entirely consume it. . . . Were evil total it would destroy itself; for the

demolition of all good—a necessary condition for evil to be
whole and entire—would cut out from under evil its very
basis.

(*ST* I.49.3)

Evil thus depends on good for its continuation. Not to be
complacent about humanity's predicament, this logic also works
in reverse: evil will continue like weeds among the wheat until
time ends. But whether one states the principle positively or
negatively, destruction is not self-subsistent but dependent on
the prior existence of created things that are good in themselves. The quasi-realities of meaninglessness and nothingness
only "are" as parasites of meaning and being. These in turn are
held in existence by the Creator (*ST* I.49.3), who promises to
preserve them in existence *even beyond destruction*, through the
bodily resurrection of individuals and the healing of the whole
creation.

White writes about these questions at some length in his
final work. Addressing the ambiguities he finds in Jung's discussions of good and evil, he admits,

For my part I have great difficulty in understanding just
what Jung *does* understand by evil, and how, intellectually,
he would have us differentiate evil from good.

(*Soul and Psyche*, p.156)

White's puzzlement is due at least party to the fact that, in
Thomistic terms, by making evil real Jung inadvertently makes
it good: Goodness and Being are interchangeable in White's
theology. He might have understood Jung better if he had seen
that Jung treats two distinguishable types of evil: evils of myth
and of history. Jung's outrage toward the latter is convincing
enough to show that he makes no equation between evil and
good in a practical context.

At the end of his life, White addressed himself mainly not
to Jungians, but to faithful Catholics who were interested in
Jung. For their benefit, in his chapter called "The Integration
of Evil," he carefully defended against a possible misunderstanding of the psychological concept, "integration of the shad-

ow." This kind of integration means the consciousness of sin, but not its toleration. It would be nonsense, he points out, to try to "integrate" moral evils into one's practical or spiritual life, since sin is "by definition . . . the privation of integrity" (Ibid, p.163).

Ironically, when insisting that moral evils must not only be recognized but also rejected by the ego, White could cite Jung's personal expressions of outrage in the face of historical evils such as genocide. Practical grounds exist for rapprochement between Jung and White on the subject of relationship to the shadow. The church's rites, White says, are "calculated to prevent unconsciousness and consequent repression of evil" (Ibid, p.162). This is exactly what had drawn Jung to psychological affirmation of the rites and dogmas of Catholicism. "Integrating evil" thus means, for both White and Jung, carrying and repenting for sin. It entails first of all an admission by the individual that one's own moral shadow is real—a real though unwanted part of the personality, with real though undesired effects.[1] This difficult first step, acknowledging personal responsibility for one's negative dispositions and behaviors, is the necessary preliminary for both psychological and spiritual wholeness.

The issues on which White and Jung cannot be brought into alignment, as we have seen, concern their treatment of God's goodness, and thus their respective warrants for hope for humanity. The subject of hope comes clearly into focus in *Soul and Psyche* in the tenth chapter, titled "Health and Holiness," where White assesses Jung's idea of the process of individuation in light of the facts of illness and death.

The confrontation with death, White says—our own death, and the death of those we love—is humanity's original lesson in hope. The fact of death forces us to choose between hope and despair. An ability to hope is thus universal, and not unique to Christians; hope is the last gift found in Pandora's box (*Soul and Psyche*, p.180). For Christians, however, the unsurpassed lesson in hope is taught, not by the universal human experience of death but by the unique events of Christ's death and resurrection. Experiences associated with individuation, and acquaintance with the universal myths about dying and rising, may give plausibility to Christian teachings about the resurrection, White grants. But real Christian hope concerns the actions of God.

> Complete, unquestioning hope in God and for God can be established solely on the power, mercies and promises of God himself. As faith is concerned with the humanly un-knowable but the divinely known, so hope is concerned with the humanly impossible but the divinely achieved.
>
> (Ibid)

Psychology takes us as far as the grave, White declares; and there its subject matter dies (Ibid, p.181). Faith takes us beyond the grave, because its subject matter is not mortal.

2. Jung on Last Things

In his turn to God's knowledge and God's promised triumph as sure warrants for Christian hope, White separates himself definitively from Jung's framework. As we have seen, Jung systematically denied the grounds for any meaningful distinction between what is divinely and humanly known, divinely and humanly achieved. His subjective starting place completely barred him from this route out of the condition of human anxiety.

Without necessarily joining Jung's epistemological bias, some theologians would admit that the problem of evil is not easily resolved by statements about Christian warrants for hope. The experienced power of evil is too vivid. Human outrage in the face of innocent suffering, for example, is not and should not be allayed by doctrinal assertions, unless these can be supported by demonstrations of an equally vivid divine goodness by which such evil is overcome. And even if God's goodness is lavishly demonstrated in the wake of evil, as occurs with hyperbole in the final narrative of Job, it would be arrogant to claim that innocent suffering and death are ever fully compensated on earth. In such situations, if one stays true to the human experience of evil, either one must be willing to follow Jung's example and call God a beast, or else a point comes when theology, like Job, has to lay its hand over its mouth. Faith cannot answer "why."

This is a silence which the Protestant theologian Karl Barth, for one, considers an appropriate response of faith. He holds that theology should not be expected to provide a comprehensive answer to every question it raises.

> All theology is *theologia viatorum*. It can never satisfy the natural aspiration of human thought and utterance for completeness and compactness. . . . It can never form a system, comprehending and as it were "seizing" the object.
>
> (*CD* III/3, p.293)[2]

The failure of theology to seize its object is especially valid, Barth says, when we come to the existence of that which "should not" exist, the absurd perversion we call evil. Barth allows evil sufficient objective reality to give it a name, *das Nichtige*. With the paradoxical power of an "impossible" existence, evil preys on creation as long as creation lasts, in spite of the fact that this "nothingness" is the chaos that God does not will (*CD* IV/2, p.398).[3]

Barth's answer, however, satisfies Jung no better than White's does, based as it is on the systematic insistence that we know God only from objective revelation, not from subjective experience. Jung's experiential bias raises the commonsense challenge: granted that the parasite cannot outlive its host, on what grounds do we assert that the host can outlive the parasite? If God wills that chaos and nothingness should *not* exist, by what power do they continue their all-too-convincing existence? Finally, if the rose is real, is the worm not real also?

Among the works of Jung's old age, *Answer to Job* is not the only one that treats apocalyptic themes. His small book, *The Undiscovered Self*[4] (German title, *Gegenwart und Zukunft*, "Present and Future"), also contemplates the modern world as it faces its next millennium.

> Today, as the end of the second millennium draws near, we are again living in an age filled with apocalyptic images of universal destruction. What is the significance of that split,

symbolized by the "Iron Curtain," which divides humanity
into two halves? What will become of our civilization, and of
man himself, if the hydrogen bombs begin to go off, or if the
spiritual and moral darkness of State absolutism should
spread over Europe?

(Self, pp.3f)

Jung is not alone, of course, in imagining a historical enactment of the eschaton. Virtually no one pretends that humanity
could not—by its own acts—put an end to itself. His concern
reflects the nightmares of an era, the Cold War and the nuclear
arms race. Since the international scenario has changed, other
apocalyptic scenarios have risen up to replace the ones he knew.
Nothing assured him then, or would assure him now, that the
needed psychological transformation would definitely occur
within humanly known history. And on his own epistemological
warrants, he cannot speculate about what may lie beyond that
history to redeem it.

As need hardly be stated, Jung's vision of "last things" is not
the same as White's. Among systematic differences, Jung's view
of the biblical theme of bodily resurrection is complicated by
the symbolic level at which he treats that claim. He does attribute importance to the theme, suggesting that whenever in
Christian history it has been prominently discussed, the psychological connotation is a celebration of bodily life as such (Visions
II, pp.305ff).[5] As a matter of personal belief, on the other hand,
Jung the empiricist puts little personal stock in the symbol of
Christ's resurrection.[6] If there is anything to hope for in life, he
implies, human beings should seek it this side of the fire, not on
some farther shore. To say that goodness or consciousness can
transcend and outlive a "last battle" with evil is simply unjusti-
fied by anything Jung recognizes as evidence.

It must be added, however, that the hope Jung entertains in
the face of possible apocalypse is neither political nor technologi-
cal, but spiritual. He places his hope in the effects of hard-won
individual consciousness (Self, pp.46f). "Virtually everything,"
he writes, "depends on the human soul and its functions" (Ibid,
p.84). If moral responsibility resides where the pain is borne, the
burden of suffering is borne, he says, not by God but by human-

ity. And it is borne not by humanity as a collective body, but by the singular human being struggling to become an individual.

The most singular human individual, from a Christian viewpoint, is Jesus Christ. In his treatment of that individual, however, Jung displays a split vision which from a theological perspective looks like defective Christology. As an empiricist, Jung puts little weight on the claim that Jesus was bodily raised from the dead. He speaks of the historical Jesus as a great spiritual examplar, but adds that as a human being, complete with shadow and unconsciousness, Jesus' vision of himself was very likely false.

The real symbol of the union of God and humanity, Jung says, is Jesus' cry of dereliction (Ibid., *CW 11*, §647). But even this union would seem only provisional, since the God who harmed Job cannot himself be harmed (*Job*, §661). God's absolute power is hard to reconcile with Jesus' total yielding to mortality. Thus, for Jung, it seems that human and divine reality cannot completely merge anywhere in earthly life, not even in the moment of Jesus' crucifixion.

Jung's image of the Christ-symbol, on the other hand, corresponds to the Self in eternal transcendent power. As an image of the Self archetype, Christ is eternal and unbounded by the particularities of human life and death. The Christ-image, as Jung reminded his friend many times, is psychically necessary; yet it, too, is incomplete, since it lacks the human shadow. As a symbol Christ thus has little to do with the real life of the man Jesus, who was mortal, limited by time, burdened with sin, and who died. The immortal archetype, the Self, cannot be lived in full by a human being.

Behind this dichotomy between the human Jesus and the symbolic Christ, Jung finds a God of power but not of love. To this God-image he himself responds with fear; and he sees fear as the inevitable response. He finds support for this position not only in the book of Job, where God is clearly dangerous, but also in the book of Revelation, which he attributes to the writer of the fourth gospel. According to Jung, John the Evangelist "felt his gospel of love to be one-sided, and he supplemented it with the gospel of fear: *God can be loved but must be feared*" (*Job*, *CW 11*, §732).[7] If this image of the terrible invulnerable deity still persists in the human psyche, as Jung says, its presence seriously (though secretly) undermines any proclamation of good news.

For solace and hope in the face of God's terrible double aspect, Jung looks—as one would guess—not to the church as an institution, but to the collective impact of individuals courageously suffering the union of opposites within themselves. Psychological morality, amounting to heroism, is the main ingredient of such hope as Jung can maintain. Perhaps even the torn political collective, about which he cares so deeply, may be saved by individuals courageously seeking their inner unity:

> Today humanity, as never before, is split into two apparently irreconcilable halves. The psychological rule says that when an inner situation is not made conscious, it happens outside, as fate. That is to say, when the individual remains undivided and does not become conscious of his inner opposite, the world must perforce act out the conflict and be torn into opposing halves.
>
> (*Aion, CW 9ii*, §126)

Curiously, despite his claim to distrust God, in his old age Jung urges "faith" as a solution to world-threatening problems. His late writings recommend that knowledge should be reunited with faith to cure the split consciousness that threatens the world (*Self*, pp.73f). But Jung's agenda goes further than that. The persistent unconsciousness of God can only be made whole, he teaches, by the persistent labor of mortals to become conscious.[8]

The "reunion of faith and knowledge" sounds very much like Victor White's agenda; but this is an instance where two people may use the same words and mean different things by them. For Jung, in the last period of his life, "faith" means participation in one's native religious myths and symbols. He urges individuals consciously to relate to mediating archetypal images and their instinctive roots. This sort of faith has nothing to do, he warns, with "rational philosophy" (Ibid, p.83) or with the goodness of a God beyond human knowledge.

By 1957, when he wrote *The Undiscovered Self*, Jung expected no more help from the theological side. He wrote that intellectual abstractions on the part of theologians and the modern practice of "demythologizing" the scriptures had convinced him that theology was psychologically useless. Formal theology, he says, merely fosters "consciousness at the expense of the unconscious" (Ibid, p.80). It ignores the symbolic sources of faith (Ibid, pp.73ff) and thus increases the splitting of inner values in the modern world. Jung had not lost hope that some form of "spontaneous religious experience" (Ibid, p.88)—might yet transform the world; but first, Christians must transform their own religion:

> I am . . . convinced that it is not Christianity, but our conception and interpretation of it, that has become antiquated in face of the present world situation. The Christian symbol is a living thing that carries in itself the seeds of further development.
>
> (Ibid, pp.62f)

A development of Christianity is only possible, however, if enough individual Christians are stricken by a sense of the world's historic crisis. Part of Jung's hope for the future resides in his conviction that the extremity of present circumstances will draw archetypal energy to the task of Christian transformation. "The activation of unconscious fantasies is a process that occurs when consciousness finds itself in a critical situation," he explains (Ibid, p.67). Under the influence of the archetype of wholeness, terrible and benign, Jung hoped that the transformation of individual souls would influence a whole society to compensate for its one-sidedness. Deadly unconscious oppositions might then be revealed as more or less conscious halves of a larger whole.

3. Werner Meyer's Eulogy

Beneath Jung's rationality and empiricism lay depths of personal religious experience in the face of which he sometimes confessed to being overwhelmed and as irrational as a child. The religious shadow of the scientist could erupt in surges of feeling and conviction. Jung tried to live in more or less conscious touch with his feeling-shadow, so that it would pose as little danger as possible to himself, his family, and his patients.[9] But his inescapable shadow made him a vulnerable human being, whose depth and complexity we can still see in his correspondence and feel in the passionate value-statements that recur in his professional writings.

It was psychologically important for Jung, the Kantian agnostic, to acknowledge consciously his "living thraldom" to the God of biblical revelation. Moreover, this acknowledgement simultaneously supported two of his theological claims: that the inner God is ambiguous; and that in encountering the power of the God-image, the ego is compelled to give up its pretense of mastery and control. Jung's experience convinced him that neither doubt nor faith was an adequate response to the encounter; there was only "immediate knowledge." When asked as an old man whether he still believed in God, he was forced to reply, after pausing, "I *know*. I don't need to believe. I know" ("Face to Face," *C.G. Jung Speaking*, p.428).

An existential commitment like Jung's confronts finitude as a special challenge. What grounds for hope does Jung's religious position provide in the face of death? The ministers and eulogists at Jung's own funeral had to face precisely this challenge. Where the knowledge of God is entirely intra-psychic, and Christ is only the locally valid image of an archetype, what can one say about the destination of the soul? Some of the existential implications of Jung's psychology are poignantly evident in words spoken in the presence of his friends and family in St. Michael's Reformed Church, Küsnacht, on 9 June 1961.[10]

Carl Gustav Jung was eulogized by three speakers. The first was Werner Meyer, a Protestant pastor and friend of the family, whom Jung had long liked and trusted while casting a mildly critical eye on Meyer's mystical tendencies.[11] Meyer's affinity for Jung's work is plain in the first eulogy. Normally Christian preachers entrust the departed soul to eternity, recalling the promise of resurrection grounded uniquely in Jesus Christ. As a Swiss Reformed pastor, Werner Meyer might have been expected to express this biblical perspective, grounding hope in events outside, beyond and prior to human experience. But in

speaking to C.G. Jung's survivors Meyer avoids any such reference to orthodox theology.

Instead he exegetes a legend about a seventeenth-century
Cabbala scholar, Christian Knorr von Rosenroth, whose writings Jung had loved (*Gedenkfeier*, p.16).[12] This legend, based
upon a daughter's vision of her dead father's soul, allows Meyer
to speak of Jung's life after death in images of an individual's
subjective experience. It may be sheer happenstance that, by
exploring the text of a woman's vision of her departed relative,
Meyer's eulogy also obliquely echoes the spiritualist theme that
had occupied Jung's first book-length research.[13]

According to legend, the spirit of the mystic appears to his
daughter as a little boy, and tells her about his after-death passage over deep waters. The scholar's soul is commanded by a
power higher than itself to seek greater wholeness, journeying
over dangerous depths toward ever greater spiritual wisdom.
As in the vision of the medieval scholar, Meyer says, Jung's soul
will now pass through new stages of learning, refining and
completing whatever was incomplete in him before death.

Meyer's eulogy carefully avoids reference to the events of
the New Testament. He does complete justice, however, to
Jung's conviction that, whatever else it may be, the image of
God is a real inner presence to be reckoned with. In his letter to
Pastor Max Frischknecht, 7 April 1945, Jung had written characteristically: "I would consider it extremely dishonest . . . if a
psychologist were to assert that the God-image does not have a
tremendous effect on the psyche" (*Letters I*, p.360). Meyer
shares Jung's confidence in the *Wirklichkeit* of the God-image,
the central symbol of transcendence, before whose power the
ego is right to tremble.

Meyer also leaves open the question of God's goodness,
when he describes the waters of divine judgment over which the
soul is about to pass. The mood of the vision is close to that of
Psalm 29, which compares the voice of God to a mighty storm
from the sea, magnificent, holy and, to mortal view, awesomely
destructive.

Aber nun muss er selbst durch die letzten grossen Wasser
hindurch, nicht nur als Forscher und Entdecker, sondern

als ein Erforschter und Entdecker. Er möge bei seinem Transitus durch das grosse Wasser sich den reinigenden Stürmen des Gerichts . . . froh und frisch entgegenwerfen. Und mag auch dies und das bei der grossen Durchforschung und Zurechtbringung . . . weggeschnitten werden, weil das Vorläufige dem Bleibenden, das Fragment dem Vollendeten zu weichen hat: Diese letzte Exkursion in unerforschte Gebiete wird die lohnendste sein. . . . [But now he himself must go through the last great waters, not only as an explorer and discoverer, but also as one who is explored and discovered. May he in crossing the great water cast himself bravely and gladly into the purifying storms of judgment. And if, in the course of this great examination and rectification, one thing or another . . . is cut away, because the passing must yield to the permanent and the part to the whole— Nevertheless, this last excursion into unexplored territories will be the most rewarding. . . .]

(*Gedenkfeier*, p.18)[14]

These are archetypal images resonant of Jung's own work—the night sea journey; the individual psyche traveling toward wholeness; the overwhelming ambiguous power of the Self which draws the soul through pain toward wholeness.

It was fitting that Jung's eulogist refrain from claims about absolute divine goodness or references to God raising the dead to life in Christ. In the light of Jung's conviction that the nature of God and the work of Christ could be affirmed only from a psychological and symbolic point of view, it would have been jarring to impose Christian orthodoxy upon ideas which Jung's teaching had left paradoxical and ambiguous.

Meyer does suggest, however, that *"dies und das"* of a transient nature—features of Jung's thought, perhaps—might be trimmed away and cleansed in the storms of judgment. By suggesting that elements in Jung's finite learning are subject to correction in the school of infinity, Meyer affirms that the Self subjects the ego to overpowering experiences that are painful from the ego's viewpoint, but still vital to the soul's learning.

This view of afterlife suggests a school for the soul. In that respect it is essentially Gnostic, for it gives the passion to *know*, no longer restricted by mortality, infinite room for self-expression after death. Meyer pictures Jung's soul in relationship with a mysterious transcendence resembling the "transcendent function" of the human psyche. Jung is now in the position of an initiate, pursuing wholeness in the form of wisdom. It is painful for the ego to experience its own relativization; but the hardship is justified by the goal, the completion of the great soul through knowledge.

Werner Meyer's experiment in framing a Jungian vision of death and afterlife was true to certain themes in Jung's own work. He made a genuine connection between Jung's psychology and his biography. Yet in picturing the soul alone on its journey, Meyer unwittingly contradicted certain ideas that Jung himself had written about the afterlife before his death.

In Chapter XI of *Memories, Dreams, Reflections*, "On Life after Death,"[15] Jung himself had restated the Gnostic theme—the soul athirst for learning, even after death. But Jung's discussion of the afterlife is characteristically cautious. He takes care not to lose sight of the limits of subjective knowledge. All he writes is rooted in the limits of what can be said from a human perspective. This approach can be contrasted with Meyer's unrestrained enthusiasm about a vision of the soul's archetypal adventure.

Jung tentatively explores a few slim suggestions or anticipations—"memories," he calls them, paradoxically—of afterlife existence, assembled through his own research. True to his caveat about human knowledge, he admits that on this subject, especially, he can "do no more than tell stories—'mythologize'" (*Memories*, p.299). The stories come not from world mythology, but from individuals' fleeting glimpses of the afterlife in recorded dreams and experiences, both his own and others'.

One reported glimpse, he says, particularly impressed him. A woman of sixty, his student, dreamed two months before her death that on arrival in the afterlife she was expected to present a lecture to a class of departed souls. Jung was struck by the excitement of her dream audience.

> The dead were extremely interested in the life experiences the newly deceased brought with them, just as if the acts and

experiences taking place in earthly life, in space and time, were the decisive ones.

(Ibid, p.305)

The souls' eagerness to hear all about a perfectly ordinary life, he speculates, shows that growth in knowledge is possible only within the mortal framework of time and space.

Based on this glimpse, Jung affirms that the souls of the dead hunger to learn; but they can learn only what the living (i.e., the newly departed) have to teach them. They depend on information derived from mortal existence, just as the archetypal sub-personalities (animus and anima, figures in dreams) are strikingly ignorant about reality, unless they are "instructed" through an ongoing dialogue with ego. Despite their numinosity, they are blind guides. Jung notes:

> Quite early I had learned that it was necessary for me to instruct the figures of the unconscious, or that other group which is often indistinguishable from them, the "spirits of the departed."

(Ibid, p.306)

This theme, "the education of souls after death," is then carried forward by Jung's discussion of his own dream a year after his wife's death. In it he saw his wife continuing to study the Holy Grail, a scholarly task she had lacked time to complete in life (Ibid, p.309). He remembers that he was comforted by this image; but he draws back from concluding that departed souls can learn things through their own efforts, as the dream seems to suggest. No growth happens in eternity, he declares, except with the help of the living. No soul, however noble, advances after death, apart from contributions gleaned from finite experience.

The community of departed spirits thus depends on the time-bound world, Jung concludes. Like the archetypes, the spirits of the dead inhabit a realm where the opposites coexist unconsciously. Nothing changes in that unconsciousness. The peace of eternity, Jung hypothesizes, is a static state, allowing no growth or learning. The growth of consciousness requires the lively conflict of opposing views. But since this condition is found only in a finite time and place, the dead must wait on the living.

> The maximum awareness which has been attained any-where forms, so it seems to me, the upper limit of knowledge to which the dead can attain. That is probably why earthly life is of such great significance, and why it is that what a human being "brings over" at the time of his death is so important. Only here, in life on earth, where the opposites clash together, can the general level of consciousness be raised.
>
> (Ibid, p.311)

Contemplating these thoughts, we see one of the reasons why Jung insists that God, as imagined both in the Bible and in the psyche, must be complex and full of contradictions. God is a living being, subject to change and growth and the opposition of life. The God of Christian orthodoxy, on the other hand, the totally good One who cannot change (or move, according to Aquinas), seems to Jung not only false but perverse. Without internal tension, contradiction, change and potentiality, even God is dead. Whatever else he thinks about God and the God-image, measured in subjective or objective terms, the God Jung meets through the psyche is alive, powerful, and full of the tension of opposites.

Werner Meyer almost certainly had not seen Jung's reflections on the afterlife; *Memories, Dreams, Reflections* was published only posthumously. If he had, he might have hesitated to talk about Jung's soul on a solitary journey through the waters of eternity. He might rather have urged the gathered mourners to imagine the spirits of the dead gathered to hear, with rapt attention, what Jung's newly arrived soul would teach them. He might also have admonished each person in the congregation to add to the sum of human wisdom as individuals, while still alive, so that they, too, might someday "bring over" into eternity the advance in consciousness for which the spirits long.

B. CHRISTIAN-JUNGIAN COLLABORATION

1. White and Jung in Retrospect

White had had only a short experience with Jungian analysis, and a brief intense exposure to Jung's writings, when he formed his proposal of a Thomistic-Jungian bridge. He had already envisioned the systematic theological foundation on which to base a new synthesis of theology and psychology. He brought to the task an epistemology which honored human interiority as well as external authority, and in keeping with this he hoped to show that orthodox Thomism could affirm a kind of experiential or "affective" knowledge. His plea for theological tolerance shows also that he could approach doctrine symbolically, even if not entirely in the Jungian sense. Nevertheless, when he contacted Jung in 1945, White did not fully know what he was getting into.

White might have succeeded better in his project if several conditions of his life and work had been other than they were. It might have helped somewhat, for example, if he and Jung had been able to engage each other more often at leisure and face to face, rather than conducting so much of their business at long distance and from such dissimilar social environments. White made himself professionally vulnerable by dedicating himself so completely to his work on the psychological-theological synthesis. If he had taken Jung's statements about the ambiguous intra-psychic God-image more seriously from the start, he might have foreseen that his work with Jung could have only limited success and approached it more cautiously. If he had aimed for a more modest goal and staked less of his professional life on the collaboration, he might have protected himself better and been less severely disappointed in the course of his career.

But these speculations overlook White's personal feeling about the project he and Jung were undertaking. He had been seized by his vision of ecclesial transformation; and his sense of urgency was of course reinforced by Jung's intuition of a moral crisis threatening the Western world.[16] Jung was already growing old when they met, so it seemed there was no time to waste on painstaking philosophical analyses of the foundations of the proposed "bridge."

Yet with hindsight we can say that longer personal and practical experience between White and Jung was probably needed, before so much was risked on their marriage of opposites. Not only White, but Jung, too, could have entered more deeply into practical experience of the other's religious world. Jung never fully understood White's view of Christian symbols, any more than White understood Jung's. They belonged not only to different conceptual worlds, but also to different religious cultures.

In this regard we should keep in mind a distinction Jung made between two kinds of understanding. German possesses two verbs meaning "to understand": *verstehen* (its root meaning "stand") and *begreifen* (its root meaning "grasp"). Jung assigned far greater value to the latter than to the former. A conceptual question, for example, requires *verstehen*, an intellectual mastery, but little or no personal commitment. One can "understand" abstractly, in this sense. When one is gripped by a question or problem addressing the whole personality, however, one must wrestle in one's totality to grasp it, in the sense of *begreifen*.

An illustration of this difference is easy to find, and may help to show its importance. Victor White, in confessing that he still did not know what Jung meant by the Self,[17] may have been referring to an inability to conceptualize or define the concept clearly in the abstract. But it is clear that he also could not quite come to grips with the profound ramifications of Jung's concept. He not only did not "understand" it, but also was unable personally to grasp or be grasped by it.

In this connection, an opinion about White's death has been current in Jungian circles for decades. It has its basis in things Jung himself said or implied at the time.[18] White's tragedy, this opinion states, was rooted in his refusal to allow his own religious foundations to be transformed. He rejected the totality of the psyche, the Self, and its implications for a historic change in the very nature of Christianity. John P. Dourley, a Catholic theologian and Jungian analyst, states the Jungian opinion squarely and, I think, correctly:

White's theology was predicated on a supernatural, self-sufficient and perfect deity, in no need of the world of created nature nor in organic continuity with it and with human consciousness. It is not surprising, then, that White could not make the transition to the sense of a more intimate relation of divinity to humanity which Jung . . . contends is the face of the human religious future. To make such a transition would have cost White his faith. His failure to make it may have cost him his life.

(*A Strategy for a Loss of Faith*, p.41)[19]

There were some refusals and inabilities to understand (in the sense of *begreifen*) on Jung's side, too. At least once in print, White noted an important difference between his cultural-religious practice and Jung's. Attempting to apply Jung's teaching about the Self to the church as a sacramental body, White noted that a Catholic

would doubtless give a more dynamic interpretation to the identification of Christ with the human *Ganzheit* than was possible in the Swiss Protestantism of Jung's upbringing. . . . [For a Catholic] the militant character of this body, the ceaseless conflict on earth between the light and the darkness, will be a more vivid reality than is perhaps possible within the framework of *sola fides* and extrinsic imputation.

("Eranos: 1947, 1948," p.399)

Here as elsewhere, White refrained from urging Jung to participate, even marginally, in Catholic practice. (An invitation to a Protestant to receive Communion with Catholics in that era would have been meaningless in any case.) Perhaps he wanted to avoid any hint of proselytizing; for as his vision shows (VW to CGJ, 3 Jan. 48), he hesitated to share even a bite of "Catholic fish" with his Protestant friend. But the collaboration might have benefited if Jung had been able to eat a little of White's "fish," to experience for himself how the body of Christ—the church—can become for participating Catholics a human sacrament.

Before he died, C.G. Jung returned many times to the theme of apparently irreconcilable opposites. In *Memories*,

Dreams, Reflections, contemplating the difficulty he had as a young man in discovering how to live with both his "Number 1" and "Number 2" personalities, he reports a profound insight that came to him through one of his early dreams. To his surprise, he discovered that his extraverted "first" personality was becoming increasingly important and valuable to him. It bore the light that showed him the way forward.

> Consciously I had done nothing to promote any such development; on the contrary, my sympathies were on the other side. Something must therefore have been behind the scenes, some intelligence, at any rate something more intelligent than myself. For the extraordinary idea that *in the light of consciousness the inner realm of light appears as a gigantic shadow* was not something I would have hit on of my own accord.
>
> (*Memories*, p.89, italics added)

Applying Jung's insight to the theoretical problems we have been considering, it may be that each of the two opposing epistemologies is the other's shadow. Seen from outside, each way of learning and knowing looks like darkness to the other. Yet each possesses a realm of light peculiar to itself. This suggestion supports the presupposition that the conflict of consciousness and shadow cannot be resolved by consciousness alone. The shadow must also contribute something to the process of integration. If it does, the contribution may come as insult or as gift, but at any rate it will come as a surprise to consciousness.

Jung impulsively addressed this fact when he called his new friend in England his "white raven." White had come to him out of the blue sky like the raven to Elijah,[20] bearing theological insights that the old religious outsider could not have provided himself. As the raven's gifts to the prophet and the prophet's to the raven became less and less digestible to each, the personal costs of their encounter mounted. When that is said, however, we should not forget that larger historical realities also influenced their work together. We cannot be sure, finally, whether in the tragedy of their struggle the seeds of a greater gift are hidden.

2. Possibilities

Jung and White were forced to abandon their unfinished bridge. If any synthesis between the two points of view is possible, it now remains for others to complete. The usefulness and feasibility of further collaboration between Jung's psychology and White's theology will be assessed variously, however, depending on the proposed starting point. Christian theology of a transcendent or "objective" kind will probably never connect with a psychology like Jung's. It will come up against the same doctrinal obstacles, concerning the nature of God and the problem of evil, and the same epistemological conflicts that were Jung's and White's nemesis.

A mediating perspective, recognizing the fundamental importance of individual experience but also claiming continuity with the church's dogmas and collective symbols, is one to which both Jung and White expressed a degree of openness. White writes that the truth of the gospel touches both faith and knowledge, both dogma and experience (*Soul and Psyche*, pp.77f). And although Jung's notion of transcendence agrees very imperfectly with White's, his doctrine of the Self includes transcendence of a limited kind. The God-image transcends the ego; the objective voice of the Self confronts and relativizes the ego's one-sidedness (*Psychology and Religion*, CW 11, §70). Jung enjoins his readers to remember that mortals are not gods. God is found within the human soul; but the process of individuation reveals that the soul is not identical with the God-image.

It has been observed (by Victor White among others) that the intellectualism and propositionalism of an exclusively transcendental theology, stressing mainly the objectivity of doctrine and the otherness of God, tend to kill affective immediacy and vitiate the power of religious symbols. But in response to this charge, theologians who hold a high doctrine of divine transcendence—transcendental Thomists, Barthians, and others—can counter that faith dies in the air of religious subjectivism, suffocated by merely human concerns and deprived of its true object.

If any lasting synthesis of Jungian and Christian understanding is possible, it must certainly begin from a perspective that is closer to the subjectivist position. Jung's epistemology consistently rules out a meeting on any other grounds. The question to be answered is whether *any* Christian theology, even one using a human experiential starting point, would be able to achieve a viable synthesis with Jungian thought and practice. This question has been considered recently by at least two Roman Catholic scholars with strong anti-transcendentalist and anti-intellectualist leanings, both Canadians, John P. Dourley and F.X. Charet.

In a little essay reflecting on the correspondence between Jung and White,[21] Charet remarks that the success of further dialogue between Jungian and Catholic thinkers will depend on the interplay of diverse schools of thought, both theological and psychological. The eclipse of Catholic neo-scholasticism and the emergence of new varieties of Thomism since the second Vatican Council, he writes, have given to Catholic thought more than one acceptable starting place and more than one possible agenda for a conversation with Jung.

Contemporary Catholic theologians inclined toward the school of "transcendental Thomism"—Charet calls it "resurrected scholasticism" ("Dialogue," p. 436)—put God's unconditioned freedom and transcendence at the center of Christian doctrine. Charet notes, correctly, that serious conversation between Jungians and neo-Thomists will probably reawaken the same issues that Jung and White found irresolvable and lead again to impasse. But he hypothesizes another scenario:

> If Catholic theology should ever disengage itself from excessive intellectualizing and take a more experiential turn toward the contemplative and the mystical, a dialogue with Jungian psychology might focus on different problems or, perhaps, tackle these same questions differently. What the Jungian response in any projected dialogue would be is as yet unclear, given the current upheaval in its own ranks. . . .
> ("Dialogue," pp.436f)

The turn toward experiential theology, toward the contemplative and the mystical, would mean that theology begins with the personal experience of religious symbols. As a Catholic theologian who long since looked in that direction, John Dourley has argued for decades that orthodox Catholic thought can tolerate a more experiential starting place. As mentioned above, Dourley is both a Catholic priest and a Jungian analyst. In his study of the implications of Paul Tillich's thought[22] for this purpose, he has gone perhaps as far as anyone could to explore the possibility that Jung's psychology can be married to Christian theology.

Dourley is prepared to go much further than Victor White in conditioning religious belief on human interiority. Unlike White, he has no ties to a Thomism that maintains God's absolute transcendence and perfection. Rather, his vision of the Christian message is thoroughly shaped by Jungian psychology. In *The Illness that We Are* Dourley explains his disagreement with Aquinas' view of God's transcendence:

> Indeed, the distance Aquinas placed between the deity and human consciousness is the ultimate antithesis of Jung's contentions that human and divine being intersect in human consciousness, and that no real distinction can be made between the reality of God and the human experience of God.
>
> (*Illness*, p.41)

Since Dourley locates the reality of God entirely in the inner life of the individual (*Illness*, p.87), he bows only selectively to classic Catholic doctrines. Like Jung, he says nothing about God's extra-psychic reality, and he offers the same challenge to ecclesial authority with its claims of an "absolute" truth.

Among Christian systematic theologies, Dourley notes, Tillich's seems one of the best suited to admit a synthesis with Jung's psychology.[23] In his study of Tillich, as expected, he finds major areas of agreement. Tillich's epistemology locates God in the intrinsic human "ground of being," as the "life within life" ("Jung, Tillich," in *Jung and Christianity in Dialogue*, p.91).[24] Dourley argues persuasively that if Tillich's theology is not the location for a Christian-Jungian bridge, no bridge is possible between Christian orthodoxy and an authentic appropriation of Jung's thought.

Significantly, however, Dourley has concluded that, once one takes seriously Tillich's commitment to Trinitarian doctrine and his stress on the extrinsic gift of grace through a unique Christ-event, his theology is revealed as basically incompatible with Jung's vision. For all their apparent similarities, Dourley concludes, Tillich's thought is less like Jung's than like White's or Buber's.[25] That is, Tillich still adheres to the doctrine of a transcendent and extra-psychic God. He cannot do otherwise, Dourley comments, and remain an orthodox Christian theologian ("Jung and Tillich Reconsidered," in *Love, Celibacy and the Inner Marriage*, p.69).[26] It seems that there is no way to bring Tillich's Trinity, which omits matter, evil and the feminine, in line with Jung's intra-psychic and quaternarian God-image. Having reached this conclusion, Dourley is forced to abandon his search for a location, within Christian church teachings, from which to build the desired bridge.

Dourley once said that he, with Jung, wanted to promote an "appreciative transcendence" of existing religion and so sponsor an organic evolution beyond Christianity.[27] But it seems clear that many Christian theologians—not only those committed to a propositionalist or intellectualist view of doctrine—would be uncomfortable with an interpretation of Christian symbols which claimed to "transcend" (even "appreciatively") the present state of the church's wisdom and authority. The decision to go "beyond" Christianity, even if one begins by affirming it, at some point unavoidably becomes its negation. Dourley has recently granted this point. He now writes that Jung strove for the "appreciative transcendence *and so undermining* of Christianity" ("Jung and Tillich Reconsidered," p.70, italics added).

I think Dourley's analysis of the direction of Jung's thought is accurate. But we should not overlook the word "appreciative" in what otherwise might be read as an invitation to abandon Christianity outright. Even if an organic synthesis between Jung's psychology and orthodox Christian theology is unlikely, Jungians concerned with Christian symbols still need to consider the importance of symbolic and spiritual continuity.

Jung did not wish to invent a new religion or to pull up old symbols by the roots. Thus he urged White to stay on at Black-friars not only to spare his friend stressful changes, but also so that White might continue to minister to his culture through teaching. The present era, Jung reminded him, still needs a psychologically informed interpretation of the Christ-symbol. Jung might have been alarmed if any theological proposal, offered in his name, threatened to demolish, rather than to gradually transform, the ancient symbols of Christian doctrine and practice.

3. Hikers in No-mans-land

Frustration is inevitable in any conversation where basic presuppositions disagree; so it is understandable if many practitioners of theology and psychology want nothing to do with conversations across the epistemological fence. But there are those who feel that neither psychological subjectivity nor metaphysical transcendence ought to be entirely excluded from consciousness; and so people keep trying to combine the viewpoints of Jung's psychology and Christian theology, if not to bridge them then at least to keep both perspectives in awareness.

It should be clear by now that anyone who attempts even a makeshift synthesis between Jung's psychology and orthodox Christianity will need to befriend some part of Jung's epistemology. There are good theological arguments, too, for keeping the subjectivity of immanent revelation in mind. If God has any connection at all to creation and the human subject, then theology cannot deny the meaning of human subjective experience; and the nature of the divine-human connection must be open to ongoing interpretation. The risk of a univocally "transcendental" theology is that it kills living faith in the effort to protect it. Religion then loses its symbolic aspect and becomes mere legalism and literalism.

The relationship of human experience with divine transcendence entails the resolution of many relative opposites—consciousness and the unconscious, body and spirit, word and flesh. Incarnational faith maintains that these pairs can mingle and coexist, even if their mingling is inarticulate and their coexistence a struggle. A religious viewpoint based in Christian witness has to be faithful to both its axes: the eschatalogical transcendence of God, and the temporal subjectivity of human experience.

Respect for these perspectives entails ongoing communication, however partial and clouded, between theories of knowledge, and suggests that wisdom springs from neither immanent nor transcendent warrants alone, but arises from the tensions in their meeting. If new insights into the meaning of these polarities are able to be shared in dialogue, they will doubtless come in fragments. St. Paul, survivor of a painful reversal of meanings touching every dimension of life, concluded that we still see God, at best, "in a glass darkly." The moment of personal enlightenment may be global and sudden; but if we would hold it long enough to share what we have witnessed, and contribute to the transformation of our culture, we must satisfy ourselves with partial statements and imperfect understandings.

The impasse that emerged between Jung and White shows how an epistemological conflict can cast a paralyzing spell that blocks mutual understanding. Such an impasse is especially likely if the dialogue is carried on in public, and if each speaker feels responsible for communal leadership. Relativization and compromise can then seem like a loss of authority. Any institution—political, ecclesial, academic, or scientific—tends to regard opposing views as errors and defections, even when they are merely news from another culture, or represent the other side of a prevailing view.

A movement to combine or overcome conflict between two schools of thought, as in Lindbeck's cultural-linguistic theory, necessarily occupies a level of abstraction higher than either of the schools whose conflict it hopes to reframe. Similarly, Bateson's proposed alternation between form and process (discussed in the first chapter) resolves the opposition between two ways of seeing by incorporating both into a meta-theory. Meta-theories, however, tend to become over-intellectualized and self-validating, unless they are grounded in practice and repeatedly challenged. They must be tested and retested, learned and relearned, experimentally and practically applied. There is not much point in a completely abstract theory, one that momentarily satisfies the intellect but has no impact on behavior and cannot be challenged in application.

But just here common experience shows the difficulty of living by even the best abstractions. Most of the time we live below the level of our wise reconciling meta-theories. In daily practice it is hard to maintain the necessary level of tension, metaphorically to translate conflicting views into a balanced dialectical whole and to remind oneself that those who are caught in a polarizing conflict are "simply speaking their own language." The social transformation of groups caught in polarized dialogue requires that numbers of people on each side grasp and be grasped personally by a new way-of-seeing, which entails an authentic way-of-living. The process requires the integration of considerable shadow and the bearing of some necessary suffering.

Meta-theories may thus be excellent aids in the exercise of *verstehen* and yet be difficult or impossible for the total personality to grasp. But if this conclusion is true it is unfortunate. One who lives out an existential commitment under the power of a harmonizing meta-theory can incarnate its reconciling vision and carry a message of co-existence into a violently divided world. We call such persons saints, and sometimes martyrs, for warring opposites usually resist being gathered under anyone's wings.

We should acknowledge that bridges between epistemic language-worlds are almost always left unfinished. Bridge-building may be a defective metaphor for the meeting of two thought-worlds, in any case. For a conceptual "bridge" is a way above obstacles, a road through the air. White's dream of the wind-guided sailboat, speeding past rocks and gliding easily up village streets, is hardly a more helpful image. Cultural-linguistic and epistemological conflicts need to be dealt with over time, patiently, imperfectly, in all their concreteness. For a true meeting of language-worlds, then, the better metaphor may be knapsack-and-boots.

Imagine two individuals who barely know one another's language, beginning to grasp the meanings of each other's words and practice through daily mutual interaction, while walking together over rocky ground. In slow increments one comes to understand or at least to recognize the other's point of view, in spite of its strangeness, while seeing the strangeness of one's own world reflected in the other's struggle to understand. As in any multi-cultural learning process, each must suffer equally by the relativizing contact to achieve a real encounter and real learning.

There is no Archimedean vantage point—Jung was right about this—from which to correct anyone's epistemology, including one's own. But imperfect understandings leave room for initiatives not of the ego's making. Sparks of meaningful questions may leap between the points of an unfinished bridge and confessions of partial understanding break the silences in no-mans-land.

Survival in no-mans-land comes down to a sort of faith, though not the sort that kills what cannot be assimilated. If we believe that meaning is to triumph over meaninglessness in the end, we will embrace the fruits of collaboration between even polarized opposites. Believers in the biblical God are enjoined to hope that the irreconcilable powers will someday embrace. Meanwhile, we are directed to look for our daily bread on the desert floor.

Is this painful way the best we can hope for? At least it is a life-supporting struggle, not a death-like peace built on suppression of conflict. It is understandable that institutions and groups with power and position are often willing to risk death by stagnation and to cast the stranger into exile, rather than face the necessity of change that comes through a confrontation with otherness. But to silence opposition in the name of institutional security is very often a sin against the Holy Spirit, a rejection of life for the sake of order.

Many who care about healing and inner transformation, and generally about the work of helping either individuals or collectivities toward wholeness and fullness of life, will honor the work of Jung and White and support others who hike together in the borderlands. For the reasons explored in these pages, however, it would be hard to predict for collaborators in other times and places more visible success, or less personal cost, than C.G. Jung and Victor White experienced in theirs.

Appendix A

The Letters of Victor White

For three decades following their deaths—apart from a time when this correspondence was lent to Gerhard Adler and Aniela Jaffé[1] to facilitate their editing the *C.G. Jung Letters*—the scores of letters that Victor White sent to C.G. Jung were kept in the family archives in Küsnacht, unavailable to researchers. They are now stored, together with copies of Jung's letters to White, in the C.G. Jung Archive[2] at the Swiss Federal Polytechnic—the ETH—in Zurich.

Early in 1986, on the advice of Dr. William McGuire, I wrote a letter to the ETH library archivist, Dr. Beat Glaus, requesting permission to study White's letters. My request, as I had been warned to expect,[3] was promptly turned down by the Jung heirs. Jung's grandson Lorenz wrote to me that White's letters were locked away on orders of C.G. Jung himself. Since there was no way to tell when the ban might be lifted, I reconciled myself to writing my dissertation without access to this primary source of information.

Clues about the content of White's letters existed, however. Most important for my research, three-quarters of Jung's letters to White were already printed in the *C.G. Jung Letters*. It was thus often possible, by reading between the lines of Jung's letters, to discern in outline the questions arising on White's side. Considerable information was available, too, in the footnotes of the *Letters*, where the two editors, Adler and Jaffé, had incorporated summaries and brief excerpts of White's most important letters to Jung.[4]

Franz Jung's letter to me, dated 30 April 1986 (a translation of which appears below), provided a glimpse—limited, to be sure, but unique at the time—into specific aspects of White's correspondence. It proved possible from these and other sources to piece together an adequate account of the two men's collaboration, separation, and reconciliation.

The Locked Archive

In 1986, replying to my original requests, Franz and Lorenz Jung each stated that, by reason of their sensitive nature, White's letters would under no circumstances be made available. Lorenz's letter of 4 February

1986 explained this refusal in terms of the Jung family obligation to preserve confidentiality, mentioning several aspects of this duty. The letters are not suited to public perusal, he said, since they concern personal questions. In his lifetime C.G. Jung expressly stated that he wished this correspondence to be kept secret. And due to their personal nature the letters were covered by a duty of "medical confidentiality."[5]

The latter phrase should not be read as saying that the relationship between Jung and White had been literally that of doctor and patient.[6] "Medical confidentiality" here means that in handling such sensitive material the Jung heirs continue to be bound—as was C.G. Jung himself—to the highest standard of confidentiality. The underlying principle governing this central duty is summarized by Lorenz Jung as a moral injunction, that "the confidence between two people not be relativized in retrospect" (4 Feb. 86).[7]

The family's firmness on this principle can be traced to C.G. Jung's own caution with emotionally freighted information. For example, in his March 1959 BBC interview, "Face to Face," Jung said he would not discuss the dreams Freud once gave him to analyze, even though by now Freud had been dead for years. "There is such a thing as a professional secret," he commented. "These regards last longer than life" ("Face to Face," p.432). In line with Jung's sense of professional privacy, his heirs have historically considered themselves bound—not absolutely, but in principle—by his wishes concerning the publication of specific bodies of material.[8]

Inevitably, Jung's professional obligation to safeguard sensitive material sometimes came into tension with his equally strong desire to further scientific learning. Where these duties conflicted, his stipulations about delays in publication could sometimes vary enormously.[9] When he was intent on absolute secrecy, however, he destroyed both sides of the correspondence (*Letters I*, p.xi). That he saved Victor White's letters suggests that he felt they would someday be useful to scholars.

In early April 1986 I answered Lorenz Jung's letter, accepting the limitations placed on my research by the need for confidentiality, but adding a pragmatic request: since I was forbidden to see this material but he was not, would he kindly read through the letters of Victor White and answer a few specific questions for me? In less than a month I received the following reply, not from Lorenz Jung but from his father. It amazed me both by its completeness and by the evidence of long and demanding study which Franz Jung had undertaken in order to write it. He had answered every one of my questions and offered suggestions for further study.

Although circumstances have changed since Mr. Jung wrote to me in the spring of 1986, his letter illustrates the Jung family's desire to support serious research on the religious aspects of C.G. Jung's life and work, while remaining true to their duty to guard the confidentiality of sensitive communications. My translation of Franz Jung's complete letter is printed here with his permission.

* * *

From Mr. Franz Jung   Küsnacht-Zürich: 30 April 1986
Re: Your letter of 4 April 1986 to Dr. Lorenz Jung
Dear Mrs. Lammers,

My son, Dr. Lorenz Jung, spoke with me about your letter concerning the correspondence between Father White and C.G. Jung and gave it to me for reply.

I have taken time to look through the entire correspondence, which is largely handwritten. It comprises approximately 80 letters, with various addenda such as case material and dreams, as well as very personal and private information, all of which, as my son told you, makes the correspondence unsuitable for publication.

Jung's heirs understandably feel themselves very much bound by their father's wish to protect a profound relationship like this one between two friends—a relationship which after all ended tragically—and not subject it to scrutiny from people who stand outside. I ask you, therefore, to base your work upon documents that are already published. It seems to me that this would also shed more light than if you were to cite new, unpublished sources that are not generally available.

I can assure you that the correspondence, insofar as it deals with general psychological or religious problems, contains nothing different from the views the writers put forward in their books, lectures, etc., at the time. Since the correspondence extends from 3 August 1945 to 8 May 1960, publications of C.G. Jung like *Aion, Mysterium Coniunctionis, Job,* etc., and those of Victor White (see the citations in Jung's works), including *God and the Unconscious,* deal with the same topics as their conversations and letters and often even use the same arguments and wordings. The themes under discussion: God-image, evil, *privatio boni,* Quaternity and Trinity, etc., are the central points of conflict where knowledge and faith could not be brought into agreement.

Since Jung has been misunderstood by so many theologians, I cannot imagine what sense it makes to try to shed new light on the irreconcilable opposites. It seems to me it would be best if you carefully studied and quoted from Jung's numerous publications and footnotes and White's various publications from 1946 to 1959, especially *God and the Unconscious,* with the Foreword by C.G. Jung and appendix by Gebhard Frei, S.M.B. I am not familiar with *Soul and Psyche.*

Returning to your specific questions, I can tell you that White's opinion about *Answer to Job* changed only in that he reacted enthusiastically when he first heard about it in conversation; but when it appeared later on in English translation he reacted critically and expressed concern about the consequences. One gathers from this, as well as from a few later statements, that White was personally not in agreement, and that he met with reproaches from his colleagues and superiors. But I could not find any suggestion that White would have been replaced as translator of the *Summa*. On the contrary, I gained the impression that White stood by his dogmatic positions with extraordinary firmness and always tested Jung's interpretations and experiences against the Thomistic standpoint.

As you know, White died very young of cancer, my father a year later of advanced old age. For insight into the final years, I suggest you read the published letters of C.G. Jung (*Briefe III* Walter-Verlag Olten),[10] especially:

16 Sept. 1959 to V. Brooke
 5 Dec. 1959 to Mr. Leonard   as well as other sources,
 6 Feb. 1960 to Mother Prioress of course, such as
29 Apr. 1960 to Mother Prioress *Memories, Dreams,*
30 Apr. 1960 to J. Rudin, S.J.   *Reflections*: the chapter
 3 June 1960 to Mrs. Ginsberg   called "Late Thoughts"
24 Aug. 1960 to W.P. Witcutt

C.G. Jung had received White's last book, *Soul and Psyche*, as he informed him on 30 April 1960. But I cannot say whether he ever read the book all the way through; it is no longer in his library. I think the final letters clearly depict the mutually disappointing development of the relationship. The standpoints of the two friends were just too different. Neither could retreat from his own convictions, nor could either understand that the other could not simply come around to his viewpoint.

It is painful and tragic, of course, that fifteen years of hard work, seeking the highest and deepest kinds of knowledge, ran into a wall of misunderstandings and ended fruitlessly; but one must say in all justice that at least the first years of this intellectual exchange brought many valuable and reciprocal learnings.

I hope that my long explanatory comments have to some extent clarified the situation as it was in those years, and that you can derive sufficient raw material for your work from the sources to which I have referred you.

Cordially, Franz Jung

P.S. You mentioned that you were going to ask the Dominican Order for
    permission to look at the letters and quote them. This effort appears

useless to me; even with agreement from that quarter, we would *not* open our archives, due to the circumstances mentioned.

* * *

Opening the Archive

In summer 1990 the *Jung-Erbengemeinschaft* decided to release White's letters. What triggered this decision was the arrival in Zurich of Victor White's recently appointed literary executor, Dr. Adrian Cunningham from the University of Lancaster, with authorization from Fr. Timothy Radcliffe, O.P., then Prior Provincial of the English Dominican Province (Victor White's legal heirs). Dr. Cunningham's mission was to take charge of all of White's documents, including the letters to C.G. Jung, on behalf of the English Province.

This request came a full three decades after the deaths of White and Jung. During this time, Franz Jung had guarded White's letters at his father's request (F. Jung, personal correspondence, 10 Dec. 92). Now, he advised the collective heirs of C.G. Jung, the time had come to release them. The considerations which he personally brought to bear on the question are outlined in his own words below:

* * *

For many years the Jung heirs, knowing the importance and sensitivity of the Jung-White letters, had kept in mind what C. G. Jung himself stipulated concerning them: he wished his heirs to handle White's correspondence as confidential and to look carefully for an editor. Eventually, it was hoped, they would find one who would understand C. G. Jung's and Victor White's deep-rooted problems and who could be trusted to treat these questions with the necessary tact and respect.

When Mrs. Ann Lammers sent her dissertation, "A Study of the Relation Between Theology and Psychology: Victor White and C. G. Jung," to me in September 1989, I read it with enormous interest and showed it also to my son, Dr. Lorenz Jung. We were impressed by the knowledge and seriousness of the work, and I encouraged Mrs. Lammers to look for a publisher right away. Even if at this time the author had not had access to the full White-Jung correspondence, I thought that such a careful study would be an important addition to the field of religion and psychology. Mrs. Lammers' work showed her expertise in two fields which unhappily often seem to lie rather far from each other. She showed special knowledge and understanding of the often difficult writings of C. G. Jung, and she handled the even more sensitive passages on Victor White's religious convictions with tact and respect.

As a result, when Prof. Cunningham requested in June 1990 to look into the correspondence of C. G. Jung and Victor White, with the possibility of later copying and editing some of it, the Jung heirs agreed unanimously to my proposal that we give permission to both interested parties to copy and read the letters: to Mrs. Lammers so that she could complete her book, and to Prof. Cunningham for the Dominican Order, so that he could edit the letters as he proposed. We thought such a happy coincidence should not be missed; and we hope our prompt decision will bring forth important new insights and understandings of these significant themes.

(F. Jung, personal correspondence, 1 Nov. 92)[11]

* * *

Permission to study the Jung-White correspondence was given to me in 1991 by both sets of heirs. I was reassured to discover on reading them that, in keeping with Franz Jung's letter of April 1986, the contents of Victor White's letters did not fundamentally contradict the evidence I had previously gathered—although they certainly added to it. Incorporating new material from White's and Jung's correspondence yields a picture of the collaboration that is far more detailed, clear and dramatic than I could have drawn when writing the dissertation on which this book is based; but in outline it is the same picture.

Selected Books and Articles
by Victor White

A list of C.G. Jung's writings and their dates of publication is part of the back matter of every volume in the *Collected Works*, and detailed information is in the *General Index* (Volume 20). The works of Victor White, on the other hand, have received less scholarly attention and are hard to find. The English Dominican quarterly, *Blackfriars* (see note below), was discontinued in 1965, and the old issues are not stored in most U.S. theological libraries. The journal White founded, *Dominican Studies*, has also ceased publication.

What follows is a partial chronology of White's published work, by date of composition. It includes all his articles and books considered in this study, and indicates libraries where sources are available. (Legend of abbreviations appears on p. 268.)

1932   "Spengler Views the Machine Age" (*Blackfriars* XIII, 1/32). [W-EDS & CUA]

"The Boom of Youth" (*Blackfriars*, XIII, 9/32): review of Wyndham Lewis, *The Doom of Youth*. [W-EDS & CUA]

1934   *Scholasticism* (London: Catholic Truth Society, #126 in the series "Pamphlets for Students"). [YDS]

1939   "Kierkegaard's Journals" (*Blackfriars* XX, 11/39). [W-EDS & CUA]

1941   "The Platonic Tradition in St. Thomas Aquinas" (chapter 5 in Part I, *God the Unknown*, 1956). [KML]

1942   "The Effects of Schism" (*Blackfriars* XXIII, 2/42). [W-EDS & CUA]

"Western and Eastern Theology of Grace and Nature" (chapter 5 in Part II, *God the Unknown*, 1956). [KML]

"Frontiers of Theology and Psychology" (Guild of Pastoral Psychology, Lecture 19). (Chaps. 4 and 5 in *God and the Unconscious*, 1952, are based on this lecture.) [KML]

1943   "Thomism and 'Affective Knowledge' " (three issues of *Blackfriars*: XXIV, 1/43 & 4/43; XXV, 9/44). [W-EDS & CUA]

1944   "St. Thomas Aquinas and Jung's Psychology" (*Blackfriars* XXV, 6/44). [NYC]

"Walter Hilton: An English Spiritual Guide" (Guild of Pastoral Psychology, Lecture 31). [KML]

1945   "Psychotherapy and Ethics" (*Blackfriars* XXVI, 8/45. Reprint by the Newman Association: "A tribute to C.G. Jung on his 70th birthday." Chapter 8 in *God and the Unconscious*, 1952.) [KML]

"Psychotherapy and Ethics: Postscript" (*Blackfriars* XXVI, 10/45. Included as the end of chapter 8 in *God and the Unconscious*, 1952. Review of Flugel's *Man, Morals, and Society*.) [W-EDS & CUA]

1947   "St. Thomas's Conception of Revelation" (*Dominican Studies*, Vol. 1, 1/48, Oxford Blackfriars). (written 3/47) [SML/Mudd]

"The Aristotelian-Thomist Conception of Man" (*Eranos- Jahrbuch 1947*). [delivered at Ascona 8/47, incorporating "St. Thomas's Conception of Revelation" as Part II.] [SML]

"The Twilight of the Gods" (chapter 1 in *God and the Unconscious*, 1952).

"The Gods Go A-Begging" (chapter 2 in *God and the Unconscious*, 1952).

"Aristotle, Aquinas and Man" (chapter 6 in *God and the Unconscious*, 1952).

"Revelation and the Unconscious" (chapter 7 in *God and the Unconscious*, 1952).

1948   "The Unconscious and God" (chapter 3 in *God and the Unconscious*, 1952).

"The Analyst and the Confessor" (*The Commonweal*. New York: 7/23/48) (chapter 9 in *God and the Unconscious*, 1952). [KML]

"Notes on Gnosticism" (Guild Lecture No. 59. London: Guild of Pastoral Psychology, 1949). Read to the York Analytical Psychology Club, 2/20/48; read to the London Guild of Pastoral Psychology, 12/10/48. Chapter 11 in *God and the Unconscious*, 1952.) [KML]

1949   "Satan" (*Dominican Studies*, Vol. 2, no.2. 4/49, Blackfriars). [W-EDS & CUA]

"Eranos: 1947,1948" (*Dominican Studies*, Vol. 2, no.4. 10/49). [SML/Mudd]

1950   "The Scandal of the Assumption" (*Life of the Spirit: A Blackfriars Review*, Vol. V, Nov/Dec 1950, pp.199–212). [KML]

"Devils and Complexes" (chapter 10 in *God and the Unconscious*, 1952).

1951   "The Dying God" (chapter 12 in *God and the Unconscious*, 1952).

"Some Recent Contributions to Psychology" (*Blackfriars* XXXII, 9/51). [W-EDS & CUA]

"Buddhism Comes West" (*Blackfriars* XXXII, 12/51). [W-EDS & CUA]

1952   "The Dying God: Pagan, Psychological and Christian" (*Blackfriars* XXXIII, 2/52). [W-EDS & CUA]

"The Dying God: Pagan, Psychological and Christian: Differences" (*Blackfriars* XXXIII, 3/52). [W-EDS & CUA]

"Four Challenges to Religion" (*Blackfriars* XXXIII) "Freud" (4/52); "Jung" (5/52); "Frazer" (6/52); "Marx" (7,8/52). [W-EDS & CUA]

"The Unknown God" (chapter 2 in Part I, *God the Unknown*, 1956). [KML]

God and the Unconscious (London: The Harvill Press). (Revised edition, Dallas: Spring, 1982). [Note: 1982 edition does not include Gebhard Frei's appendix. The 1952 edition is available at KML.]

1953   "Religious Tolerance" (*The Commonweal*, NYC: 9/4/53, pp.531–34). [KML]

"Good and Evil" (*Harvest*, vol.12. London: Analytical Psychology Club, 1966). [KML]

1954   "Review of Jung's *Psychological Reflections*, ed. Jolande Jacobi." (*Blackfriars* XXXV, 1/54). [W-EDS & CUA]

Review of *CW 7* & *CW 12*; Jung's *Von den Wurzeln des Bewusstseins*; and Progoff's *Jung's Psychology and its Social Meaning* (*Blackfriars* XXXV, 3/54). [W-EDS & CUA]

1955   Review of *CW 17*; and de Forest's *The Leaven of Love* (*Blackfriars* XXXVI, 2/55). [W-EDS & CUA]

"Jung on Job" (*Blackfriars* XXXVI, 3/55; also appears, revised, as Appendix V in *Soul & Psyche*, 1960). [NYC or W-EDS & CUA]

"Good Friday" (*The Commonweal* LXI:26. New York, 4/1/55, pp.674-76).

"Kinds of Opposites" (*Studien zur Analytischen Psychologie, Festschrift zum 80. Geburtstag C. G.Jungs*. Zürich: Rascher Verlag). [KML]

"Charles Gustave Jung" (*Jung at Eighty*, special edition of *Time and Tide: The Independent Weekly*. Vol. 36, no. 30, 7/23/55. London, pp.962f). [KML]

"Two Theologians on Jung's Psychology" (*Blackfriars* XXXVI, 10/55). [W-EDS & CUA]

1956   *God the Unknown & other essays* (London: Harvill Press). [KML]

1957   Review of *Eranos-Jahrbuch, 1955, Band XXIV* (*Blackfriars* XXXVIII, 2/57). [W-EDS & CUA]

Review of Tillich's *Biblical Religion and the Search for Ultimate Reality*; and Robinson's *Christ and Conscience* (*Blackfriars* XXXVIII, 3/57). [W-EDS & CUA]

1958   "Holy Teaching: The Idea of Theology According to St. Thomas Aquinas" (Aquinas Paper No. 33, Blackfriars Publications, for the Aquinas Society of London). [YDS]

Review of Hostie's *Religion and the Psychology of Jung* (*Journal of Analytical Psychology*, Vol. III, London: Tavistock Publ., pp.59–64). [KML]

1959   "Some Recent Studies in Archetypology" (*Blackfriars* XL, 5/59). [W-EDS & CUA]

1960   Review of Jung's *CW 9i* & *CW 9ii*; Jacobi's *Complex, Archetype, Symbol in the Psychology of C. G.Jung*; and Philp's *Jung and the Problem of Evil* (*Blackfriars* XLI, 1,2/60). [W-EDS & CUA]

Soul and Psyche: An Enquiry into the Relationship of Psychotherapy and Religion (NYC: Harper & Brothers). [KML & YDS]

"Theological Reflections" (*Journal of Analytical Psychology*, Vol. V, London: Tavistock Publications., pp.147–54). [KML]

Thomas Gilby's review of *Soul and Psyche* (Blackfriars XLI, 5/60). [W-EDS & CUA]

"PERSONAE: Victor White, O.P. († May 22, 1960)" (Unsigned obituary. *Blackfriars* XLI, July/Aug.1960). [W-EDS & CUA]

Additional Essays by White on Diverse Topics in BLACKFRIARS:

1933:   Review of current writings on sexual ethics.

1935:   "Reunion in Germany" (Protestant clergy entering Roman Catholic Church); and "The Case for Italy" (condemning the invasion of Abyssinia).

1936:   Two articles on ecumenism.

1937:   Discussion of the Pope's statements on Communism.

1938:   Two articles on the Church of England. A review of Maritain's *Humanisme intégrale* (*True Humanism*).

1939:   "Christian Revolution" (on war and pacifism). Article on the reunion of churches.

1941:   Essay on ecumenism, quoting Yves M.-J. Congar's *Chrétiens désunis* (*Blackfriars* XXII, 9/41, p.469).

1957:   Review of Aldous Huxley's *Adonis and the Alphabet*.

BLACKFRIARS: A Monthly Review

Much of Victor White's writing appeared originally in *Blackfriars: A Monthly Review* (edited by the English Dominicans). For a time *Blackfriars* incorporated *The Catholic Review*. It published from 1920–65, superseded by the *New Blackfriars*. Complete collections are available at the combined libraries of Weston College and the Episcopal Divinity School, Cambridge, MA, and at the library of Catholic University of America, Washington, D.C. White's obituary (Vol. XLI, Nos. 482–83, 7,8/60) thanks him for thirty years of loyal service to the publication, i.e., 1930-60. His earliest *Blackfriars* article leads the January 1932 issue (Vol. XIII). His last appears in the May 1959 issue (Vol. XL).

Legend: Locations of Libraries Mentioned Above

CUA: Catholic University of America (Washington, D.C.).

KML: Kristine Mann Library (Analytical Psychology Club of New York, New York, NY).

NYC: New York Public Library (New York, NY).

SML: Sterling Memorial Library (Yale University, New Haven, CT).

SML/Mudd: Mudd Library (Yale University, New Haven, CT).

W-EDS: Weston College and Episcopal Divinity School (Cambridge, MA).

YDS: Yale Divinity School (Yale University, New Haven, CT).

Appendix C

A Note on Aelred Squire

I met Father Aelred Squire through a mutual friend, Brother William Brown, O.H.C., in the nick of time as I was trying to complete my dissertation for Yale in the summer of 1987. The conversation that told me of Father Aelred's existence, and led to our first meeting, happened entirely by chance at a time when Brother William was just on the point of leaving California, having recently finished his term as prior at a small ecumenical priory in Berkeley.[1]

One fine Sunday in June I took a break from my dissertation to worship at Grace Cathedral in San Francisco. After the service I fell into conversation with Brother William, who had served that morning in the chancel. He spoke with his usual friendly interest about my work, and asked how my research was going. I lamented that despite my best efforts so far I had yet to find anyone who could give me first-hand information about Victor White's days at Blackfriars, Oxford.

"I know someone who was White's student," Brother William announced with a twinkle: "Aelred Squire. He's Camaldolese now, but used to be Dominican. He'll be coming up to Berkeley from Big Sur in two weeks. Shall I give him your name?"

This book draws in many ways upon Aelred Squire's knowledge and wisdom. He helped me to perceive the theological context that framed the final years of White's career and to understand the daily circumstances and atmosphere in which White taught and wrote. Fr. Aelred's memories of that era, though often incomplete, suggested directions for research. In the absence of a published account, he kindly provided a brief written overview of the history of Blackfriars, Oxford. And from his fund of theological and historical knowledge he deepened my contextual understanding of concepts such as "experience," basic to White's theological project—a project in whose spirit Squire himself to a large degree shared.

It is natural to want to know the background and bias of anyone who contributes so much to a project like this one. Readers may therefore want to know something about Aelred Squire's scholarly work, as well as his relationship to the monastic world in which both he and Victor White struggled with their often complex vocations. Since I would have been at a

269

disadvantage in trying to tell Squire's story, not being well enough versed in the history and terminology of the monastic orders, the following account is the product of collaboration. Most of its substance was written by the historian best informed about the events it describes.

Fr. Aelred Squire was born in Streatham, London S.W., on 6 December 1921 and baptized Kenneth in the local Anglican parish church. His reading as a schoolboy made him a convinced Catholic in his heart by the time he was in his teens. At that time he had already adopted the practice of saying daily the so-called Little Office of our Lady in Latin. But it was only when, as a conscientious objector in wartime, he was working for the Hertfordshire War Agricultural Committee in Berkhamstead, that it became clear to him that he should ask for instruction and reception into the Catholic Church.

As Oxford was accessible by bus, he arranged to be instructed by a well-known Blackfriars Dominican, Fr. Conrad Pepler, who received him into the Catholic Church at St. Peter's, Eynsham, in 1943. His contact with the Dominicans thus gave the first concrete shape to interests about which he had so far only read, and it was natural for him to think of asking to join them. But in the year of his reception, he also began to visit the Benedictine house of Prinknash in the hills above Gloucester, which produced a strong counter-pull in his imagination. This reawakened something in an older experience. A first rather mysterious acquaintance with religious life had occurred much younger in Squire's life when, around the age of seven or eight, he came across the ruins of a small Cluniac priory not far from the south-coast town to which his family had moved by then, where he spent many afternoons sitting and taking in things.

This attraction to a contemplative life was unwittingly strengthened by the suggestion of the prioress of a Carmelite convent, then at Woodcock Hill near Berkhamstead, with whom he had come into contact through Dominican connections.[2] She suggested that he might care for a time to help the convent out with their need for a gardener to work the large kitchen garden, and for someone to fulfill the duties of an outside "turn sister." (The "turn sister" normally lived in a room outside the enclosure, a few steps down from the opening through which incoming goods and messages were passed in a revolving "turn.")

It was thus by moving up the hill from his former lodgings that Squire came to meet Victor White, many years before they lived in the same house in Oxford. White came to the convent from time to time to give spiritual direction or retreat conferences. On these occasions Squire tried to make conversation with White as they ate breakfast together after

Mass in Squire's room; but he found his visitor laconic to the point of muteness.

Meanwhile, Squire found the silent life of the Sisters congenial. Further visits to Prinknash led to his asking the abbot of the time to accept him as a novice when it should be possible; and he was given a positive response. When this became known, a friend he had made was outraged at the possible waste of Squire's promising gifts if he became a monk, and strongly urged Dominican life as more suitable for him. This threw Squire into deep conflict. In the end, he wrote to the abbot saying that he thought he ought to become a Dominican.

Thus in September 1946, still with many serious misgivings, he entered the Dominican novitiate then at Hawkesyard Priory in Staffordshire, a house no longer in existence. It was usual at that time to give candidates a new name at their clothing. Exceptionally, Squire was offered a choice of three names, one of which was Aelred, after the twelfth-century Cistercian monk in whom he was already interested. So he asked for that name, by which he has been known ever since. In 1947 he made his simple profession for three years.

The making of his solemn profession for life in 1950 was a more difficult matter. In continuing anguish Squire followed the advice of the confessor he consulted. His study of the Rule of St. Benedict, of which he had begun to paint an illustrated copy as a novice, had given him a high regard for the virtues of obedience and humility. He did not feel prepared to say that his preference for his future was better than that of others, many of whom insisted that Dominican life was meant to be radically contemplative. Thus he made his solemn profession with a continuing sense of tension; yet he feels he can still say that he has never, under obedience, been asked to do something against his conscience.

With this inner conflict unresolved, Squire moved to Oxford Blackfriars to continue his studies in theology, having completed three years of philosophy at Hawkesyard. Victor White now became his professor in dogmatic theology, whose many terse asides in class suggested a sympathetic and compelling mind. Although at the time there was a certain formal separation between teachers and students, it was not unusual for a student to approach any priest for confession or spiritual advice. During the four years in which they both lived at Blackfriars, Squire made a determined effort to know White, though he often found "Vicky" as taciturn as he had been at Woodcock Hill.

That a meaningful relationship nevertheless developed is suggested by the fact that Fr. Victor agreed to be Squire's assistant priest at his ordination in October 1952. That day, as Squire mentions in the foreword to his *Summer in the Seed*,[3] White gave him "with a wry smile" the two volumes of the *I Ching* in Richard Wilhelm's translation, so much admired by Jung.

On completing his theological studies in 1954, Squire was given his Lectorate in Sacred Theology (STLr), Victor White being among his examiners. It was then decided that he should do a research degree in the university of Oxford, and he was accepted to work under the historian Richard Southern. Soon after Squire began to work on this degree, his Provincial of the time, Fr. Hilary Carpenter, felt compelled to ask him to fill a gap at the Dominican preparatory school at Llanarth in Wales.[4] He taught there for a time, until he was recalled to teach ascetical theology in the Dominican theological school at Blackfriars, Oxford.

From this point onward exact dating sometimes becomes a little difficult, owing to an unexpected development in Fr. Aelred's health. During various hospital admissions for the surgical repair of a physical defect he had had from birth, a nervous breakdown occurred in which the hidden conflict in his life played no small part. The stress of his schedule in this period, combining the duties of student and teacher with the full round of liturgical offices and preaching, no doubt also predisposed him to illness. To the surprise of his doctors, Fr. Aelred even suffered a temporary paralysis that was due to a stroke, though not recognized as such at the time.[5]

That he made a relatively rapid recovery and was able to receive his degree of Bachelor of Letters (B.Litt.) in the university in November 1958, Fr. Aelred attributes to the support, understanding and kindness of his then prior, Fr. Hildebrand James, and of the many friends who helped him in various ways. He was sent to Belgium temporarily to rest. On his return he was soon lecturing in liturgy and church history, as well as ascetical theology, for the Blackfriars studium. He was even occasionally used as an examiner in Canon Law, though this was not his subject.

Squire's sense for canonical matters led him, in the latter part of this time, to consult his confessor as to whether it would now be right to ask for a papal indult to be exclaustrated[6] in order to test his calling to more solitude. This was approved and in due course granted.[7] In August 1965 Squire left for a small German-speaking village in the Belgian Ardennes, to live as a hermit under the supervision of the neighboring parish priest and the Bishop of Liège. He took up residence in a few rooms of an otherwise abandoned priest's house and said Mass for the farming community.

As the two years of exclaustration drew to an end it seemed unwise to Squire to remain where he was, as he did not wish to become involved in the life of a diocesan priest. He therefore returned to teach at St. Catherine's Centre,[8] which had been founded by the confessor who helped him at the time of his breakdown. St. Catherine's Centre was located at the

Dominican Sisters' convent in Portobello Road, West London. Here Squire lived and revised his teaching in ascetical theology, which eventually became his *Asking the Fathers* (1973).[9] His first book, *Aelred of Rievaulx, a study*, which was the fruit of his Oxford research, appeared in 1969.

That year, as a result of a conversation in London with the Dominican Vicar Provincial for Scandinavia, Squire paid his first visit to Norway, where they felt they would like to have an Englishman work with them, on account of the ancient connections between the two countries. He was so enamoured of what he saw that he asked if he might transfiliate to the Dominicans in Paris, since Dominicans working in Scandinavia were under that province. Permission was granted on both sides, and Squire left for Oslo in 1970.

He asked his bishop there, a former Cistercian monk, to be his spiritual director. After Squire had served for one year as a Novice master in Oslo, one of the smallest and remotest parishes in the diocese fell vacant by a sudden death. The bishop asked the Dominicans to take it over; but this they did not feel they wanted to do. It was then that Fr. Aelred asked his Vicar Provincial if he might offer himself to the bishop for that purpose, since it sounded as though the place might offer a good deal of the solitude anyone could desire. The bishop (who had *not* inspired the idea) was grateful and installed Squire, still a Dominican, as parish priest in Lillehammer.

In this small-town parish serving a very scattered community, many of Squire's few parishioners lived in remote places several hours' journey away. Thus, for the greater part of the year, especially in winter, Fr. Aelred was able to lead a quiet, primarily monastic life. His only commitment, aside from visiting his widely dispersed people regularly in the winter months, was to teach a seminar on the great world religions at the neighboring Nansen School, Norway's humanist academy. Here, with enough time to do his research and gather the books he needed, Squire wrote his most developed literary work, *Summer in the Seed* (London, 1980).

In the middle 1970s an invitation to be part of a two-week seminar on his patron Aelred at the Abbey of Gethsemani in Kentucky opened Fr. Aelred's first real connection with monastic life in the United States. One of the monks present—not a Trappist—later told him of the little monastery of Christ in the Desert, New Mexico, which he had joined. For the first time Fr. Aelred felt clearly that he ought to consider transferring to a purely monastic life, if anyone would take him at his age. His request to transfer his solemn vows to the Rule of St. Benedict was granted by the Holy See. He renewed his vows to the Benedictine Rule on the Feast of the Annunciation, 1982, at the monastery of Christ in the Desert.

Following this, various circumstances brought him into contact with the Camaldolese Benedictine congregation at Big Sur on the mid-California coast. After the canonical three years required for someone already a Benedictine, he completed transfiliation to them in 1986. Their life, which is lived as a combination of solitude and community, older than that of the Carthusians, seems to have brought all the broken pieces of his life together.

Fr. Aelred feels that the decision to leave Norway in search of monastic life was, humanly speaking, the most difficult he has ever taken. However he retains many friendships with people there, as he does with several Dominicans among his generation. Indeed, he often thinks with affection of the quiet, rural priory in England where he spent his first four years with them, and where he laid the foundations of his patristic and monastic studies. His most recent book, *Fathers Talking*,[10] is a small collection of patristic translations, representative of many he has made since living in America.

Notes

CHAPTER ONE: BUILDERS OF BRIDGES

[1] Victor White, *Soul and Psyche: An Enquiry into the Relationship of Psychotherapy and Religion* (New York: Harper & Brothers, Inc., 1960).

[2] C.G. Jung, *Answer to Job* (*Collected Works, Volume 11: Psychology and Religion: West and East*. Second Edition. Translator, R.F.C. Hull. Princeton: Princeton University Press, 1958/1969). Hereafter cited as *Job, CW 11*. (Volumes of the *Collected Works* are cited throughout using the abbreviation *CW*, followed by volume number.) *Antwort auf Hiob* was first published in German in 1952. It appeared in English translation in 1954.

[3] Victor White pointed out metaphysical aspects of Jung's psychology in his first published lecture on Jung's thought, "The Frontiers of Theology and Psychology" (Lecture 19, The Guild for Pastoral Psychology. Oxford: 1942). The lecture is discussed at length below in Chapter Two.

[4] Marilyn Nagy, *Philosophical Issues in the Psychology of C.G. Jung* (Albany, NY: State University of New York Press, 1991). Cited hereafter as Nagy.

[5] C.G. Jung, "Approaching the Unconscious" (*Man and his Symbols*. Edited by C.G. Jung and M.-L. von Franz. London: Aldus Books Limited, 1964).

[6] C.G. Jung, "Freud and Jung—Contrasts" (*Modern Man in Search of a Soul*. New York: Harcourt Brace Jovanovich, n.d.; originally published 1933). Hereafter cited as "Contrasts."

[7] C.G. Jung, "The 'Face to Face' Interview" (with John Freeman, BBC Television, 22 Oct. 1959), in *C. G. Jung Speaking: Interviews and Encounters* (Editors, William McGuire, R.F.C. Hull. Princeton: Princeton University Press, 1977), p.431.

[8] Gregory Bateson, *Mind and Nature: A Necessary Unity* (New York: Bantam Books, 1979). The two moments in this zigzag ladder usually go by turns, Bateson explains, as in the feedback mechanism of a thermostat, the act of shooting a shotgun, or the processes of natural selection. Alternating in their "zigzag ladder," process (or feedback) and form (or calibra-

tion) function in complementarity to enable an activity or development that neither alone could sustain.

⁹ C.G. Jung, *Collected Works, Volume 7: Two Essays on Analytical Psychology* (Second edition. Translator, R.F.C. Hull. Princeton: Princeton University Press/Bollingen: 1953/1956), §111. Hereafter cited as *Two Essays, CW 7*).

¹⁰ Victor White, "Thomism and 'Affective Knowledge' " (*Blackfriars*, Oxford: Vol. XXIV, Jan. '43, pp.8–16; April '43, pp.126–31; Vol. XXV, Sept. '44, pp.321–28). This important three-part essay is discussed at length below (Chapter Two).

¹¹ George Lindbeck, *The Nature of Doctrine: Religion and Theology in a Post-Liberal Age* (Philadelphia: Westminster Press, 1984).

¹² Throughout this book the word "Self" is capitalized, departing from the usage established in the Princeton edition of the *CW*, to help keep this crucial concept of Jung's psychology distinct from other usages of "self," as in a phrase such as "self-centered." This distinction between the personal self and the transpersonal Self is crucially important to Jung, as we shall see below (Chapter Five).

¹³ Victor White, *God and the Unconscious* (Revised edition. Dallas: Spring Publications, 1952/1982). In the Foreword, C.G. Jung explores in a sympathetic vein some of the most basic challenges of the collaboration between himself and White.

¹⁴ For the typology that views religious discourse variously as "propositional," "experiential-expressive," and "cultural-linguistic" I am indebted to George Lindbeck and his book *The Nature of Doctrine*. My use of the "language" metaphor in this book owes much to discussions with Mr. Lindbeck and other doctoral students, when we studied his typology in the Yale theological seminar of spring 1984. I have bent the model to my purpose, however, by identifying the "syntax" in White's and Jung's respective languages with the epistemology that underlies each.

¹⁵ At its most formal and minimal, Lindbeck's cultural-linguistic criterion invites comparison with the idea of sheer structural coherence, as conveyed in a modern linguistic invention, "boinguage." (I first encountered this entertaining pseudo-language in 1968 at Columbia University, in a class at Teachers College.) Boinguage enables one to generate sentences with a grammatical pattern but no distinguishable content, e.g.: "The boinging boings boinged over the unboinged boing." Thus a possible danger entailed in the cultural-linguistic theory is that it may, despite itself, tend to view theology as "boinguage": a language exercise making no truth claims apart from the purely formal one of grammatical coherence.

¹⁶ I am indebted to Lindbeck's analysis of these questions in Chapter 3 of *The Nature of Doctrine*, "Many Religions and the One True Faith." Also

to his discussion in Chapter 6, "Towards a Post-Liberal Theology," which applies Clifford Geertz's notion of "thick description" to the explication of meaning in religious discourse.

[17] Victor White, "Religious Tolerance" (*The Commonweal*. New York: 4 Sept. 53), discussed below in Chapter Two.

[18] C.G. Jung, *Letters, Volume I: 1906–1950*; *Volume II: 1951–1961* (Selected and edited by Gerhard Adler and Aniela Jaffé. Translator, R.F.C. Hull. Princeton: Princeton University Press, 1973). Hereafter cited as *Letters I* and *Letters II*.

[19] Victor White, "Kinds of Opposites" (*Studien zur Analytischen Psychologie C.G. Jungs. Festschrift zum 80. Geburtstag von C.G. Jung*. Band I: "Beiträge aus Theorie und Praxis." Herausgegeben vom C.G. Jung Institut Zürich. Zürich: Rascher-Verlag, 1955), pp.141–50.

[20] This statement, which occurs in one of Victor White's last letters to C.G. Jung, appears also as an excerpt quoted in the footnotes to the *C. G. Jung Letters* (*Letters II*, p.518n). Significant brief excerpts from White's letters were incorporated into the footnotes of the *Letters* by Adler and Jaffé. Apart from that, the letters from White to Jung are unpublished as the present work goes to press. A volume with both sides of the correspondence is scheduled to appear soon, edited and with an introduction by Adrian Cunningham. Pending the appearance of that volume, material from the unpublished letters is cited with the initials of writer and recipient and the letter's date.

[21] This essay is reviewed in depth below (Chapter Two).

[22] Raymond Hostie, S.J., *Religion and the Psychology of Jung* (Translator, G.R. Lamb. London & New York: Sheed and Ward, 1957).

[23] Victor White, "Review of *Religion and the Psychology of Jung* by Raymond Hostie, S.J." (*The Journal of Analytical Psychology*, Vol. III. London: Tavistock Publications, Ltd., 1958). Hereafter cited as "Hostie."

[24] C.G. Jung, *Collected Works*, Volume 9ii: *Aion: Researches into the Phenomenology of the Self* (Second edition. Translator, R.F.C. Hull. Princeton: Princeton University Press/Bollingen, 1973).

[25] Ludwig Feuerbach, *The Essence of Christianity* (Translator, George Eliot; Foreword by H. Richard Niebuhr; Introduction by Karl Barth. New York: Harper & Row, 1957. Originally published in 1841).

[26] Jung in fact cites Feuerbach's maxim, "Der Mensch ist, was er ißt" (though he attributes it to Moleschott) as a perfect example of reductive materialism, the characteristic attitude of what he calls "negative thinking," whose "habitual mode is expressed by the two words 'nothing but' " (*Collected Works, Volume 6: Psychological Types*. Translator, H.G. Baynes, revised by R.F.C. Hull. Princeton: Princeton University Press, 1971; §593).

[27] C.G. Jung was born 26 July 1875, and died 6 June 1961. Victor White was born 21 October 1902, and died 22 May 1960. They were 27 years apart in age.

[28] Jung wrote to White, 8 January 1949, suggesting that White try to find asympathetic friend, as Jung had done. "If you feel isolated in England, why don't you make one of your *fratres* into a real brother in the spirit? When I came to Zurich, the most materialistic city of Switzerland, there was nobody ready-made for my needs. I then shaped some for me" (*Letters I*, p.517).

[29] From Gerhard Adler's report (private correspondence, 3 June 86) and evidence in White's letters, as well as the fact that he was invited to lecture to Jungian audiences in England, Switzerland and the United States, it is evident that White's connections with the Jungian world were important to him. Fr. Aelred Squire recalls that White had a circle of Jungian friends about whom he was quiet with colleagues at Blackfriars. Around the time of White's death he was cared for by friends in his Jungian circle, including Mrs. C.K. Ginsberg, at whose house he died (*Letters II*, p.563). Doris Layard, the former wife of White's analyst, John Layard, visited White several times in his final illness and brought other friends to see him, including Aelred Squire and Richard Kehoe.

Another devoted friend was Mother Michael of the Blessed Trinity. She was by all accounts a remarkable woman, trained as a medical doctor before entering the Carmelites and serving as prioress in her order for some decades. In 1959 she wrote to inform Jung of White's near-fatal motorcycle accident. They corresponded again at the time of White's cancer diagnosis and death (*Letters II*, pp.516, 536f, 546f, 552, and 603f).

[30] The frustration which gave rise to Jung's snappish comment was not without cause at this point in the relationship. But his polemical use of exaggeration should not obscure the underlying point: Victor White was in fact bound by oath (a required part of the STM ceremony he took part in, in 1954) to teach only what his superiors considered authentic Catholic doctrine. Anticipation of this oath-swearing had generated agonized doubts in two of White's letters to Jung, written in November 1953 and March 1954. Jung's replies to these exceptionally painful letters are among his longest, most heartfelt epistles to his friend (*Letters II*, pp.133ff, 163ff).

[31] Apparently Philp shared Jung's letter with White, who quotes this statement from it in *Soul and Psyche*, Appendix VIII, "The Polemic on Evil, Continued."

[32] Gerhard Adler guesses that White first became interested in Jung's writings through John Layard. It was Adler, however, who suggested that White contact Jung directly (Gerhard Adler, private correspondence, 3 June 1986).

[33] Victor White, "The Frontiers of Theology and Psychology" (Lecture 19 for the Guild of Pastoral Psychology. London: Guild of Pastoral Psychology, 1942).

[34] Victor White, "St. Thomas Aquinas and Jung's Psychology" (*Blackfriars*, Vol. XXV. Oxford: Blackfriars, June 1944).

[35] Victor White, "Psychotherapy and Ethics" (*Blackfriars*, Vol. XXVI. Oxford: Blackfriars, August 1945).

[36] Now printed together as Chapter 8 of White's *God and the Unconscious*.

[37] This was not Jung's only pun on White's name. At the end of a letter of 4 Feb. 47, White referred to what must have been a pun in Jung's previous letter (unfortunately now lost): "I admire your proficiency in Anglo-Saxon! Still, if ever you should care to write again, I should like it very much if you were to drop both WHITE and WIGHT & just call me Victor—." White's own humor was a dimension of his personality that sometimes emerges in anecdotes and letters, but rarely in his published writing. For example, Aelred Squire recalls "Vicky" showing him a snapshot of himself and Jung at Bollingen (see frontispiece), showing Jung in full sunlight and White in half-shade, with the quip—playing on the title of White's first book—"There's God and the Unconscious" (A.S., 7 July 1987).

[38] Victor White's essay "Psychotherapy and Ethics" (*Blackfriars* XXVI, August 1945. Reprinted by the Newman Association in Honor of C.G. Jung's 70th Birthday) describes the collaboration that White thinks should be undertaken between Jung's psychology and Thomistic theology, for the good of the world. It concludes: "The task before us is gigantic indeed" (p. 12).

[39] White had asked if he might visit Jung that summer, assuring him (in joking reference to a passing complaint of Jung's about his socialist critics), "I would attire myself in a disguise which would forestall any unseemly comments from the Totalitarian Left!" (1 April 1946).

[40] When White visited Jung he seldom wore clericals, according to Franz Jung (interview, 17 Aug. 91). The Bollingen retreat called for camp clothes. White did wear clericals once, however, when he visited one of the famous religious houses nearby—the monastery at Einsiedeln or the convent at Eschenbach. The photo of White and Jung together by the tower (mentioned above), showing White in his clerical collar, was presumably taken that day.

[41] White's dream text reads, in part: "I 'knew' that there was no danger, not so much because you were at the wheel, but because the *Wind* was taking care of us and would never wreck the pair of us." Continuing at high speed, the dream journey ends in a coastal town,

where "the boat, with you calmly at the wheel and smoking your pipe, imperceptibly mounted the shore and sailed down the streets dexterously missing all the buildings and the traffic. She was amphibious!" White's next paragraph begins, "I hope this is 'all right', and not inflation" (VW to CGJ, 13 Oct. 46).

CHAPTER TWO: THOMISM AND THE WARRANTS OF EXPERIENCE

[1] At many points in this chapter and the next I am indebted to Fr. Aelred Squire, O.S.B., Camaldolese (cited hereafter as A.S.). Fr. Aelred first met Victor White in the 1940s, before entering the Dominicans. He made his profession with the Order in 1947 and studied with White from 1950 to 1954. Aelred Squire himself taught at Blackfriars between 1956 and 1965 and was among the few friends from Oxford who visited White during the latter's final illness. He is now a Camaldolese Benedictine, living at New Camaldoli Hermitage in Big Sur, California. He is the author of *Aelred of Rivaulx* (1969), *Asking the Fathers* (1973), and *Summer in the Seed* (1980). His career is told in Appendix C.

Further information and consultation concerning events in Victor White's professional life were generously supplied by Adrian Cunningham, the scholar appointed by the English Dominican Province in 1990 to be White's literary executor. Dr. Cunningham (cited hereafter as A.C.) is chair of the theology department at the University of Lancaster.

[2] *The New Catholic Encyclopedia* (Editors: Catholic University of America, Washington, D.C., New York: McGraw Hill, 1967). Here cited as *NCE*.

[3] An anecdote may illustrate. Aelred Squire remembers an exchange with his student master in the early 1950s. He had been sent a book by a Cistercian friend which was "markedly anti-scholastic and made much of the early Cistercian appeal to experience . . . in Bernard and all that school." The student master commented, "Once you begin to talk about experience you are almost in heresy." Aelred ventured that a Catholic was "permitted *not* to be a neo-Thomist," and received the curt reply, ". . . Just" (A.S., 3 Aug. 87).

[4] One modern index lists occurrences of the word *experientia* in 28 articles of the *Summa Theologiae* (Deferrari, Roy J. and Sister M. Inviolata Barry, *A Complete Index of The Summa Theologica of St. Thomas Aquinas*. Catholic University of America Press, 1956). An older Latin word-index identifies three significant contexts for Thomas' use of the word: on how angels think (1a. Q54, 5; 1a. Q58, 3); on hope and despair (1a2ae. Q40,

5); and on the working of grace (1a2ae. Q112, 5) (S. Thomae Aquinatis, *Summa Theologica*. Editio nono. Nicolai, Sylvii, Billuart et C.-J. Drioux. Sequentia Supplementi. Londini: Apud Davidem Nutt, Bibliopolam, 1875. Volume 8, p. clxxxviii.)

⁵ For the parallel between the Cistercian use of *experientia* and modern usage, I will refer once again to Aelred Squire. He observes that seven centuries elapsed after *experientia* ceased to be used by Catholic theologians in the twelfth-century Cistercian sense (which can be understood, loosely phrased, he adds, as "the personal impact of the natural world and, especially, the world of other people"). The term would not reemerge in anything like that sense until Pope Paul VI's encyclical on the Church during the second Vatican Council.

⁶ St. Thomas Aquinas, *Summa Theologiae: Latin Text and English Translation* (Editors, Thomas Gilby, et al. London & New York: Blackfriars, in conjunction with Eyre & Spottiswode and McGraw Hill, 1964). This, the Blackfriars edition, is hereafter cited as *ST*.

⁷ It would be possible, of course, to create other typologies of Thomism in the twentieth century. A book that develops a typology of philosophical schools of modern Thomism is Helen James John's *The Thomist Spectrum* (New York: Fordham Press, 1966). In Section One she groups three major writers under the heading "Thomism as Christian Philosophy": Garrigou-Lagrange, Maritain, and Gilson. Her grouping is based on philosophical perspective. White's interest—and mine here—is in theology. White quotes Maritain frequently, and Gilson almost as often. He is not so sympathetic with Garrigou-Lagrange.

⁸ An unsigned article titled, "PERSONAE: Victor White, O.P. († May 22, 1960)" (*Blackfriars*, Vol. XLI, Nos. 482–83, 7,8/60, hereafter cited as Obituary): "Irony indeed is one of the things that [White's] prose lacks. It is unalterably serious; every phrase is forthright, and, when he hesitates, this too is expressed unambiguously" (Obituary, pp.283f). The style of this obituary, which praises White's theology at the expense of his psychology, suggests the hand of Thomas Gilby, O.P., who was prior at the Cambridge house when White went there in his final illness. His comments are fair to Victor White as a human being, but less than sympathetic to his work. Gilby, whose Thomism is more conservative than White's, took over the translation of the Blackfriars *Summa Theologiae* when White died. He also reviewed White's last book, *Soul and Psyche* (*Blackfriars*, Vol. XLI, 5/60).

⁹ White may never have a proper biography since, due to a series of decisions, oversights and accidents, few of his personal papers remain to be studied. Adrian Cunningham was not named White's literary executor until 1990. By then it was already too late to retrieve most of White's

letters, appointment books, photographs, journals and other private papers. Some documents were lost simply because no particular value had
been placed on them by the Order; some were casually thrown out because they took up needed space. According to a story that may never be
substantiated, Mrs. C.K. Ginsberg, who nursed White at the end of his
life, destroyed all the personal papers he had with him at his death (A.C.,
25 Aug. 91).

[10] A different view of White's social and emotional environment is
held by Adrian Cunningham, who sees White as having had close friendships with a few members of the Order, such as Gerald Vann and Richard
Kehoe (up to the latter's departure). But the evidence for saying that White
was in close and confiding relationships with other men seems tenuous,
and the distinct memories of one sympathetic eye-witness are positive to
the contrary. White's letters to Jung, too, complain of deep loneliness and
of not feeling at home at Blackfriars—even before the decision of the
Order in 1954 ended his teaching career in that setting.

[11] In his letters to Jung, White describes the busy schedule he is
keeping as a teacher at Blackfriars, his duties in the classroom and chapel,
and the demands that are made by various souls needing counsel (VW to
CGJ, 19 Jan. 47). Although he complains that the schedule is exhausting
(Ibid), he admits that he finds it hard to write for personal reasons as well:
"External circumstances and interior inhibitions alike seem to conspire to
prevent my getting down to a sustained and serious book!" (VW to CGJ,
23 October 45).

[12] Victor White, *God the Unknown & Other Essays* (London: Harvill
Press, 1956).

[13] White's first article in *Blackfriars* is dated January 1932. His last is
dated January/February 1960. His obituary writer recognizes his "thirty
years of loyal service" to the journal (Obituary, p.284). White was not an
editor for the full thirty years, however. A footnote to a 1955 journal
article describes him as "former editor of *Blackfriars*" ("Good Friday,"
Commonweal LXI:26, New York: 4/1/55, p.674n).

[14] White's first review in *Blackfriars* is written in a remarkably arch,
mannered style in comparison to his later work. It is studded with capitalized phrases, such as "our Machine Age" and "conflict of Nature and Art"
("Spengler Views the Machine Age," *Blackfriars*. Oxford: Blackfriars, January 1932, pp.9, 12).

[15] Another official church doctrine that White found problematic,
although it is plainly present in Aquinas, concerns the omniscience of
Jesus Christ. White's own conviction being that the historical Jesus was
humanly fallible (and therefore subject to ignorance), he could not personally endorse the official teaching. For years, to avoid speaking against

authorized doctrine, he kept silent on the subject (VW to CGJ, 4 March 54).

16 Victor White, *Scholasticism* (London: Catholic Truth Society, 1934; #R 126). The essay, which appeared as a small pamphlet in the series "Studies in Comparative Religion," was later republished in another CTS series, "Pamphlets for Students." It is cited hereafter as *Scholasticism*.

17 Chapter V, "The Platonic Tradition in St. Thomas Aquinas," appeared in *The Eastern Church Quarterly* in 1941 (*God the Unknown*, Author's Preface, p.vii).

18 Eugene TeSelle argues in *Augustine the Theologian* (New York: Herder & Herder, 1970) that in denying human perfectibility and expounding the resurrection of the body, Augustine firmly rejects the Platonic depreciation of material reality (*Augustine the Theologian*, pp.252, 263f).

19 George Lindbeck's article, "The *A Priori* in St. Thomas' Theory of Knowledge" (*The Heritage of Christian Thought: Essays in Honor of Robert Lowry Calhoun*. Editors, Robert E. Cushman and Egil Grislis. New York: Harper & Row, 1965). Lindbeck attributes the concept of "participation" to Aquinas' Aristotelian side; unlike White, he does not see a connection to Augustine or Plato. On the other hand, he does give White leeway for a modest "platonizing" of Aquinas when he writes "Aquinas rejected only that part of his Platonic heritage which he explicitly says he did: he rejected only *a priori* objects of knowledge, and he continued to accept, in the form of a non-objectifiable *a priori*, a good deal more Platonism than is immediately apparent" ("The *A Priori* in St. Thomas' Theory of Knowledge," p.46).

20 The letter in question, dated 3 Jan. 48, is discussed in Chapter Three under "Obstacles."

21 Victor White, "Thomism and 'Affective Knowledge' " (*Blackfriars*, Oxford: Vol. XXIV, Jan. '43, pp.8–16; April '43, pp.126–31; Vol. XXV, Sept. '44, pp.321–28). Hereafter cited as "Affective Knowledge" I, II, and III.

22 We will see that this principle is extremely important to White from the beginning in his work with Jung, but that it later becomes an obstacle between them when he tries to apply it in their debate about evil.

23 In the first Question (I.1,6 ad 3) Aquinas makes a distinction between two ways by which one may know God: one is Wisdom, which the soul receives *per modum inclinationis*, the second is Theology, which is "acquired by patient study" ("Affective Knowledge," p.12). St. Thomas announces that he uses only the second kind of knowledge in the work at hand. So White concludes, "*Ex professo* the *Summa* is to be conducted on purely scientific, logical lines" (Ibid.). The alternative method of knowing God—

involving the soul's inclination and love—is at home in endeavors other than theology.

²⁴ White quotes here from Aquinas' *Commentary on the Sentences*, I.XV,ix,4 ad 3.

²⁵ The passage cited is *ST* IIa IIae.xlv,2.

²⁶ Lindbeck's essay, "The *A Priori* in St. Thomas' Theory of Knowledge," also takes up the question of whether there is a meeting place for St. Thomas' epistemology and a "deobjectivized" Kantian subjectivity, in accord with existentialist thought. White's position in relation to Lindbeck's analysis is a bit of a puzzle. The intellectual movement that Lindbeck describes has developed theoretical agreement between the thought of Aquinas and a modified Kantian epistemology. This is surely a movement White belongs to in spirit. On the other hand, Lindbeck differentiates the philosophical work of this movement from that of Gilson and Maritain, White's standard-bearers. White might admire the historical and theological work of Gilson and Maritain, and yet disagree with them—as Maréchal does according to Lindbeck—on epistemological grounds.

²⁷ White's warning against the substitution of the thought (intellective knowledge) for the thing (affective knowledge) had a significant contemporary parallel. In his 1937 Terry Lectures Jung had commented on the same theme (see note 13, Chapter Three). Contrasts in the way this important theme is handled are presented in Chapter Three under "Obstacles."

²⁸ Victor White, "Holy Teaching: The Idea of Theology According to St. Thomas Aquinas" (Aquinas Paper No. 33, Blackfriars Publications, for the Aquinas Society of London, 1958).

²⁹ Victor White, "Religious Tolerance" (*The Commonweal*, New York: Sept. 4, 1953). Hereafter cited as "Tolerance."

³⁰ Two years after this, in 1955, John Courtney Murray, an American Jesuit, was silenced by the authorities in Rome. White also mentions the work of Jacques Maritain and other French theologians who had participated in a recent symposium on the subject of religious tolerance.

³¹ Had White lived to read George Lindbeck's *The Nature of Doctrine* (op. cit.), he might have recognized in Lindbeck's cultural-linguistic category a sympathetic proposal. In distinction from what Lindbeck calls "propositional" truth (which, White warns, produces an "idolatry of the dogma"), in this essay White makes *right practice* of Christian faith a test or proving ground for the truth of doctrine.

³² See C.G.Jung, "Why I am Not a Catholic" (*Collected Works, Volume 18: The Symbolic Life*. Translator, R.F.C. Hull. Princeton: Princeton University Press, 1976; §1466ff). This statement about Jung's relation to faith and the church is discussed in Chapter Four.

CHAPTER THREE: AT THE WIND'S MERCY

¹ C.G. Jung, "Psychotherapists or the Clergy" (*Modern Man in Search of a Soul*, translated by W.S. Dell and Cary F. Baynes. New York & London: Harcourt Brace, 1933. Later published in R.F.C. Hull's translation, *CW 11: Psychology and Religion*, §488–538).

² C.G. Jung, "Psychoanalysis and the Cure of Souls" (*CW 11: Psychology and Religon*), §539–552.

³ Victor White, "The Frontiers of Theology and Psychology" (Lecture 19 for the Guild of Pastoral Psychology. London: Guild of Pastoral Psychology, 1942). Hereafter cited as "Frontiers." A note below the title reads: "The following paper was read to a group of psychologists, clergy and others which meets regularly at Oxford under the chairmanship of Mr. J. Layard. It is hoped that it may stimulate more thorough and detailed exploration of the practically uncharted territory of which it is offered as a preliminary and very inadequate survey" ("Frontiers," p.3).

⁴ White had been in analysis with John Layard for some months, at least, before this lecture was written. He continued to see Layard for analytic work occasionally during the following years, as letters to Jung indicate. Eventually White came to see Layard as a man with serious problems who needed further analytic help himself (VW to Marie-Jeanne Schmid, 11 Dec. 46).

⁵ Victor White, "Walter Hilton: An English Spiritual Guide" (Guild of Pastoral Psychology, Lecture 31).

⁶ White cites a collection of Jung's essays, *The Integration of the Personality* (Translator, Stanley M. Dell. New York; Farrar & Rinehart, 1939), Chapter 6, "The Development of Personality," p.287. Jung later complained to White (*Letters I*, p.386) that this book had been rushed into print in the American edition. Jung's 1932 lecture, on which the chapter was based, was included (revised and retranslated) in *CW 17: The Development of Personality* (Translator, R.F.C. Hull. Princeton: Princeton University Press, 1954), §284ff.

⁷ Jung's famous dictum, that none of his patients in the second half of life were psychologically healed until they developed a "religious outlook" ("Psychotherapists or the Clergy," in *Modern Man in Search of a Soul*, p.229), was of course familiar to White ("Frontiers," p.4).

⁸ C.G.Jung, "Freud and Jung—Contrasts" (chapter 6 in *Modern Man in Search of a Soul*), p. 117. The article was written in 1929 at the special request of a German editor (Translator's Preface, p.ix, note 1).

⁹ White's acquaintance with Freudian theory included *The Future of an Illusion*, *Totem and Taboo*, and *Moses and Monotheism*. When White first contacted Jung in September 1945, he was reviewing a book that he criti-

cized as being too Freudian in its deterministic materialism. His criticisms sound much like Jung's attacks on Freud's causal theory. White's review, a "Postscript" to "Psychotherapy and Ethics," appeared in *Blackfriars* and then became the last section of a chapter in *God and the Unconscious* (pp.158ff).

¹⁰ Although White's sweeping reference to "[Jung's] published writings" ("Frontiers," p.3) implies that he has read everything Jung has published to date, the endnotes to his lecture refer only to *Modern Man in Search of a Soul*, *Two Essays in Analytical Psychology* (especially the first of the two, *On the Psychology of the Unconscious*), *The Secret of the Golden Flower*, *Psychological Types*, *The Integration of the Personality*, and Jolande Jacobi's *The Psychology of C.G. Jung*. He had also read Jung's unpublished lecture "Die Psychologie der Trinitätsidee" ("Frontiers," pp.24ff).

¹¹ White quotes from *The Psychology of the Unconscious* (1912), a section of Jung's book whose original title is *Wandlungen und Symbole der Libido*. This work constituted Jung's irrevocable departure from Freudian theory. A much revised version appears in the Bollingen Series of Princeton University Press, titled *Symbols of Transformation* (*CW 5*).

¹² White arrives at this definition as the logically necessary conclusion of Jung's "qualifications and amplifications . . . in *The Psychology of the Unconscious* and in the first of the *Two Essays*" ("Frontiers," p.6).

¹³ The Terry Lectures, which Jung presented at Yale University in 1937, were originally published in English under the title *Psychology and Religion* (New Haven, CT: Yale University Press, 1938). They were later revised and translated into German for a Swiss edition. Retranslated into English by R.F.C. Hull, the revised version of the lectures is now found in *CW 11*, *Psychology and Religion: West and East*, where "Dogma and Natural Symbols" is printed as §56–107. Hereafter cited as *Psychology and Religion*, with paragraph numerals as printed in *CW 11*.

¹⁴ How White missed this important piece of Jung's early writing on the relation between psychology and religion, if he did, is a puzzle. Of course, one cannot prove that he had not seen the Terry Lectures from his failure to quote them. But it was characteristic of White to refer in print to a significant writing by Jung soon after he first read it. No mention of *Psychology and Religion* appears in White's published work or letters until the letter he wrote to Jung on 3 Jan. 48, which is discussed below.

¹⁵ Jung's description of one who undergoes this spiritual harrowing sounds like himself: "If a Protestant survives the complete loss of his church and still remains a Protestant, that is, a man who is defenseless against God and is no longer shielded by walls or communities, he has the unique spiritual chance of immediate religious experience" (*Psychology and Religion*, p.62; *CW 11*, §86).

[16] In 1947 Jung invited White to become a co-founder of the C.G. Jung Institute in Zurich (*Letters I*, pp.481f), an act that reflected the very high esteem in which he held his theological colleague at the time.

[17] This footnote on "kinds of opposition," following the same outline as White's 1955 paper "Kinds of Opposites," is found in the Blackfriars edition of *Summa Theologiae*, Ia. Q48, 1. Discussion of White's philosophical and theological distinctions and their implications for his disagreements with Jung is found in Chapter Six, below.

[18] In Hull's translation: "The Protestant is left to God alone. For him there is no confession, no absolution, no possibility of an expiatory *opus divinum* of any kind. He has to digest his sins by himself. . . ." (*CW 11*, *Psychology and Religion*, §86).

[19] White's play on words takes Jung's "Demut" (humility) and contrasts it with "Armut" (poverty).

[20] No bibliographical reference is available for this letter, since as of this writing the letters White sent to Jung have not yet been published. Unpublished letters are cited by sender, receiver, and date, as here.

[21] Jung's letter of 19 Dec. 47 (*Letters I*, pp.479ff) said that he felt compelled from within to write about Christ, and that he was suffering sleeplessness and anxiety about it. This work became his lecture "Über das Selbst" and eventually made up the main part of the book *Aion* (*CW 9ii*).

[22] Adrian Cunningham provides this characterological detail, based on the report of one of White's contemporaries (interview, 25 August 91). The gist of the story is supported by a passage in one of the letters White wrote to Jung about his vocational dilemma. Here White complains of severe anxieties and a nightmare, and adds, "I couldn't go to sleep again, developed the deuce of a stomachache and a mild temperature; and frankly hoped I was going to be able to retire from the whole conflict into a nice long neurotic illness" (VW to CGJ, 8 Nov. 53).

[23] Adrian Cunningham kindly allowed me to see this private ordination announcement of Gerald Vann, which is among Victor White's few surviving personal papers. In Gill's engraving, originally titled "The Nuptuals of God," the crucified body of Christ is hidden, except for his outstretched arms and thorn-crowned head, by the female figure superimposed on it. The woman is depicted as kissing the mouth of Jesus, her arms stretched out almost in line with his. Her hair flows down to cover her body; but one hip, uncovered, indicates that she is naked. On Vann's ordination announcement card the engraving is titled "Christ and the Church." Dr. Cunningham remarks: "Gill's engraving originally appeared in the hand-printed Ditchling journal, *The Game*, in 1922 and produced a rift between Gill and Vincent McNabb, so Vann's choice of it is even more interesting" (A.C., private correspondence, 5 June 92).

²⁴ In the warmest terms, White recommended Richard Kehoe to Jung as a contributor to an Eranos conference: "When she [Frau Fröbe] told me that the "Menschensohn" [Son of Man] was a desired subject, I at once thought of my colleague, Fr. Richard Kehoe (of whom I have told you). He is a splendid lecturer, and his psychological exegesis of Scripture is most exciting" (VW to CGJ, 27 Dec. 47).

²⁵ Some evidence is available, although its significance must remain ambiguous. Given the nature of his work and his religious setting, we can be sure that whatever caused White to seek the help of a Jungian analyst in 1940 or 1941 can only have been something of shattering personal importance. Certainly it was more than the fact that he had suddenly been asked to step down as editor of *Blackfriars* (A.C., interview, 25 Aug. 91). Another bit of negative evidence, purely suggestive, can be found in the collected correspondence. It is plain that Jung carefully preserved the majority of White's letters to him. Yet he—or someone—seems to have lost at least four. From internal evidence in the letters, it is clear that one letter has been lost that White sent toward the end of 1947; two others date to late fall of 1948, and one to January or early February of 1952. Until and unless these missing letters turn up, as they may, we must consider the possibility that a few letters were deliberately destroyed. Letters can also disappear by accident, of course. Franz Jung recalls that his father would sometimes start the fire at Bollingen with whatever was in his pockets (Franz Jung, 16 Aug. 91); so we can imagine a few letters going, accidentally or deliberately, into the fire in the stone tower.

²⁶ In an early letter to Jung's secretary (to whom White often wrote when he did not wish to disturb Jung himself) he declared: "I hope that people over here will soon cease to regard me as a sort of unofficial agent for Zürich!" (VW to Marie-Jeanne Schmid, 16 Oct. 46).

²⁷ White's important dream of the fast-sailing boat, which he dreamed after visiting Bollingen for the first time and sent to Jung in his letter of 27 Aug. 46, is discussed more fully in Chapter One.

²⁸ This probable scenario can be deduced from comments about the book occurring in White's letters to Jung over the following four years. It is certain that White visited Bollingen in 1951 (VW to CGJ, 17 July 1951). We can gather that this was the occasion (since there would have been no other convenient time) when Jung discussed the recently completed book with White and promised to let him read it once it was published (VW to CGJ, 30 March 52).

²⁹ The history of the argument between Jung and White on the subject of evil and the theological and psychological implications of their debate are themes explored in later chapters. But, as the term *privatio boni* recurs frequently and becomes almost a shorthand reference to the di-

lemma that stumped the collaborators, its meaning should be clarified here.

The idea of "privation of good" was first proposed by Augustine in his *Confessions* as the best way to think about the fact of evil in the world without impugning the goodness and power of God. Aquinas later developed the idea more fully. The theory that evil should be defined as a "privation," having no being or power in itself, is an opinion still widely held and taught in Catholic tradition.

In June 1952, Jung demanded to know from White whether the *privatio boni* teaching was a Catholic dogma, or only a *sententia communis*—a commonly held opinion (*Letters II*, p. 71). White assured him there was "no dogma about the *privatio boni*, any more than there is about the *meaning* of many other words included in dogmas" (VW to CGJ, 9 July 52). This reassurance did not alleviate their argument, which turned on a disagreement about whether the Judeo-Christian God can be seen as capable of doing evil—acting unjustly, unconsciously, cruelly, etc.

The *privatio boni* definition of evil turns on the conviction that God, who is all-good and all-powerful, creates exclusively good things. But these good things are obviously subject, as God is not, to change and loss. Evil is not a created "being"; it has no self-sustaining existence or source of its own power. It can best be understood as a lack or loss or distortion of good in the creation. Evil is thus said to have no *nature* or *being* as such. Evil phenomena are real and observable, as created things suffer distortion and loss; therefore real evils must be dealt with in history. But the orthodox Christian belief is that evil ultimately has no place, as at the end of things God has promised to restore the original wholeness of creation.

[30] Victor White was not the only Jungian anticipating trouble from an English language edition of *Answer to Job*. No American edition appeared until 1956, and then it was not published by Bollingen Press but by the Pastoral Psychology Book Club in Great Neck, New York. Jung wryly comments on the hesitation of the Bollingen editors in a 1955 letter to Upton Sinclair: "My *Answer to Job* was left by the Bollingen Press to the English publishers, since they were apparently afraid of something like 'Unamerican activity' and the loss of prestige presumably" (*Letters II*, p.231).

[31] This letter to Dr. E. V. Tenney, 23 February 1955, was written just before White's review of *Answer to Job* made further collaboration virtually impossible. Jung commented on White's struggle in the context of his scholastic training. The passage begins: "Another aspect of this concretism is the rigidity of scholastic philosophy, through which Father White is wriggling as well as he can. He is at bottom an honest and sincere man

who cannot but admit the importance of psychology, but the trouble is that he gets into an awful stew about it. . . ." (*Letters II*, p.228).

[32] In response to White's letter of March 1954, Jung devoted a great deal of ink and paper to White's Christology (*Letters II*, pp.164f). In this, Jung's longest letter to his friend (20 pages in the handwritten draft), he demonstrates unexpected perspicacity as a spiritual advisor within White's own theological context. Beside psychological interpretations, Jung offers a capable argument about the Christian idea of Christ's two natures; and he designates the cross as the best symbolic resolution of White's personal struggle between "irreconcilable opposites" (Ibid, p.166).

[33] A discussion of this definition of "experience" (*Soul and Psyche*, p.274, note 1) and its impact on White's theology is included above in Chapter Two.

[34] Jung was convinced that a new religious orientation for the world was slowly emerging. He predicted this change would come to fruition in "about six hundred years" (Max Zeller, "The Task of the Analyst," *Psychological Perspectives* 6/1/75:74–78. Quoted by Murray Stein in *Jung's Treatment of Christianity: The Psychotherapy of a Religious Tradition*. Wilmette, IL: Chiron Publications, 1985; p.188).

[35] As one who was present when Fr. Victor and the second candidate received the STM degree, and who later reacted with dismay when the new regent of studies was appointed, Aelred Squire remembers the two events as being linked. Although evidence exists that the decision to pass over White for the regency was taken in Rome after the STM ceremony, Squire remembers feeling that the unusual double ceremony had ominous implications. His account follows: "Just as when the gifted Fr. Daniel Callus moved to Oxford in 1932 he must have seemed the natural man to implement the desire of the modern founder of Blackfriars, Oxford, to make that house a centre of learning and studies, so when in 1954 Dr. Callus was due to retire as regent of studies there—a post which he had held since 1942—there was a widespread and perhaps natural expectation that Victor White might be his successor, though representing theological learning of a rather different kind. This did not in fact happen. In the event two men were given the Dominican degree of Master of Theology, of whom Victor White was one, the other being appointed as regent. It is difficult to know how this decision was reached—personal rivalry may certainly be excluded. I remember how embarrassing it was to Fr. Victor's friends to be present at the conferring of these degrees and believe that its implication must have entailed a strong sense of rejection of the work of Fr. Victor by his own Dominican Province" (A.S., correspondence, 3 Aug. 87).

[36] This date was kindly supplied by Paul Parvis, Subprior at Blackfriars, Oxford (Correspondence, 26 Aug. 87).

³⁷ Information about these events in Rome, summer 1954, is from original documents in the archives of the English Dominican Province (Adrian Cunningham, 29 Sept. 92).

³⁸ One Dominican priest who knew White in California in 1954–55, when White was living at St. Albert's College, Oakland, recalls that while there White gave no sign of inner conflict. Fr. Moreno, a senior professor at the Dominican School of Philosophy and Theology in Berkeley, recalls that White seemed cheerful during those months. He was always ready to go out to dinner if invited, but kept to himself much of the time. No sign of a vocational struggle was visible (Fr. Antonio Moreno, O.P., interview, 23 Jan. 87).

³⁹ The decision of the English Provincial to name the second STM recipient in White's place was at best a short-term solution to the emergency created by this news from Rome. The other man was not well suited to the office and in fact was relieved of it again in 1958 when his four-year term was up. Lacking a younger candidate at that time to replace him, the Province then brought Daniel Callus out of retirement and reappointed him to his old position (A.C., private correspondence, 5 June 92).

⁴⁰ Richard Kehoe, "Review of *Antwort auf Hiob*" (*Dominican Studies*, Vol. V, 1952), pp.228–31. There may be a connection between the fact that Richard Kehoe felt freer than White to publish a sympathetic review of Jung's *Job*, and the fact that he left Blackfriars shortly after he wrote it. The year of Kehoe's departure is recorded in the Dominican archives as 1951 (A.C., 13 Feb. 92). Kehoe remained a member of the Order, however, until his death. Assuming, as is likely, that the typescript of Jung's book was available for prepublication review, Kehoe perhaps wrote his brief article and submitted it to White's journal before he left Blackfriars. The review is signed, "Richard Kehoe, O.P."

⁴¹ Victor White, "Jung on Job" (*Blackfriars*, Vol. 36. Oxford: March 1955), pp.52–60.

⁴² White shares theoretical grounds for these opinions about Jung and *Answer to Job* with at least one modern scholar, Jeffrey Satinover, whose reading of Jung's psychological woundedness takes almost this form. (E.g., "Jung's Lost Contribution to the Dilemma of Narcissism." Unpublished typescript. New Haven, CT: Yale University, Department of Psychiatry, 1985.) Satinover, whose theoretical orientation began with Jung but shifted toward Freud, takes an explicitly reductive approach, seeking Freudian etiological explanations both to Jung's theory and to his personal psychology.

⁴³ In the spring of 1955 Emma Jung was diagnosed as having a small cancerous lesion in the stomach. After it was removed, her doctors said she should still have a few years of life. During White's stay in Zurich that

May she was convalescing at home and required a great deal of care (*Letters II*, p.251). Early in November, however, she came down with what seemed like an ordinary cold and died within two weeks (Franz Jung, 17 Aug. 91).

⁴⁴ To those who know something of C.G. Jung, the code of scientific discovery that governed his thought and his sense of responsibility for bringing religious consciousness to a higher level, it may seem incredible that White could have persuaded himself that Jung would suppress *Answer to Job*. Franz Jung (interview, 17 Aug. 91) remembers that his father's attitude toward *Answer to Job* was, from the beginning, that writing this book had literally saved his life. He thought it his most important piece of work, and there was never the slightest doubt that he would publish it. Central to Jung's belief system was the connection between his own subjective experience and the world of objective knowledge. He would not have suppressed the fruit of his life-and-death struggle with the problem of evil and the image of Christ, whether for fear of scandal or any other reason.

⁴⁵ In a letter dictated before his death White returned to this theme: "I think and hope you know that when you first showed me 'Antwort auf Hiob' I loved and admired it very much, especially when you told me the conditions under which you had written it and what it had done for you. I still do love your picture of Job, because I love you. But in those days you were emphatic that it was not to be published, and I had never supposed that you would publish so personal a document without any analysis in personal terms" (VW to CGJ, 6 May 60).

⁴⁶ Mother Michael of the Blessed Trinity, prioress of the Carmelite nuns at Presteigne in Wales, was the mutual friend who in 1959 conveyed to Jung the word of White's accident and carried Jung's message of concern back to White. She kept Jung informed of White's welfare through the last months of White's life. White had been a visiting priest at the Carmelite convent for many years while it was located in Woodcock Hill, Northchurch, Berkhamstead, and continued to visit after the community moved, under Mother Michael's leadership, to Presteigne in Wales (A.S., 17 Oct. 91).

⁴⁷ On evidence available to him, Dr. Cunningham informs me that the near-fatal accident, usually referred to as White's "motorcycle accident," actually involved a motor-scooter (A.C., correspondence, 5 June 92). White's mind may have been distracted by many things in the spring of 1959. He had had, in any case, a history of close shaves. On at least one occasion, Aelred Squire recalls, White terrified a passenger who rode with him through Oxford on his motorcycle, by cutting so close to trucks on the narrow streets.

⁴⁸ White's review of Volume 7, the first volume to appear in the Bollingen series, appeared in 1954 ("Review of Jung's *Collected Works*, Volumes 7 and 12; Jung's *Von den Wurzeln des Bewusstseins*; and Progoff's *Jungs Psychology and its Social Meaning. Blackfriars*, Vol. 25, March 1954, pp.125–27). It would have been bizarre for White to attack Jung in this review, when he was relying so much on Jung's help to deal with his vocational struggle. Also, White had read Jung's *Two Essays on Analytical Psychology* with appreciation since his earliest exposure to Jung's work. His review in fact praises the "Two Essays" that compose Volume 7: "In them we find Jung as a writer at his crispest and clearest, and least inclined to deviate from the narrow path of strictly psychological exposition, as well as most ready to meet the prejudices of his medical colleagues and the general public" (p.126).

⁴⁹ Mrs. Catherine K. Ginsberg's letter to Jung after White's death attests to White's mental state in his final illness. Mrs. Ginsberg, a member of the Jungian community in England, took Victor White into her household in London during the final six weeks of his life to nurse and care for him. She wrote to Jung on 28 May 60 to tell him the manner of White's death (*Letters II*, p.563). Mrs. Ginsberg's letter, written (typed) in German, has remained together with the collected Jung-White correspondence. In it she informs Jung that, in spite of great physical suffering, White's mind remained "extraordinarily lively."

⁵⁰ Not all the handwritten notations that appear in the margins of White's letters to Jung are in the latter's handwriting; some were clearly written by others who handled the letters at one time or another after Jung's death. But the concise notation in the margin of White's letter of 18 March 60, directing attention to White's statement of apology in May 1955, is clearly Jung's holograph.

⁵¹ Both White and Jung use the Latin phrase for "stumbling block," or literally, "rock of scandal." Since in this letter of 8 May 60 White mentions that he dictated the previous one, enclosed, it seems likely that this letter, too, was dictated. Thus the odd mistake in the Latin word for "rock" (spelled *petrus* rather than *petra*) probably reflects a typist's error.

A reader with a theory of synchronicity might find significance in the misspelling, as Petrus (Peter), leader of Christ's apostles, is thought of as the first Bishop of Rome (for Roman Catholics, therefore, the original Pope). White evidently proofread the letter before signing it, as shown by two small handwritten corrections—an added comma and a line separating two words typed as one. He did not change "petrus" to "petra," perhaps because he enjoyed the humorous irony of the misspelling.

⁵² Despite the anxiety White expressed in this letter, written at a time of intense self-doubt, it was not the case that all who looked to him for

spiritual advice ended by leaving either the church or the Order. In Aelred Squire's words, "it was he who helped me to remain a Dominican for at least ten years after my final profession. . . ." (6 Dec. 91).

CHAPTER FOUR: JUNG'S RELATIONSHIP TO CHRISTIAN THOUGHT

[1] Marilyn Nagy, *Philosophical Issues in the Psychology of C.G. Jung* (Albany, NY: State University of New York Press, 1991). (Also cited in Chapter One.)

[2] We have seen how White defines the term "experience." Jung's definition is close to the meaning White assigns to the word, for White's dictionary definition stresses both consciousness and subjectivity (*Soul and Psyche*, p. 274, note 1). The concept of experience is further complicated for Jung, however, by the fact that he views the psyche as both subject and object of its own experiential knowledge. And some of what the psyche knows through its experience has origins in the unconscious, i.e., the unknown "other half" of reality ("Tavistock," *CW 18*, §8).

[3] An exception is the word-association experiment which Jung devised early in his career, using quantitative measurements, a clearly defined method, and definite rules of interpretation. Based (among other things) on the reliability of this experiment, with its predictable and quantifiable results, Jung's hypothesis of the psychological "complex" almost immediately became a widely accepted theory.

[4] C.G. Jung, "On the Nature of the Psyche" (*Collected Works, Volume 8: The Structure and Dynamics of the Psyche*. Second Edition. Translator, R.F.C. Hull. Princeton: Princeton University Press, 1960/1969).

[5] The footnote to which Jung directs White's attention was dropped from later editions (*Letters I*, p.384, note 4).

[6] Without depending on William James' notion of pragmatism in the same systematic way that he depends on Kant's epistemology, Jung owes something to James in all his discussions of "reality." Pragmatism is especially evident in Jung's assertions that evil is "real." Jung mentions his debt to James in several places, but especially in a substantial (17-line) quotation from James' *Pragmatism* which opens Chapter VIII of *Psychological Types* (*CW 6*), §505ff. In a 1936 essay Jung again honors "William James, whose psychological vision and pragmatic philosophy have on more than one occasion been my guides" ("Psychological Factors Determining Human Behavior," *CW 8*, §262).

[7] For example, in the second part of *Answer to Job* Jung traces the psychological connections of Christological imagery in two directions, one

leading toward the feminine image of Godhead (Sophia, Mary), the other toward the masculine image of the *Logos spermatikos*. The images are apparently logically incoherent and mutually exclusive. This apparent confusion between masculine and feminine images has been elegantly untangled by a Jungian biblical scholar, Joan Chamberlain Englesman, in *The Feminine Dimension of the Divine* (Wilmette, IL: Chiron Press, 1987). Her analysis confirms Jung's observations, pointing out further that the Logos language conceals and replaces the Sophia (Wisdom) tradition on which the early Christian community drew. Masculine images suit the gospel writer's Christological purposes; but hidden feminine imagery continues to exist beneath the masculine, yielding the anomaly of genders which Jung's phenomenology uncovered but did not fully explain.

[8] Jung admonishes Hugo Rahner, who represents for him a "medieval" thinker, that the classical conception of archetypes is so different from his own as to be irrelevant to him (*Letters I*, p.374). (See also note 36, Chapter Four.)

[9] C.G. Jung, "The Development of Personality" (*Collected Works, Volume 17: The Development of Personality*. Translator, R.F.C. Hull. Princeton: Princeton University Press, 1954). Hereafter cited as "Personality." Jung compares the inner voice which reveals a person's vocation with "the lion that fells him. . . . Only in this sense is he entitled to speak of 'his' vocation, 'his' law" ("Personality," *CW 17*, §304). In the same passage he mentions the objectivity of psychic facts such as an imagined cancer—one of his favorite illustrations of the power of the unconscious over consciousness.

[10] This portion of a letter Jung wrote to H. Irminger, a Roman Catholic theologian, is now printed as "Why I am Not a Catholic," in *Collected Works, Volume 18: The Symbolic Life* (Trans. R.F.C. Hull. Princeton: Princeton University Press, 1976), §1466ff. It is discussed in some detail below.

[11] A full discussion of the antecedents and implications of this principle is found in Part I of Nagy's book, *Philosophical Issues in the Psychology of C.G. Jung*, which is titled "To Know Only the Soul: Jung's Epistemology."

[12] This lecture, first delivered in Vienna in 1932 with the title, "Die Stimme des Innern," condemns Enlightenment rationalism but is marred in turn by a dark echo of the Romantic era, a tendency to idealize the "personality" of the nation. This regrettable tendency was one Jung shared with many intellectuals of his time who had not yet fully understood the nature of Hitler's rule, or who still hoped against hope that in this leader Germany had found its psychologically necessary center of personality ("Personality," *CW 17*, p.168n). That Jung was not blind to the potential viciousness of rising nationalism, however, is indicated in the lecture by his repeated

warnings about "psychic epidemics," "Caesarean madness" and "the Roman devil-worship of power" ("Personality," *CW 17*, §302–309).

[13] Letter to Albert Oeri, 4 January 1929: "I wonder which devil Karl Barth (with his absolute God) worships in practice. It's very likely one of them has him by the collar" (*Letters I*, p.58).

[14] C.G. Jung, "A Psychological Approach to the Dogma of the Trinity". (*CW 11*. Hereafter cited as "Trinity.") Quoting from an essay by an Old Testament scholar, Jung also mentions that Barth refers to the Holy Ghost as "the combination of father and son, . . . the *vinculum caritatis*" ("Trinity," *CW 11* §177).

[15] "Amplification" is one of Jung's primary methods of interpreting dream symbology and psychological symptoms. It is related to his confidence in the archetypal level of the unconscious. Unlike Freudian association, it insists that *all* meanings are connected to an original symbol or image that is rooted in the collective symbolic thought-world.

[16] Karl Barth, *The Humanity of God* (Atlanta: John Knox Press, 1982). See especially the second essay, "The Humanity of God," written in 1956.

[17] C.G. Jung, "Transformation Symbolism in the Mass" (*CW 11*), §296–448. Hereafter cited as "Mass."

[18] C.G. Jung, *Memories, Dreams, Reflections* (Recorded and edited by Aniela Jaffé. Translators, Richard and Clara Winston. New York: Random House, 1961; Vintage, 1965). Hereafter cited as *Memories*.

[19] Catholic readers could be excused for mistaking Jung's personal intentions, since his own family members were misled sometimes. Seeing his father's intense interest in the doctrines and rituals of the Catholic Church, Franz Jung asked him once, "Bist du ein katholischer Mann?" The father answered, giving his deep laugh, "Um Gottes willen . . . !" ("Are you a Catholic?"—"For heaven's sake . . . !") The father's belly laugh was demonstrated in the son's telling (Franz Jung, interview, 17 Aug. 92).

[20] In Jung's somewhat exasperated reply to H. Irminger, 22 Sept 1944, he explains that it is an error to think that he would become a Roman Catholic if only he understood the doctrines better. He adds that he has been courted also by alchemists and by Hindus, each group under the impression that he understood their beliefs almost well enough to join them (*Letters I*, pp.346f).

[21] Jung's brief for Catholicism in this essay is clearly psychological and pragmatic, not theological: "So long as a defence works I shall not break it down, since I know that there must be cogent reasons why the patient has to think in such a narrow circle. . . . *In the same way and for the same reason I support the hypothesis of the practicing Catholic while it works for him*" (*Psychology and Religion, CW 11*, §79, emphasis added).

²² For a fine example of Jungian thought about neighbor-love, see Ann Belford Ulanov's application of Jungian categories in her essay, "The Two Strangers" (*Union Seminary Quarterly Review*. New York: Union Theological Seminary, 1973). Like Jung, she argues that love for "the stranger within" has psychological priority; without an inner reconciliation with the shadow, love for the outer "stranger" or enemy is impossible.

²³ The eulogies and prayers from Jung's funeral service are printed in a limited edition, a copy of which may be found at Yale University in the Beinecke Rare Book and Manuscript Library. The officiant at the service was Dr. Hans Schär, a Swiss Protestant theologian, who also officiated at the funerals of Emma Jung and Toni Wolff (*Letters II*, p.28n). The eulogy by Werner Meyer meditates in visionary fashion on the journey of Jung's soul after death (Werner Meyer, Hans Schär, Eugen Böhler, *Zur Erinnerung an Carl Gustav Jung: Gedenkfeier anlässlich der Bestattung*. Freitag, 9 Juni 1961, in der reformierten Kirche in Küsnacht. Limited edition, Gedenkschriften-Verlag Zürich).

²⁴ Victor White, for one, fully acknowledged the reality of Jung's Protestantism; but he tended to see it as a limitation. For example, when White applies Jung's concept of the Self to the sacramental body of the church, he acknowledges that "a Catholic would doubtless give a more dynamic interpretation to the identification of Christ with the human *Ganzheit* than was possible in the Swiss Protestantism of Jung's upbringing" ("Eranos: 1947, 1948," *Dominican Studies*, Vol. 2, No. 4. Oxford: Blackfriars Publications, 10/49, p.399). White's review of Jung's "Über das Selbst" is discussed below in Chapter Five.

²⁵ In "Marriage as a Psychological Relationship" (*Collected Works, Volume 17: The Development of Personality*. Translator, R.F.C. Hull. Princeton: Princeton University Press, 1954), Jung observes that children live out the "unlived life" of their parents ("Marriage," *CW 17*, §328). Jung's adventurous work on religious subjects, using many of the tools from his father's toolbox, is a case in point.

²⁶ Another interpreter might point out the obverse side of the dream image. It seems very important to Jung in the dream to *try*, at least, to imitate his father's reverence, even though he cannot uncritically subscribe to his father's complete submission. Jung's interpretation emphasizes his failure to bow completely; one might equally well emphasize his attempt.

²⁷ What Jung means by "God-image" (*Gottesbild*) is different in significant ways from what theologians mean by *imago Dei*. When this distinction is observed, serious confusion can be avoided. The term *imago Dei* is sometimes used by moral theologians as a kind of shorthand for the moral dignity and autonomy of persons, in light of their creation by God. Jung might find this anthropology congenial, if it did not lean too much on the

doctrine of God's intrinsic goodness. Jung's "God-image" arises from his observation of psychological imagery and behavior. It can become highly problematic in relation to classic theological statements about the nature and activity of God.

[28] C.G. Jung, "The Relations Between the Ego and the Unconscious" (*CW 7*, Part II). Hereafter cited as "Ego and Unconscious."

[29] Jung's great-grandfather was reportedly converted by Schleiermacher.

[30] Murray Stein catalogues the ways followers and critics of Jung have characterized his relation to Christianity. In the first chapter of his book *Jung's Treatment of Christianity: The Psychotherapy of a Religious Tradition* (Wilmette, IL: Chiron Publications, 1985), Stein describes the limitations of the following categories which have been variously assigned to Jung: empirical scientist (pp.4ff); heretic, philosopher, prophet (pp.8ff); hermeneutical revitalist (pp.10ff); doctor of individual souls (pp.12ff); "modern man" (pp.14ff). Stein's own interpretation of Jung's work with Christian symbols and themes is discussed briefly below. Hereafter cited as Stein.

[31] Stein oversimplifies somewhat by demarcating this phase of Jung's work so sharply, since Jung's interest in the Western church and its symbols is already in evidence before that year. Two major essays in *Psychology and Alchemy* (C.G. Jung, *Collected Works, Volume 12: Psychology and Alchemy*. Second Edition. Translator, R.F.C. Hull. Princeton: Princeton University Press, 1953. Original publication in German, 1944), dating from the Eranos meetings of 1935 and 1936, contain discussions of the psychological meaning of Christ which clearly anticipate *Aion* and *Answer to Job*. (See especially "The Lapis-Christ Parallel," the fifth chapter in Part III, "Religious Ideas in Alchemy.")

[32] Reinhold Niebuhr, in *Moral Man and Immoral Society: A Study in Ethics and Politics* (New York: Charles Scribner's Sons, 1932/1960), defines Christian love in terms of self-sacrifice, and thinks only individuals are capable of it. Collectives—groups or governments—can get as far as the rough justice that balances selfish interests. But to realize *agape* requires a singlehearted, selfless regard for others which only the individual—by grace—can achieve. The conviction that groups are morally inferior to individuals has obvious parallels in Jung's thought.

[33] Jung's thinking also unconsciously parallels Kierkegaard's (see for example, Kierkegaard's *Works of Love*) in their common emphasis on the moral autonomy of the individual and the ethically ambiguous experience of the individual God-relation. Strikingly, both Jung and Kierkegaard illustrate the terrible ambiguity of the personal God-relation by referring to the story of Abraham's duty to sacrifice Isaac (Jung's "Transformation Symbolism in the Mass," *CW 11*, §397f, and Kierkegaard's *Fear and Trem-*

bling. Translator, Alexander Dru. New York: Harper & Brothers, 1958/ 1959, *passim*).

³⁴ Jung's 1916 essay, "The Structure of the Unconscious," underwent revisions over the following two decades and now appears under the title "The Relations Between the Ego and the Unconscious," Part II of *Two Essays, CW 7*.

³⁵ For a review of ethical views on self-love, see Gene Outka, *Agape: An Ethical Analysis* (New Haven: Yale University Press, 1972), especially Chapter 2, "Agape and Self-Love," pp.55ff. Differentiating between ethical and psychological egoism, Outka points out that the latter makes the former redundant: if the psyche is egoistic, no principle of egoism is needed. One need not shout to a person falling past one's window, "Go down!" (Gene Outka, "Religious Ethics and Moral Issues," lectures, Yale University, 1985, 1986).

³⁶ In his 4 Aug. 45 letter to Hugo Rahner, a Catholic theologian whose help he had engaged before he met White, Jung explains that the classical conception of archetypes is irrelevant to him. "I fully appreciate your objections if I accept the Scholastic premise, but it seems to me that the Scholastic standpoint is neither adequate nor suitable for the needs of an empirical science," Jung writes, referring to a "radically altered view of the world" which no longer understands classical thought-forms (*Letters I*, p.374).

³⁷ Barbara Hannah, *Jung: His Life and Work—A Biographical Memoir* (New York: G.P. Putnam's Sons, 1976). In 1937 Jung spoke to followers in New York about Christ as a human being. He called Jesus' cry of dereliction from the cross "a moment of utter failure, when he saw that the life he had led according to his best convictions and with such integrity had been largely based on illusion." However, Jung added, "he had lived his life with such devotion that, in spite of this, he won through to a resurrected body." Jung exhorted his hearers, "We should go and make our mistakes; for there is no full life without error; no one has found the whole truth; but if we would only live with the same integrity and devotion as Christ, he hoped we would all, like Christ, win through to a resurrected body" (Hannah, p.239).

CHAPTER FIVE: JUNG'S REVISIONS OF CHRISTIAN DOCTRINE

¹ William McGuire, private communication.

² The priest is identified in editorial notes by Adler and Jaffé (*Letters I*, p.300n).

[3] C.G. Jung, "A Psychological Approach to the Dogma of the Trinity" (*CW 11*, §169–295) [1948].

[4] In other contexts Jung does attribute a moral defect to "medieval" thinking, namely, habitual blindness to the genuine possibility of one's own evil. Failure to become conscious of one's shadow and identification with a totally good God-image are characteristics of what Jung calls the medieval mentality of many theologians.

[5] A passage where this thought is developed—i.e., the virtual equation of psychological repression, neurotic one-sidedness, and unconscious sin— is found in the third Terry Lecture, "The History and Psychology of a Natural Symbol," which is concerned with fourfold symbology and the mandala (*Psychology and Religion*, CW 11, §129).

[6] This important dream of Victor White's is discussed above, Chapter One.

[7] White's material helps Jung make two points, first, that "the Third Person of the Trinity, unlike Father and Son, has no personal quality" ("Trinity," *CW 11*, §276) and second, that the Spirit's gift of revelation is related only ambiguously to human morality ("Trinity," *CW 11*, §289).

[8] C.G. Jung, "Zur Psychologie der Trinitätsidee" ["Toward a Psychology of the Idea of the Trinity"] (*Eranos-Jahrbuch 1940/1941*. Editor, Olga Fröbe-Kapteyn. Zürich: Rhein-Verlag, 1942). Hereafter cited as "Trinitätsidee."

Because Jung's original lecture has not been translated and differs so much from the revised and expanded essay (now printed in the eleventh volume of the *Collected Works* under the title "A Psychological Approach to the Dogma of the Trinity"), there is no authorized translation of many passages found in the original lecture. Where that is the case, it is sometimes helpful to resort to the German text.

[9] The second sentence of the statement is no clearer in German than in translation. In Jung's defense one must admit that serious theological writing on the subject of the Trinity can become equally confusing. The term *perichoresis* —*circumincession* in its Latin form—refers to the reciprocal existence and closeness uniting the three Persons who are, together, one God.

[10] As explained below, Jung uses the term "evil" in two different though related ways. The "evil" that Jung wants to include in the Christian Godhead is not in the first instance what we will call the "evil of history" (though he holds God accountable for some of that) but rather it is the "evil of myth." Indeed, the evil located in the God-image *must* be at one level a mythic and archetypal kind of evil, since the image of God is an archetypal image.

[11] Jung's footnote refers us to Montague Rhodes James, *The Apocryphal New Testament* (Oxford, 1924), p.33.

¹² C.G. Jung, "Über das Selbst" (*Eranos-Jahrbuch 1948, Band XVI.* Zweite Folge. Editor, Olga Fröbe-Kapteyn. Zürich: Rhein-Verlag, 1949), pp.285–315: "*Christ exemplifies the archetype of the self*" (*Aion, CW 9ii,* §70). The wording of Jung's lecture "Über das Selbst" changed so little when Jung incorporated it into Chapters IV and V of *Aion* that most passages from the original text which appear in that book can be quoted in the Hull translation without loss of accuracy.

¹³ Jung himself traces his christological work to this year. "As early as 1944, in *Psychology and Alchemy*, I had been able to demonstrate the parallelism between the Christ figure and the central concept of the alchemists, the *lapis*, or stone" (*Memories*, p.210).

¹⁴ In an essay written in 1971, Marie-Louise von Franz makes the same point about the "stages" of individuation neatly summarized in the early chapters of *Aion*: "Was Jung in den genannten drei Stufen der Individuation durch klassifizierende Begriffe zu ordnen versucht hat, bedeutet in Wirklichkeit einen unendlich langwierigen Prozeß, der bei jedem einzelnen Analysanden individuell variierende Formen annimmt" ("Die Selbsterfahrung bei C.G. Jung" in Heidland, Mann, von Franz, *C.G. Jung und die Theologen: Selbsterfahrung und Gotteserfahrung bei C.G. Jung.* Radius-Projekte 49. Stuttgart: Radius-Verlag, 1971, p.26). ("What Jung has attempted to organize under the classifying concepts of the three stages of individuation, signifies in reality an endlessly difficult process, which assumes uniquely varied forms with each particular analysand.")

¹⁵ Edward F. Edinger's *Ego and Archetype: Individuation and the Religious Function of the Psyche* (Baltimore: Penguin Books, 1972) explores in depth the relationships, positive and negative, that can exist between these two separate and unequal centers within the psyche—the ego and the Self. He also studies in depth the psychological and symbolic parallels between this primary intrapsychic relationship and the symbolic imagery of relationship between human beings and God. In categories drawn from Jung, and in the light of imaginal work by Western artists and poets, Edinger analyzes crucial representations of the divine-human relationship as known in Jewish-Christian biblical tradition, including the expulsion from Eden, the story of Job, and the mythic symbolism of Christ's birth, death, and resurrection.

¹⁶ "Autochthonous" means, literally, "rooted in one's own ground." This psychic "ground"—the history and language in which symbols are rooted—may be either individual or collective; but Jung views individual religious experience as the more compelling. So, for example, in one passage he defines archetypes as "forms or images which occur practically all over the earth as constituents of myths and at the same time as auto-

chthonous, individual products of unconscious origin" (*Psychology and Religion*, *CW 11*, §88).

[17] Franz Jung remembers his father's solemn conviction that writing *Antwort auf Hiob* was necessary to his recovery from a serious illness, which was recognized at the time as being partly psychosomatic in origin (F. Jung, interview, 17 Aug. 92). Jung mentioned the episode in letters at the time. To Aniela Jaffé he wrote that the way the book was written was "like the spirit seizing one by the scruff of the neck" (*Letters II*, p.20). To Dr. H. in Germany: "In the spring I was plagued by my liver, had often to stay in bed and in the midst of this *misère* write a little essay. . . ." (*Letters II*, p.21). The second verb, "write," follows "had to": Jung's liver compelled him to stay in bed and write *Job*. The intellectual origins of the book, meanwhile, are spelled out in the "Prefatory Note" to *Job*, where Jung advises us that the book tackles problems raised in *Aion*, particularly the *privatio boni* (*Answer to Job*, pp.ixf).

[18] White calls Jung's theory of the Self a "quasi-Manichaean dualism . . . heavy in its consequences for psychology itself and more especially for the understanding of the Christian warfare" ("Eranos: 1947, 1948," p.399).

[19] At the very end of his life, White stated that perhaps he did not fully understand what Jung meant by the doctrine of the Self. By claiming uncertainty on this central point, he implied that the rift between himself and Jung was due to misunderstanding rather than to outright disagreement, and thus granted a possibility that better understanding might yet bridge the abyss between their positions. White's uncertainty and his degree of genuine disagreement about the meaning of the Self are discussed below in Chapter Six.

[20] The Hebrew verb *bara'* is normally translated, as here, "to create." This verb occurs with no other subject but God, and always conveys echoes of the first verse of Genesis: "In the beginning God created (*bara'*) the heavens and the earth." Hebrew has verbs of similar meaning which can apply to human subjects. Two of these verbs (rendered in English as "make" and "form") actually occur in this verse. Thus we are reminded that the poet has a choice; his use of language is significant. The conclusion is unavoidable that the poet of Second Isaiah specifically refers darkness and evil back to God's original creation.

[21] Jung included his lecture "Über das Selbst" in *Aion* as Chapters IV and V. The first two-thirds of the 1948 lecture are incorporated verbatim into Chapter IV, "The Self." Into this chapter Jung interpolated a few new paragraphs but made few other changes. The last third of the lecture becomes the basis of Chapter V, titled "Christ, A Symbol of the Self." This chapter contains considerable interpolated material.

²² In a footnote to *Soul and Psyche* (p.296, note 43) White points out the distinction in Neoplatonist philosophy between *me on* ("not something") and *ouk on* ("nothing"). The position of Christian theologians, following Augustine, that evil is not a real "being" (*ousia*) does not pretend that it is "nothing" in the second sense, but only says that it is "not something." Jung discounts the distinction, however, since he wants to base his conclusions not on fine points in philosophy, but on how he believes ordinary people understand the doctrine in a practical sense.

²³ "Perfect" and "complete" (in German, *vollkommen* and *vollständig*) must be read as terms of art in this context. Sticklers for etymology sometimes protest that the two terms Jung used both mean the same thing in English (referring to a state of being "finished"), and so they should be interchangeable. Jung's distinction is certainly artificial from this point of view. But the differentiation between an attitude that splits off the shadow (perfection) and one that takes ownership of it (completeness) has profound theoretical and practical ramifications.

²⁴ C.G. Jung, *The Visions Seminars* (two volumes). Zurich: Spring Publications, 1987).

²⁵ In Chapter V of *Aion*, on the other hand, Jung closely studies the notion of perfection as it arises in early Christian writings. He concludes that *teleiosis* might most satisfactorily be read as a condition of striving toward, rather than being identified with, the goal of perfection. When "perfection" is understood in this processive sense, rather than as a static condition, Jung gives it a positive interpretation. "To strive after teleiosis in the sense of perfection is not only legitimate but is inborn in man as a peculiarity which provides civilization with one of its strongest roots" (*Aion, CW 11*, §123). Jung finds such a similarity between the early Christian concept of *teleiosis* (in the sense of "striving toward a goal") and his own concept of psychological "completeness," that in another passage he equates the two terms (*Aion, CW 9ii*, §171).

²⁶ "And because individuation is an heroic and often tragic task, the most difficult of all, it involves suffering, a passion of the ego. . . . The analogous passion of Christ signifies God's suffering on account of the injustice of the world and the darkness of man" ("A Psychological Approach to the Dogma of the Trinity," *CW 11*, §233).

²⁷ His argumentation is weak not simply on account of its repetitiveness; the problem goes even to the quality of his "experiential" warrants. Jung says he became interested in the *privatio boni* doctrine because he once had a Protestant patient who used it to justify moral laxness (Foreword to *God and the Unconscious*, pp.xxf). The case no doubt occurred. Yet it is very odd for a psychologist to attack a particular doctrine because one of his patients has used it to rationalize acting-out.

[28] What Jung means by "the opposites" and what a theologian like Victor White may mean by that term are two very different things. The implications of their divergent treatment of this concept are discussed in the following chapter.

[29] Jung admits that a privative theory of evil has had authority in the church since the second century, but he points out that other theories have coexisted with it. In Chapter IV of *Aion* he quotes passages from Augustine and Origen calling evil a privation of good, and then adds a string of similar statements by other ancients: Theophilus of Antioch, Basil the Great, Titus of Bostra, John Chrysostom, Dionysius the Areopagite (§81–88), and finally Aquinas (§91–93). Then he cites writers from the history of world religions, whose positions offer a challenge to Christian orthodoxy on this subject: Pseudo-Clement, the Ebionites, the apocalyptic "Ascension of Isaiah," Jakob Böhme, Taoism, diverse rabbinical midrashim, and the book of Job (*Aion*, *CW 9ii*, §99–112).

Thus he documents the existence of contrasting, and to his mind preferable, descriptions of evil which coexisted for centuries with the church's official teaching. With one exception, the writings Jung introduces in this chapter as positive examples lie outside the realm of Christian orthodoxy. The book of Job represents Jung's one example from within the biblical canon—i.e., a canonical witness that makes the image of God—in Jung's eyes—dangerous and unconscious.

[30] James Hillman's comments on the archetypal or mythical dimension of evil are especially illuminating. He writes in *Insearch: Psychology and Religion* (Irving, TX: Spring Publications, Inc., 1979): "The more that evil is archetypal, the more we experience it as impersonal. . . . When evil takes on godly form (Loki, Lucifer, Hermes-Mercury, the Trickster), it has a double nature and, like the spirit, can blow for good or ill" (*Insearch*, p.90). But in historical manifestations, embodied in concrete human acts and choices, evil is morally repulsive. Hillman writes: "It is the human element in the Devil that gives evil its full reality. . . . This implies that the archetypal shadow never achieves full reality until it is linked in a pact with the human" (*Insearch*, p.90).

[31] Austin Farrer, *Love Almighty and Ills Unlimited* (London: Collins/Fontana Library Edition, 1966), p.7 and *passim*.

[32] The definition of evil as "that which ought not to be," suggested by Richard Norris, recognizes better than the term "privation" the *experiential reality* of evil, even while it acknowledges its metaphysical wrongness and agrees with Farrer's "outrage." Dr. Norris, an Anglican theologian and patristics scholar, suggests that the real meaning of evil for Jung is not "the fourth" but the splitting of opposites (Lecture, Church of St. Luke in the Fields, New York, NY, spring 1982). This

view, which I think is well-founded, is taken up below under "Teleology and Privation."

³³ Jung resists making humankind the "birthplace of all evil" (*Aion*, *CW 9ii*, §62), as that fiction only creates a monstrous psychic inflation; but it is obvious that he also refuses to take the whole burden off human shoulders, since the highest level of responsibility for moral consciousness rests with mortals.

³⁴ Aurelius Augustine, *The City of God* (Translator: Marcus Dods. New York: Random House, 1950). In XXII.8 where Augustine discusses two miraculous cures, he omits the actual names of the sufferers and substitutes these allegorizing names, which I take to be—in context—a theological commentary on the "undeserved" nature of physical disease and similar *malum poenae*.

³⁵ Aelred Squire, *Summer in the Seed* (New York: Paulist Press, 1980).

³⁶ From von Rad's *Wisdom in Israel* (London, 1972), p.221. Squire's discussion of *Answer to Job* in his chapter titled "Leviathan" is to a large extent built upon the intrinsic agreements between Jung's point of view in *Job* and von Rad's reading of Hebrew Wisdom writings (*Summer*, Chapter Six).

³⁷ In *The City of God* Augustine associates the fact of "innocent" suffering with original sin. He argues that *malum poenae* should be understood in the long run as a consequence of *malum culpae*—though he means the fault not of individuals but of humanity as a whole. In no case would Augustine have applied this fault, as Jung does, to God.

³⁸ This passage is from Richard Kehoe's "Review of *Antwort auf Hiob*," op. cit., p.230.

³⁹ Victor White meant by "privation of good" "a *defectus boni quod natum est et debet haberi*, the absence of a good which is naturally there and should be there" (*Soul and Psyche*, p.153, quoting from *ST* I.49.1).

⁴⁰ C.G. Jung, *Dream Analysis: Notes of a Seminar Given in 1928-1931* (Editor, William McGuire. Princeton: Princeton University Press, 1984).

CHAPTER SIX: THEODICY

¹ Victor White, "Kinds of Opposites," *Studien zur Analytischen Psychologie C.G. Jungs. Festschrift zum 80. Geburtstag von C.G. Jung.* Band I: "Beiträge aus Theorie und Praxis" (Herausgegeben vom C.G. Jung Institut Zürich. Zürich: Rascher Verlag, 1955), p.148. The full statement reads: "Aquinas was well aware that the recognition of opposites was the indispensable requisite for advance in consciousness, or, as he would have put it, in the pursuit of truth or reality. . . . He explains that the attain-

ment of truth is like the disentangling of a knot, the knots which bind the mind are its 'doubts', and their knottiness or doubtfulness must be faced and examined before they can be untied or resolved."

² Adler and Jaffé provide this translation of the passage, which they attribute to Fathers of the English Dominican Province, 1947, Vol. I, p.747 (*Letters II*, p.213n). Victor White adverted to this passage again when he wrote, "Aquinas himself recognizes that to the unreflecting apprehensions of the psyche, the privation which is evil . . . has the character of a certain kind of entity—and is a positive contrary" (*Soul and Psyche*, p.156).

³ Primary locations of St. Thomas' discussions of evil: *ST* I.48–49 and I.75. Also in the *Summa Contra Gentiles* [*On the Truth of the Catholic Faith*] (Translator: Vernon J. Bourke. Garden City: Hanover House, 1956), especially in Book III, Part 1, "Providence."

⁴ White particularly focuses on the kinds of opposition mentioned by Aquinas in *ST* I.75.7.

⁵ A fifth category, "Pythagorean pairs," is not included in White's paper; it is mentioned by Aquinas only to be discarded [*ST* I.48.1]. Jung's theory of good and evil often seems to fit this category, because like the Pythagoreans he reifies evil, seeing it as a *natura* ("cause of motion" in Aristotle, ST I.48.1, p.108n).

⁶ For example, Jung writes: "The relative abolition of the ego affects only those supreme and ultimate decisions which confront us in situations where there are insoluble conflicts of duty. This means, in other words, that in such cases the ego is a suffering bystander who decides nothing but must submit to a decision and surrender unconditionally" (*Aion, CW 9ii*, §79).

⁷ White describes Christ's agony as "intensely conscious inner realization of the opposition in all their [sic] extremity" ("Opposites," p.145). The crucial word in White's definition is "conscious." One might raise questions about the practical difference between "agony" and "conflict," suggesting that White strains these terms, or allows Aquinas to strain them. But Jung's interpretation of "sacrifice" agrees closely with the distinction White draws between "agony" and "conflict." At a certain point when duties conflict, as Jung notes, the ego must give up and be a "bystander"; then moral "conflict" is over, even if "agony" remains.

⁸ Aquinas writes: "Moreover, 'good' has the same extension as 'being': since it can be predicated of everything, it cannot be used as a differential term for any specific kind, as Aristotle makes clear. Nor can 'bad' be a differential term, since evil is a privation and not an entity" (*ST* Ia.IIae. 54,3.2). The Blackfriars edition adds a footnote to stress the logical convertibility of the concepts: "*whatever is good is a being, and whatever is a being is good*" (*ST*, vol. 22, p.104n, emphasis added).

⁹ It is noteworthy that St. Augustine, who coined the phrase *privatio boni*, decries the Stoics because they deny that evil is real. He catalogues the miseries of human life and natural disasters, repeating, "Certainly there is a mighty force in these evils" (*City of God* XIX.4ff), and adds, "Let every one, then, who thinks with pain on all these great evils, so horrible, so ruthless, acknowledge that this is misery" (*City of God* XIX.7).

¹⁰ Appendix 12, "Esse," in Volume 22 of the Blackfriars *Summa Theologiae* includes the following comments: "St. Thomas treats as a special case the 'is' which occurs in a sentence such as 'James is blind'. There is no form which is *being blind*; to be blind is simply to lack the form *being sighted*. So the predicate of 'James is blind' does not signify any sort of *being*. Similarly, there is no form which is *being bad*, or *being a bad P*. If a knife is a bad knife because it has no handle, its badness is not its possessing the form *having no handle*, but simply its lacking the form *having a handle*" (*ST* Vol. 22, p.133).

¹¹ The reference is to Augustine's *Enchiridion* 12 (*ST* I.48.5, p.124, note 3).

¹² Victor White, "Good and Evil" (*Harvest*, Volume 12. London: Analytical Psychology Club, 1966), pp.16–34, typescript. Published with special permission from the Harvill Press, Ltd.

¹³ Victor White, "Eranos: 1947, 1948" (*Dominican Studies*, Volume II, no.4, 10/49. Oxford: Blackfriars Publications), pp.394–400.

¹⁴ Victor White, "Theological Reflections" (*The Journal of Analytical Psychology*, Vol. V. London: Tavistock Publications, 1960), pp.147–54.

CHAPTER SEVEN: HOPE AND POSSIBILITY

¹ In lectures given in the 1930s on the visions of a young woman patient, Jung comments on the necessity of assimilating the shadow before encountering what he calls "the real non-ego": "Most people are still wrestling with their shadows; they have not yet been able to experience the fact that their shadows are real, they have the greatest trouble with that. But only when they have understood it can they encounter the wider non-ego. . . . The true encounter with the collective unconscious can happen only after you have integrated the shadow, thereby completing the ego" (C.G. Jung, *The Visions Seminars*. Book Two. Zurich: Spring Publications, 1976, pp.294f).

² *Church Dogmatics* Vol. III, Part 3. *The Doctrine of Creation* (Translator, G.W. Bromiley. Edinburgh: T.& T. Clark, 1960, p.293).

³ *Church Dogmatics*, Vol. IV, Part 2: *The Doctrine of Reconciliation*. Translator, G.W. Bromiley. Edinburgh: T.&T. Clark, 1958, p.398).

⁴ C.G. Jung, *The Undiscovered Self* (Trans. R.F.C. Hull. Boston: Little, Brown and Company, 1957, 1958). Hereafter cited as *Self*.

⁵ C.G. Jung, *The Visions Seminars*, Book One and Book Two (From the notes of Mary Foote. Zurich: Spring Publications, 1976). Cited here as *Visions I* and *II*.

⁶ As noted, when Jung used the metaphor of resurrection in a talk given to friends in 1937, he urged his listeners to live "with the same integrity and devotion as Christ . . . even if it is based on a mistake" and expressed the hope that they would then, "like Christ, win through to a resurrected body" (Hannah, *Jung*, p.239). Again, in a brief writing in 1954, Jung indicated that he respects resurrection as an essential element in the myth of Jesus as a God-man. He dismisses the historical claim, however, and says that belief in bodily resurrection shows the "primitivity" of the early church and the surprising survival of a "pagan" materialism among modern Christians ("On Resurrection," *CW 18*, §1558–74).

⁷ Jung did not swerve from this teaching that the fear of God is a necessary and primary response; he treats the theme again in *Memories, Dreams, Reflections*, and in other late works.

⁸ As a contemporary theologian and Jungian, John P. Dourley writes: "In effect, Jung made human consciousness the second moment or principle in divine life. Mythically, theologically and metaphysically, this means that historical consciousness has come to realize that the unresolved split in the Godhead seeks its recognition and resolution in human consciousness. . . . Humanity and divinity are engaged in a process of mutual redemption" (*Love, Celibacy and the Inner Marriage*. Toronto: Inner City Books, 1987, p.71).

⁹ Stories of his interaction with some of his women patients, such as Sabina Spielrein, suggest that Jung did not learn to carry this feeling shadow easily or without significant cost to himself and others. (Aldo Carotenuto, *A Secret Symmetry: Sabina Spielrein between Jung and Freud*. Translators, Arno Pomerans, John Shepley, Krishna Winston. New York: Pantheon Books, 1984.)

¹⁰ Werner Meyer, Hans Schär, Eugen Böhler. *Zur Erinnerung an Carl Gustav Jung, 1875–1961: Gedenkfeier Anlässlich der Bestattung, Freitag, 9. Juni 1961 in der reformierten Kirche in Küsnacht* (Zürich: Gedenkenschrift-Verlag, 1961). Werner Meyer's eulogy, the first and longest of the three addresses, opens with a prayer based on psalms (mainly Psalm 8). Hans Schär, the officiant, next focuses on the high points of Jung's biography and empha-sizes his character as a healer. Last Eugen Böhler, representing the Eidgenössische Technische Hochschule (ETH), honors Jung as a scientist and scholar.

¹¹ In a letter to Pastor Wegmann, 20 November 1945, Jung refers to Meyer's "catholicizing" tendency and the "streak of mysticism" seen in Meyer's recently published work, *Leib Christi*. Jung also compares Meyer's perspective to his own, though he notes that Meyer tends to be "caught up uncritically in his visionary world" (*Letters I*, p.391).

¹² The cabbalist is mentioned only a few times in the text of Jung's writings on alchemy, but often in the footnotes. A quotation from Christian Knorr von Rosenroth serves as the epilogue to Jung's 1946 essay, "The Psychology of the Transference" (*Collected Works, Volume 16: The Practice of Psychotherapy*. Trans. R.F.C. Hull. Princeton: Princeton University Press, 1954; §353–539).

¹³ C.G. Jung, "On the Psychology and Pathology of So-Called Occult Phenomena," in *Psychiatric Studies* (Second Edition. *Collected Works*, Vol. 1. Translator, R.F.C. Hull. Princeton: Princeton University Press/Bollingen, 1957/1970), Jung's doctoral thesis.

¹⁴ This translation of a passage from Werner Meyer's eulogy is my own.

¹⁵ Meyer is not to be blamed for failing to take this passage into account; he could not have seen it, since the "autobiography" that Jung dictated to Aniela Jaffé did not appear until months after his death (*Memories*, p.xiv).

¹⁶ Many statements are on record showing Jung's feeling of urgency about the fate of humanity in the latter half of the twentieth century. In addition to those cited in earlier chapters, an excellent example comes up in the "Face to Face" interview with John Freeman of the BBC: "We need more understanding of human nature, because the only real danger that exists is man himself. He is the great danger, and we are pitifully unaware of it. . . . His psyche should be studied, because we are the origin of all coming evil" ("Face to Face," *C. G. Jung Speaking*, p.435).

¹⁷ At the end of his life (in "Theological Reflections," discussed above), White confessed he was still not sure what analytical psychology meant by the Self.

¹⁸ See Jung's letter about White's death, sent to Mother Michael of the Blessed Trinity (*Letters II*, p.604). In an essay on the Jung-White and Jung-Buber conversations (cited immediately below), John P. Dourley highlights Jung's cryptic final statement in this letter. Jung says that White had come to a crossroads, "where the way bifurcates to the land of Hereafter and to the future of mankind and its spiritual adventure" (Ibid, p.605). In Jung's view, White had a moral (though half-conscious) choice between dying on his familiar spiritual path, or undergoing a radical inner transformation that would allow him to serve the future of humanity. Like many who have confronted such a choice in our era, Jung

suggests, White could not bear the transformation; but then no other way lay open to him except death.

[19] John P. Dourley, "Jung and the White, Buber Exchanges: Exercises in Futility," in *A Strategy for a Loss of Faith: Jung's Proposal* (Toronto: Inner City Books, 1992).

[20] The biblical context from which Jung drew in declaring to the theologian, "you are to me a white raven," is perhaps not so familiar to contemporary readers as it was to White and Jung. The statement invokes a poignant moment in the Old Testament story of Elijah, in which the prophet, fleeing from his enemy Ahab, is miraculously saved from death in the wilderness: "And the word of the Lord came to Elijah, 'Depart from here and turn eastward, and hide yourself by the brook Cherith, that is east of the Jordan. You shall drink from the brook, and I have commanded the ravens to feed you there.' So he went and did according to the word of the Lord; he went and dwelt by the brook Cherith that is east of the Jordan. And the ravens brought him bread and meat in the morning, and bread and meat in the evening; and he drank from the brook" (1 Kings 17:2–6, RSV).

We need not dwell on the layers of meaning and possible irony implicit in Jung's comparison of himself to Elijah, the militant monotheist who fiercely opposed his people's movement to accommodate the gods of their neighbors. We should note, however, that in calling his raven "white," Jung not only made a pun on Victor White's name but also negated the dark symbolism usually associated with ravens.

[21] F.X. Charet, "A Dialogue between Psychology and Theology: The correspondence of C.G. Jung and Victor White" (*The Journal of Analytical Psychology*, October 1990, Vol. 35, No. 4, pp.421–441). Charet explains that although the grip of neo-scholasticism ended during the intellectual revolution of the 1960s, a "resurrected scholasticism under the modern designation, transcendental Thomism" (represented by Rahner and Lonergan) has begun to assume a similar role in defining Roman Catholic orthodoxy (*Dialogue*, p.436).

[22] A powerful sample of Tillich's thought is in his brief classic, *Dynamics of Faith* (New York: Harper & Row, 1957).

[23] John P. Dourley's earlier works on the possibilities for a synthesis between Christian theology and Jungian psychology include *The Psyche as Sacrament: A Comparative Study of C.G. Jung and Paul Tillich* (Toronto: Inner City Books, 1981); and *The Illness that We Are* (Toronto: Inner City Books, 1984), hereafter cited as *Illness*.

[24] John P. Dourley, "Jung, Tillich, and Aspects of Christian Development" (ed. Robert J. Moore and Daniel J. Meckel, *Jung and Christianity in Dialogue: Faith, Feminism and Hermeneutics*, New York & Mahwah, NJ: Paulist Press, 1990).

²⁵ This argument is fully developed in Dourley's recently published essay, "Jung and the White, Buber Exchanges: Exercises in Futility" (in *A Strategy for a Loss of Faith: Jung's Proposal*, op. cit.).

²⁶ John P. Dourley, *Love, Celibacy and the Inner Marriage* (Toronto: Inner City Books, 1987).

²⁷ John Dourley, interview, May 1987.

APPENDIX A

¹ From 1962 to 1972 the Jung-White letters were in the care of Frau Jaffé and Dr. Adler, as she edited the German edition of the *C.G. Jung Letters* and he the English. Apart from that, until 1991 they were kept in Küsnacht; since 1991 Dr. Beat Glaus has kept them in the C.G. Jung Archive at the ETH library (F. Jung, personal correspondence, 10 Dec. 92).

² The C.G. Jung Archive at the ETH in Zurich became the repository for most of Jung's scientific papers and letters in August 1980, after the Swiss Federal Government accepted them as a gift from the Jung family in 1977 (Ibid).

³ Beate Ruhm von Oppen, correspondence, 20 Sept. 1985.

⁴ About half of White's letters are paraphrased or quoted in the footnotes. Meanwhile, of Jung's correspondence with White, about three-quarters of the letters are printed in this collection, the rest being judged by the editors as "too private" for publication (*Letters I*, p.450n). The complete collection—i.e., all the letters now held in the Jung archives—is missing a few documents on both sides. It is possible that, Aniela Jaffé and Gerhard Adler both now having died, a search of their papers at some future time may turn up documents that belong to the correspondence.

⁵ "[Es] werden in [den Briefen] doch zum grossen Teil äusserst persönliche Fragen berührt, die der *ärztlichen Schweigepflicht* unterstehen" (Lorenz Jung, private correspondence, 4 Feb. 86; emphasis added).

⁶ The phrase used by Lorenz Jung in his letter for the "duty of medical confidentiality" [*ärztliche Schweigepflicht*] does not mean that Jung was literally White's doctor. Victor White was in analysis with John Layard in Oxford, starting in 1941, according to G. Adler (personal correspondence, 3 June 86), a fact also mentioned in White's 1953 lecture, "Good and Evil." The medical principle of confidentiality to which Jung subscribed, and which still binds his family, covers sensitive information that emerged within relationships of all sorts, including Jung's conversations with many who, like White, were not actually his patients.

⁷ "C.G. Jung hat aus obigen Gründen seinerzeit nicht gewünscht, dass dieser Briefwechsel publiziert wird und deshalb wollen wir ihn auch

jetzt nicht freigeben, *denn das Vertrauen zwischen zwei Menschen soll nicht im nachhinein relativiert werden"* (Ibid, emphasis added).

[8] Jung's desire to withhold correspondence from publication had previously been reversed in one important case. Gerhard Adler's Introduction to the *C.G. Jung Letters* records that Jung forbade publication of his correspondence with Freud for a period of 30 years after his death, a period which he later changed to 20 years. Jung wrote in 1956, "Separate treatment of this correspondence is justified, because it touches in parts upon very personal problems. . . . I consider it inopportune to expose the personal material as long as the waves of animosity are still running so high" (*Letters I*, pp.xif). Notwithstanding, in 1970—less than ten years after Jung's death—the heirs of Jung and of Freud agreed to exchange the two sides of this historic correspondence, so that it could be prepared for publication while people who had known both men were still living to edit the work.

[9] William McGuire notes that in the case of the Freud correspondence, "Jung had left conflicting instructions about restrictions on publication—for thirty years, for twenty, for fifty, for one hundred, or until 1980" (*The Freud/Jung Letters: The Correspondence between Sigmund Freud and C.G. Jung.* Editor, William McGuire. Translators, Ralph Mannheim and R.F.C. Hull. Princeton: Princeton University Press, 1974, p.xxxiii).

[10] The corresponding volume in English is *Letters II*, Princeton University Press.

[11] As Franz Jung is uniquely able to comment on the Jung heirs' decision to release White's letters, he kindly supplied this statement (original in English) about the reasons for that decision. Those reasons go to a history that sheds light not only on the particular treatment given to the Jung-White correspondence, but also on the family's sense of guardianship over Jung's whole literary deposit.

APPENDIX C

[1] William Brown, an Anglican monk in the Order of the Holy Cross, and Aelred Squire, a Catholic monk in the Camaldolese branch of the Order of St. Benedict, were known to each other in 1987 through a rather unusual ecumenical arrangement. For thirteen years, 1980–93, Incarnation Priory in Berkeley, CA, housed two monastic communities. Joined by a friendship covenant, monks from the Camaldolese part of the Roman Catholic Benedictine family and monks in the Anglican Order of the Holy Cross had their own respective priors and daily offices; but they worshiped together weekly, and their common life fostered a lively exchange.

[2] The Carmelite prioress who befriended Aelred Squire as a young man was also White's friend, Mother Michael of the Blessed Trinity (Chapter One, n.29; Chapter Three, n.46).

[3] Aelred Squire, *Summer in the Seed* (New York: Paulist Press, 1980), p.xiii.

[4] Squire had unusual success, evidently, as a teacher of boys. After his first term at Llanarth, to the surprise of the rest of the staff, his pupils gave him a book-token as a spontaneous sign of appreciation.

[5] A neurologist has subsequently confirmed that Squire suffered a stroke, though as far as he recalls this was not admitted at the time. In the absence of timely physical therapy, he suffered some minor residual loss of function, never regaining his ability to write legibly as before.

[6] A papal indult of exclaustration may be given to a subject under solemn vows for a number of possible reasons. It has the effect of withdrawing the subject, for a specified period of time or reason, from the superior to whom he is normally bound by obedience, and transferring him to a higher one—in this case the Pope or someone, often a bishop, acting in his name. Thus it was possible for Aelred Squire to fulfill his vows as a Dominican while living as a solitary religious.

[7] In the same month of the same year Thomas Merton received his abbot's permission to retire regularly to a hermitage in the abbey grounds. He and Squire were briefly in correspondence, though they never met in the flesh.

[8] St. Catherine's Centre in London was founded for the broader training of sisters, in the light of the thought of the Second Vatican Council.

[9] The first edition of Squire's *Asking the Fathers* came out in 1973 and was twice reprinted in England and the U.S. It has recently appeared in a charming Italian edition, *Alla scuola dei padri* (Brescia, 1990) and a new American edition is scheduled to be published in the near future.

[10] Aelred Squire, *Fathers Talking: An Anthology* (Cistercian Studies Series: Number Ninety-Three. Kalamazoo, MI: Cistercian Publications, 1986).

Bibliography

A. THEOLOGY

1. Victor White: Primary*

White, Victor, O.P., "The Analyst and the Confessor." *The Commonweal*, 7/23/48. New York: Commonweal Foundation.

———. "The Aristotelian-Thomist Conception of Man." *Eranos-Jahrbuch 1947*, Band XV, *Der Mensch*. Editor, Olga Fröbe-Kapteyn. Zürich: Rhein-Verlag, 1948.

———. "Charles Gustave Jung" (sic). *Time and Tide, The Independent Weekly*. Special Issue: *Jung at Eighty*. Vol. 36, July 23, 1955. London.

———. "The Dying God: Pagan, Psychological and Christian." *Blackfriars*, Vol. XXXIII, 2/52. Oxford: Blackfriars Publications.

———. "The Dying God: Pagan, Psychological and Christian: Differences." *Blackfriars*, Vol. XXXIII, 3/52. Oxford: Blackfriars Publications.

———. "The Effects of Schism." *Blackfriars*, Vol. XXIII, 2/42. Oxford: Blackfriars Publications.

———. "Eranos: 1947, 1948." *Dominican Studies*, Vol. II, 10/49. Oxford: Blackfriars Publications.

---

*Note: Where works by Victor White and C.G. Jung are listed, the date of composition or original publication, if available, appears in brackets after the copyright date.

————. "Four Challenges to Religion." *Blackfriars*, Vol. XXXIII: "Freud" (4/52); "Jung" (5/52); "Frazer" (6/52); "Marx" (7,8/52). Oxford: Blackfriars Publications.

————. "The Frontiers of Theology and Psychology." Guild Lecture no. 19. London: Guild of Pastoral Psychology, 1942.

————. *God and the Unconscious*. Foreword by C.G. Jung. Appendix by Gebhard Frei. London: The Harvill Press, 1952.

————. *God and the Unconscious*, revised edition. Introduction by William Everson. Foreword by C.G. Jung. Dallas, TX: Spring Publications, 1952/1982.

————. *God the Unknown & other essays*. London: Harvill Press, 1956.

————. "Good and Evil." *Harvest*, Vol. 12. London: Analytical Psychology Club, 1966. [1953]

————. "Holy Teaching: The Idea of Theology According to St. Thomas Aquinas" (Aquinas Paper no. 33). Oxford: Blackfriars Publications for the Aquinas Society of London, 1958.

————. Editor & translator. " 'How to Study' by St. Thomas Aquinas." (Inaugural lecture for academic year 1944–45.) *Blackfriars*. Oxford: Blackfriars Publications, 1947.

————. "Jung on Job." *Blackfriars*, Vol. XXXVI, 3/55. Oxford: Blackfriars Publications.

————. "Kierkegaard's Journals." *Blackfriars*, Vol. XX, 11/39. Oxford: Blackfriars Publications.

————. "Kinds of Opposites." *Studien zur Analytischen Psychologie C.G. Jungs. Festschrift zum 80.Geburtstag von C.G. Jung.* Band I: "Beiträge aus Theorie und Praxis." Herausgegeben vom C.G. Jung Institut Zürich. Zürich: Rascher Verlag, 1955.

————. "Notes on Gnosticism." Guild Lecture no. 59, pamphlet. London: Guild of Pastoral Psychology, April 1949.

———. "The Platonic Tradition in St. Thomas Aquinas." *God the Unknown & other essays*. London: Harvill Press, 1956. [1941]

———. "Psychotherapy and Ethics." *Blackfriars*, Vol. XXVI, August 1945. Oxford: Blackfriars Publications.

———. "Psychotherapy and Ethics: Postscript." *Blackfriars*, Vol. XXVI, October 1945. Oxford: Blackfriars Publications.

———. "Religious Tolerance." *The Commonweal*, September 4, 1953. New York: Commonweal Foundation.

———. "Review of *Eranos-Jahrbuch 1955*, Band XXIV." *Blackfriars*, Vol. XXXVIII, 2/57. Oxford: Blackfriars Publications.

———. "Review of *Religion and the Psychology of Jung* by Raymond Hostie, S.J." *Journal of Analytical Psychology*, Vol. III. London: Tavistock Publications, 1958.

———. "Review of Jung's *Psychological Reflections*, ed., Jolande Jacobi." *Blackfriars* XXXV, 1/54. Oxford: Blackfriars Publications.

———. "Review of Jung's *CW 9i* & *CW 9ii*; Jacobi's *Complex, Archetype, Symbol in the Psychology of C.G. Jung*; and Philp's *Jung and the Problem of Evil*." *Blackfriars*, Vol. XLI, 1–2/60. Oxford: Blackfriars Publications.

———. "Review of Tillich's *Biblical Religion and the Search for Ultimate Reality*; and Robinson's *Christ and Conscience*." *Blackfriars*, Vol. XXXVIII, 3/57. Oxford: Blackfriars Publications.

———. "St. Thomas Aquinas and Jung's Psychology." *Blackfriars*, Vol. XXV, 6/44. Oxford: Blackfriars Publications.

———. "St. Thomas's Conception of Revelation." *Dominican Studies*, Vol. I, 1/48. Oxford: Blackfriars Publications. [3/47]

———. "Satan." *Dominican Studies*, Vol. II, 4/49. Oxford: Blackfriars Publications.

———. "The Scandal of the Assumption." *Life of the Spirit: A Blackfriars Review*, Vol. V, 11–12/50. Oxford: Blackfriars Publications.

————. *Scholasticism*. Pamphlet, No. R 126. London: Catholic Truth Society, 1934.

————. "Some Recent Contributions to Psychology." *Blackfriars*, Vol. XXXII, 9/51. Oxford: Blackfriars Publications.

————. "Some Recent Studies in Archetypology" *Blackfriars*, Vol. XL, 5/59. Oxford: Blackfriars Publications.

————. *Soul and Psyche: An Enquiry into the Relationship of Psychotherapy and Religion*. New York: Harper & Brothers, 1960.

————. "Spengler Views the Machine Age." *Blackfriars*, Vol. XIII, 1/32. Oxford: Blackfriars Publications.

————. "Theological Reflections." *Journal of Analytical Psychology*, Vol. V. London: Tavistock Publications, 1960.

————. "Thomism and 'Affective Knowledge.' " Parts I and II in *Blackfriars*, Vol. XXIV, 1/43, 4/43; Part III in *Blackfriars*, Vol. XXV, 9/44. Oxford: Blackfriars Publications.

————. "Walter Hilton: An English Spiritual Guide." Guild of Pastoral Psychology, Lecture 31. London: Guild of Pastoral Psychology, 1944.

————. "Western and Eastern Theology of Grace and Nature." *God the Unknown & other essays*. London: Harvill Press, 1956.

2. Victor White: Secondary

Dourley, John. Interview, May 1987. Private correspondence, February 1993.

Gilby, Thomas, O.P. "PERSONAE: Victor White, O.P. († May 22, 1960)." (Unsigned obituary, attributed to Gilby) *Blackfriars*, Vol. XLI, 7–8/60. Oxford: Blackfriars Publications.

————. "Review of White's *Soul and Psyche*." *Blackfriars*, Vol. XLI, 5/60. Oxford: Blackfriars Publications.

Lefébure, Marcus. Private correspondence, July 1986.

Moreno, Antonio, O.P. Interview, January 1987.

Parvis, Paul M., O.P. Private correspondence, August 1987.

Squire, Aelred, O.S.B., Cam. Private correspondence and interviews, 1987–92.

von Oppen, Beate Ruhm. Private correspondence, September 1985.

3. Historical Theology

Aquinas, St. Thomas. *On the Truth of the Catholic Faith. Book Three: Providence. Part I (Summa Contra Gentiles).* Translator, Vernon J. Bourke. Garden City, NY: Hanover House, 1956.

———. *Summa Theologiae: Latin Text and English Translation.* London & New York: Blackfriars, in conjunction with Eyre & Spottiswode and McGraw-Hill, 1964.

———. *Theological Texts: Selected and Translated with Notes and an Introduction by Thomas Gilgy.* Durham, NC: The Labyrinth Press, 1955.

Augustine, Aurelius, St., of Hippo. *The City of God.* Translator, Marcus Dods. New York: The Modern Library/Random House, 1950.

———. *Confessions.* Translator, R.S. Pine-Coffin. New York: Penguin Books, 1961.

———. "The Free Choice of the Will." *The Fathers of the Church, Volume 59.* Translator, Robert P. Russell, O.S.A. Washington, DC: The Catholic University of America Press, 1968.

———. *On the Spirit and the Letter.* Translator, W.J. Sparrow Simpson. London: SPCK, 1925.

Calvin, Jean. *Institutes of the Christian Religion. The Library of Christian Classics, Vol. XX and XXI.* Editor, John T. McNeill. Translator, Ford Lewis Battles. Philadelphia: The Westminster Press, 1960.

Feuerbach, Ludwig. *The Essence of Christianity.* Translator, George Eliot. Introduction, Karl Barth. Foreword, H.R. Niebuhr. New York: Harper & Row, 1957.

Kierkegaard, Søren. *Fear and Trembling*. Translator, Alexander Dru. New York: Harper & Brothers, 1958.

————. *The Journals of Kierkegaard*. Translator, Alexander Dru. New York: Harper & Brothers/Harper Torchbooks, 1958/1959.

————. *Works of Love: Some Christian Reflections in the Form of Discourses*. Translator, Howard Kong. New York: Harper & Row/Harper Torchbooks, 1962.

4. Modern Theology, Philosophy and Ethics

Barth, Karl. *Church Dogmatics, Vol. III, Parts 2 and 3: The Doctrine of Creation*. Translator, G.W. Bromiley. Edinburgh: T.&T. Clark, 1960.

————. *Church Dogmatics, Vol. IV, Parts 1 and 2, and Part 3, first half: The Doctrine of Reconciliation*. Translator, G.W. Bromiley. Edinburgh: T.&T. Clark, 1956 (IV/1), 1958 (IV/2), and 1961 (IV/3,1).

————. *The Humanity of God*. Atlanta: John Knox Press, 1960.

Bateson, Gregory. *Mind and Nature: A Necessary Unity*. New York: Bantam Books, 1979.

Brown, Peter. *Augustine of Hippo*. Berkeley & Los Angeles: University of California Press, 1967.

Buber, Martin. *The Eclipse of God: Studies in the Relation Between Religion and Philosopy*. New York: Harper & Brothers, 1952.

Burrell, David. *Aquinas: God and Action*. Notre Dame, IN: University of Notre Dame Press, 1979.

Dourley, John. *Paul Tillich and Bonaventure: An Evaluation of Tillich's Claim to Stand in the Augustinian-Franciscan Tradition*. Leiden, Netherlands:E.J. Brill, 1975.

Farrer, Austin. *Love Almighty and Ills Umlimited*. London: Collins/Fontana Library Edition, 1966.

Frei, Hans W. *The Eclipse of Biblical Narrative: A Study in Eighteenth and Nineteenth Century Hermeneutics.* New Haven and London: Yale University Press, 1974.

———. *The Identity of Jesus Christ: The Hermeneutical Bases of Dogmatic Theology.* Philadephia: Fortress Press, 1975.

Griffin, David Ray. *God, Power, and Evil: A Process Theodicy.* Philadelphia: The Westminster Press, 1976.

John, Helen James. *The Thomist Spectrum.* New York: Fordham Press, 1966.

Hick, John. *Evil and the God of Love,* revised edition. San Francisco: Harper & Row, 1966/1978.

Homans, Peter. *Theology after Freud: An Interpretive Inquiry.* Indianapolis & New York: The Bobbs-Merrill Company, Inc., 1970.

Lewis, C.S. *The Four Loves.* New York: Harcourt Brace Jovanovich, Inc., 1960.

Lindbeck, George. "The *A Priori* in St. Thomas' Theory of Knowledge." *The Heritage of Christian Thought: Essays in Honor of Robert Lowry Calhoun.* Cushman and Grislis, editors. New York: Harper & Row, 1965.

———. *The Nature of Doctrine: Religion and Theology in a Postliberal Age.* Philadelphia: Westminster Press, 1984.

Kehoe, Richard, O.P. "Review of *Antwort auf Hiob.*" *Dominican Studies,* Vol. V. Oxford: Blackfriars Publications, 1952.

Kurtz, Lester. *The Politics of Heresy: The Modernist Crisis in Roman Catholicism.* Berkeley: University of California Press, 1986.

McFague, Sallie. *Metaphorical Theology: Models of God in Religious Language.* Philadelphia: Fortress Press, 1982.

Mooney, Christopher, S.J. Interview, 29 May 1986.

The New Catholic Encyclopedia. Editors: Catholic University of America, Washington, D.C. New York: McGraw-Hill, 1967.

Niebuhr, Reinhold. *Moral Man and Immoral Society: A Study in Ethics and Politics*. New York: Charles Scribner's Sons, 1932/1960.

Norris, Richard. "Evil" (Lecture). Church of St. Luke in the Fields. New York City, Spring 1982.

Otto, Rudolf. *The Idea of the Holy: An Inquiry into the nonrational factor in the idea of the divine and its relation to the rational*, second edition. Translator, John W. Harvey. London, Oxford, New York: Oxford University Press, 1923/1950.

Outka, Gene. *Aqape: An Ethical Analysis*. New Haven: Yale University Press, 1972.

Ricoeur, Paul. *Interpretation Theory: Discourse and the Surplus of Meaning*. Fort Worth, TX: The Texas Christian University Press, 1976.

Squire, Aelred, O.S.B., Cam. *Summer in the Seed*. London: SPCK, 1980.

TeSelle, Eugene. *Augustine the Theologian*. New York: Herder & Herder, 1970.

Tillich, Paul. J. *Dynamics of Faith*. New York: Harper & Row, 1957.

―――. *The New Being*. New York: Charles Scribner's Sons, 1955.

―――. *Systematic Theology*. (In three volumes.) Chicago: University of Chicago Press. Vol. I, 1951; Vol. II, 1957; Vol. III, 1963.

Tracy, David. *Blessed Rage for Order: The New Pluralism in Theology*. New York: Seabury Press, 1979.

Wartofsky, Marx W. *Feuerbach*. Cambridge: Cambridge University Press, 1977.

Windsor, Pat. "Häring fears 'psychological exodus' from church." *National Catholic Reporter*, April 28, 1989.

Wood, Charles. *The Formation of Christian Understanding: An Essay in Theological Hermeneutics*. Philadelphia: Westminster Press, 1981.

B. PSYCHOLOGY

1. C.G. Jung: Primary*

Jung, Carl Gustav. *Aion: Researches into the Phenomenology of the Self (CW 9.ii)*. Second Edition. Translator, R.F.C. Hull. Princeton: Princeton University Press (Bollingen), 1959. [1951]

————. *Answer to Job. Psychology and Religion: West and East (CW 11)*. Translator, R.F.C. Hull. New York: Bollingen Foundation, 1958. [1952]

————. *C.G. Jung Speaking: Interviews and Encounters*. Editors: William McGuire, R.F.C. Hull. Princeton: Princeton University Press, 1977.

————. *Collected Papers on Analytical Psychology*, Second Edition. Editor, Constance E. Long. New York: Moffat Yard & Co., 1917.

————. *The Development of Personality (CW 17)*. translator, R.F.C. Hull. Princeton: Princeton University Press, 1954.

————. "The Development of the Personality." *The Integration of the Personality*. Translator, Stanley M. Dell. New York: Farrer & Rinehart, 1939. [1932]

————. *Dream Analysis: Notes of the Seminar Given in 1928–1930*. Editor, William McGuire. Princeton: Princeton University Press, 1984.

————. "The 'Face to Face' Interview" (With John Freeman, BBC Television, 22 Oct. 1959). *C.G. Jung Speaking: Interviews and Encounters*. Editors, William McGuire, R.F.C. Hull. Princeton: Princeton University Press, 1977.

————. "Freud and Jung: Contrasts." *Modern Man in Search of a Soul*. New York: Harcourt Brace Jovanovich, 1933. [1929]

---

*Note: *The Collected Works of C.G. Jung,* published by Princeton University Press (Bollingen Series XX) in twenty volumes, are listed here in abbreviated form: *CW* and volume number. The executive editor of the series is William McGuire. Translator, publication information, etc., are given for each volume listed here.

——— and Sigmund Freud. *The Freud/Jung Letters: The Correspondence between Sigmund Freud and C.G. Jung.* Editor, William McGuire. Translators, Ralph Mannheim, R.F.C. Hull. Princeton: Princeton University Press, 1974.

———. "Good and Evil in Analytical Psychology." *The Journal of Analytical Psychology,* Vol. V. London: Tavistock Publications, 1960.

———. "Jung and Religious Belief." *The Symoblic Life (CW 18).* Princeton: Princeton University Press, 1976. [1957]

———. *Letters. Volume I: 1906–1950. Volume II: 1951–1961.* Translator, R.F.C. Hull. Editors, Gerhard Adler and Aniela Jaffé. Princeton: Princeton University Press, 1973.

———. *Man and his Symbols.* Co-editor, M.-L. von Franz. Coordinating editor, John Freeman. London: Aldus Books Limited, 1964; also New York: Doubleday & Co., Inc., 1964.

———. "Marriage as a Psychological Relationship." *The Development of Personality (CW 17).* Princeton: Princeton University Press, 1954. [1925]

———. *Memories, Dreams, Reflections.* Recorded and edited by Aniela Jaffé. Translated by Richard and Clara Winston. New York: Random House, 1961; Vintage Books, 1965.

———. *Modern Man in Search of a Soul.* New York: Harcourt Brace Jovanovich, Inc., 1933.

———. "On the Nature of the Psyche." *The Structure and Dynamics of the Psyche (CW 18).* second edition. Translator, R.F.C. Hull. Princeton: Princeton University Press, 1953/1968. [1947/1954]

———. "On Resurrection." *The Symbolic Life (CW 18).* Princeton: Princeton University Press, 1976. [1954]

———. "A Psychological Approach to the Dogma of the Trinity." *Psychology and Religion: West and East (CW 11),* second edition. Translator, R.F.C. Hull. Princeton: Princeton University Press, 1958/1969. [1948]

——. *Psychological Types (CW 6)*. Translator, H.G. Baynes, revised by R.F.C. Hull. Princeton: Princeton Unversity Press, 1971. [1921]

——. *Psychology and Alchemy (CW 12)*, second edition. Translator, R.F.C. Hull. Princeton: Princeton University Press, 1953/1968.

——. *Psychology and Religion, West and East (CW 11)*, second edition. Translator, R.F.C. Hull. Princeton: Princeton University Press, 1958/1969.

——. "Psychology and Religion." (Terry Lectures.) New Haven: Yale University Press, 1938. [1937]

——. "Psychotherapists or the Clergy." *Psychology and Religion: West and East (CW 11)*, second edition. Translator, R.F.C. Hull. Princeton: Princeton University Press, 1953/1968. [1932]

——. *The Structure and Dynamics of the Psyche (CW 8)*. Translator, R.F.C. Hull. Princeton: Princeton University Press, 1960.

——. *The Symbolic Life (CW 18)*. Translator, R.F.C. Hull. Princeton: Princeton University Press, 1976.

——. *Symbols of Transformation: An Analysis of the Prelude to a Case of Schizophrenia (CW 5)*, second edition. Translator, R.F.C. Hull. Princeton: Princeton University Press, 1956/1967. [1912: *Wandlungen und Symbole der Libido*, Part I of volume.]

——. "Transformation Symbolism in the Mass." *Psychology and Religion: West and East (CW 11)*, second edition. Translator, R.F.C. Hull. Princeton: Princeton University Press, 1953/1968. [1940]

——. *Two Essays on Analytical Psychology (CW 7)*, second edition. Translator, R.F.C. Hull. Princeton: Princeton University Press, 1953/1966.

——. "Über das Selbst." *Eranos-Jahrbuch 1948*, Band XVI (Zweite Folge). Editor, Olga Fröbe-Kapteyn. Zürich: Rhein-Verlag, 1949. [1948]

——. *The Undiscovered Self.* Translator, R.F.C. Hull. Boston: Little, Brown & Co., 1957.

————. *The Visions Seminars* (Book One and Book Two). Zurich: Spring Publications, 1976.

————. "Why I am Not a Catholic." *The Symbolic Life (CW 18)*. Translator, R.F.C. Hull. Princeton: Princeton University Press, 1976. [1944]

————. "Zur Psychologie der Trinitätsidee." *Eranos-Jahrbuch 1940/1941*. Editor, Olga Fröbe-Kapteyn. Zürich: Rhein-Verlag, 1942. [1940]

2. *C.G. Jung: Secondary*

Analytical Psychology Club of New York Incorporated, ed. "Memorial Meeting for Dr. Jung, October 20, 1961." *Bulletin*. New York: November 1961.

Carotenuto, Aldo. *A Secret Symmetry: Sabina Spielrein between Jung and Freud*. Translators, Arno Pomerans, John Shepley, Krishna Winston. New York: Pantheon Books, 1984.

Clift, Wallace B. *Jung and Christianity: The Challenge of Reconciliation*. New York: Crossroad, 1983.

Collins, Brendan. "Wisdom in Jung's *Answer to Job*." *Biblica Theology Bulletin*, Vol. 21, No. 3, Fall 1991.

Cox, David. *Jung and St. Paul: A Study of the Doctrine of Justification by Faith and its Relation to the Concept of Individuation*. London: Longmans, Green & Co., 1959.

Dourley, John. "The Challenge of Jung's Psychology for the Study of Religion." *Studies in Religion/Sciences Reliqieuses*. Vol. 18, No. 3, Summer 1989. Waterloo, Ontario: Wilfrid Laurier University Press.

————. *The Illness that We Are: A Jungian Critique of Christianity*. Toronto: Inner City Books, 1984.

————. "Jung, Tillich, and Aspects of Western Christian Development." *Jung and Christianity in Dialogue: Faith, Feminism, and Hermeneutics*. Editors, Robert L. Moore and Daniel J. Meckel. New York & Mahwah: Paulist Press, 1990.

————. *Love, Celibacy and the Inner Marriage*. Toronto: Inner City Books, 1987.

————. *The Psyche as Sacrament: A Comparative Study of C.G. Jung and Paul Tillich*. Toronto: Inner City Books, 1981.

————. *A Strategy for a Loss of Faith: Jung's Proposal*. Toronto: Inner City books, 1992.

Edinger, Edward F. *Ego and Archetype: Individuation and the Religious Function of the Psyche*. Baltimore: Penguin Books, Inc., 1972.

Englesman, Joan Chamberlain. *The Feminine Dimension of the Divine*. Wilmette, IL: Chiron Press, 1987.

Evans-Wentz, W.Y. (ed.). *The Tibetan Book of the Dead*, third edition. Translator, Lama Kazi Dawa-Samdup. Psychological commentary by C.G. Jung. London: Oxford University Press, 1927/1949/1957.

Jaffé, Aniela. "The Creative Phases in Jung's Life." Translator, Murray Stein. *Spring: An Annual of Archetypal Psychology and Jungian Thought*. New York, 1972.

Halpern, Stefanie. "A Human Meeting with Death." *The Arms of the Windmill: Essays in Analytical Psychology in Honor of Werner H. Engel*. New York: C.G. Jung Foundation, 1984.

Hannah, Barbara. *Jung: His Life and Work—A Biographical Memoir*. New York: G.P. Putnam's Sons, 1976.

Hillman, James. *The Dream of the Underworld*. New York: Harper & Row, 1979.

————. *Insearch: Psychology and Religion*. Irving, TX: Spring Publications, Inc., 1979.

————. "Psychology: Monotheistic or Polytheistic?" *Spring: An Annual of Archetypal Psychology and Jungian Thought*. New York: Spring Publications, 1971.

————. *Re-Visioning Psychology*. New York: Harper & Row, 1975.

———. *Suicide and the Soul.* Irving, TX: Spring Publications, Inc., 1964/ 1976.

Homans, Peter. *Jung in Context: Modernity and the Making of a Psychology.* Chicago & London: University of Chicago Press, 1979.

Hostie, Raymond. *Religion and the Psychology of Jung.* Translator, G.R. Lamb. New York: Sheed & Ward, 1957.

Kerenyi, Carl, et al. *Evil.* Edited by the Curatorium of the C.G. Jung Institute, Zurich. Evanston, IL: Northwestern University Press, 1967.

Kirsch, James. "Reconsidering Jung's So-Called Anti-Semitism." *The Arms of the Windmill: Essays in Analytical Psychology in Honor of Werner H. Engel.* New York: C.G. Jung Foundation, 1984.

Koltuv, Barbara Black. "Lilith." *Quadrant,* Vol. 16, no. 1. New York: C.G. Jung Foundation, Spring 1983.

Lowe, Walter. *Evil and the Unconscious.* Chico, CA: Scholars Press, 1983.

Maag, Victor. "The Antichrist as a Symbol of Evil." *Evil.* Edited by the Curatorium of the C.G. Jung Institute, Zurich. Evanston, IL: Northwestern University Press, 1967.

Massell, Sylvia Perera. "The Scapegoat Complex." *Quadrant,* Vol. 12, No. 2. New York: The C.G. Jung Foundation, Winter 1979.

Meyer, Werner, Hans Schär, Eugen Böhler. *Zur Erinnerung an Carl Gustav Jung: Gedenkfeier anlässlich der Bestattung.* Freitag, 9. Juni 1961, in der reformierten Kirche in Küsnacht. Gedenkschriften-Verlag Zürich.

McGuire, William. Private correspondence, 1985–87.

Nagy, Marilyn Jean. *Philosophical Issues in the Psychology of C.G. Jung.* Albany, NY: State University of New York Press, 1991.

Neumann, Erich. *Depth Psychology and a New Ethic.* Translator, Eugene Rolf. New York: Harper & Row/Harper Torchbooks, 1969.

————. *The Origins and History of Consciousness*. Translator: R.F.C. Hull. Princeton: Princeton University Press, 1954.

Read, Herbert. *Zum 85. Geburtstag von Professor Dr. Carl Gustav Jung: 26. Juli 1960*. Zürich: Rascher & Cie AG, 1960.

Satinover, Jeffrey. " Jung's Lost Contribution to the Dilemma of Narcissism." Unpublished typescript. New Haven, CT: Yale University, Department of Psychiatry, 1985.

Spiegelman, J. Marvin, ed. *Catholicism and Jungian Psychology*. Phoenix, AZ: Falcon Press, 1988.

Stein, Murray. *Jung's Treatment of Christianity: The Psychotherapy of a Religious Tradition*. Wilmette, IL: Chiron Publications, 1985.

Tillich, Paul J. Address (untitled). *Carl Gustav Jung: A Memorial Meeting, 1 December 1961*. New York: Analytical Psychology Club of New York, 1961.

Ulanov, Ann Belford. Lectures: "Depth Psychology and Theology." New York: Union Theological Seminary, Fall 1980.

————. "The Two Strangers." *Union Seminary Quarterly Review*. New York: Union Theological Seminary, 1973.

von Franz, Marie L., Ulrich Mann, Hans-W.Heidland. *C.G. Jung und die Theologen: Selbsterfahrung und Gotteserfahrung bei C.G.Jung*. Herausgeber: Wolfgang Boehme. Stuttgart: Radius-Verlag, 1971.

Wehr, Gerhard. *Jung: A Biography*. Translator, David M. Weeks. Boston & London: Shambhala, 1987.

3. Freudian Psychology

Freud, Sigmund. *Beyond the Pleasure Principle. The Complete Psychological Works of Sigmund Freud*. Vol. XVII, Standard Edition. Translator, James Strachey. London: The Hogarth Press and the Institute of Psycho-analysis, 1955. [1920]

————. *Civilization and its Discontents*. Translator, James Strachey. New York: W.W. Norton & Co., 1961. [1930]

————. *The Ego and the Id. The Complete Psychological Works of Sigmund Freud*, Vol. XIX, Standard Edition. Translator, James Strachey. London: The Hogarth Press and the Institute of Psycho-analysis, 1961. [1923]

————. *The Future of an Illusion*. Translator, James Strachey. New York: Norton & Co., Inc., 1961.

————. *The Interpretation of Dreams*. Translator, James Strachey. New York: Avon Books/Discus, 1965. (Reprinted from *Standard Edition, Volumes IV and V*, London, 1953.)

————. *New Introductory Lectures on Psychoanalysis*. Translator, James Strachey. New York: W.W. Norton & Co., Inc., 1965. [1933]

————. *Three Case Histories*. Translator not identified. Editor, Philip Rieff. New York: Collier Books/Macmillan, 1963.

————. *Totem and Taboo: Some Points of Agreement between the Mental Lives of Savages and Neurotics*. Translator, James Strachey. New York: W.W. Norton & Co., Inc., 1950.

Leavy, Stanley. "A Footnote to Jung's 'Memories.' " *The Psychoanalytic Quarterly*, Vol. XXXIII, 1964.

————. Lectures: "Introduction to the Clinical and Theoretical Writings of Sigmund Freud." New Haven: Yale University, Fall 1982.

————. "Questioning Authority: The Contribution of Psychoanalysis to Religion." *Cross Currents*. Summer 1982.

MacIsaac, Sharon. *Freud and Original Sin*. New York: Paulist Press, 1974.

Rieff, Philip. *Freud: The Mind of the Moralist*, third edition. Chicago: University of Chicago Press, 1959/1961/1979.

————. *The Triumph of the Therapeutic: Uses of Faith after Freud*. New York: Harper & Row/Harper Torchbooks, 1966.

Siirala, Aarne. *The Voice of Illness: A Study in Therapy and Prophecy*. Foreword by Paul J. Tillich. Introduction by Gotthard Booth, M.D. New York and Toronto: The Edwin Mellen Press, 1964.

C. THE JUNG-WHITE DIALOGUE

Adler, Gerhard. Private correspondence, June 1986.

Arraj, James. "Jungian Spirituality: The Question of Victor White." *Spirituality Today*, Vol. 40, No. 3, Autumn 1988. Chicago: Dominicans, Province of St. Albert the Great.

Charet, F.X. "A Dialogue between Psychology and Theology: The Correspondence of C.G. Jung and Victor White." *The Journal of Analytical Psychology*, Vol. 35, No. 4, October 1990. London: Society of Analytical Psychology.

Cunningham, Adrian. Private correspondence, 1992–93. Interviews, 1991–92.

———. "Victor White and C.G. Jung: The Fateful Encounter of the White Raven and the Gnostic." *New Blackfriars*, Volume 62, 1981.

Dourley, John P. "The Jung, Buber, White Exchanges: Exercises in Futility." *Studies in Religion/Sciences Reliqieuses*. Vol. 20, No. 3, Summer 1991. Waterloo: Ontario: Wilfrid Laurier University Press.

Henderson, Joseph. Interview, 2 February 1987.

Jung, Franz. Private correspondence 1986–1992. Interviews, 17–21 August 1991.

Jung, Lorenz. Private correspondence, February 1986.

Lammers, Ann Conrad. *A Study of the Relation between Theology and Psychology: Victor White and C.G. Jung*. Doctoral dissertation, Yale University, 1987. Ann Arbor, MI: UMI (University Microfilms International), 1988.

Index

A *priori*, Kantian: in Aquinas, 283n.19; archetypes as, 119–20; Self as, 169
"absolute truth": and magisterial authority, 23, 66–70, 136–37, 251–52; and transcendence, 251–52; and unconscious, 141–42; and violence, 26, 67, 136–38, 178–79. *See also* Perfection; Roman Catholic Church; *Summum Bonum*
Actus purus: and J's concept of libido, 77–78; and Aquinas' concept of motion, 80–81
Adler, Gerhard (co-editor, *C.G. Jung Letters*), 37, 38, 257, 311nn.1,4; advised W to contact J, 278n.32
Affective knowledge: epistemological limits of, 62–63; and J's psychology, 60, 82–83; and love of God, 59–60; and *Summa Theologiae*, 283–84n.23, 284n.27; and *Summum Bonum*, 83–84; and W's Thomism, 17, 30, 56–65, 69, 91, 245. *See also* Epistemology; Experience; Thomism
Analytical Psychology. *See* Jung, Carl Gustav—Psychology of
Anima and animus, 19; integration of, 165–66; as scientific hypothesis, 166; and evil, 174
Apologetics: and W's Thomism, 35, 57, 58, 71–75; in Aquinas, 65–66; J's investment in, 137
Aquinas. *See* Thomas Aquinas, Saint
Archetypes: ambiguity of, 119, 169, 219; in amplification of dreams, 296n.15; classical, 295n.8, 299n.36; and dogma, 12; and evil of myth, 180–81; not directly known, 119–20, 125–26, 129–31; and participation, 76–77; and religious experience, 12, 226, 301–02n.16; and transcendence, 75–76; unconsciousness of, 119, 243–44
Augustine, Saint: anti-Platonism of, 55,

283n.18; influenced Aquinas, 51, 54–55, 59, 64–65; on crucifixion, paradox of, 188; on historical evils, 206, 303n.22, 307n.9; on innocent suffering, 185, 305n.34; on original sin, 305n.37; Platonism of, 51–52; *privatio boni*, his proposal, 172, 222, 288–89n.29; *Summum Bonum*, his formulation, 226; theodicy, 187; his influence on W, 23, 51–52, 228

Barth, Karl: on evil, 234, on theology, limits of, 189–90, 234; transcendent theology of, 128–29, 143, 296n.13
Bateson, Gregory: meta-theory of, 17, 28, 254, 275–76n.8
Blackfriars, Oxford (Dominican college): history of, 43–44, 269; and regent of studies, 98–99, 290n.35, 291n.39; W's departure from, 99–101. *See also* White, Victor, O.P.
Blackfriars: A Monthly Review (Dominican periodical), 45; character of, 46–47; W's 30-year service to, 46, 110, 268, 282n.13, 288n.25
Buber, Martin, 115, 252

Callus, Daniel, O.P., 290n.35, 291n.39
Catholicism. *See* Roman Catholic Church; Thomism
Charet, F.X., 250
Christ: and Antichrist, 164–65, 177, 221; and crucifixion, 187–88, 303n.26; as incomplete image of Self, 94, 154–55, 163–65, 167, 173, 177, 220–21, 223, 236, 239–40, 301n.15; J's developing work on, 287n.21, 298n.31, 301n.13; and Jesus, 204–05, 236, 299n.37; needed by modern world, 96, 149, 178, 220–221, 245–46, 253; and Satan, 172–73, 224; image, shadow in, 96, 151, 219; and Sophia and Logos,

331